DIVERSITY IN ORGANIZATIONS

DIVERSITY IN ORGANIZATIONS

CONCEPTS AND PRACTICES

Edited by

Mary Ann Danowitz

Professor and Head of the Department of Leadership, Policy, and Adult and Higher Education, North Carolina State University, USA

Edeltraud Hanappi-Egger

Professor and Head of the Department of Management, Vienna University of Economics and Business, Austria

Heike Mensi-Klarbach

Assistant Professor, Vienna University of Economics and Business, Austria

palgrave
macmillan

First published 2012 by
PALGRAVE MACMILLAN

Palgrave Macmillan in the UK is an imprint of Macmillan Publishers Limited,
registered in England, company number 785998, of Houndmills, Basingstoke,
Hampshire RG21 6XS.

Palgrave Macmillan in the US is a division of St Martin's Press LLC,
175 Fifth Avenue, New York, NY 10010.

Palgrave Macmillan is the global academic imprint of the above companies
and has companies and representatives throughout the world.

Palgrave® and Macmillan® are registered trademarks in the United States,
the United Kingdom, Europe and other countries.

ISBN 978–0–230–36131–7

This book is printed on paper suitable for recycling and made from fully
managed and sustained forest sources. Logging, pulping and manufacturing
processes are expected to conform to the environmental regulations of the
country of origin.

A catalogue record for this book is available from the British Library.

A catalog record for this book is available from the Library of Congress.

10   9   8   7   6   5   4   3   2   1
21   20   19   18   17   16   15   14   13   12

Printed in China

CONTENTS

FIGURES

TABLES

PREFACE

Welcome to *Diversity in Organizations: Concepts and Practices*. This book has been specifically written to meet the needs of advanced undergraduate and post-graduate courses. It is also filled with useful insights and practices that will assist managers and other organizational employees to implement and improve diversity management programmes, and help them engage with diversity in their daily work. We assume no previous knowledge of diversity management or diversity in organizations; instead each chapter provides fundamental material for the accompanying content and can function as a stand-alone resource.

This book has developed out of the research, teaching and consulting work of experts from seven leading European business schools on the subjects of diversity in organizations and diversity management. It is a collaborative effort intended to equip students with frameworks, material and tools to understand and develop inclusive and diverse organizations in a context that is not only linguistically, ethnically and culturally heterogeneous, but also rapidly changing. To this end *Diversity in Organizations: Concepts and Practices* follows two distinct, and we hope worthwhile, aims: To reframe current approaches to the realization of inclusive organizations as *strategic* processes of diversity management, and to increase individual sensitivity to cultural and diversity issues by outlining concepts and practices which can address the challenges of societal and demographic transformation within Europe and throughout the global economy.

Mary Ann Danowitz
Edeltraud Hanappi-Egger
Heike Mensi-Klarbach

ACKNOWLEDGEMENTS

This book is the culmination of a collaborative process of work and research that was initiated in Vienna in March 2010 at the first meeting of the 'Gender and Diversity Management' Faculty Group of the CEMS Global Alliance in Management Education. During the next year and a half, faculty experts from seven leading European business schools conceived, designed and taught two CEMS blocked seminars on 'Gender and Diversity Management: Towards Inclusive Organizations' to students from 18 nations, who took part in the intensive week-long seminars at the Vienna University of Economics and Business.

During, between and after the seminars, faculty members worked to develop a text that would explore in detail the issues surrounding diversity in organizations, offering current and future employees (in particular managers) useful knowledge and examples of good practice to help them grasp the value of inclusivity, and thus encourage them to implement and improve diversity management programmes, and to engage with diversity in their daily working lives. By exchanging chapters for review and comment before publication, the editors have tried to ensure that the book's content is both coherent and consistent. At the same time we have striven to exploit the expertise of each contributor, and thus achieve a consistently high standard from beginning to end.

We believe that diversity in organizations is a multidisciplinary subject that calls for in-depth knowledge from scholars working in a wide range of specialist areas. Therefore, as editors we feel our greatest debt of gratitude is to the individual contributing authors. Their collective expertise and diverse perspectives have enriched the text far beyond that which any one author could achieve. Moreover, it was their willingness to find time in busy schedules to write and revise the various chapters, all within a rather tight deadline, which allowed this book to see the light of day.

We would like to thank Patrick Spath, an excellent participant in the 2011 CEMS seminar, who helped with clerical tasks while casting a critical eye over the text from the perspective of the student reader. Many thanks also to Derek Henderson for the final proof-reading and for agreeing to work against the clock.

We are deeply grateful to Ursula Gavin at Palgrave Macmillan for endorsing the project and lending expert guidance on structure and content from the early phase of conceptualization through to completion and to Ceri Griffiths for her support and diligent attention to details at the production phase. During the book's development, Palgrave Macmillan circulated proposals and manuscripts to an extensive and thorough group of peer reviewers. We are greatly indebted to these anonymous 'early' readers, who offered many insightful and thoughtful suggestions. We would also like to express our thanks to the copyright holders for agreeing to the reproduction of selected images and tables.

Vienna   MARY ANN DANOWITZ
                                               EDELTRAUD HANAPPI-EGGER
                                                 HEIKE MENSI-KLARBACH

The authors and publishers are grateful to the following for permission to reproduce copyright material:

Academy of Management for Figure 6.2, 'Strategic responses for managing diversity and their implementation', from P. Dass and B. Parker (1999) 'Strategies for Managing Human Resource Diversity: From Resistance to Learning', *Academy of Management Executive*, 13 (2), p.74.

M. N. Akinola and D. A. Thomas for Figure 6.4, 'Factors influencing the effectiveness of organizational diversity activities', from M. N. Akinola and D. A. Thomas (2008) 'Defining the Attributes that Enhance the Effectiveness of Workforce Diversity Initiatives in Knowledge Intensive Firms', HBS Working paper 07-019. p. 6. [Copyright 2006, 2008 by M. N. Akinola and D. A. Thomas. Reproduced by permission of the owners.]

European Commission, DG of Justice, Mrs Serdynska Joanna, for Figure 3.4 'Business benefits of diversity' and Figure 3.7 'Measurement framework for diversity' from European Commission, Final report "Methods and Indicators to Measure the Cost-Effectiveness of Diversity Policies in Enterprises", October 2003, catalogue number: KE-55-03-899-EN-N'.

Hewlett-Packard for Figure 6.1, 'The Hewlett-Packard diversity value chain'.

Taylor & Francis Group, LLC for Table 8.1, 'Symptoms of resistance to diversity', from K. M. Thomas (2008) *Diversity Resistance in Organizations*, New York, N Y.: Lawrence Erlbaum Associates, p. 6.

Every effort has been made to contact all the copyright-holders, but if any have been inadvertently omitted the publishers will be pleased to make the necessary arrangement at the earliest opportunity.

ABOUT THE EDITORS

Mary Ann Danowitz holds an Ed.D. in Higher Education. She is Professor of Higher Education and Head of the Department of Leadership, Policy, Adult and Higher Education at North Carolina State University in the United States. Previously she was a Lise Meitner Austrian Science Fund Senior Research Fellow with the Department of Management at the Vienna University of Economics and Business (WU). The focus of her research is gender, diversity and equality in the areas of leadership, governance, management, organizational change and careers, particularly regarding the higher education sector in the United States and Europe. She has held professorial and administrative posts at the University of Denver, Ohio State University and Pennsylvania State University, was a Fulbright Professor in Austria and Indonesia, and has served as a Visiting Professor and/or consultant in Australia, England, Germany and Malaysia. Her publications include four books and monographs, as well as more than 120 articles, book chapters and scientific papers.

Edeltraud Hanappi-Egger holds a Ph.D. in Computer Science. She is Professor for Gender and Diversity in Organizations and Head of the Department of Management at the Vienna University of Economics and Business (WU). A guest researcher at several international institutions, since 2008 she has been a member of the University Board of the Technical University of Graz and of the 'Young Faculty' of the Austrian Academy of Sciences. Edeltraud Hanappi-Egger has published more than 250 articles, books and book chapters on gender and diversity, organization studies and diversity management.

Heike Mensi-Klarbach studied Business Administration at Vienna University of Economics and Business (WU) and went on to obtain a Ph.D. in 2009 on the business case for diversity. Currently she is Assistant Professor with the Gender and Diversity Group at the WU. In 2006 she was awarded a DocTeam fellowship from the Austrian Academy of Sciences. The main focus of her research is diversity in organizations, especially in top management teams. In addition, she lectures on selected topics of gender and diversity management, business ethics and organizational behaviour. Her publications include a monograph, and several articles and book chapters.

ABOUT THE CONTRIBUTORS

Alexandra Beauregard holds a Ph.D. in Organizational Behaviour. She is a lecturer in the Department of Management at the London School of Economics, where she teaches courses in Diversity Management and Organizational Behaviour. The main focus of her research is on gender and diversity issues surrounding the interface between paid work and home life. She is on the editorial boards of the *Journal of Organizational Behavior*, the *British Journal of Management* and *Equality, Diversity and Inclusion: An International Journal*. Alexandra Beauregard is also an associate member of the Diversity and Equality in Careers and Employment Research Centre based at Norwich Business School (University of East Anglia).

Marie-Thérèse Claes, Ph.D., is Professor of Intercultural Management at the Louvain School of Management (University of Louvain). In addition, she holds guest professorships at several other universities in Europe, Asia and the United States of America, and has been Dean of the Faculty of Business at the Asian University Thailand. She has worked as a consultant to various companies and is a former president of the Society for Intercultural Education, Training and Research (SIETAR Europa) and the European Women's Management Development International Network (EWMD). She is also a fellow of the Royal Society of Arts, and a Fulbright and a Japan Foundation alumna.

Julia Nentwich was awarded a Ph.D. from the University of Tübingen in Germany. She is a senior lecturer in Organizational Psychology and Gender Studies at the University of St Gallen, Switzerland, where she is responsible for the teaching programme 'Gender and Diversity'. Her research at the Institute for Organizational Psychology focuses on issues around gender, diversity and change in organizations from social constructionist and discursive perspectives. She has published widely on these topics, both in English and German.

Henriett Primecz is Associate Professor at Corvinus University of Budapest in the Department of Organizational Behaviour. She was awarded a Ph.D. from the University of Pécs (formerly Janus Pannonius University) on the subject of multi-paradigm perspectives on cross-cultural management, and has lectured graduate and postgraduate students on organizational theory, organizational culture, cross-cultural management and gender issues. Currently Henriett Primecz is leading a research project entitled 'Employee Friendly Organizations. Myth or Reality' and, together with Laurence Romani and Sonja Sackmann, is editing a book to be called 'Cross-Cultural Management in Practice: Culture and Negotiated Meaning'.

Robyn Remke, Ph.D., is Associate Professor at the Department of Intercultural Communication and Management and co-director of the EngAGE (Engaged, Applied, Global Education) programme at Copenhagen Business School. Motivated by questions of social and organizational injustice and discrimination, her research uses a critical/feminist lens to explore the gendered nature of organizations and organizing. Her research focuses on the ways in which organizational members embody organizational practices such as leadership, diversity management programmes and parental leave policies through communication. In addition, she investigates alternative forms of organizational structure and gendered identity in the workplace. Robyn Remke is also President of the Organization for the Study of Communication, Language and Gender.

Annette Risberg holds a Ph.D. from Lund University, Sweden and is Associate Professor at Copenhagen Business School, Denmark. Since 2007 she has co-ordinated and taught a master's level course on Diversity Management. Within the field of diversity she is particularly interested in practices of diversity management; currently she is undertaking a field study of diversity management in practice in Sweden.

Gudrun Sander was awarded a Ph.D. from the University of St Gallen Switzerland, where she is currently Senior Lecturer in Gender Studies as well as Strategic Management, Controlling and Leadership. She is responsible for the executive education programme, 'Women Back to Business' and is vice-director of the Executive School of Management, Technology and Law (University of St Gallen). The focus of her research is on issues around gender, diversity and change management in organizations. She has published widely on these topics, mostly in German.

Janne Tienari, who holds a Sc.D. in Organizations and Management, is Professor of Organizations and Management at Aalto University, School of Economics,

Finland, where he teaches CEMS courses on Strategy, Work and International Human Resource Management. His other courses include Gender, Organizations and Management. Janne Tienari's research interests encompass multinational corporations and academic institutions, cross-cultural studies of gender and management, local translations of diversity management, media representations, and the language of global capitalism.

INTRODUCTION
Diversity in Organizations: Concepts and Practices

The workforce of the twenty-first century is characterized by ever increasing diversity in terms of ethnic background, lifestyle, intergenerationality and, of course, the participation of women. In view of all of these trends, it is necessary that managers and indeed all employees develop a greater awareness of concepts and practices that can remove obstacles to the full participation and contribution of workers. A positive approach to diversity, in which organizational systems and practices are fully inclusive, will serve to improve effectiveness and performance.

Diversity in organizations first became recognized as a significant issue in the United States, and therefore has been part of the culture of North American corporations and the curriculum of universities for some time. More recently, an increasing number of European companies have grasped the benefits of inclusive organizational structures, so that on this side of the Atlantic diversity in organizations has also become an urgent topic.

A recurring shortcoming of diversity and diversity management, however, is the difficulty of applying concepts and approaches developed in one particular field to novel settings. In this book we minimize the problem by primarily focusing on policies and legislative practices within Europe, specifically the member states of the European Union (EU). To this restricted field we carefully introduce concepts, research findings and practices that tackle diversity and inclusivity while taking account of diverse historical, political, social and cultural contexts.

Another feature of the book is that it draws on a wide range of recent scholarly work on diversity and inclusivity in organizations to determine how best to establish and sustain inclusive organizations. This focus on *inclusivity* is in contrast to the preoccupation with *difference* found in other publications in this field, which runs the risk of reaffirming static systems of categorization (for example male and female, homosexual and heterosexual, Christian and Muslim). This merely serves to reproduce certain stereotypes and further stigmatize specific groups. In contrast, the current book adopts a more integrative and practical approach by undertaking a comprehensive organizational analysis of how exclusion is subtly and indirectly created and maintained, without ignoring the historically determined structural discrimination of specific groups.

Current trends in society, in the business world and the public sector are reflected in the increasing attention paid to diversity issues in organizations and in the field of economics. Thus companies are forced to create inclusive structures in order to maintain a competitive advantage, as a means to refining their pool of talent and to critically analyse and reflect on organizational practices and ways of 'doing'. Rather than simply pointing to 'problem groups' (such as women, ethnic minorities or disabled people) and trying to find a suitable organizational response, they must attempt to reveal underlying discriminatory practices or obstacles to inclusivity. A more holistic approach is required that takes account of the various levels at which exclusive processes are manifested, that is, the individual employee, the managerial level, the organization itself (by analysing its values and structures) or indeed the societal level in which the organization is located.

The right qualifications, **knowledge and skills** are necessary to deal with such highly complex issues. More specifically, the management of diversity and the creation of a culture of inclusion – two essential ingredients to build a sustainable business for the future according to the European Commission – require individual self-awareness, diversity competence and strategic managerial skills. By presenting current research in the fields of diversity policy, legislation and good practice, the intention is to assist all employees, and in particular managers, to actively shape organizations to become more inclusive. Europe, as one of the world's most diverse regions, provides the framework for our discussion. More specifically, we will investigate how diversity and the goal of inclusion are tackled within the European Union, a unique organization of 27 member states, a combined population of more than 500 million, and whose agencies employ 23 working languages. Problems and practices will be illustrated by real-life examples in order to help readers develop effective diversity and inclusive practices for themselves and the organizations in which they work.

Thus, the book is also designed as a useful guide and resource for for all those who wish to gain knowledge of diversity issues in order to boost organizational performance, in particular managers who wish to increase their organization's effectiveness by optimizing diversity and increasing inclusivity.

The editors hope that students of the subject will benefit from an approach which stresses a *strategic management perspective* to achieving inclusivity in organizations, as well as the impact of *individuals* who are sensitive to issues of culture and diversity, and thus who understand the opportunities and challenges of current societal trends (in Europe: an ageing society, increased ethnic diversity, dissolution of the nuclear family, and so on) and the repercussions on the workplace and our global economy. These two primary concepts can be said to form the scaffolding to our book, *Diversity in Organizations: Concepts and Practices*.

THE STRUCTURE OF THE BOOK

At the beginning of each chapter you will find the following:

- *Chapter objectives*, highlighting the practical and theoretical knowledge to be gained by the end of the chapter;
- *Chapter outline*, signaling the main topics;
- An *Introduction*, establishing the main issues discussed in the chapter and how these relate to inclusiveness.

In each chapter you will also find:

- *Key concepts and terms*, boxed or highlighted to assist readers to communicate effectively about the topics;
- An *on-page glossary* to give easy access to key definitions;
- *Visual aids including figures and tables* to help explain concepts and highlight salient information;
- *Case studies with questions* to provide additional concrete illustrations of the theoretical discussion, and encourage readers to think about their likely actions in certain scenarios and cultural contexts;
- *Stop and reflect questions* to encourage students to reflect critically on differences in perceptions and to assess their own attitudes and beliefs;
- *Review questions* to check comprehension and internalization of the material;
- *Top ten references (*)* are identified to focus readers' attention on the leading academic and practical resources on the topic under discussion.

The final chapter summarizes the most important issues, concepts and practices identified in the course of the book, while a glossary of key terms can be found at the end.

CONTENT OF THE BOOK

Diversity in Organizations: Concepts and Practices is divided into three interrelated parts, taking the reader from an overview of diversity and inclusion and its European context to specific issues regarding the implementation of diversity management.

Part One provides a framework for diversity in organizations and diversity management. Diversity in organizations is positioned within the nexus of organization *theory*, organizational *behaviour* and organization *studies*. The historical background to diversity studies is outlined, followed by a discussion of current concepts and theories.

In the first chapter, entitled 'Theoretical Perspectives on Diversity in Organizations', *Edeltraud Hanappi-Egger* presents an overview of various theoretical strands relevant to a discussion of gender and diversity. She disentangles the historical roots of current scholarly work on diversity and organizations, while introducing the main concepts used throughout subsequent chapters.

In 'Diversity in Europe: Its Development and Contours' *Mary Ann Danowitz* and *Marie-Thérèse Claes* highlight the societal, cultural and political circumstances and backgrounds of diversity management in order to understand the specific opportunities and challenges of organizational inclusivity.

Heike Mensi-Klarbach closes this first part by examining some apparently contradictory arguments in favour of diversity management, namely the 'business case rationale' and the purely 'ethical rationale'. In this discussion of the 'business and moral cases', it becomes clear that a strict either–or approach must be abandoned when seeking to develop sustainable forms of inclusivity in organizations. Instead, ethical and business arguments must *both* be taken into consideration.

After this initial presentation of the book's main themes, we turn in the second part to the question of 'individual and cross-cultural diversity', specifically the necessity of raising awareness of diversity and of critical self-reflection.

In the chapter entitled 'Gender and Diversity Across Cultures', *Marie-Thérèse Claes*, *Edeltraud Hanappi-Egger* and *Henriett Primecz* discuss the vital role of the cultural context. The authors show how culturally constructed meanings of diversity and difference impact on organizational processes (particularly decision-making) in cross-cultural settings.

In the fifth chapter, *Janne Tienari* and *Julia Nentwich* present the approach known as 'doing gender/doing difference'. They demonstrate how inclusive and exclusive practices and attitudes are embedded in organizational structures, hierarchies and ways of doing.

The third part of the book takes a practical turn by examining how inclusive organizations are established in reality, and which steps should be undertaken to ensure that diversity management is sensitive to both context and culture.

The next chapter, by *Mary Ann Danowitz* and *Edeltraud Hanappi-Egger*, explores how different interpretations of diversity produce correspondingly different diversity strategies. The authors describe several leading models of diversity management in terms of strategic and evolving processes.

Based on the notion of diversity as strategy, *Heike Mensi-Klarbach* and *Edeltraud Hanappi-Egger* then turn to the important issue of 'organizational analysis'. They present specific methods and tools which diversity managers can exploit to produce the data and insights necessary to design an optimal diversity model for their individual organizations.

In the following chapter *Annette Risberg*, *Alexandra Beauregard* and *Gudrun Sander* focus on 'organizational implementation' by providing examples of diversity initiatives as management instruments with the potential to trigger structural change. The authors also describe resistance to diversity and ways of dealing with this.

In the ninth chapter, entitled 'Work, Life and a Culture of Care', *Robyn Remke* and *Annette Risberg* emphasize the importance of reflecting critically on the nature of traditional workplace policies and practices. The authors argue that contemporary workplaces must be better adapted to the specific lifestyles and familial circumstances of employees in order to ensure their 'wellness'.

Finally, in the tenth chapter, *Mary Ann Danowitz*, *Edeltraud Hanappi-Egger* and *Heike Mensi-Klarbach* highlight the key points of each chapter, providing an overview of what it means to foster inclusivity in organizations from a management perspective.

PART ONE

FRAMEWORK FOR DIVERSITY

Contents

CHAPTER

THEORETICAL PERSPECTIVES ON DIVERSITY IN ORGANIZATIONS

Edeltraud Hanappi-Egger

Chapter Objectives

After completing this chapter, you should be able to:

- explain the meaning of scientific management in the Industrial Revolution and its role in the gender-specific division of labour;
- describe some early gender topics recognized by management theorists;
- identify the most important scholarly work in organization theory relating to gender and diversity;
- describe how the issue of diversity is tackled from the perspective of organization theory, organizational behaviour and organization studies;
- explain what is meant by difference-oriented diversity and indicate the main points of critique;
- explain the basic ideas behind intersectional diversity;
- explain the difference between gender neutrality and gender blindness in organizations;
- discuss the main arguments for and against diversity management;
- explain the three levels of a relational diversity concept.

Chapter Outline

- Introduction
- Concepts of gender and diversity in organizations
- Studying gender and diversity in organizations
- Implications for the study of organizations
- Bridging the gap: establishing inclusive organizations
- Chapter review questions
- Case study
- References

INTRODUCTION

In early writings in organizational studies one can discern the unspoken assumption that organizations and work are non-gendered. Since the majority of employees were men, and male authors were primarily writing for a male readership (Calás and Smircich, 1991; 2009), the male experience and perspective were considered to be *universally* applicable (Acker, 1992). However, as more and more women joined the paid workforce and feminist scholars began investigating issues around organizations, work and management, the relevance of gender and diversity became clear. Recent demographic and societal changes have provoked a steadily growing interest in the topics of gender and diversity within organizations. To understand how the associated field of research has evolved and changed over time, we must first return to the roots of organization theory and management.

The Industrial Revolution, early gender topics and scientific management

When reviewing early scientific studies which looked at the phenomena of management and organizations, it is obvious that interest in these topics was stimulated by the emergence of large-scale productive units during the Industrial Revolution of the eighteenth century (Hanappi-Egger, 2011). One of the first books to examine the coordination and synchronization of factory work was Adam Smith's *The Wealth of Nations*, written in 1776, while another much later, yet equally salient, work in this field was Henri Fayol's *Administration Industrielle et Générale* of 1916. Of course, one of the most famous books to question the ideology of capitalism and point out its exploitative nature was *Capital* by Karl Marx, first published in 1867.

These early studies of work, work flow and management only made oblique reference to gender and diversity topics. At best they distinguished between men's, women's or children's work, for example in Adam Smith's famous description of how to optimize the production of needles (Hanappi-Egger, 2004), or referred to 'class identity' as the most important feature of the workforce (Zanoni, 2011; Hanappi and Hanappi-Egger, 2011). Thus the first substantial classification in terms of 'diversity' was that of workers versus capitalists, while any further sub-division or alternative form of classification was not explicitly raised.

> *Scientific management* (also called *Taylorism*) refers to an understanding of management as a scientifically informed process of organizing work as efficiently as possible. 'Scientific' in this context refers to a neutral and objective form of management that does not take account of any hidden assumptions, such as those regarding gender and diversity.

Other early publications that touched on the question of gender did so in terms of the working conditions of women, focusing on their special requirements while promoting the idea that women's work should be matched to their physical constitutions (Beblo, Krell, Schenieder and Soete, 1999). The gender gap in income and the moral risks of mixing the two sexes at the workplace were also discussed. Several studies on working women published in the early 1920s examined the 'specific needs' of women, whereby such 'needs' were derived purely from biological considerations. Edgeworth (1922, p. 457) discussed the question of equality of pay for women as follows:

> To sum up; equal pay for equal work, in the sense of equal competition between the sexes, has been advocated, with some reservations and adjustments. Desperate disordered competition, tending to the degradation of labour, is supposed to be excluded. There are suggested compensations to families for the loss sustained by the male breadwinner through the increased competition of women.

Apart from these isolated contributions on the role of women at work, mainstream organization theories remained *gender* and *diversity neutral*, either expressly or implicitly, instead focusing on the economic performance of organizations. This claim of objectivity will be re-visited later in the chapter. Here it is important to emphasize the development of a supposedly 'scientific' form of management based on the popular philosophy of rationalism (Taylor, 1911), in which the advantages of the scientifically based coordination and synchronization of machines and workers were promoted. This led, for instance, to attempts to optimize output by carefully designing tools and intelligently positioning workers on the assembly line. Such arrangements were derived from mathematical modelling, fed by the raw data of precise time and motion studies (Hanappi-Egger, 2004).

Such supposedly 'objective' approaches gave managers the possibility of defending and legitimizing their decisions by referring to efficiency equations devised by scientific experts. This helped eliminate any political dimension to management concepts (along with critical reflection) by asserting the objectivity and truth of scientific investigations fully backed by the precepts of natural science (Mills, Simmons and Mills, 2005). One finds frequent reference to 'natural science' and 'objective facts' in writings on scientific management, and these terms also crop up time and again in discussions on gender and diversity (Hanappi-Egger, 2011). In this context 'objective' links are drawn between some characteristic of diversity, such as skin colour or sex, to some particular work-related skill or aptitude.

> *Rationalism* is a school of thought which emphasizes the importance of intellect and empirical fact in opposition to feelings, intuition, coercive power or religious conviction.

When one considers the societal and political circumstances in Europe at the dawn of the Industrial Revolution, when the aristocracy still held the reigns of power, it is easy to understand how an emerging resistance to feudal power (implying brute force) fostered a keen interest in transparency and rationality. *Rationalism*, and much later *bureaucracy*, became hot topics in organization theory. One of the most important scholars of this stream was the sociologist Max Weber (1864–1920), who taught scholars to view organizations as rational systems, exemplified in his work on bureaucracies (Weber, 1980). The main organizational elements which Weber saw necessary to ensure transparency and objective decision-making were a clear determination of tasks and responsibilities, a strongly hierarchical structure and a clearly articulated system of rules. It is true to say that rationality has remained a central concept in management thinking since the mid-eighteenth century. In particular, mainstream economics has made frequent use of the 'homo oeconomicus' as a synonym for the 'rational decision maker' (Hanappi-Egger, 2011).

Since Weber's early examination of bureaucracy, various theories of the organization have emerged, ranging from classical theories that view organizations as machines, via neo-classical theories on the social aspects of work, to postmodern perspectives which even question our belief in an objective reality (Hanappi-Egger, 2004; Mills et al., 2005). Step by step, these theories have undermined the notion of the 'objective' or 'neutral' organization (Benschop and Doorewaard, 1998), while at the same time highlighting the social and political dimensions. This has led to an abandonment of the 'machine' metaphor and the attempt to optimize organizational processes while ignoring the people who carry them out. Today we view organizations as socio-political systems; the role of workers, their identities, their interests, preferences, wishes and motives have moved to the forefront of organization studies. Doorewaard and Benschop (2003), for example, highlight the importance of emotions in organizations, whether the satisfaction that comes with work well done, or the anger and frustration engendered by a lack of promotion. And, of course, harassment and discrimination based on social categories will greatly disturb the social relations of employees, and thus negatively influence teamwork, promotion and competition (Zanoni, Janssens, Benschop and Nkomo, 2010).

The field of organization studies clearly encompasses a large range of topics. These are sometimes positioned under the rubric 'organization theories' and sometimes under 'organizational behaviour'.

Organization studies, organization theories and organizational behaviour: different concepts, or one and the same?

When trying to define which topics are relevant to the study of organizations, we are confronted by a long and varied list of approaches and potential fields of investigation. Although a clear and unambiguous distinction cannot be made, in general *organization theories* deal with the structural phenomena of organizations (such as hierarchies, culture, and norm systems), while *organizational behaviour* deals with topics related to agents (such as leadership and motivation). More specifically, organizational behaviour involves 'the systematic study of behaviour at work that provides concepts, theories and models to help us make sense of a range of activities from the mundane to the critical.' (Mills et al., 2005, p. 9) This means that some scholars turn to structural analysis to determine hierarchies, norms (that is specific standards of behaviour) and rules, while others focus on the question of how individuals deal with these structures, and how they negotiate the meaning of these rules and norms. Recent research in organization studies has attempted to overcome this distinction between 'structure' and 'agency' by emphasizing the mutual dependencies existing between the given organizational structure and the scope of actions of organizational members. Thus structure refers to a framework that strongly determines the capacities of organizational members to act, while at the same time the agents themselves are continuously re-shaping, producing and reproducing these organizational structures (Giddens, 1997; Bourdieu, 1985).

Organization studies are systematic investigations of structures, practices and ways of 'acting' in organizations. These include:
- *Organization theories*, which deal with the structural framework of organizations and industries (the macro-level), and
- *Organizational behaviour*, which concerns the actions and interactions of individuals and groups (the micro-level).

As Martin and Collinson (2002, p. 246) have pointed out:

> Organization studies is fragmented by the different academic units within which faculty members are located and the different theories and interests they favour. Organization studies, a phrase used more on the European than North American side of the Atlantic, encapsulates multiple disciplinary interests. In general, the phrase stands for management units in UK business schools and management and organization behaviour foci in US business schools.

Hence we should be aware that even though these research fields have slightly different foci, it is difficult to make a sharp distinction between organization studies, organization theories and organizational behaviour. Furthermore, it is important to remember that scholars in organization studies are themselves embedded in specific cultural settings and geographical locations. Again, Martin and Collinson (2002) have highlighted the diversity and fragmentation of research found among academics who investigate organizations, emphasizing that mainstream organization theories and management sciences that are already well established in US academic circles tend to exclude alternative approaches: 'Consequently, critical scholars, those who question the claims of logico-rational depictions of organizations, work in a more hostile climate in the USA than in the UK and Europe' (Martin and Collinson, 2002, p. 250). The authors also point to the development of 'gendered organization theories' (Mumby and Ashcraft, 2006; Britton, 2000; Mills and Tancred, 1992; Acker 1990) as emerging from parallel and divergent disciplines, which address topics from alternative perspectives and with diverse methodological approaches.

> If we assume that organizations are not gender-neutral but that gender plays an indirect, implicit, subtle and often invisible role, then theories of 'gendered organizations' refer to these inherently gendered sub-structures within organizations.

While acknowledging the existence of multiple divergent approaches to gender and diversity, the following section will highlight the most influential work on the role and impact of these issues within organizations.

As a first step the main terms and concepts of gender and diversity will be explained as they relate to organization studies. At the same time we intend to investigate the hidden intentions of commonly used terms in order to stress the importance of questioning taken-for-granted knowledge.

CONCEPTS OF GENDER AND DIVERSITY IN ORGANIZATIONS

Is gender in organizations only a matter of women's studies?

For our purposes the term *sex* refers to a classification by purely biological indicators, while *gender* is understood to refer to socially constructed meanings of being a man or a woman. Often this distinction is forgotten, so that the artificial aspect of gender is overlooked and a manifold concept is reduced to a strict male/female dichotomy. From their earliest years children are labelled as 'boys' or 'girls' on the basis of a biological classification, while purely *social constructions* of femininity and masculinity are attributed and matched with the nature of 'being a man' or 'being a woman'. Thus a relatively strict dualistic gender system is dominant in many cultural contexts, and alternative concepts such as those evinced by inter- or transgender individuals are disregarded.

Over the last few decades some scholars have come to question the 'natural' sex-based ordering of societies, identifying this as a social construction and introducing the concept of 'gender' to argue that the subordination of women is not due to mere physical subjugation, but rather to societal inequalities as socially generated phenomena. Some scholars have argued that since gender is not derived from but merely related to sex, an 'either–or' perspective of strict dualism is unsupportable (Wetterer 1995). Furthermore, it has even been claimed that the concept of sex is itself the result of specific social processes: the biological definition of sex, and in particular the rigid distinction between the two sexes leading to marginalization of other forms as 'abnormal' (such as inter- or transgender individuals), is said to be the result of societal power relations and conventions (Butler, 2004; Ferber, Holcomb and Wrentling, 2008).

Questions relating to gender and diversity in organizations are commonly ascribed to the field of 'women's studies'. Indeed, early investigations of diversity in management and organization saw the role of women from the perspective of organization theory. As Mills et al. (2005) found when reviewing leading textbooks on management published over the previous twenty years in Canada, very few dealt with race and ethnicity.[1] More recent publications have indeed emphasized the importance of diversity, defining the concept as 'everyone other than white males' (ibid., p. 23). This tendency towards gender and diversity bias in scholarly work in organization studies – namely considering the white male as the only or primary representative of society, and disqualifying the majority of people as 'the others' – has come under a great deal of criticism. As far back as 1974 Acker and van Houten re-analysed two classical studies, the Hawthorne studies carried out in the USA and Crozier's work on French bureaucracies, to determine that sex differences may be more a result of organizational structures and processes than of biology, socialization, attitudes or values. Acker and van Houten's work was the first to show that sex-related inequality of power shapes organizational processes such as recruitment, a fact that today is well supported in research and unfortunately still exists in practice.

Moving from gender to diversity in organizations

While gender remains an important topic in organizations, more and more scholars are turning to the role of diversity. This rather elastic concept is often defined using social categories such as age, ethnicity, beliefs or religion, disability and sexual orientation. These categories refer to historically shaped

---

[1] Note: In German-speaking countries the term 'Rasse' ('race') is highly controversial due to its association with Nazi ideology. Hence, in several European countries the reference to 'ethnicity' or 'colour' is preferred.

groups that have been subjected to discrimination. The European Union (EU) has formulated an anti-discrimination guideline (see Chapter 2) based on this classification, and most companies that address the topic of diversity adopt these categories when attempting to build inclusive organizations. Kandola and Fullerton (1998, p. 7) define diversity as follows: 'The basic concept of diversity accepts that the workforce consists of a diverse population of people. The diversity consists of visible and non-visible differences which include factors such as sex, age, background, race [see footnote 1], disability, personality and work-style.'

There exists various approaches to the topic of diversity and how, if at all, the groups who should benefit from measures to reduce discrimination and exclusion should be specified. In this context we can identify two main schools of thought: the difference-oriented approach and the intersectional/anti-categorical approach.

Difference-oriented approaches

Since it is assumed that diversity implies *difference*, a fundamental question to be answered is: what kind of difference are we dealing with? Which differences can prove advantageous or a hindrance in various social settings? Analysis and discussion regarding inclusiveness and exclusiveness are commonly carried out on the basis of social categories.

Social categories refer to a system of classifying individuals in terms of social categories such sex, religion, age and so on.
  Diversity dimension (or *diversity marker*) refers to one of these specific social categories.

Various ways of classifying individuals have been adopted, such as the following:

- Visible (race, gender . . .) and invisible (religion, sexual orientation . . .) diversity dimensions (Voigt, 2001).
- Person-immanent diversity (sex, sexual orientation, education, background . . .) and behaviour-immanent diversity (behaviour as a consequence of person-immanent diversity; a person's background is believed to determine how they behave in certain situations) (Thomas, 2001).
- Internal dimensions (which are usually permanent, such as sex, sexual orientation or age), external dimensions (which are in some way selected, and thus may be subject to change, such as education or religion) and work-related diversity dimensions (seniority, division, functional belonging, and so on) (Gardenswartz and Rowe, 1994).

- Historically discriminated groups (defined by sex, sexual orientation, age, ethnicity, disability, religion) (European Anti-Discrimination Law: Verloo, 2006).

The various approaches can be distinguished by the social categories which they adopt, and how these are labelled or grouped (Table 1.1).

Consider how you would classify yourself according to these categories. Which difficulties do you encounter with this kind of classification system? Why?

These so-called *essentialist* classification systems are frequently criticized for imposing rather static distinctions between individuals to create mutually exclusive groups (Lorbiecki and Jack, 2000), while internal homogeneity is assumed to exist within each group. Additional dubious assumptions are introduced to strengthen the classification, so that all 'homosexuals', for example, are viewed as possessing similar identities, or 'men' are assigned various physical and mental traits considered typical of the male sex, regardless of the validity in each case. Specific attributions are imposed on such 'target groups', which can serve to reproduce stereotypes.

Essentialism refers to the idea that people have an immutable 'essence' which is the root cause of their behaviour. In particular, it is assumed that biological traits are responsible for social behaviour (for example gender-specific skills).

Table 1.1 Classification systems of diversity dimensions

Diversity dimension	Classification systems
age	internal dimension, visible, person-immanent, historically discriminated
sex	internal dimension, visible, person-immanent, historically discriminated
sexual orientation	internal dimension, visible, person-immanent, historically discriminated
ethnicity	internal dimension, visible? (physical characteristics), person-immanent, historically discriminated
physical ability	internal dimension, visible? (physical aids . . .), person-immanent, historically discriminated
class	external dimension (?), invisible, behaviour-immanent
education	external dimension, invisible, behaviour-immanent
religion/beliefs	external dimension, visible? (signs, dress codes), historically discriminated
parental status	external dimension, invisible, behaviour-immanent
management status	organizational dimension, invisible, behaviour-immanent?
work content	organizational dimension, invisible? (visible in dress codes)

There is a heated debate amongst scholars studying diversity in organizations as to whether these specified groups do actually possess internal homogeneity. Thus it has been argued, for example, that 'women' or 'Catholics' or 'the French' do not truly exist as definable groups; these categorizations are said to be based on stereotypes that simply cannot be applied to individuals who are supposed to share a group characteristic. This means that even if Susan can be labelled as 'a woman', it cannot then be assumed that she displays the range of characteristics attributed to 'being a woman' (in stereotypical terms such as being relation-oriented, emotional or intuitive). Similarly, it has been argued that such social labelling imposes a static characterization independent of the relevant social context. Such approaches which focus on these group labels are called *difference-oriented* approaches (or *essentialist* approaches), and to those adopting such approaches it appears relatively straightforward to develop such a system of social classification.

However, it is easy to see that such a rigid classification in terms of social categories does not adequately capture the complexity of self-understandings which most people hold. For example, what does it mean to be a 50-plus French Muslim single gay man? How do we decide which social categorization is relevant to each situation?

To overcome this restrictive assumption that individuals can be uniquely assigned to one social group, several scholars have introduced the notion of *intersectionality* into diversity studies (McCall, 2005; Knapp, 2005; Eberherr and Hanappi-Egger, 2010).

Intersectional/inter-categorical approaches

The term *intersectionality* was first introduced by Crenshaw (1989) to emphasize the fact that black women's experience of oppression is complex and multi-level rather than a simple fusion of sexism and racism. If we agree that individual forms of oppressions can overlap to create a complex system of multiple forms of discrimination, then intersectionality can either be taken to refer to the interplay of several social categories (such as gender, age and ethnicity) within organizations (Collins, 1998) or it can refer to 'inequality regimes' as defined by Acker to be 'loosely interrelated practices, processes, actions and meaning that result in and maintain class, gender and racial inequalities within particular organizations.' (Acker, 2006, p. 443)

Such inter-, intra- and anti-categorical approaches are becoming ever more widely adopted by scholars investigating diversity. An inter-categorical perspective examines the relationship *between* categories: if, for instance, a job vacancy is announced, and the resulting applications are from a local man, a man with a migration background, a local woman and a woman with a migration background, then an inter-categorical analysis might focus on how the human resource manager goes about choosing whom to hire given that all applicants are equally qualified.

An intra-categorical perspective means highlighting the differences *within* a specific category, such as the above mentioned male applicants and their social backgrounds.

Anti-categorical approaches are deconstructionist and post-structuralist analyses of practices which create inequalities. An example would be to study a company's formal and informal recruiting procedures in order to uncover subtle exclusion mechanisms. Scheduling meetings in the evenings, for instance, excludes people with caring obligations, who in most cases are women (see Chapter 8).

The idea of intersectionality is to try to encompass various aspects of oppression or subordination, as well as the mutual influences and commonalities of different forms of discrimination.

Although these more complex, less essentialist, approaches are frequently referred to in scholarly works on diversity studies, their application in the case of individual organizations is difficult and challenging. As Boogaard and Roggeband (2010) have pointed out, the 'operationalization' of intersectional analyses presents particular difficulties.

McDowell (2008) has expressed concern regarding an increase in fragmentation as well as the reluctance of researchers to adopt multiple approaches in work studies related to intersectionality. She writes: 'But still an anxiety remains. Is the theoretical and practical consequence of fragmentation, the emphasis on difference and diversity, a neglect of the commonalities facing the new global proletariat, making it more difficult to organize across space and scale, across differences of locality, gender and lived experiences?' (McDowell, 2008, p. 505) This highlights the dangers of focusing too narrowly on differences per se and of trying to identify group commonalities, so that unifying elements *between* such groups and commonly shared living contexts are ignored or lost.

Another concept strongly linked to diversity in organizations is *diversity management*. This rather popular term refers to the notion that, in reaction to a growing diversity within organizations, managers must maintain an awareness of the different needs and requirements of their workforce. They should also be responsible for the elimination of discrimination and the unfair treatment of minority groups, and consequently should establish inclusive structures.

Diversity management can be defined as a management concept which, acknowledging the value of difference, strategically and systemically strives to promote equity among its workforce in order to create added value.

Diversity management: solution or problem?

Kandola and Fullerton (1998, p. 7) define diversity management to be 'founded on the premise that harnessing these differences [social categories such as gender, sexual orientation, religion, age, disability and ethnicity] will create a productive environment in which everyone feels valued, where their talents are being fully utilized and in which organizational goals are met.'

This raises several important issues relevant to any discussion of diversity in organizations: First, the definition assumes that diversity is already present in organizations due to an underlying heterogeneity in the societal environment. This relates to the idea of organizations as *open systems*, that is, products of their societal environment which, in turn, reshape this environment (Scott, 1986). Secondly, it identifies several social categories which determine social opportunities and a risk of discrimination. Third, it opens up the business case of diversity management by referring to the utilization of diversity for organizational goals. This is the view that diversity, if managed properly, can contribute to the economic success of an organization (see Chapter 3).

As these aspects can be interpreted as both pros *and* cons, diversity management is a subject of contentious debate regarding the validity of some underlying assumptions:

Thus it is often argued that the focus solely on management is skewed by ignoring the contribution of all organizational members.

Also the rather functionalist belief that diversity can be 'managed' has come under criticism. A functionalist view sees diversity merely as a resource that is a means by which to optimize performance.

Finally, the business case approach is often posited as being in opposition to the efforts of anti-discrimination movements (Kelly and Dobbin 1998).

It is strange that despite the strong case that can be made for the economic benefits of diversity management (such as cost-savings and increased productivity), many companies have not yet begun tackling diversity in a more strategic and sophisticated way. Hanappi-Egger and Hofmann (2012) provide an explanation for this by emphasizing that organizations are open systems which re-create and reproduce societal hierarchies in terms of gender and diversity. They point out that gender-specific phenomena observed on the labour market (such as the majority of workers in social/caring professions being women, while men continue to dominate engineering and technological fields) are reflected in a parallel dynamic within organizations (secretaries are mostly women and the vast majority of CEOs men).

Hence, organizations do not *invent* but rather *reproduce* gender and diversity relations such as the gender segregation of working fields and structural discrimination based on ethnicity, religion, sexual orientation, age and disability. It is important to bear in mind when working through this book that the way people perceive diversity, and how and why they make sense of diversity, always depends on the social context. This underlines the importance of considering the societal environment when attempting to understand and design a diversity strategy. For example, Grimes (2002) has challenged the colour bias in diversity research which, due to the prevalence of white researchers, continues to assume white to be the ethnic norm; or consider the ongoing discussion on the cultural bias of the concepts of diversity and diversity management with regard to US-American roots. Syed and Özbilgin (2009) have discussed how the sociodemographic setting in Europe differs from that of the USA, arguing that diversity management in the latter is not simply transferable to the European context since the legal frameworks, as well as cultural backgrounds, are quite different (Verloo, 2006). Additionally the business-case view of diversity has been criticized (Hanappi-Egger, Köllen and Mensi-Klarbach, 2007; Mensi-Klarbach, 2010) and closely examined in relation to business ethics and theories of empowerment (Wetterer, 2002; Wrench, 2005; Noon, 2007).

The implementation of diversity management in organizations

Several studies on the implementation of diversity management have shown that organizations adopt the concept of specific target groups when attempting to improve under-representation (Krell, Riedmüller, Sieben and Vinz, 2007). However, efforts to recruit and include representatives of socially disadvantaged groups sometimes end up reproducing stereotypes and stigmatization (Gilbert, Stead and Ivancevich, 1999). The specification of target groups for diversity management and the introduction of measures to foster acceptance and integration often leads to effects very different to those intended. In fact they may even provoke counter-reaction and backlash, as well as resistance by groups in power and those being questioned (Johnson, 2006; Dwyer, Richard and Chadwick, 2003).

This means that an explicit focus on specific target groups for diversity management may be more problematic than at first appears. On the other hand, postmodern approaches that emphasize a *fluid* identity construction (referring to the complexity, dynamism, temporality and context-dependency of identity) have been criticized from an anti-discrimination perspective. Such approaches, it is claimed, neglect the historical and systematic discrimination of groups based on race/ethnicity, gender, sexual orientation and religion as well as the male bias (Brodribb, 1992).

This dilemma of how to specify historically discriminated groups without merely reproducing stereotypes cannot be easily resolved. However, for *analytical* purposes it is certainly helpful to refer to those social groups that historically have suffered some form of discrimination, while at the same time bearing in mind this risk of reproducing stereotypes.

The managers of a food company located in Germany decide to hire a sales person from the immigrant Turkish community in order to better serve Turkish clientele. In addition to the obvious benefits that the new employee's language skills will bring, it is assumed that he or she will be familiar with Turkish culture, and consequently better able to identify with what 'Turkish people want'.

Consider which stereotypes are being reinforced by this approach. What expectations might be placed on the Turkish employee, and which roles might he or she be forced to adopt? Which problems could the employee face? How might the other workers react to this measure?

Can you find similar examples from your own environment in which such stereotypical assumptions are held?

STUDYING GENDER AND DIVERSITY IN ORGANIZATIONS

After highlighting various approaches and perspectives on gender and diversity, we now turn to another important question: what is the best way to investigate gender and diversity topics in organizations in order to identify and address problems of discrimination and exclusion? Which approaches are useful, and which methods can be adopted? Here only a brief overview of various approaches will be given, with more detailed discussion and examples offered in later chapters.

But first let us try to answer a question we posed earlier: are organizations neutral in the sense that social categorization is irrelevant? We shall begin our investigation with the topic of gender:

Why organizations are not gender-neutral

Doubts are often expressed whether the concept of gender is in any way relevant to the functioning of organizations, since the main features of organizational practices are to focus on performance, excellence and quality. These indicators are assumed to be completely unrelated to gender, instead depending on skills, qualifications and other 'objective' factors. The argument is frequently heard that, regardless of their sex, sexual orientation, religious beliefs and the like, individuals basically have the same opportunities for employment or promotion if they meet the qualification requirements.

In contrast to this view, several scholars have theorized that organizations are gender *blind* rather than gender *neutral*. This means that although it may appear as if gender does not play any role in organizational practices, a deeper investigation reveals the presence of hidden gender dimensions. Gender-blindness thus refers to the *neglect* of gendered phenomena. For example, training courses that many companies offer to their employees are often scheduled for the evenings or weekends. Sometimes they are held in locations outside the workplace, or even abroad. At first glance it seems that all workers who are selected and show interest can participate; therefore, the measure appears gender-neutral.

A closer look, however, reveals that this kind of further training opportunity can cause tremendous problems for people who have private obligations which reduce their flexibility. Employees with caring responsibilities which cannot be delegated are indirectly excluded from participation – and these are more likely to be women.

Thus the proposed further training is not gender-neutral but gender-blind, meaning that it ignores the living circumstances of employees and the wider social implications.

Dana Britton (2000) has highlighted some of the pathbreaking contributions to the discussion around 'gendered organizations' from the previous few decades. Perhaps the most influential work in this field has been that published by Kanter (1977) and Acker (1990). Rosabeth Moss Kanter investigated the influence of power, opportunities and workforce sex ratios within organizations. She explored the repercussions on sex and gender, including how roles and jobs are typically assigned to men and women so that the former are more likely to hold management jobs and enjoy greater power. In related work, Joan Acker (1990; 1992) investigated the gendered processes and practices found in organizations that serve to reproduce gender relations and maintain traditional power structures. The most important of these are the gender-specific divisions of tasks, certain symbols (such as dress codes for men and women), employee interaction and 'doing gender' (see Chapter 5), the actions of individuals (for example following these dress codes) and internal rules and standard practices (for example scheduling meetings in the evenings).

Fletcher and Ely (2003, p. 5) have described the various approaches of gender scholars to management and organizations topics. These are formulated as follows:

- 'Fix the women'
  In this approach gender is defined as socialized sex differences. The focus of interest is on the dubious assumption that women lack the skills and knowledge of how to 'play the game'. Gender equity is to be achieved by the elimination of differences between the sexes, meaning that women are to be encouraged to adopt male-typical characteristics.
- 'Celebrate differences'
  Here gender is understood to be socialized sex differences along with separate spheres of activities. The problem is identified as the low regard for women's skills, with the solution being to recognize and value these differences in order to assure a plurality of values, both feminine and masculine.
- 'Create equal opportunities'
  Here sex differences in treatment, access to resources and opportunity are assumed to stem from unbalanced structures of power. Thus, a more equal

distribution of power between men and women is viewed as a fundamental step to ensuring a more objective and less sexist treatment of the workforce.

- 'Revise work culture'
  Here gender is considered to be a central organizing feature of social life, embedded within belief systems, knowledge systems and social practices. Although social practices are designed by and for white, heterosexual, class-privileged men, these are masked to appear neutral. This hidden gender bias should be identified and underlying access barriers eliminated.

Review Questions

How would you classify the following measures in terms of Fletcher and Ely's list?

- a training course for women aimed at increasing their self-confidence to apply for top management jobs;
- the introduction of a women's quota;
- a promotional campaign to ensure 'more power for women in political decision-making';
- the development of a new company mission statement regarding the handling of diversity.

Explain your decisions. Based on your own experiences, can you identify other examples of organizational measures or programmes which could be placed in these four categories?

IMPLICATIONS FOR THE STUDY OF ORGANIZATIONS

The approach that aims to 'revise work culture' highlights an important issue: Gender should not be viewed as an individual, static phenomenon, but rather understood as a multidimensional set of social relations continually being reshaped by organizational structures and practices (and vice versa), thus contributing to the sense-making of gender in organizational interactions. This means that gender should be viewed as a process of 'doing gender', as defined by West and Zimmermann (1987).

From gender to diversity in organizations

Turning to scholarly work on diversity, Merrill-Sands, Holvino and Cumming (2003, p. 327) identify several different 'lenses' that provide a theoretical framework to the topic of diversity in organizations:

The *social difference lens* looks at organizational demography (Nkomo and Cox, 1996) to examine how differences among group identities affect work behaviour and outcome, in view of the fact that individuals 'do not leave their racial, gender or ethnic identities at the door when they enter an organization' (ibid., p. 342). Thus, for example, the focus of interest turns to those mechanisms that lead to the gender-specific division of labour in a company.

The *cultural difference lens* examines 'cultural differences of diverse nationalities or ethnic groups'. This can help to identify subtle exclusion mechanisms, for example, when an organization holds a Christmas party while ignoring other religious groups and their celebrations.

Finally, the *cognitive-functional lens* emphasizes task-relations, highlighting the different skills, work styles and expertise of organizational members (Jehn, Northcraft and Neale, 1999). This can be useful, for example, when analysing team work that involves specialists from different professions, such as engineers and artists collaborating in the development of video games.

In a similar fashion to the discussion on how best to investigate gender in organizations, the various aspects and approaches to diversity in organizations can be described as follows.

Although diversity can be investigated using the various lenses outlined above, the primary distinction can be said to lie between the notions 'fix the group' and 'celebrate the difference', namely classifying workers into social categories and studying how they contribute to organizational outcomes. This is particularly true in regard to social and cultural differences. The question of cognitive-functional differences is tied to work styles and skills, which are not necessarily related to socio-demographic aspects, although some stereotypes and prejudices might exist regarding, say, discipline and cultural background (punctuality as a German characteristic, for example). Evidently such stereotypical thinking should not play a role in professional management.

As we can see, there are multiple approaches to the meaning of diversity in organizations and how best to analyse it. Each involves different assumptions while also identifying and addressing different problems. However, experts in this field generally concur with the view that it is urgently necessary to eliminate highly exclusive organizational frameworks that systematically reproduce dominant views, and thereby promote specific groups while disadvantaging others. The following section, and other chapters in this book, will discuss how this can be achieved.

BRIDGING THE GAP: ESTABLISHING INCLUSIVE ORGANIZATIONS

Organizations form complex social spaces inhabited by human beings. Thus they present a multitude of challenges and opportunities regarding diversity, such as a web of power relations, competitive situations, prejudices (meaning the attribution of stereotypical characteristics) and diverse goals. Embedded in larger societal environments, organizations are also shaped by external value systems. On the one hand this means that the historic and systematic discrimination of specific groups cannot be ignored when analysing an organization. On the other hand such a difference-oriented approach runs the risk of reproducing stereotypes, thereby stigmatizing so-called 'problem-groups'. Diversity management is a *functionalist* approach (adopting an instrumentalist view of difference) which deals with diversity in organizations by assuming that diversity can be consciously *utilized* for economic benefit. It is clear that organizations reproduce societal power structures, which have to be challenged when attempting to overcome discrimination. The commitment of those in power is necessary if exclusion is to be eliminated and employees given an opportunity to increase their empowerment.

The wide-ranging scholarly debate on the sense and nonsense of diversity management has stimulated the development of a new concept that tries to overcome various difficulties and reduce the resistance of empowered groups. This is the concept of *inclusion*, meaning the establishment of organizational structures which do not disadvantage any one specific group.

While a rigid focus on *diversity* might serve to maintain a 'majority group' (representing the norm) by making continual reference to it, the idea behind inclusion is the attempt to repudiate such a majority–minority mindset by establishing inclusive internal structures and processes. To make this more practicable, Syed and Özbilgin (2009, p. 2440) have proposed a multi-level, relational approach to organization and organizational practices (italics by the chapter author):

> *The macro-national level* involves structural conditions including social stratification and beliefs, and the social conception of law, education, family and work that either inhibits or enhances equality of opportunity for
> individuals.
>
> *The meso-organizational level* involves the organizational processes and approaches to diversity which mediate employment opportunities according to individual abilities and contextual circumstances.
>
> *The micro-individual level* involves factors including individual agency, identity and various forms of human capital as key influences on individual capabilities and opportunities.
>
> It is, nevertheless, acknowledged that the layers defined here do not reside in different geographies but are irreducibly interdependent and interrelated: hence the term "relational". The inclusion of multiple levels of analysis allows for an examination of diversity and equal opportunity as a negotiated process, which is socially and historically embedded.

In terms of inclusion this means creating a culturally sensitive inclusive working environment in organizations, which takes the specific societal context into consideration.

Inclusion means enabling and valuing the participation of all employees so that they contribute fully to the organization.

Roberson's (2004, p. 215) argument that 'inclusion represents a person's ability to contribute fully and effectively to an organization' clearly focuses on the individual level while disregarding the question of organizational structures. On the other hand, Pless and Maak (2004, p. 130) have pointed out that 'diversity management has to be built on solid normative grounds, on founding principles, understood as pillars of a culture of inclusion.[...] We argue, therefore, that in order to unleash the potential of workforce diversity, a culture of inclusion needs to be established.'

Here the authors make clear the necessity of providing a structural framework for the individual contribution. However, it is vital that the individual, the structural and the interactional level are all taken into consideration when attempting to establish inclusive working conditions.

At this point it is perhaps useful to mention two basic tenets underlying all the contributions to this book. First, the avoidance of any attempt to pinpoint 'victims' or 'offenders' in the discussion around diversity, instead analysing social mechanisms as well as organizational processes and practices which produce and reproduce discriminatory situations. Second, to consider the role of individual behaviour as well as the interactional level (interface). Thus the establishment of inclusive organizations is seen a multi-layered, relational and multi-faceted process.

Based on this reasoning, the following chapters will examine these various levels of organizational analysis in order to identify the main barriers to the establishment of inclusive structures, while providing insights and practices to prepare managers for the important task of diversity management.

Chapter Review Questions

- What was the original impulse giving rise to the field of scientific management, and which role did gender and diversity play?
- How did early scholarly writings on management address the topic of gender?
- What is the main difference between organization theory and organizational behaviour?
- How would you describe 'gender blindness'?
- What is meant when we speak of 'doing gender'?
- What are the main critiques of diversity management?
- What is meant by 'inclusive organizations'?

The following example will give an idea of how organizations, in particular companies, are dealing with societal changes and the increasing importance of diversity.

Case Study

The constant change and dynamism in our understanding of diversity and inclusion at the societal level have had a remarkable impact on companies. Here we consider the example of Propharma, a key player in the pharmaceutical industry, with headquarters in Germany and more than 150 subsidiaries around the world. Several decades ago Propharma's leadership identified the management of human resources as crucial to maintaining international competitiveness. This led to the establishment of a department for women's issues and an explicit focus on the diverse needs of employees, reflected in a range of activities. A childcare centre was opened in 1973, an agreement for part-time working arrangements drawn up in 1984, a project group on equal opportunities set up in 1988, and in 1990 family-oriented policies were implemented to foster special working arrangements for parents.

From 1990–95 the focus shifted from families to issues directly affecting women, resulting in several initiatives such as awareness-raising activities, mentoring programmes and network building.

From 1996–2000 the emphasis shifted towards 'dialogue between men and women' and the advancement of women to top management positions. In 1997 the relevant department was renamed the 'Department for Equal Opportunities'. From 2001 the company promoted several issues related to diversity, for which the following definition was adopted: 'Diversity encompasses gender, age, cultural background or nationality, lifestyle, education and professional biography.'

This led to various positive steps such as initiatives to support gay and lesbian employees, the organization of social events for employees from different cultures, an open discussion of generational diversity, the introduction of diversity management, as well as the contracting of outside providers to offer household services such as laundry pick-up and delivery to company offices.

The company mission statement was reformulated in 2001 to include the aim of establishing 'an organizational structure that allows employees to deploy their abilities and potentials and allow a good work-life-balance.' Propharma subsequently received several awards, both at home and abroad, for its fostering of equal opportunity.

Test Your Understanding

1. How did this company's understanding of 'diversity' change over time?
2. How would you compare and contrast these understandings or approaches to diversity?
3. What might have been the underlying reasons for these changes?
4. What are the most significant aspects of this case?

REFERENCES

J. Acker (1990) 'Hierarchies, Jobs, Bodies: A Theory of Gendered Organizations', *Gender & Society*, 4 (2), 139–58.

J. Acker (1992) 'Gendering Organizational Theory' in A. Mills and P. Trancred (eds) *Gendering Organizational Analysis* (Newbury Park /London/New Dehli: Sage), pp. 248–60.

*J. Acker (2006) 'Inequality Regimes: Gender, Class, and Race in Organizations', *Gender & Society*, 2006/20 (4), 441–64.

J. Acker and D. R. van Houten (1974) 'Differential Recruitment and Control: The Sex Structuring of Organizations', *Administrative Science Quarterly*, 19 (2), 152–63.

M. Beblo, G. Krell, K. Schenieder and B. Soete (1999) *Ökonomie und Geschlecht* (München Mering: Rainer Hampp).

*Y. Benschop and H. Doorewaard (1998) 'Six of One and Half a Dozen of the Other: The Gender Subtext of Taylorism and Team-based Work', *Gender, Work and Organization*, 1 (5), 5–18.

B. Boogaard and C. Roggeband (2010) 'Paradoxes of Intersectionality: Theorizing Inequality in the Dutch Police Force through Structure and Agency', *Organization*, 17 (1), 53–75.

P. Bourdieu (1985) *Praktische Vernunft. Zur Theorie des Handelns* (Frankfurt: Suhrkamp).

D. M. Britton (2000) 'The Epistemology of the Gendered Organization', *Gender & Society*, 14, 418–34.

S. Brodribb (1992) *Nothing mat(t)ers: A Feminist Critique of Postmodernism* (North Melbourne: Spinifex Press).

J. Butler (2004) *Undoing Gender* (London and New York: Routledge).

M. Calás and L. Smircich (1991) 'Voicing Seduction to Silence Leadership', *Organization Studies*, 12 (4), 567–602.

M. Calás and Smircich, L. (2009) 'Feminist Perspectives on Gender in Organization Research: What is and is Yet to be' in D. A. Buchanan and A. Bryman (eds) *The SAGE Handbook of Organizational Research Methods* (London: Sage), pp. 246–69.

P. Collins (1998) *Fighting Words: Black Women and the Search for Justice* (Minneapolis: University of Minnesota Press).

K. Crenshaw (1989) 'Demarginalizing the Intersection of Race and Sex: A Black Feminist Critique of Anti-discrimination Doctrine, Feminist Theory and Anti-racist Politics', *HeinOnline*, University of Chicago Legal Forum, 139–68.

H. Doorewaard and Y. Benschop (2003) 'HRM and Organizational Change: An Emotional Endeavor', *Journal of Organisational Change Management,* 16 (3), 272–86.

S. Dwyer, O. Richard and K. Chadwick (2003) 'Gender Diversity in Management and Firm Performance: The Influence of Growth Orientation and Organizational Culture', *Journal of Business Research*, 56 (12), 1009–19.

H. Eberherr and E. Hanappi-Egger (2010) 'The Role of Diversity and Intersectionality in City Councils', *European Journal of Cross Cultural Competence and Management,* 1 (2/3), 266–80.

F. Y. Edgeworth (1922) 'Equal Pay to Men and Women for Equal Work', *The Economic Journal*, 32 (128), 431–57.

*A. K. Ferber, K. Holcomb and T. Wrentling (2008) *Sex, Gender, and Sexuality* (The New Basics Oxford: Oxford University Press).

J. Fletcher, and R. J. Ely (2003) 'Introducing Gender: Overview' in R. J. Ely, G. Foldy and M. Scully (eds) *Reader in Gender, Work, and Organization* (Malden: Blackwell), pp. 3–9.

L. Gardenswartz and A. Rowe (1994) *Diversity Teams at Work* (Irwin: McGraw-Hill).

A. Giddens (1997) *Die Konstitution der Gesellschaft* (Frankfurt/New York: Campus).

*J. A. Gilbert, B. A. Stead and J. M. Ivancevich (1999) 'Diversity Management: A New Organizational Paradigm', *Journal of Business Ethics*, 21, 61–76.

D. S. Grimes (2002) 'Challenging the Status Quo? Whiteness in the Diversity Management Literature', *Management Communication Quarterly*, 15 (3), February 2002, 381–409.

H. Hanappi and E. Hanappi-Egger (2011) 'Exploitation Re-visited: New Forms, Same Ideologies?' Presentation at the AHE-conference, Nottingham, Great Britain, 6–9 July 2011.

E. Hanappi-Egger (2004) 'Einführung in die Organisationstheorien unter besonderer Berücksichtigung von Gender- und Diversitätsaspekten' in R. Bendl, E. Hanappi-Egger and R. Hofmann (eds) *Interdisziplinäres Gender- und Diversitätsmanagement, Einführung in Theorie und Praxis* (Vienna: Linde international), pp. 21–42.

E. Hanappi-Egger (2006) 'Gender and Diversity from a Management Perspective: Synonyms or Complements?', *Journal of Organisational Transformation & Social Change*, 3 (2), 121–34.

*E. Hanappi-Egger (2011) *The Triple M of Organizations: Man, Management and Myth* (Vienna/New York: Springer).

E. Hanappi-Egger and R. Hofmann (2012) 'Diversitätsmanagement unter der Perspektive organisationalen Lernens: Wissens- und Kompetenzentwicklung für inklusive Organisationen' in R. Bendl, E. Hanappi-Egger and R. Hofmann (eds) *Diversität und Diversitätsmanagement* (Vienna: Facultas), pp. 327–49.

E. Hanappi-Egger, T. Köllen and H. Mensi-Klarbach (2007) 'Diversity Management: Economically Reasonable or "only" Ethically Mandatory?', *The International Journal of Diversity in Organisations, Communities and Nations*, 7 (3), 159–68.

K. A. Jehn, G. B. Northcraft and M. A. Neale (1999) 'Why Differences Make Difference: A Field Study of Diversity, Conflict, and Performance in Workgroups', *Administrative Science Quarterly*, 44, 741–63.

*A. Johnson (2006) *Privilege, Power and Difference*, 2nd ed. (Boston, Mass.: McGraw Hill).

R. Kandola and J. Fullerton (1998) *Managing the Mosaic: Diversity in Action*, 2nd ed. (London: Institute of Personnel Development).

R. M. Kanter (1977) *Men and Women of the Corporation* (New York: Basic Books).

E. Kelly and F. Dobbin (1998) 'How Affirmative Action Became Diversity Management', *American Behavioral Scientist*, 4 (7), 960–84.

G. Knapp (2005) 'Race, Class, Gender: Reclaiming Baggage in Fast Travelling Theories', *European Journal of Women's Studies*, 12 (3), 249–65.

G. Krell, B. Riedmüller, B. Sieben and D. Vinz (2007) *Diversity Studies. Grundlagen und disziplinäre Ansätze* (Frankfurt/M: Suhrkamp).

A. Lorbiecki and G. Jack (2000) 'Critical Turns in the Evolution of Diversity Management', *British Journal of Management*, 11, Special Issue, 17–31.

P. Martin and D. Collinson (2002) ' "Over the Pond and Across the Water": Developing the Field of "Gendered Organizations" ', *Gender, Work and Organisation*, 9 (3), 244–65.

L. McCall (2005) 'The Complexity of Intersectionality', *Signs. Journal of Women in Culture and Society*, 30 (3), 1771–80.

L. McDowell (2008) 'Thinking Through Work: Complex Inequalities, Constructions of Difference and Trans-national Migrants', *Progress in Human Geography*, 32 (4), 491–507.

H. Mensi-Klarbach (2010) *Diversity und Diversity Management- die Business Case Perspektive. Eine kritische Analyse* (Hamburg: Kovac).

D. Merrill-Sands, E. Holvino and J. Cumming (2003) 'Working with Diversity: A focus on Global Organizations' in R. Ely, E. Foldy and M. Scully (eds) *Reader in Gender, Work and Organization* (Malden: Blackwell), pp. 327–42.

A. J. Mills, T. Simmons and J. H. Mills (2005) *Reading Organization Theory* (Aurora: Garamond Press).

*A. J. Mills and P. Tancred (1992) *Gendering Organizational Analysis* (London and New Delhi: Sage).

D. Mumby and K. Ashcraft (2006) 'Organizational Communication Studies and Gendered Organization: A Response to Martin and Collinson' *Gender, Work and Organization*, 13 (1), 68–90.

S. Nkomo and T. Cox (1996) 'Diverse Identities in Organizations' in S. Clegg, C. Hardy and W. Nord (eds) *Handbook of Organization Studies* (London and Thousand Oaks: Sage), pp. 338–56.

M. Noon (2007) 'The Fatal Flaws of Diversity and the Business Case for Ethnic Minorities', *Work, Employment and Society*, 21, 773–84.

*N. M. Pless and T. Maak (2004) 'Building an Inclusive Diversity Culture: Principles, Processes and Practice', *Journal of Business Ethics,* 54, 129–47.

Q. Roberson (2004) 'Disentangling the Meanings of Diversity and Inclusion in Organizations', *Group & Organization Management*, 31 (2), 212–36.

W. R. Scott (1986) *Grundlagen der Organisationstheorie* (Frankfurt/Main: Suhrkamp).

A. Smith (2002) 'An Inquiry into the Nature and Causes of the Wealth of Nations', in N. W. Biggart (ed.) *Readings in Economic Sociology* (Malden: Blackwell Publishers Inc), 6–17.

*J. Syed and M. Özbilgin (2009) 'A Relational Framework for International Transfer of Diversity Management Practices', *The International Journal of Human Resource Management*, 20 (12), December 2009, 2435–53.

F. Taylor (1911) *The Principles of Scientific Management*, republished by Forgotten Books, 2008, http://www.forgottenbooks.org, date accessed 9 March 2010.

R. Thomas (2001) *Management of Diversity – Neue Personalstrategien für Unternehmen* (Wiesbaden: Gabler).

M. Verloo (2006) 'Multiple Inequalities, Intersectionality and the European Union', European Journal of Women's Studies, 13 (3), 211–28.

B. Voigt (2001) 'Measures & Benchmarks. Komparatives Diversity-Measurement', presentation at 3rd International Managing Diversity Conference, 5–6 July 2001, Potsdam, Germany.

W. Weber (1980) *Wirtschaft und Gesellschaft. Grundriß der verstehenden Soziologie* (Tübingen: Suhrkamp).

C. West and D. Zimmerman (1987) 'Doing Gender', *Gender & Society*, 1 (2), 125–51.

A. Wetterer (1995) *Die soziale Konstruktion von Geschlecht in Professionalisierungsprozessen* (Frankfurt/Main, New York: Campus).

A. Wetterer (2002) 'Strategien rhetorischer Modernisierung', *Zeitschrift für Frauenforschung und Geschlechterstudien*, 3/2002, 129–48.

F. M. Wilson (2003) *Organizational Behaviour and Gender* (Aldershot, Burlington: Ashgate).

J. Wrench (2005) 'Diversity Management Can be Bad for You', *Race Class*, 46 (3), 73–84.

P. Zanoni (2011) 'Diversity in the Lean Automobile Factory: Doing Class through Gender, Disability and Age', *Organization*, 18 (1), 105–27.

*P. Zanoni, M. Janssens, Y. Benschop and S. Nkomo (2010) 'Unpacking Diversity, Grasping Inequality: Rethinking Difference Through Critical Perspectives', *Organization*, 17 (1), 9–29.

CHAPTER

2

DIVERSITY IN EUROPE: ITS DEVELOPMENT AND CONTOURS

Mary Ann Danowitz and Marie-Thérèse Claes

Chapter Objectives

After completing this chapter, you should be able to:
- discuss the historical, cultural and legal contexts of gender and diversity management in the European context;
- identify major areas covered by anti-discrimination law;
- outline key guidelines related to equality and anti-discrimination;
- highlight some of the complexities associated with the EU and its member states especially in relationship to anti-discrimination;
- describe perceived benefits of diversity management for businesses and the European workforce.

Chapter Outline

- Introduction
- The EU: An overview
- The EU, business and the workforce
- Conclusion
- Chapter review questions
- Case study
- References

INTRODUCTION

In order to obtain an accurate understanding of diversity in organizations, it is first necessary to investigate issues of culture, history, politics and law in Europe as they relate to equality, non-discrimination and diversity. The European Union is a starting point for perspectives on Europe because all member states are required to transpose EU directives into national law. Furthermore, countries that are not, or not yet, members of the European Union see these directives as a benchmark for their own legislations. Efforts to create a pan-European market and political understanding and harmony following the devastation of the Second World War led to a new valuing of diversity. A shift in attitudes, as well as the introduction of important legal provisions to secure the rights of minorities, was first stimulated by women's efforts to achieve equality and increased participation in the workforce. Since the 1990s, EU guidelines and initiatives, as well as growing demographic diversity, have encouraged ever more employers to turn to diversity management. At the same time, EU enlargement to 27 countries has brought unprecedented social and political diversity – if intelligently and sensitively handled, such diversity can bring great economic and other benefits.

This chapter will systematically explore several key external factors that influence organizational practices regarding equality, diversity and workforce participation. We must turn to the macro context for a discussion of particular policies and legislation, as well as the history and influence of social identity groups. These are the factors that determine the relative importance of diversity issues, and the attention that is paid to particular groups over time (Prasad, Pringle and Konrad, 2006).

THE EU: AN OVERVIEW

After the horrors of the Second World War, in which more than 48 million people, mostly civilians, perished (War Chronicle, 2011), European leaders were determined to prevent such a catastrophic conflict from ever happening again. They decided to secure peace among Europe's victorious and vanquished nations by bringing them together as equals, closely cooperating within shared institutions.

On 5 May 1949, in the early years of the Cold War, the leaders of Belgium, Denmark, France, Ireland, Italy, Luxembourg, the Netherlands, Norway, Sweden and the United Kingdom created the Council of Europe ('a kind of United States of Europe' in the words of Winston Churchill) following several years of discussion. One of the first acts of this new body was to draft the European Convention on Human Rights (see the Appendix), one of the leading international legal instruments to protect human rights. Today the Council of Europe has 47 members and aims to 'develop throughout Europe common and democratic principles based on the European Convention on Human Rights and other reference texts on the protection of individuals' (Council of Europe, 2011; see also Figure 2.1). One of the Council's earliest challenges, and a recurring problem for all European institutions, was to decide which languages to adopt. In the end English and French were chosen as official languages, and German, Italian and Russian as working languages. Although the Council of Europe is completely separate from the 27-member EU, it should be noted that no country has joined the EU without first joining this older institution.

In 1951 Belgium, France, Germany, Italy, Luxembourg and the Netherlands signed the treaty founding the European Coal and Steel Community (ECSC). The aim was to bring Europe's steel and coalmining industries under common management in order to prevent the production of weaponry for wars of aggression.

In 1957 the same six countries signed the Treaty of Rome, thereby creating the European Economic Community (EEC), a common market for the free movement of people, goods and services. From 1973 onwards several other European countries were accepted into the EEC. Finally, in 1993, the EEC was transformed into the European Union with the signing of the Maastricht Treaty.

1949	Council of Europe	1993	Maastricht Treaty establishing
1951	European Coal and Steel Community		the European Union
1958	Treaty of Rome, European Economic Community	2009	Treaty of Lisbon, constitution

Today the EU consists of 27 countries, and its agencies use 23 official and working languages. It is a critical mass of people and resources, with a total population of more than 500 million inhabitants, 7 per cent of the world's population, spread over an area of 4,324,782 km^2 (1,669,807 mi^2). The EU is the world's biggest exporter and second largest importer (Europa, n.d.). According to the International Monetary Fund (2011), in 2010 the EU generated US$16.282 trillion, or 20 per cent of the global economy based on purchasing power parity.

Today the European Union is the most important agent for change in contemporary policy-making and governance in Europe, with EU agreements affecting both member countries and neighbouring states (Wallace, Wallace and Pollack 2005). Although not members of the EU, Iceland, Liechtenstein and Norway participate in the European Economic Area, while Switzerland maintains similar links to the EU through bilateral treaties (European Commission, n.d.).

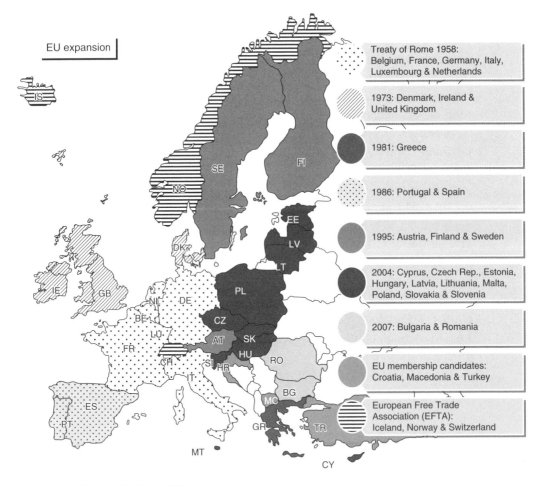

Figure 2.1 Map of EU expansion

Migration

Europe has seen significant of immigration since the second half of the twentieth century. As elsewhere in the world, economic and political pressures drive such migration patterns. During the 1950s, and particularly in the 1960s, the number of foreign workers recruited into the economies of northwestern European grew rapidly (Organization for Economic Co-operation and Development, OECD, 2011), mostly due to the burgeoning demands of European Coal and Steel Community and the development of heavy industry. The Treaty of Rome, considered the foundation of the European Union, is based on a philosophy of the free movement of workers within the European area. Since 1957, numerous directives, recommendations, conventions or treaties have helped to further ease the movement and settlement of economic migrants and their families. From the early 1960s to the early 1970s, more than 30 million migrants from outside the EEC arrived to work in member countries (although this number includes temporary workers and multiple entries).

By the early 1980s the resident foreign population in western Europe had effectively tripled over the previous three decades to reach 15 million. In 2000 more than 20 million foreigners were living in the European Economic Area (EEA), accounting for 5.4 per cent of the total population, with only small variations between countries (Garson and Loisillon, 2003). In the period 1992–2001 some 5,855,000 people were naturalized in the EU-15 group of countries (SOPEMI, 2004).

The picture across Europe is rather diverse (Indexmundi, 2011). Some countries, such as the Netherlands, Germany and Switzerland have seen a decrease in their net migration (the difference between the number of persons entering and leaving a country during the year per 1,000 persons). For example, in Germany net migration fell from +2.2 in 2010 to +0.54 in 2011). In other countries net migration has risen. Spain and Italy, for instance, have seen dramatic increases in recent years due to political instability in some North African states; in Italy immigration rose from +2.1 in 2010 to +4.86 in 2011.

Despite the recent financial crises, there is every indication that Europe's appetite for economic migrants will increase in the coming decades. Labour and skills are predicted to grow (Boswell, 2005), not least due to a rapidly ageing European population in most parts of Europe.

European countries have often introduced special provisions to deal with migrants from ex-colonies or overseas territories. Such post-colonial migration has produced at times severe conflict both in France and the UK, where the children and grandchildren of immigrants from former colonies feel they are still not regarded as full and equal citizens (see section on Immigration and Citizenship Laws and Policies).

Language and culture

Europe displays the greatest linguistic and cultural diversity in the western world. However, the common history, geography and socio-political evolution of the European continent (including the shared experience of a colonial heritage) has formed the basis for a pan-European culture that contrasts – sometimes sharply – with the USA, as well as other regions of the western world such as Australia and New Zealand (Eupedia, 2011).

> *Culture* consists of explicit and implicit patterns of behaviour (knowledge, language, values and customs) and the complex interaction of symbols, values and behaviours of distinct human groups.

The meaning of diversity in the EU has a lot to do with the existence of multiple cultures, languages and nationalities. For example, one of the first decisions made by the European Economic Community was regarding the choice of languages to adopt in publications and meetings:

> The policy of official multilingualism as a deliberate tool of government is unique in the world. The EU sees the use of its citizens' languages as one of the factors that make it more transparent, more legitimate and more efficient. Multilingualism is a value for intercultural dialogue, social cohesion and prosperity. It plays an important role in lifelong learning, media and information technologies, as well as in the EU's external relations. (Multilingualism in the EU, 2011)

When joining the EU, each member state stipulates which language(s) it wishes to be included in the current list of 23 official languages. In total Europe has about 220 to 230 indigenous ethnic groups and more than 90 minority groups that can be distinguished on a linguistic basis (Europa, 2011a).

Some languages are given official recognition at the regional level only. Thus in Spain four languages are recognized locally: Castilian Spanish, Galician (Galego), Basque (Euskara) and Catalan. The Sami languages, spoken by around 24,500 inhabitants of Norway, Sweden, Finland and Russia, have official status in all these countries apart from Russia (Omniglot, 2011).

It is EU policy to protect and promote regional and minority languages. Today the European Commission employs English, French and German as official and working languages, while the European Parliament provides translations into various languages according to the needs of its members. Documents may be sent to EU institutions and a reply received in any of the member states' official languages (Europa, 2011b).

Europe can be broadly divided into cultural groups defined by language, whether Germanic (German, Dutch, English and the Scandinavian languages), Latin/Romance (French, Italian, Spanish and Portuguese) or Slavic (Russian, Polish, and so on) (Claes and Gerritsen, 2011). Of course this does not mean that all cultures in these distinct groups are identical, but rather that they display some similarities. For example, Latin cultures tend to be more hierarchical and collectivistic than Germanic cultures. Or it can be observed that Slavic cultures tend to use a more indirect style of communication than Germanic cultures. These are generalizations, or tendencies; one could also say that they are working hypotheses which can be verified (or proved wrong) when interacting with people from these cultures.

While generalizations and stereotyping have helped generations of Europeans live and work across borders they have also contributed to discrimination and unfair treatment. Over the centuries they have even been used as an excuse for extreme intolerance, leading to conflicts and wars on the basis of religion, ethnicity, language, regional identity and cultural autonomy. As recently as the 1990s, the disintegration of Yugoslavia became the trigger for violent ethnic conflict. This history, along with increasing freedom of mobility within the EU and its eastern enlargement in 2004, has given impetus to the EU's strong policies regarding social cohesion, equality and, anti-discrimination, as well as its advocacy of diversity.

Anti-discrimination and diversity

We begin with a general discussion of diversity from recent European perspectives in order to help us pinpoint meanings and strategies that aim to increase diversity and inclusivity in organizations. Also, by understanding the multiple meanings of diversity within Europe, we will show the difficulties that arise when such a concept, originating in the cultural and political context of the United States, is exported.

When notions of diversity as a business practice made their way from North America across the Atlantic in the early 1990s, a common reaction from European practitioners was that Europe, due to its many countries, languages and cultures, was already fully aware of diversity. In general, Europeans have frequent and close contacts with people of other nationalities, who maintian distinct customs, habits, languages and work styles. From an early age they can easily travel relatively short distances to a foreign country for school trips, holidays, family or business reasons. This creates a basic awareness of differences in languages, food, architecture, religion and culture across the continent. Also, most Europeans speak at least one foreign language in addition to their mother tongue; throughout Europe it is compulsory to learn a second language from primary school age.

The signatories of the Treaty of Rome (1957) that founded the European Community, recognized the importance of various dimensions of diversity among the member states, and the need to affirm and protect this diversity. These intentions were fleshed out by the EEC Treaty, which provided for the establishment of a common market, a customs union and common policies. Articles 2 and 3 of the Treaty directly address these three issues, and specify which measures must be undertaken to achieve the stipulated objectives.

The European Union calls on members to establish 'the foundations of an ever closer union among the European peoples', based upon a notion of fundamental human rights. Adhering to the 1948 UN Universal Declaration of Human Rights, the EU commits its member states to promote, respect and observe rights and fundamental freedoms for all, without regard to race, colour, sex, language or religion.

The preamble of the Treaty of Rome (1957) declares that in establishing the European Community, members countries are:

- determined to lay the foundations of an ever closer union among the peoples of Europe;
- resolved to ensure the economic and social progress of their countries by common action to eliminate the barriers which divide Europe;
- affirming as the essential objective of their efforts the constant improvements in the living and working conditions of their peoples;
- recognizing that the removal of existing obstacles calls for concerted action in order to guarantee steady expansion, balanced trade and fair competition;
- anxious to strengthen the unity of their economies and to ensure their harmonious development by reducing the differences existing between the various regions and the backwardness of the less-favoured regions;
- desiring to contribute, by means of a common commercial policy, to the progressive abolition of restrictions on international trade;
- intending to confirm the solidarity which binds Europe and the overseas countries and desiring to ensure the development of their prosperity, in accordance with the principles of the Charter of the United Nations;
- resolved, by thus pooling their resources, to preserve and strengthen peace and liberty, and calling upon the other peoples of Europe who share their ideal to join in their efforts.

EU's protection of individual rights in the workplace began as an initiative to improve living and working conditions, and to strengthen competition. Article 119 of the Treaty of Rome established the principle of equal pay for men and women. This strictly work-related principle was one repercussion of a more general philosophical commitment to equality for all citizens that arose in the aftermath of the Second World War (Rees, 1998). The idea of equal pay for equal work emerged as part of a range of post-war democratic measures in western Europe to expand the welfare state, to reduce social inequality and, most markedly in the case of France, to extend full political rights to women. However, the exact interpretation of social progress was highly divergent, especially when one looks at the cases of Germany, the Netherlands and France, where differences can be attributed to alternative conceptions of the roles of men and women, of the family unit, and the nature of economic development. Ultimately, members of the European Community reached an agreement to reduce unequal competition, ensuring that those countries with lower wages for women could not exploit this market advantage (Frader, 2010). These early divergent positions, negotiations and compromises are still reflected in the reality of contemporary national differences, as well as paving the way for the current process of the 27 member states to reach agreement on a wide range of legislative issues.

Changing priorities regarding diversity

Originally the EU's valuing of diversity focused on preserving the national cultural diversity among member states. However, with the accession of nine nations in 2004, including several Eastern European countries, a second strand of diversity became prominent in which renewed attention was paid to supra or sub-national minorities and the need to preserve minority cultures and languages such as those of the ethnic Hungarians in Romania and Slovakia, as well as the ethnic Russians living in Estonia, Latvia and Lithuania (Thiel and Prügl, 2009). This recent history, as well as the EU's ever increasing legislative authority, must be borne in mind when trying to understand the workings of the EU regarding individual rights in the areas of employment and society. Here EU legislation has profoundly influenced anti-discrimination and diversity practices in organizations.

Although they share a common cultural heritage, the peoples of Europe lack the shared identity and values of citizens of the United States. Certainly we look in vain for any meaningful pan-European identity in contrast to the very strong national pride felt by US Americans. Identification in Europe mainly occurs at the national level, where shared culture and language are powerful integrative forces (Stuber, 2007).

At a political level no consistent European anti-discrimination policy existed until the Amsterdam Treaty (signed in 1997) introduced measures to combat discrimination on the grounds of age, ethnicity, disability, gender, race, religion or sexual orientation (Stuber, 2007). As we will see in the section discussing the EU and business, this has been accompanied by parallel initiatives within communities and companies to reduce discrimination and foster diversity. It is clear that organizations must respond to, and deal with, cultural and linguistic diversity, especially in the public sector and non-governmental organizations (NGOs). Such forms of diversity are also important in the private sector, as they can increase sensitivity to customers' needs as well as having an impact on recruitment and staff training.

Case study in good practice

When immigrant communities in the British county of Yorkshire started to expand, police and partner agencies found they lacked translators for more than 50 languages spoken locally. In some cases members of the public had to wait for over four hours for an interpreter to be found. In response, West Yorkshire police developed an imaginative marketing campaign targeting students. The campaign used internet-based advertising to recruit young people to train to become an interpreter and translator for their own communities. The candidates had to be over the age of 18, fluent and literate in English and at least one of the locally used languages. Through a highly effective strategy of 'pop up' and static adverts on web pages, as well as community events and direct marketing to social clubs and places of worship, the campaign elicited a huge response from minority communities. From over 1000 applications, 160 successfully met the interview and training requirements. As of November 2011, 40 new interpreters have been registered and 29 additional students should soon be accepted onto the National Register for Public Service by successfully passing an examination qualifying them as public sector interpreters and translators. Interpreters are now available in Yorkshire to facilitate communication in such diverse languages as Bengali, Hungarian, Ndebele or Tamil, whereas, previously such specialist interpreters had to come from London.

Source: Adapted from West Yorkshire Police (2010).

The legal framework of equal opportunities and anti-discrimination

What distinguishes the EU as a legislative body is the double level of governance it employs, that is the supranational and the national. As Wallace, Wallace and Pollack explain:

> Country-defined policy demands and policy capabilities are set in a shared European framework to generate collective regimes, most of which are then implemented back in the country concerned … In other words, the EU policy process is one which has differentiated outcomes, with significant variations between countries. (Wallace, Wallace and Pollack, 2005, p. 7)

The EU enacts policies and legislation conferred by treaties. All 27 EU member states must agree upon proposals unanimously before they enter the statute books. This takes place through an EU institutional structure in which the individual states are active participants.

The EU has several means of influencing social or business practice through legislation. Two of these – regulations and directives – are binding, and thus highly relevant to the issues of equality and diversity in organizations.

EU regulations have binding legal force throughout all member states. States usually do not have to take actions themselves to implement regulations, which override any conflicting domestic law or decision.

Directives require states to achieve a certain outcome by a certain date, but leave it to the national authorities to choose how they go about implementing the provisions.

The EU allows member states to adapt their laws to best meet the goals of a directive (Eurofound, 2007). If a state implements a directive incorrectly or incompletely, it still has a legal duty to comply with the directive. Most EU legislation dealing with employment and industrial relations is in the form of directives (Eurofound, 2010). Other measures are often called 'soft laws' (Eurofound, 2011).

Soft law encompasses other EU measures such as guidelines, declarations and opinions that are not legally binding, but which are a more flexible means to achieve policy objectives by influencing practice.

This brings us to specific EU provisions regarding equality, anti-discrimination and diversity.

EU guidelines: promoting equality and anti-discrimination

For many years the focus of EU action in the field of non-discrimination was on preventing discrimination on the grounds of race/ethnic origin and sex. Article 13 of the Treaty of Amsterdam, which came into force in 1999, granted the Community new powers to combat discrimination on the grounds of sex, racial or ethnic origin, religion or belief, disability, age or sexual orientation. This important milestone led to a series of related measures and resolutions, summarized in Table 2.1.

The directives allow for a few selected forms of acceptable discrimination, such as in insurance and banking services where knowledge of age and disability can be essential to the assessment of risk, and therefore regulates the price of certain products. Such an assessment must, however, be based on accurate data and statistics.

> *Direct discrimination* is the unfair treatment of an individual or group solely on the grounds of a personal characteristic such as age, disability, ethnic origin or racial, religion or beliefs or sexual orientation.

Table 2.1 EU rights and directives on equality and anti-discrimination

	Racial Equality Directive
2000	Equal treatment between people irrespective of racial or ethnic origin
	Employment Equality Directive
2000	Equal treatment in employment and training irrespective of religion or belief, sexual orientation and age
	The European Union Charter of Fundamental Rights
2009	(see the Appendix) Sets out in a single text the whole range of civil, political, economic and social rights of European citizens and all persons resident in the EU.
	These rights are divided into six sections: <ul><li>dignity</li><li>freedoms</li><li>equality</li><li>solidarity</li><li>citizens' rights</li><li>justice</li></ul> These are based, in particular, on the fundamental rights and freedoms recognized by the European Convention on Human Rights, the constitutional traditions of the EU member states, the Council of Europe's Social Charter, the Community Charter of Fundamental Social Rights of Workers as well as other international conventions to which the European Union or its member states are parties.

Indirect discrimination is a more complex phenomenon in which a rule or practice that *appears* neutral has a negative impact upon a person or a group of persons who display a specific characteristic. The author of the rule or practice may be unaware of these repercussions.

Harassment is a particular form of discrimination which encompasses verbal or written comments, gestures or other forms of behaviour regarded as intimidating, humiliating or offensive by the recipient.

By the beginning of 2011 all 27 member states had transposed EU anti-discrimination directives into national law by putting into place enforcement mechanisms and adopting specific measures. The degree of implementation varies from country to country; according to the Academy of European Law (2011) there still exist some gaps where the measures are insufficiently or incorrectly implemented (Chopin and Gounari, 2009; Academy of European Law, 2011).

Disability refers to a physical, mental or psychological impairment that can hamper work performance or hinders the participation of a person in following their chosen professional life.

Anti-discrimination directives at the nation state level: the case of disability anti-discrimination

In the EU employers have an obligation to provide reasonable workplace accommodation for people with disabilities. Failure to do so is considered a form of discrimination, although the exact requirements and regulations in each case will depend on how the national government has chosen to implement EU directives and which provisions it has adopted. Disability is also the social field where we find the largest number of positive action measures in place. Table 2.2 gives an overview of disability provisions across three member states, all of which have strict regulations regarding, for example, workplace accommodation, as well as a number of incentives. In the examples that follow, we can see that Spain is the only country to have introduced a wide-ranging quota system. The regulations that are in place in Ireland apply only to the public sector, while Latvia has no specific anti-discrimination measures or incentives for either the public or private sectors (Academy of European Law, 2011).

The body of EU anti-discrimination law serves as a benchmark for several countries outside the Union. For example, although Turkey currently lacks any specific anti-discrimination or equal treatment legislation, a preliminary draft of a law to combat discrimination and establish an equality council was sent in March 2010 to various universities and non-governmental organizations across the country in order for them to express their opinions. This draft

Table 2.2 Disability: anti-discrimination initiatives of three EU member states

	General principle	Reference text	Obligatory measures	Incentives
Ireland	Anti-discrimination law	Employment Equality Acts of 1998 and 2004, Equal Status Act (2000 to 2004).	Only public administration regulated. Reasonable accommodation: premises and equipment adaptations, patterns of working time.	–
Latvia	Anti-discrimination	Medical and Social Protection of Disabled Persons Act (1992) which regulates the social security of disabled persons. Concept of 'Equal opportunities for all' (1998). Labour law (2004).	–	–
Spain	Employment obligation	Spanish Constitution of 1982 on Social Integration of Disabled Persons. Law 51/2003: Equal opportunities, non-discrimination and universal access for persons with a disability. Law 62/2003 of fiscal, administrative and social order.	Quotas: public and private employers with 50 or more employees, disabled persons with over 33 per cent incapacity. Non-fulfillment: compensation allowance taxes. Workstation adaptation (reasonable accommodation).	Grants for recruiting disabled persons. Tax relief.

was apparently inspired by EU legislation, in particular Directives 2000/43 and 2000/78, although the material scope of the Turkish draft legislation is even wider than the respective EU legislation (see European Network of Legal Experts in the Non-discrimination Field, n.d.).

Equal opportunities, positive action and mainstreaming

A trio of concepts – equal opportunities, positive action and mainstreaming – are necessary to understand the measures that organizations in Europe introduce as part of diversity management, including the prevention or remedying of discrimination and the achievement of equality.

Equal opportunities refers to an equal distribution of opportunities for education, training, employment, career development and the exercise of power, so that individuals are not disadvantaged on the basis of their sex, race, language, religion, economic or family situation, or any other factor.

Positive action refers to proportionate measures intended to foster full and effective equality for members of groups that are socially or economically disadvantaged, or otherwise face the consequences of past or present discrimination.

Mainstreaming seeks to promote equality at all levels and in all areas by taking equality issues into account during policy formation, implementation and evaluation.

The concept of mainstreaming originated in the more restricted form of *gender* mainstreaming, with a particular focus on the public sector (Rees, 1998). More recently, however, private sector organizations have modified the concept to apply it to the mainstreaming of diversity.

Distinguishing between positive action and mainstreaming

Although positive action and mainstreaming may have similar goals, their practical approaches are rather different: whereas the former involves targeted measures that, inter alia, attempt to compensate for specific disadvantages, the latter seeks to change the *mindset* of policymakers in order to make equality a central concern. If successful, this approach is likely to prompt this important group of actors to consider taking positive action. An example of mainstreaming is the decision by the governing board of a national museum that wishes to boost the number of visitors to consider whether certain groups are currently under-represented (such as Muslim women). Once this issue is placed on the agenda, the museum's executive management might respond by designing positive action measures like publicizing its exhibits and activities in media outlets utilized by the target group or sending promotional materials to Muslim women's organizations and mosques.

Source: European Commission (2009a).

Recent international comparative studies have shown that the legal, cultural, and social context of each EU member state will shape the ways in which companies approach diversity management as a means to comply with EU legislation. For example in Germany (Bruchhagen, Grieger, Koall, Meuser, Ortlieb and Sieben, 2010), the Netherlands (Bleijenbergh, van Engen and Terlouw, 2010), France (Bender, Klarsfeld and Laufer, 2010) and Sweden (Kalonaityte, Prasad and Tedros, 2010) companies take account of local conditions to apply a wide range of both anti-discrimination measures and positive action to institutionalize equality at work.

National contexts and citizenship diversity

Policies and laws on immigration and citizenship

It is clear that immigration policies and laws on citizenship will greatly influence the employment and social conditions of ethnic minorities. At the same time we must remember that collective attitudes to nationality – what it means to be a citizen – will in turn have an impact at the political level. In particular, Weldon's (2006) research on EU citizens' tolerance at the individual level, in particular their attitudes towards minorities, shows that tolerance is closely associated with political policies of migration and citizenship across the three citizenship regimes shown in Table 2.3.

Tolerance: a fair, objective and permissive attitude towards opinions and practices that differ from one's own.

In general, political institutions design citizenship laws and government policies which 'embody cultural traditions about who is a legitimate member of the nation-state' (Weldon, 2006, p. 332).

When trying to understand the differences and similarities between nation states regarding the treatment of immigration and citizenship, it is useful to take a closer look at two factors: the legal traditions of a country and its historic experience of immigration and emigration (Weil 2001, p. 18).

Review Questions

- Investigate the citizenship and immigration laws of your home country.
- How would you classify them?
- If your home country is one listed in Table 2.3, do you agree with the classification? Explain your reasoning.

- Compare your findings with those of another country. How do that nation's citizenship and immigration laws fit into the classification of Table 2.3?

Racism and xenophobia

A worrying trend seen in several European countries is the resurgence of racism and extreme nationalist political movements. In the 1990s many governments became increasingly concerned about the low social inclusion of their immigrant and ethnic minority communities, set against a backdrop of rising racist violence and xenophobia (Swiebel, 2009). This was also a time of major economic, social and political change, partly driven by the forces of globalization. While new immigrants continued to arrive from outside Europe, resident ethnic communities and their descendants faced a future of menial work or long-term unemployment. Such low socio-economic attainment, which remains true today, cannot solely be attributed to poor language fluency or the lower education levels of such groups. Instead, we must admit that this troubling situation is largely (if not entirely) due to persistent forms of discrimination (Vertovec and Wessendorf, 2009).

Table 2.3 Classification of policies on migration and citizenship

Differential exclusion	Immigrants are seen as guest workers (*Gastarbeiter/in*) and are denied full political rights. Citizenship is defined by *jus sanguinis* (bloodline descent)
	Naturalization is possible for non-nationals, but requires that other citizenships be relinquished and candidates meet the criteria for cultural norms and affiliation with the country
	Examples of this type: Austria, Belgium*, Germany, Luxembourg and Switzerland. For instance, ethnic Germans from Eastern Europe who have never lived in Germany have easier access to citizenship than second-generation Turkish migrants born and educated in Germany.
Assimilation	Immigrants are awarded full citizenship and are expected to assimilate to cultural norms. Those born in the nation's territory are automatically given citizenship. Dual nationality is not encouraged. New citizens can be incorporated with relative ease. The underlying approach discourages the identification of ethnic origin in national registers or at work.
	Examples of this type: Denmark and France (in the 1960s).
Pluralism / Multiculturalism	Immigrants have full rights while maintaining some cultural differences. Dual nationality is permitted. Official recognition is given to different ethnic group identities. Although loyalty to the nation state is expected, different cultures and norms are accommodated.
	Examples of this type: The Netherlands, Sweden, and the UK.
	*Belgium does not require renunciation of prior citizenship.
	*Weldon (2006) categorizes the UK as pluralistic/multicultural or individualistic-civic while Kirton and Greene (2011, p. 251) add a fourth category – pragmatic pluralic – to describe British society since the 1970s. This is similar to pluralism/multiculturalism but without a legally defined policy perspective.

Sources: Adapted from Wrench (2007, p. 77), Weil (2001) and Weldon (2006).

Recently the extreme right has become prominent in the political landscapes of some central-eastern European countries, namely the Czech Republic, Slovakia, Poland and Hungary (Mareš, 2006). As more and more workers in Europe face an insecure future, other extreme nationalist groups have gained voter support. In 2010 Sweden elected 20 members of the nationalist party 'The Sweden Democrats' to the country's parliament. This party, which holds anti-immigration and anti-Muslim policies, calls for authoritarian solutions to Sweden's growing social problems. Also, Europe's Roma communities have in recent years come under increasing pressure in several countries, in some cases resulting in acts of violence.

Europe's Jewish and other minority groups have become alarmed by the success of parties such as the Dutch 'Freedom Party', the 'Freedom Party' in Austria (FPO), the 'Danish People's Party', the 'British National Party' and 'Jobbik' in Hungary (Byron, 2009).

Other indicators across Europe show that public opinion seems to be turning against the idea of multiculturalism. In the UK the focus of discussion is now on the problems of 'too much diversity', while Germans have a fear of 'parallel societies' and some Italians detect a 'dismembering of society'. Even in those countries with a strong multicultural tradition and anti-discrimination policies such as Sweden and the Netherlands, we can detect a 'shift away from group emancipation towards an emphasis on individual integration' (Vertovec and Wessendorf 2006, p. 185). In response to this backlash against multiculturalism, EU agencies have come under pressure to take strong action in the fight against racial discrimination (Swiebel, 2009). This has led to the drafting of directives and legislation described in this chapter, including Articles 21 and 22 of the EU Charter of Fundamental Rights adopted at the 2001 Nice European Council, as well as Council Framework Decision 2008/913, which combats certain forms of racism and xenophobia through criminal law.

The process of 'Europeanization' (meaning the dissemination and adoption of European norms and social practices) supports the EU's proactive measures on equality and anti-discrimination, helping to provide a framework and resources to fully incorporate EU directives into each member state's legal system. At the same time the integration of EU provisions also depends upon the culture, history, laws, policies and domestic actors of each individual member state. Such factors will ultimately determine the local interpretation and application of directives, especially in regard to diversity management.

THE EU, BUSINESS AND THE WORKFORCE

National anti-discrimination law in most EU member states exceeds the requirements of European law, whether regarding the definition of discrimination, the scope of protection or the responsibilities of the relevant equality agencies. Such legislation has a major impact on the operations of companies across the continent. All employers throughout the EU must:

- provide equal access to employment;
- treat their workers fairly and equally, for example when offering training opportunities or access to benefits;
- make sure that disabled people can work comfortably.

Workforce participation

No minority or discriminated group will experience the job market in the same way, and these differences should be examined from the perspective of both employer and employee. Employers will often have preferences and particular requirements for certain employees, primarily in terms of their skills and qualifications, but also regarding other less relevant characteristics. Workforce participation in terms of age and sex is seen to vary *between* countries and *within* individual countries. According to Eurostat statistics (December 2010), the EU-27 employment rate for workers aged 55 to 64 was 46 per cent in 2009, a rise of 6 per cent from 2001. There are 11 member states with employment rates of 50 per cent or higher for older workers, with the highest employment rates found in Sweden (70 per cent) and Estonia (60.4 per cent).

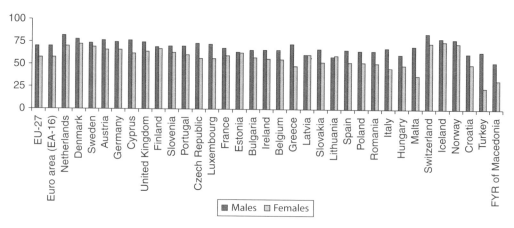

Figure 2.2 Employment rates by sex, 2009
Source: Eurostat, 2010.

Looking at the relative workforce participation of the two sexes, the average employment rate for workers aged 20 to 64 was 70.7 per cent for men and 58.6 per cent for women (Eurostat, December 2010). However, the picture changes dramatically when one examines the rates within particular minority groups. For example, Roma women are four times more likely to be unemployed than women from other ethnic groups.

Figure 2.2 illustrates the variations in employment rates of the two sexes at the national level. It can be seen that (regarding EU member states) Lithuania, Estonia and Latvia have the lowest percentage of men in the workforce, while Malta, Italy and Greece show the lowest levels of female employment. The picture is, of course, complicated by the fact that many more women work part-time than men: in 2009 an average of 34.4 per cent of women held part-time jobs compared to only 8.1 per cent of men.

Women's relatively low participation in the workforce can be attributed to several factors: the challenge of reconciling work with family and private obligations, employers' negative attitudes towards the hiring of women, and insufficient governmental support in improving the work-life balance (Chapter 9).

Figure 2.3 shows how parenthood affects employment. Mothers' participation in the workforce is 11.5 per cent lower than women without children, whereas for fathers the rate is 8.5 per cent higher than men without children. Nearly one third of women with caring responsibilities report that they work part-time or are not in paid employment, due to a lack of care services for children or other dependents (often elderly or disabled relatives). The provision of high-quality, affordable care is an important step in offering parents, particularly women, a real choice to engage in full-time employment (European Commission, Justice, 2011). Tax and benefit systems, cultural attitudes and economic conditions vary considerably across member states, and these factors

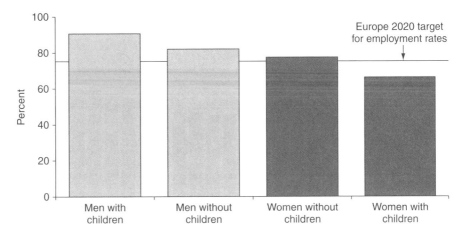

Figure 2.3 Employment rates of women and men (aged 25–49), with and without children under the age of 12
Source: Eurostat, 2010.

will also have very profound and diverse effects on male and female participation in the job market.

Low rates of female employment are closely linked to lower pay for women in comparison to men. Recognizing this pay gap, the Treaty of Rome affirmed the principle of equal pay for men and women some 50 years ago. Yet even though all EU member states have subsequently adopted relevant legislation, current data on pay differentials still shows that, on average, women earn 17.5 per cent less than men (see Figure 2.4). This figure varies widely across member states: from nearly 31 per cent in Estonia to only 5 per cent in Italy.

> A narrow gender pay gap may be explained by the fact that the female employment rate is low, and that those who are working earn higher salaries (level of education, profession) ... The underlying causes remain numerous and complex, not only reflecting discrimination on the grounds of sex but also inequalities linked to education, the horizontal and vertical segregation of the labour market, the difficulty of reconciling work, family and private life, the unequal distribution of family in domestic responsibilities, the lack of pay transparency and the impact of gender roles influencing the choice of education and vocational training courses. (The European Commission, *Justice*, 2011, p. 9)

1. What are the main reasons for the different rates of workforce participation for women and men?
2. Which stakeholders have the power to change this situation?
3. What are the participation rates in your home country? Can you pinpoint the significant factors which contribute to these patterns?
4. What are explanations for the pay gap? What should be done to reduce the gap?

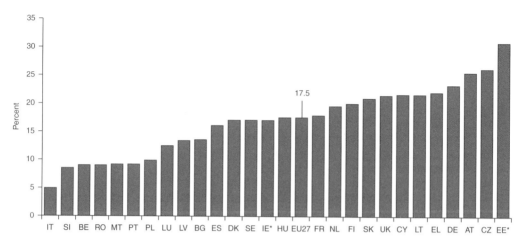

Figure 2.4   Pay gap between women and men in EU member states, 2008
Source: Eurostat (2010).

Business practices and benefits

Although the notion of managing and developing diversity has been on the political and business agenda at both the EU and national levels since the 1990s, there exists a variety of interpretations regarding its meaning. Recent research in 16 countries shows that in some cases diversity management is closely linked to equality and non-discrimination legislation (Klarsfeld, 2010). In countries such as France, Germany and Sweden it is used to institutionalize equality at work, whereas in Belgium diversity management is regarded as a tool to improve business efficiency and provide a competitive advantage (Klarsfeld, 2010, p. 1f).

For nearly a decade the European Union has systematically encouraged businesses to diversify their workforce in order to increase competiveness. At the same time it has assisted efforts to comply with anti-discrimination directives, often by documenting current practices and providing information about available resources and good practices. *The Costs and Benefits of Diversity* (European Commission, 2003) was one of the earliest reports to systematically document the activities and expectations of European companies regarding diversity. It showed that although the business case for diversity was gradually becoming more widely accepted due to the advocacy of a small number of leading enterprises, its development was still in the early stages and rather sporadic. The report discussed the cost-effectiveness of diversity policies in 200 enterprises spread over four countries, while providing case studies for six countries. One of its important contributions was to clearly point out to companies the crucial benefits that can issue from diversity policies, in particular the strengthening of human and organizational capital to create a competitive advantage (Chapter 6).

Two years later *The Business Case for Diversity: Good Practices in the Workplace* (European Commission, 2005) was published, confirming that an increasing number of European companies were adopting diversity and equality measures. The report described how major initiatives regarding diversity were more frequently implemented in companies located in the EU 15 group of nations, particularly in northern Europe. Two surveys covering 919 responses from about 1000 companies of the European Business Test Panel (EBTP) in 25 member EU nations showed that nearly half of these companies were actively engaged in promoting workplace diversity and anti-discrimination for a variety of ethical, legal and business reasons. The main reported benefits were: (1) actual or projected improvements in staff shortages and increased recruitment and retention of high quality employees; (2) enhancement of the company's reputation, image and standing with local communities; and (3) improved innovation, leading to new products, services and possibly new markets.

Diversity management in SMEs

Research on diversity management has largely been concerned with medium and large-sized companies. Yet to understand its impact in Europe we must examine the situation of *all* businesses. In the EU the reality is that 99 per cent of companies are small and medium-sized, so that this socially and economically crucial sector provides an astonishing 90 million jobs (European Commission Enterprise and Industry, 2011). Another report, *Continuing the Diversity Journey*, focuses on small and medium-sized enterprises (SMEs) in the private non-primary sector (industry and services) employing less than 250 persons. According to the Observatory of European SMEs, there are 19.3 million SMEs in the European Economic Area and Switzerland, providing more than 75 per cent of all jobs in Europe (European Commission, 2008a). Some 92 per cent of these companies are micro enterprises employing nine persons or less. The report therefore supplies important information about companies that contribute the greater share of Europe's jobs.

Survey responses from more than 1200 companies in the EU-27 (along with follow-up interviews) showed that although 56 per cent reported having some kind of equality and diversity policies in place, it was the larger companies that are more likely 'to have led in this respect' (European Commission, 2008b, p. 18). This can be attributed to the fact that SMEs with fewer than 50 employees often employ family members, are financially insecure and have no formal human resource management processes in place (Gallup Organization, 2007).

A large majority (79 per cent) of those surveyed for *Continuing the Diversity Journey* confirmed that they were aware of the benefits of employing and supporting a diverse workforce (although this figure may be unrepresentative of

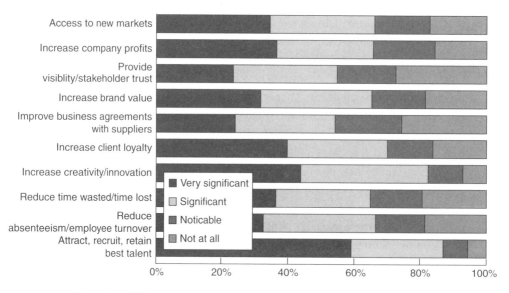

Figure 2.5 SME business benefits associated with diversity
Source: 2008 Diversity Survey, in European Commission, 2008b.

the SME business sector in general). The perceived benefits of diversity as listed in Figure 2.5 suggest some areas of company organization and structure where diversity management could benefit the majority of small and medium-sized enterprises. For example, 60 per cent of respondents indicated that diversity policies help to recruit and retain high quality employees in the face of labour market shortages and competition between SMEs and larger firms. The second benefit recognized by 40 per cent of those surveyed was that individuals with diverse backgrounds can bring different approaches to problems, thereby contributing to creativity and innovation.

Diversity charters

Businesses are increasingly turning to new initiatives to improve their handling of diversity. One recent innovation in this field intended to encourage and support efforts in the implementation and development of diversity policies is the so-called *diversity charter*. These charters follow a strategic approach to diversity management, aiming to communicate and create an internal and external organizational commitment to diversity (Chapter 5).

A *diversity charter* is a short document voluntarily signed by a company or a public institution outlining measures it will undertake to promote diversity and equal opportunities in the workplace, regardless of race or ethnic origin, sexual orientation, gender, age, disability and religion.

Diversity policies developed under a diversity charter recognize, understand and value people's similarities and differences as representing huge potential sources of innovation, problem-solving capability, improved customer relations and so on. Companies commit themselves to the systematic introduction of diversity initiatives, whilst governmental agencies exchange and share good practices, strategies and resources to improve diversity and inclusion.

The first diversity charter was drawn up in 2004 in France by the French company AXA. This charter has since attracted 2895 signatories, ranging from large multinationals such as L' Oréal, Carrefour and BNP PARIBAS to numerous small and medium-sized enterprises and even micro-enterprises. This French model has been adapted and adopted in six other EU countries: Belgium in 2005, Germany in 2006, Italy, Spain and Sweden in 2009, Austria in 2010 and finally Norway in 2011.

Charter of diversity

Promoting pluralism and seeking diversity through recruitment and career development is an opportunity for companies to progress. Such strategies improve efficiency and contribute to a better social climate. They can also have a positive impact on the way a company is viewed by customers, suppliers and consumers, in France and overseas.

The Charter of diversity, adopted by our company, is intended to demonstrate our commitment in France to cultural, ethnic and social diversity within our organization.

In accordance with this Charter, we undertake to:

1. *Raise awareness of non-discrimination and diversity issues among top management and staff involved in recruitment, training and career development and to educate them in these matters.*

2. *Respect and promote the application of all aspects of the principle of non-discrimination at every stage of human resources management, in particular in the recruitment, training, promotion and career development of employees.*

3. *Endeavour to reflect the diversity of French society, particularly in its cultural and ethnic dimension, at every level of our workforce.*

4. *Make all our employees aware of our commitment to non-discrimination and diversity, and keep them informed of the practical results of this commitment.*

5. *Make the development and implementation of the diversity policy a subject of dialogue with employees' representatives.*

6. *Insert a chapter in the annual report describing our commitment to non-discrimination and diversity, including details of the measures implemented, our internal procedures and the results achieved.*

Source: Diversity Charter, 2011.

The European Commission has recognized that diversity charters can help fight discrimination in the workplace and promote equality. Therefore it is funding a platform for EU-level exchange between organizations that are in the process of promoting and implementing national diversity charters. The platform is part of a larger project that aims to support voluntary initiatives of diversity management in the workplace. The EU-level exchange platform allows the promoters of existing diversity charters to meet on a regular basis, to share their experiences and develop common tools (European Commission, 2009b).

CONCLUSION

This chapter has given an overview of the historical, cultural and legal context of gender and diversity management in Europe. In order to understand the meaning of diversity, inclusion and diversity management in the EU, we need to be aware of the complex web of legal, political and cultural traditions at all levels of governance, particularly as these relate to the issue of anti-discrimination.

Scholars and practitioners in Europe have a different understanding of diversity from their counterparts in the USA. The great multiplicity of languages and cultures living side by side on the European continent has shaped the understanding of and response to diversity over many centuries. Thus commercial treaties were required at an early stage as a counterweight to this diversity, ensuring the free movement of goods and people. Of course, priorities have shifted over time, from the protection of workers to equality of treatment regardless of race, ethnic background, religion or belief, sexual orientation and age.

While the core of the diversity management argument – that diversity offers a competitive advantage in the marketplace – is similar in the US and Europe (Holvino and Kamp, 2009), the US framing of diversity management is not particularly suited to Europe's history and traditions. Diversity management in the US is a strategy to cope with the backlash against affirmative action and the resulting dismantling of affirmative action programmes. In Europe diversity management is associated with a rising awareness of diversity and the implementation of strict anti-discrimination directives. These laws, as well as social and cultural norms, provide the context in which diversity management is developed and implemented (see Chapters 6 and 7). As Wrench (2007, p. 138) has aptly described the situation in Europe: 'Diversity management operates best in the context of strong anti-discrimination law, and within diversity management policies themselves there must be anti-discrimination elements. Diversity management is a way of mainstreaming anti-discrimination activities, not a substitute for them.'

Chapter Review Questions

- Which key steps in the formation and development of the European Union have affected employment?
- How do we distinguish between anti-discrimination, positive action and mainstreaming? Give an example of the three working together.
- What are some differences in the workforce participation of men and women, and which major factors contribute to those differences?
- Which major areas are covered by EU anti-discrimination directives?
- If you were a manager how would you go about ensuring that your company is in full compliance with EU anti-discrimination directives?
- What is a diversity charter? What are some of its advantages and disadvantages?

Case Study

The Roma

On October 25th, 2005, in the flat of an ethnic Romanian man in Bucharest, police discovered the body of an 11-year-old Roma girl who had been raped, killed and cut into hundreds of pieces. A Romanian newspaper, *Adevarul*, published the news on October 26th. Had the victim been Romanian and the murderer Roma, and bearing in mind the country's long tradition of racially-motivated pogroms, one can only speculate as to what bloody manifestations of collective punishment might have been meted out as a consequence. The Hadareni atrocities of 1993 (in which four Roma men were murdered and 10 houses burned) serve as a grim reminder of what can happen (Pro Europa 2000). In the evening of October 26th a talk show on the Romanian TV station OTV included two items related to Roma: one concerning the rape and murder of the Roma girl, and the other about a fight involving Roma. During the broadcast, several commentators suggested that the murder was related to the fact that Roma parents are unable to take care of their children. Comments on the fight involving Roma included the suggestion from a caller carried live on TV that "Gypsies should be shot dead". (Nicolae, 2006)

With a total population of approximately 10 to 12 million, the Roma are the EU's largest ethnic minority. Although they can be found in almost all member states, around two-thirds live in Eastern Europe. The largest group of 1.8 to 2.5 million (an unofficial estimate) lives in Romania, constituting approximately eight to ten per cent of the population (http://www.romsaction.org/site/index.php/Qui-sont-les-roms).

They call themselves 'Romani Cel', which means 'gypsy people'. In France they are known as 'Gens du voyage' or 'travelling people', while in Spain they are called 'Gitanos'. In eastern and central European countries they are simply called 'Rom'. The French Roma aside, they are generally sedentary, holding the citizenship of the country in which they reside. Normally they also adopt the national religion, so that the Roma of Romania are Orthodox Christian, those in France are Catholic and the Roma of Bosnia, Muslim.

The Roma have their own language, called Romani. This is an Indic language, indicating the Indian sub-continent as the original home of the Roma. After leaving these homelands in the eighth to ninth century, the Roma arrived in Europe several hundred years later.

Recent waves of anti-Gypsy sentiment in Europe (Nicolae, 2006), particularly in England, Italy and France, can be attributed to a clash of culture rather than ethnic tensions, although the effects are the same: violent clashes in Slovakia, Romania and Hungary, and the dissolution of social bonds.

Nicolae argues that anti-Roma feelings are not based on race or ethnicity, but on stereotypes and historical prejudice. This is reflected in the discrepancies between the public's estimation of the numbers of Roma and the actual figures given in official censuses, which are considerably lower (see Council of Europe, 2000). According to Nicolae (2006),

anti-Gypsyism manifests itself not only through racial categorization, which postulates the inferiority of Roma, but mainly through straight-forward dehumanization of Roma, because prejudice against the Roma clearly goes beyond racist stereotyping whereby the Roma are associated with negative traits and behaviour. Through dehumanization, the Roma are viewed as less than human; and, being less than human, they are perceived as not morally entitled to human rights equal to those of the rest of the population.

The Roma are frequently the victims of virulent forms of ethnic racism in both political and public discourse (OSCE, 2005). Violence and acts of discrimination, including state-sponsored harassment, which are rare in the case of other minorities, still occur in the case of Europe's Roma communities. For example, in the summer of 2001 the UK government established a 'pre-clearance' check of air passengers at Prague airport in order to identify Romani passengers and prevent them from boarding airplanes destined for the UK (BBC, 2001). As recently as 2010 France repatriated dozens of Roma to Romania. After the French authorities were widely criticized for their action, the European Commission against Racism and Intolerance

(ECRI) held a round table in Paris to combat racist violence and discrimination in France.

Research shows that the Roma continue to suffer the highest levels of discrimination across the EU, particularly in the areas of education, employment, housing and healthcare (European Agency for Fundamental Rights, n.d.). Due to the low average age of the Roma (only 25 years compared to the EU average of 40), they make up a growing share of the working-age population. However, being less well trained and qualified to find work, there is little market demand for Roma employees. This almost certainly forces them to turn to informal economic activities such as begging or even petty crime to survive (European Agency for Fundamental Rights, n.d.).

The Europe 2020 strategy has set a target of 75 per cent of the working age population (20 to 64 years) to be in paid employment, compared to the existing rate of 68.8 per cent. The employment rate for Roma is around 26 per cent lower, based upon World Bank research in Bulgaria, the Czech Republic, Romania and Serbia (Europa,n.d.). The World Bank (2010) has estimated that full integration of the Roma into the workforce would generate an extra €0.5 billion each year for some countries.

With the support of EU funding, actors at all levels of society, from state employment agencies and community leaders to local experts and prospective employers, are undertaking initiatives to integrate the Roma population into the workforce. One such project, the Hungary-Romania Cross-Border Co-operation Programme 2007–2013, analysed the employment situation of Roma communities residing in the neighbouring counties of Bihor in Romania and Hajdú-Bihar in Hungary, assessing the professional abilities and skills of 300 Roma participants.

The results of the study showed that a lack of training and/or a high-school diploma were inhibitors for employment, even for those participants that were obviously highly intelligent. So-called 'second chance' employment training programmes and counselling centres have been set up to tackle this problem by assisting participants to find suitable work (Hungary-Romania Cross-Border Co-operation Programme 2007–2013 website, 2011).

Interviews and workshops were conducted with employers, employment agencies, Roma leaders and experts. To match prospective employees with employers, two fairs were organized in cooperation with local Roma communities, NGOs and state employment agencies.

Test Your Understanding

1. European Commission country reports often condemn the existence of structural racism (the system of public policies, institutional practices, cultural representations and other norms reinforce ways that perpetuate group inequality) against Roma in countries of central and Eastern Europe, yet some of those countries are already EU members. Why has it proved so difficult to eradicate such discrimination?

2. Does the Roma's lack of formal education explain the discrimination and exclusion they suffer in the EU? Would education and employment training remedy the situation?

3. Are there Roma in your country (or a minority group of a similar status)? What is their status and position in society? How are they treated by the press and public opinion?

4. In your opinion, which actors should have responsibility to improve the situation of minority groups, such as the Roma, who suffer persistent discrimination?

REFERENCES

*Academy of European Law (2011) Implementation of EU Anti-discrimination Law in the Member States: A Comparative Approach, http://www.era-omm.eu/oldoku/Adiskri/01_Overview/2011_04%20Chopin_EN.pdf, date accessed 2 November 2011.

BBC (2001) UK gets tough on Czech immigrants, http://www.news.bbc.co.uk/1/hi/world/europe/1445494.stm, date accessed 18 January 2012.

A. F. Bender, A. Klarsfeld and J. Laufer (2010) 'Equality and Diversity in the French context' in A. Klarsfeld (ed.) *International Handbook on Diversity Management at Work* (Cheltenham: Edward Elgar), pp. 83–108.

A. Bleijenbergh, M. L. van Engen and A. Terlouw (2010) 'Laws, Policies and Practices of Diversity Management in the Netherlands' in A. Klarsfeld (ed.) *International Handbook on Diversity Management at Work: Country Perspectives on Diversity and Equal Treatment* (Cheltenham: Edward Elgar), pp. 179–97.

C. Boswell (2005) *Migration in Europe* (Policy Analysis and Research Programme of the Global Commission on International Migration: Hamburg: Migration Research Group Hamburg Institute of International Economics).

V. Bruchhagen, J. Grieger, I. Koall, M. Meuser, R. Ortlieb and B. Sieben (2010) 'Social Inequality, Diversity and Equal Treatment at Work: The German Case' in A. Klarsfeld (ed.) *International Handbook on Diversity Management at Work* (Cheltenham and Northampton: Edward Elgar), pp.109–38.

*Business & Disability (n.d.) Business & Disability: European Case Studies, http://www.businessanddisability.org/case_studies/UK.pdf, date accessed 2 November 2011.

J. Byron (2009). 'Jewish Group Alarmed by Success of Extreme-right Parties throughout Europe', *European Jewish Press*, 9 June 2009.

I. Chopin and E. M. Gounari (2009) Developing Anti-Discrimination Law in Europe. The 27 EU member states compared, http://www.migpolgroup.com/publications_detail.php?id=282, date accessed 22 July 2011.

M.-T. Claes and M. Gerritsen (2011) *Culturele waarden en communicatie in internationaal perspectief* (Bussum: Coutinho).

Council of Europe (2000) Legal Situation of the Roma in Europe, http://www.assembly.coe.int/Documents/WorkingDocs/Doc02/EDOC9397.htm, date accessed 17 October 2011.

Council of Europe (2011) European Convention on Human Rights (1950), and its Five Protocols (1952), http://www.hri.org/docs/ECHR50.html, date accessed 5 October 2011.

Diversity Charter (2011) The French Diversity Charter in European languages, http://www.diversity-charter.com/diversity-charter-other-languages.php, date accessed 19 January 2012.

Eupedia (2011) What differentiates Europeans from Americans, http://www.eupedia.com/europe/cultural_differences_europe_usa.shtml, date accessed 5 September 2011.

Eurofound (2007) Directives, http://www.eurofound.europa.eu/areas/industrialrelations/dictionary/definitions/directives.htm, retrieved 18 July 2011.

Eurofound (2010) Regulations, http://www.eurofound.europa.eu/areas/industrialrelations/dictionary/definitions/regulations.htm, date accessed 18 July 2011.

Eurofound (2011) Soft Law, http://www.eurofound.europa.eu/areas/industrialrelations/dictionary/definitions/softlaw.htm, date accessed 18 July 2011.

Europa (2011a) Regional and Minority Languages in the New Member States, http://www.ec.europa.eu/languages/documents/euromosaic-study-comparative-summary_en.pdf, date accessed 19 January 2012.

Europa (2011b) EU Languages, http://www.ec.europa.eu/education/languages/languages-of-europe/doc135_en.htm and Language Policy, date accessed 14 September 2011.

Europa (n.d.) About the EU>Facts and Figures> The Economy, http://www.europa.eu/about-eu/facts-figures/economy/index_en.htm, date accessed 20 July 2011.

European Agency for Fundamental Rights (n.d.) Roma and Travellers, http://www.europa.eu/about-eu/facts-figures/index_en.htm, date accessed 21 January 2011.

European Commission (2003) Costs and Benefits of Diversity, http://www.eiro.eurofound.eu.int/2003/11/feature/eu0311208f.html, date accessed 14 July 2011.

*European Commission (2005) *The Business Case for Diversity: Good Practices in the Workplace* (Brussels: Directorate-General for Employment, Social Affairs and Equal Opportunities).

European Commission (2008a) The Observatory of European SMEs, http://www.ec.europa.eu/enterprise/policies/sme/facts-figures-analysis/sme-observatory/index_en.htm, date accessed 23 November 2011.

European Commission (2008b) *Continuing the Diversity Journey: Business Practices, Perspectives and Benefits* (Luxembourg: Office for Official Publication of the European Communities).

European Commission (2009a) International Perspectives of Positive Action – A Comparative Analysis in the European Union, Canada, the United States and South Africa, http://www.ec.europa.eu/social/main.jsp?catId=738&langId=en&pubId=180&furtherPubs=yes, date accessed 2 November 2011.

European Commission (2009b) Working for Good Practices across Nation States, http://www.diversity-charter.com/diversity-charter-project-2009.php, date accessed 11 September 2011.

European Commission (n.d.) The European Economic Area, http://www.eeas.europa.eu/eea/, date accessed 18 July 2011.

European Commission Enterprise and Industry (2011) Small and Medium-sized enterprises (SMEs), http://www.ec.europa.eu/enterprise/policies/sme/facts-figures-analysis/sme-definition/index_en.htm, date accessed 3 November 2011.

European Commission, Justice (2011) *Report on Progress on Equality between Women and Men in 2010. The Gender Balance in Business Leadership* (Brussels: European Commission).

European Network of Legal Experts in the Non-discrimination Field (n.d.), http://www.non-discrimination.net/content/european-network-legal-experts-non-discrimination-field, date accessed 3 November 2011.

Eurostat (2010) European Union Labour Force Survey – Annual Results 2009, http://www.epp.eurostat.ec.europa.eu/cache/ITY_OFFPUB/KS-QA-10-035/EN/KS-QA-10-035-EN.PDF, date accessed 3 November 2011.

L. Frader (2010) *Gender Equality in the New Europe: France and the European Economic Community in the 1950s World War II*, Paper presented at the 2010 Conference on the Council of European Studies.

Gallup Organization (2007) 'SME Observatory Survey. Summary', *Flash EB Series*, 196, study conducted upon the request of Directorate-General for Enterprise and Industry, http://www.ec.europa.eu/public_opinion/flash/fl196_sum_en.pdf, date accessed 23 November 2011.

J.-P. Garson and A. Loisillon (2003) *Changes and Challenges. Europe and Migration From 1950 to the present*, Conference jointly organized by The European Commission and the OECD, Brussels, 21–2 January 2003.

*E. Holvino and A. Kamp (2009) 'Diversity Management: Are We Moving in the Right Direction? Reflections from Both Sides of the North Atlantic', *Scandinavian Journal of Management*, 2009 (25), 395–403.

Hungary-Romania Cross-Border Co-operation Programme 2007–13 (2011), http://www.huro-cbc.eu/en/project_info/160, date accessed 4 November 2011.

Indexmundi (2011) Net Migration Rate in Europe, http://www.indexmundi.com/map/?v=27&r=eu&l=en, date accessed 23 November 2011.

International Monetary Fund (2011) Report for Selected Country Groups and Subjects, http://www.imf.org7external7pubs/ft/weo/2011/01/weodata/weorept.aspx?sy=2009&ey=2016&scsm=1&ssd=1&sort=country&ds=.&br=1, date accessed 17 June 2011.

V. Kalonaityte, P. Prasad and A. Tedros (2010) 'A Possible Brain Drain? Workplace Diversity and Equal Treatment in Sweden' in A. Klarsfeld (ed.) *International Handbook on Diversity Management at Work: Country Perspectives on Diversity and Equal Treatment* (Cheltenham: Edward Elgar).

G. Kirton and A.-M. Greene (2011) *The Dynamics of Managing Diversity*, 3rd edn (Amsterdam and London: Elsevier).

*A. Klarsfeld (2010) 'Perspectives for 16 Countries on Diversity and Equal Treatment at Work: An Overview and Transverse Questions', in A. Klarsfeld (ed.) *International Handbook on Diversity Management at Work* (Cheltenham and Northampton: Edward Elgar): 244–62.

M. Mareš (2006) *Transnational Networks of Extreme Right Parties in East Central Europe: Stimuli and Limits of Cross-Border Cooperation*, 20th IPSA World Congress, Fukuoka, 9–13 July 2006.

Multilingualism in the EU (2011) Multilingualism in the EU, http://www.eur-lex.europa.eu/en/dossier/dossier_11.htm, date accessed 4 September 2011.

V. Nicolae (2006) Towards a Definition of Anti-Gypsyism, http://www.ergonetwork.org/media/userfiles/media/egro/Towards%20a%20Definition%20of%20Anti-Gypsyism.pdf, date accessed 5 November 2011.

OECD (2011) *Graph 4.3. Migration, in Society at a Glance 2011* (OECD Publishing).

Office for National Statistics (2011), http://www.ons.gov.uk/ons/rel/migration1/migration-statistics-quarterly-report/august-2011/msqr.html, retrieved 18 October 2011.

Omniglot (2011) Sámi languages, http://www.omniglot.com/writing/saami.htm, date accessed 19 January 2012.

OSCE (2005) *Anti-Gypsyism in the European Mass-media* (Organization for Security and Cooperation in Europe: Warsaw).

P. Prasad, J. Pringle J. and A. Konrad (2006) 'Examining the Contours of Workplace Diversity' in A. Konrad, P. Prasad and J. Pringle (eds) *The Handbook of Workplace Diversity* (London, Thousand Oaks and New Delhi: Sage): 1–10.

T. Rees (1998) *Mainstreaming Equality in the European Union* (London and New York: Routledge).

Roms Action (n.d.) Qui sont les roms? http://www.romsaction.org/site/, date accessed 5 November 2011.

SOPEMI (2004) *Organization for Economic Co-operation and Development (OECD) Trends in International Migration* (Paris: OECD).

*M. Stuber (2007) 'Rethinking Diversity for a Global Scope: A European/EMEA Perspective', *The Diversity Factor. The Changing Currency of Diversity*, 15 (1), 17–25.

J. Swiebel (2009) The European Union's Policies to Safeguard and Promote Diversity, http://www.jokeswiebel.nl/pdf/39.pdf, date accessed 23 November 2011.

*M. Thiel and E. Prügl (2009) 'Understanding Diversity in the European Integration Project' in E. Prügl and M. Thiel (eds) *Diversity in the European Union* (Basingstoke and New York: Palgrave Macmillan): 3–20.

S. Vertovec and S. Wessendorf (2009) 'Assessing the Backlash Against Multiculturalism in Europe', MMG Working Paper WP 09-04, http://www.mmg.mpg.de/documents/wp/WP_09-04_Vertovec-Wessendorf_backlash.pdf, date accessed 23 November 2011.

*H. Wallace, W. Wallace and M. Pollack (2005) *Policy Making in the European Union*, 5th edn (Oxford: Oxford University Press).

War Chronicle (2011) Estimated War dead World War II, date accessed 17 October 2011, http://warchronicle.com/numbers/WWII/deaths.htm.

P. Weil (2001) 'Access to Citizenship: A Comparison of Twenty Five Nationality Laws' in T. Aleinkoff and D. Klusmeyer (eds.) *Citizenship Today: Global Perspectives and Practices* (Washington DC: Carnegie Endowment for International Peace), pp. 17–35.

S. Weldon (2006) 'The Institutional Context of Tolerance for Ethnic Minorities: A Comparative, Multilevel Analysis of Western Europe', *American Journal of Political Science*, 50 (2), 331–49.

World Bank (2010) Economic Costs of Roma Exclusion, http://www.web.worldbank.org/WBSITE/EXTERNAL/COUNTRIES/ECAEXT/EXTROMA/0,,contentMDK:22526807~pagePK:64168445~piPK:64168309~theSitePK:615987,00.html, date accessed 21 January 2012.

*J. Wrench (2007) *Diversity Management and Discrimination: Immigrants and Ethnic Minorities in the EU* (Aldershot: Ashgate Publishing).

CHAPTER 3

DIVERSITY MANAGEMENT: THE BUSINESS AND MORAL CASES

Heike Mensi-Klarbach

Chapter Objectives

After completing this chapter you should be able to:

- explain the different concepts of functionally and morally-based diversity management;
- pinpoint various diversity goals;
- distinguish between the business case for diversity management and the business case for diversity;
- build value chains to evaluate diversity management;
- explain how indicators and methods are employed to measure the impact of diversity management;
- discuss likely pitfalls of the business cases.

Chapter Outline

- Introduction
- Linking the business and moral reasons for equal opportunities
- About the moral and the business cases
- The business and the moral case: conflicting aims?
- The business case: challenges in evaluating diversity management
- Conclusion
- Chapter review questions
- Case study
- References

INTRODUCTION

If at first glance it appears that the business and moral cases for diversity lie at opposite ends of a continuum, in fact these rationales are often closely linked in arguments surrounding diversity management. As already outlined in the first chapter of this book, diversity management aims to reduce or eliminate the discrimination of certain social groups in order to foster inclusiveness and thereby boost performance and productivity. Of course, it could be posited that the moral case for the eradication of discrimination is sufficient unto itself, whether or not it brings economic benefits; and that a business motivation can be purely aimed at securing greater productivity or higher profits from diversity, oblivious to any secondary moral considerations. However, it is generally true that these cases are interlinked: one does not work without the other. All investments made by for-profit organizations – including those in diversity management – have to be legitimized in terms of profit-making. Therefore, the attempt is usually made to justify diversity measures in terms of the financial benefits they bring, such as lower costs and improved efficiency. Such arguments are, however, not always easy to back up with detailed profit projections because the implementation of strategic diversity plans is a costly process whose results may not be immediately visible due to a delay between introduction and impact. Thus only a small fraction of 'diversity aware' organizations actively evaluate these initiatives in terms of costs and benefits. Instead diversity management is often legitimized by moral arguments, even while economic and business reasons are continuously sought.

Note: diversity aware organizations are those which view diversity among their stakeholders as important, and therefore implement measures to foster inclusion and remove discriminatory practices.

This chapter will examine the historical roots of diversity management in order to show that moral arguments for equity (originating in the civil rights movement in the United States of America (USA)) very soon became intertwined with business reasons for improving diversity at the workplace. While we will argue that a strict separation between the moral and the business arguments for diversity is not always feasible or useful in organizational practice, we nonetheless intend to isolate and discuss some of these arguments in order to highlight their respective context and goals. The economic evaluation of diversity management (the business case for diversity management) will be outlined as a basic element of strategic diversity management: 'When confronted with a need to convince a reluctant management group about the need to manage diversity, you should start by referring to the business case and to an understanding of the value and benefits of a diverse work force' (Wheeler, 1997). Accordingly, several tools and concepts to calculate the costs and benefits of diversity management will be presented and critically examined.

LINKING THE BUSINESS AND MORAL REASONS FOR EQUAL OPPORTUNITIES

Most descriptions of the developments leading up to diversity management begin with the African-American civil rights movement in the USA. From the mid-1950s activists worked to eliminate many overt discriminatory practices from society, including those affecting the workplace, leading to the Civil Rights Act of 1964 and the establishment of the Equal Employment Opportunity (EEO) Commission (Vedder, 2006): 'Title VII of the Civil Rights Act made it illegal for employers with 100 or more employees to discriminate on the basis of race, color, religion, sex, or national origin' (Dobbin, Sutton, Meyer and Scott, 1993, p. 402). Several years later the act was expanded to ban discrimination based on age and physical or mental disability.

In the 1960s presidents Kennedy and Johnson mandated so-called Affirmative Action (AA) to go beyond anti-discrimination measures by requiring federal contractors and subcontractors to draw up detailed plans on how they intended to support women and minority groups to redress the effects of past discrimination. Such plans included stipulated goals to be met within a given timeframe, with evaluation programmes put in place to monitor progress (Dobbin et al., 1993). When the Supreme Court made clear that even firms that *unintentionally* discriminated against women and minorities could be sued (for example in the case Griggs vs. Duke Power Company from 1971) (Kelly and Dobbin, 1998), companies began to appoint affirmative action officers and affirmative action offices (Edelmann, 1990).

WEBLINK

Visit http://www.northcarolinahistory.org/commentary/297/entry for more information on the case Griggs vs. Duke Power Company.

In reaction to the increased risk of being sued for discriminatory practices, *Harvard Business Review* published an article in 1974 showing how organizations could make themselves 'court-proof': '[…] management does not have to wait for the impetus of litigation before developing a sensible affirmative action program that will provide excellent protection' (Chayes, 1974, p. 81). Here the avoidance of litigation was viewed as a matter of good business sense, as any court case would impose high legal costs and run the risk of incurring damages.

Organizations developed three anti-discrimination strategies to cope with the new legislation: quota systems, tests designed to objectively evaluate the qualifications of job candidates, and rules to formalize hiring and promotion procedures (Dobbin et al., 1993). The first of these was intended to boost the workforce participation of formerly disadvantaged groups, a form of 'positive' discrimination which in the 1970s led to allegations of reverse discrimination against the white male (Thomas, 1990). Such negative publicity encouraged some personnel managers to reject these schemes (Dobbin et al., 1993). On the other hand the refinement of evaluation systems to find the best qualified candidates and the formalization of hiring and promotion rules were seen to comply with good business principles. To summarize, it made good business sense to introduce affirmative action programmes in order to avoid litigation costs, while also improving efficiency in personnel decisions by adopting more objective selection and promotion procedures.

Business arguments for affirmative action:
1. avoid litigation costs;
2. opportunity to increase the efficiency of personnel decisions (Dobbin et al., 1993, p. 405).

Exercise 3.1

Consider the following questions:
How is discrimination defined in your country's
  legal code?

Do you know of any cases of litigation due to
  discrimination at the workplace?
Are organizations in your country at risk of
  being sued for employee discriminatory
  practices?

Several authors have claimed that Johnston and Packer's study (1987) on future workforce diversity was a trigger for the development of diversity management. By predicting that fundamental demographic shifts would lead to a shortage of qualified workers and an increasing share of the workforce made up by minorities, women and immigrants, this work reminded organizations that they urgently needed to focus on the management of diversity (Kelly and Dobbin, 1998).

In the USA anti-discrimination legislation and later the demographic prognoses by Johnston and Packer (1987) had a huge impact on the development of diversity management and its moral and business arguments.

In other parts of the world, however, we have to take account of the very different contexts in order to understand how diversity management has evolved, and how the moral and the business rationales are intertwined. While the roots of diversity management were laid in the USA, the concept subsequently travelled around the world, all the time being altered and adapted to meet local conditions (Ahonen and Tienari, 2009). In Europe employment legislation has evolved over the years in various ways and at various speeds in different countries, yet it can be stated that the first step in reducing discrimination at the workplace has generally been to secure equality between women and men (Singh and Point, 2004). Other factors such as age, religion, disability, ethnicity and sexual orientation have also been the focus of anti-discrimination laws in European countries (Chapter 2).

European Union (EU) rights and responsibilities in fighting discrimination:
The EU has some of the most advanced anti-discrimination laws in the world. European legislation in this field is based on *Article 19 of the Treaty of Lisbon* (formerly Article 13 of the Treaty of Amsterdam) which gives the EU powers to combat discrimination on the grounds of racial or ethnic origin, religion or belief, disability, age, sex or sexual orientation. (For Diversity. Against Discrimination, 2011)

WEBLINK

Visit http://www.ec.europa.eu/justice/fdad/cms/stopdiscrimination/fighting_discrimination/Rights_and_Responsibilities/?langid=en for detailed information on EU actions to prevent discrimination.

The issue of diversity affects every European nation differently, depending on the particular historical development and traditions. Those with a history of colonialism, for example the United Kingdom, France or the Netherlands, have a long familiarity with different cultures and ethnicities, and thus diversity already plays a crucial role in their national identities (Singh and Point, 2004). By contrast, countries such as Germany and Austria have only comparatively recently experienced an influx of so-called 'guest workers', invited in the 1970s and 1980s to maintain their vibrant economic growth (Bendl, Eberherr and Mensi-Klarbach, 2011). In more dramatic fashion, upheaval in one country can easily affect the diversity policies of another, as vividly illustrated by the flood of refugees in the 1980s and 1990s within the very heart of Europe, a result of the conflicts that arose following the disintegration of Yugoslavia. Finally, the EU expansions in 2004 and 2007 increased awareness of diversity by bringing countries with different cultural backgrounds in much closer economic and social contact.

Note: As the labour costs in those countries which joined the European Union in 2004 and 2007 were much lower than the EU average, a transitional directive was drawn up to regulate the flow of migrants from these new members states located in Eastern Europe.

WEBLINK

Visit http://www.ec.europa.eu/internal_market/services/services-dir/guides_en.htm for extensive background information.

The EU Services Directive is intended to develop a joint market for services in order to enhance competitiveness and growth within the union. Try to come up with some moral, political and business arguments for and against the transitional directive regulating the flow of migration from acceding countries.

The flow of services within the EU has of course enhanced diversity in national workforces, serving to increase ethnic, cultural and to some extent religious diversity. Furthermore, the issue of diversity has risen in importance as the forces of globalization have encouraged the growth of many new multinational companies in Europe. Organizations all around the world are being directly confronted with increasing diversity in their stakeholders, especially employees. Within the EU only one legal framework is in place to deal with the repercussions of diversity at work. At the same time individual regions and countries have to deal with a range of diversity issues determined by their regional and national backgrounds (Chapter 2).

> The moral case for diversity aims at combating discrimination by legal means while fostering social diversity in the workplace.

When companies are forced to comply with anti-discrimination legislation they must integrate what is called the moral case into their organizational practices. That is not to say that companies will not promote equity and equal opportunity (EO) without legal prescriptions, or go beyond the basic measures contained in anti-discrimination law. But in many cases, especially in commercial organizations, economic reasoning is required to justify any actions which exceed those stipulated by law.

In 2003 the European Commission (EC) published a major study on *Methods and Indicators to Measure the Cost-Effectiveness of Diversity Policies in Enterprises*. This was the only example of the effort to make organizations aware of the economic impact of anti-discrimination and diversity measures. The European Commission found that legal prescriptions were insufficient to ensure the sustainable development of a diverse workforce free of discrimination:

> But legislation alone may not be enough to ensure that all of the EU's citizens enjoy equality of opportunity in the workplace and that, ultimately, labour market outcomes are more equitable. To achieve these wider policy goals, additional action is needed to recruit, retain, and develop a diverse workforce. Such policies are specific to the situation and needs of each business, and are designed to implement competitive strategy. (European Commission, 2003, p. 2)

It is clear that in order to make diversity issues relevant to management they must be discussed in business terms such as improved efficiency and performance. The study tried to reveal underlying economic considerations by spotlighting several enterprises that had already set up diversity programmes with the aim of raising efficiency (European Commission, 2003).

These companies with active diversity policies perceived the following potential business **benefits** of diversity initiatives as the most relevant (European Commission, 2003, p.27):

- strengthening cultural values within the organization (74 percent of respondents);
- enhancing corporate reputation (69 per cent);
- attracting and retaining highly talented people (62 per cent);
- higher productivity arising from improved motivation and efficiency of existing staff (58 per cent);
- improving innovation and creativity amongst employees (57 per cent);
- enhanced service levels and customer satisfaction (57 per cent);
- helping to overcome labour shortages (57 per cent).

The same companies indicated that the following costs arose in connection with diversity policies (European Commission, 2003 p. 31f.):

- education and training costs (66 per cent of respondents);
- costs of providing additional staff (59 per cent);
- diverting management time (57 per cent);
- productivity shortfalls in the initial stage (50 per cent).

This pinpointing of potential costs and benefits gives a clear picture of the experiences that companies made with active diversity policies. By making these public and discussing them in a wider context of other organizational practices (encompassing the business motives and practices of small, medium and large-sized enterprises) we can help to develop a more generalized 'business case' for diversity, which in turn can encourage organizations to go further than merely comply with anti-discrimination legislation.

> Try to come up with some familiar arguments to those listed above that could encourage organizations to introduce additional diversity measures exceeding those required by current legislation? Consider whether legal prescriptions are in themselves sufficient to deal with diversity.

Even though the arguments listed above concerning costs and benefits of diversity management are based on the practical experiences of companies, we must remember that still, only relatively few organizations actively implement, monitor and evaluate diversity initiatives.

ABOUT THE MORAL AND THE BUSINESS CASES

The idea of equal opportunity programmes was, and is, to give all people the same opportunities at work, regardless of their socio-demographic background, their gender, age, sexual orientation, religion, ethnicity or disability. As discussed above, a great deal of legislation to eliminate discrimination is already in place, in some cases ensuring equity within the workforce by means of 'positive' discrimination. This notion of equality of opportunity has often been labelled the *moral case for diversity*, contrasted with economic considerations such as avoiding litigation costs or the benefits of increased efficiency. It is often claimed that legislation alone will not lead to full equality, but that diversity management programmes must take steps that go further than mere compliance with anti-discrimination legislation (European Commission, 2003, p. 2). As Thomas has stated: 'And precisely this is why we have to learn to manage diversity – to move beyond affirmative action, not to repudiate it' (Thomas, 1990, p. 109). The problem is no longer to get women and minorities into employment, but rather to encourage a heterogeneous workforce to work together efficiently and thereby help women and minorities move up the career ladder (ibid., 1990). In terms of economic reasoning, the underlying idea is to benefit from a heterogeneous knowledge base, to value differences and commonalities and thereby to prepare for changes to come.

If we understand diversity management as a strategy to foster inclusion, then it is crucial to evaluate and monitor the success of diversity initiatives. Such evaluating and monitoring of initiatives means checking whether the moral and the business goals are being met.

The following example of a mission statement from Nestlé shows how companies often link moral and business reasons for their commitment to diversity:

Exercise 3.1: *diversity at Nestlé*

From creating hundreds of *the world's leading brands* to offering *an amazing variety of career options to our employees*, it is clear that Nestlé's businesses are exceptionally diverse.

So it should come as no surprise that we value diversity in our people just as much as we do in our products.

It is our policy to provide an environment where respect is shown to all individual employees and where employees are valued, recognised and rewarded on the basis of their talent and their contribution rather than any consideration of age, gender, race, sexuality, religion or disability. As an organisation, we are opposed to any form of unfair discrimination and believe that an inclusive approach will be of maximum benefit to all our employees as well as our wider business goals and the society in which we live.

This ethos can be summed up in the following statement:

We believe that to succeed we must recruit and retain talented individuals and value and respect the differences each of those individuals brings with them.

In addition, we have a strong ongoing commitment to developing policies, procedures and practices that will actively promote equality of opportunity and optimise the abilities of our workforce. Decisions relating to the recruitment, employment, training, progression, assessment and retention of our people will always be supported by these principles of equality of opportunity.

Source: Nestlé homepage, 2011.

As this example from Nestlé shows, organizations generally assume that they will draw *economic* benefit from the establishment of policies and procedures to promote equality in addition to purely *moral* considerations.

Exercise 3.2

Find some diversity statements issued by companies in your country and analyse whether they refer primarily to business or moral considerations, or a mix of the two.

Evaluating diversity – the core business case

Three different ways of assessing the impact of diversity initiatives can be identified (Kossek, Lobel and Brown, 2006, p. 58). These are to examine the relationship between:

1. diversity practices and workforce diversity;
2. workforce diversity and individual, group and organizational outcomes;
3. diversity practices and individual, group and organizational outcomes.

The first link (Figure 3.1) refers to the goal of achieving equity within the workforce by implementing certain diversity practices. Investigating the results means, in this case, evaluating the impact of diversity programmes on the workforce composition. This can be regarded as part of the moral case, as the focus is on non-economic results expressed in concrete quotas. Still, it has to be said that many organizations define quotas as business goals, either due to legal prescriptions or their own particular business policy.

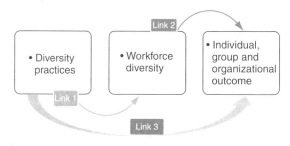

Figure 3.1 Evaluating diversity practices: Link 1
Source: Adapted from Kossek, Lobel and Brown (2006, p. 58).

Example 3.2: *Hewlett-Packard: Diversity and Inclusion*

A workforce that includes men and women from different nations, cultures, ethnic groups, generations, backgrounds, skills, and abilities gives Hewlett-Packard a competitive advantage. A diverse and inclusive workplace is essential to understanding and reflecting the values and demographics of our customers, and is vital to attracting and retaining the best employees.

Performance
We track gender diversity globally and ethnic diversity in our US workforce ...

Executive diversity
In 2010, 19.8 per cent of our top US executives (director level and above) were women, compared with 17.2 per cent in 2009. In the United States, minorities constituted 16.3 per cent, compared with 15.0 per cent in 2009.

Source: Hewlett-Packard home page: Diversity and Inclusion, 2011.

As can be seen from the example of Hewlett-Packard, numerical representation can be used to systematically evaluate measures that increase workforce diversity within organizations. And, of course, in order to set quotas it is first necessary to analyse the status quo and lay down specific goals. It can therefore be stated that quotas have a twofold relevance: First, by requiring that the current situation be reviewed and relevant goals set and, second, by evaluating diversity practices in terms of their impact on the workforce composition. However, merely counting heads may be of limited help when it comes to evaluating the inclusiveness of organizations and their practices.

The second link (see Figure 3.2) according to Kossek, Lobel and Brown (2006) is intended to measure whether a diverse workforce adds significant value to individual, group and organizational outcomes. In this case specific diversity practices are neglected, and the question of merit is reduced to the general benefit bestowed by diversity (Mensi-Klarbach, 2010). This can be called the *business case for diversity*, as it focuses on the value-added by a diverse workforce, while the role of diversity management to deal with non-economic aspects of a diverse workforce is disregarded. The potential economic, efficiency and performance benefits of a diverse workforce are often highlighted in order to convince organizations to promote and value diversity within their organizations (Meriläinen, Tienari, Katila and Benschop, 2009; Robinson and Dechant, 1997).

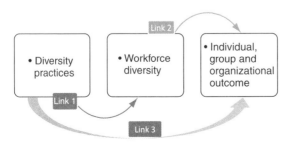

Figure 3.2   Evaluating diversity practices: Link 2
Source: Adapted from Kossek, Lobel and Brown (2006, p. 58).

Recent studies on this topic have shown, for example, that corporations with the highest number of women on their board of directors outperform companies with the fewest in terms of their return on invested capital by up to 60 per cent (Carter and Wagner, 2011). Similarly, the Swedish NUTEK study came to the following conclusion: 'The effect of having a representatively balanced labour group, with both women and men from each educational category normally employed by the company, appears to be stable. The greater the deviation from this norm, the greater the adverse effects both on earning power and on productivity.' (NUTEK, 2011). In another study Krishnan and Park (2005) found a positive correlation between organizational performance and the number of women in top management teams.

However, it cannot simply be concluded that there exists a direct causal relation between the demographic composition of the workforce, or the top management team, and financial performance (Carter and Wagner, 2011; Mensi-Klarbach, 2010). For example, Roberson and Park (2007) argue that a U-shaped curve links diversity and performance, concluding that in order to secure financial benefits from (here: racial) diversity, a certain threshold percentage of racial diversity in a company's leadership must be exceeded (about 50 per cent). Taking contextual factors into account, though not specifying them directly, Herring concluded from his study that 'Within the proper context, diversity provides a competitive advantage through social complexity at the firm level' (Herring, 2009 p. 220).

Gonzales and Denisi (2009) have introduced *diversity climate* as a moderating variable, finding significant support for their hypothesis that such climate influences the relationship between performance and the factors gender, race and ethnicity diversity.

Diversity climate is a shared understanding among organization members of an organization's diversity-related structures and actions. It comprises the perception of fairness regarding inclusion and exclusion of people from diverse backgrounds.

Thus, apart from the scope and particular form of diversity, empirical studies have shown that moderating variables – in a particular diversity climate – will influence whether or not an enterprise can exploit its workforce diversity.

Bearing this in mind, an often expressed criticism of the business case for diversity is that it implies that diversity should only be promoted if it adds value to a group or organization, not taking conditions as the climate into account (Mensi-Klarbach, 2011). However, as diversity is an issue that cannot be ignored, we can query the necessity of legitimizing diversity initiatives in terms of increased value-added (Litvin, 2006). Instead of asking whether diversity adds value, it is

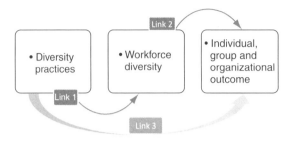

Figure 3.3 Evaluating diversity practices: Link 3
Source: Adapted from Kossek, Lobel and Brown (2006, p. 58).

crucial to look at how existing diversity can best be dealt with, while highlighting the conditions under which an organization can benefit from diversity. This idea refers to the third link (see Figure 3.3).

The third link examines the relationship between diversity practices and individual, group and organizational performance. This can be called the *business case for diversity management*, as it concentrates on the business merit of strategically managing diversity in organizations, and thus is the core argument when evaluating diversity management (Robinson and Dechant, 1997). It has been maintained that organizations are already well aware of the impact that diversity initiatives might have on their bottom line (Lockwood, 2005). Yet at the same time a pan-European study has shown that less than one-third of the surveyed companies effectively linked their diversity initiatives to productivity measures (European Commission, 2008). Currently, a lack of empirical evidence on the financial impact of diversity initiatives may be hindering the sustainability of diversity management in organizations (Hanappi-Egger, Köllen and Mensi-Klarbach, 2007): 'Without this evidence, especially in the context of budget constraints forced by the economic downturn, diversity programs may come under the same scrutiny routinely turned on most business functions' (Hansen, 2003, p. 30). To conclude, the business case for diversity management is promoted in order to make diversity management a sustainable management concept legitimized in terms of economic rationales.

The *business case for diversity* focuses on the intrinsic value-added offered by diversity, for instance a positive relation between the number of female board members and board effectiveness.

The *business case for diversity management* concentrates on the economic benefits stemming from diversity programmes and practices, such as a positive relation between training in diversity and productivity.

THE BUSINESS AND THE MORAL CASE: CONFLICTING AIMS?

The business and moral cases for diversity seem to pursue different aims, at least at first glance. However, if the primary aim of strategic diversity management is a state of *inclusion* within an organization, then the moral and the business cases can both be seen as intermediate goals on the way to achieving such inclusion.

> The *moral case* argues that discriminatory structures and practices be eliminated in order to achieve equality of opportunity. The business case formulates concrete economic goals to be realised by implementing diversity practices.

As already stated, these cases cannot be considered in isolation: they are indissolubly tied together. Let us first look at potential business benefits from diversity before turning to the goals of diversity management (see Figure 3.4). In so doing we will see that the moral and business goals are not necessarily conflicting.

The European Commission (2003) has identified two types of economic benefit derived from diversity management that can be defined as principal goals:

1. Strengthening long-term 'value drivers', that are the tangible and intangible assets that allow companies to be competitive, to generate stable cash flows, and to satisfy their shareholders.
2. Generating short and medium-term opportunities to improve cash flows, for instance by reducing costs, resolving labour shortages, opening up new markets, and improving performance in existing markets. These are also known as "return-on-investment" (ROI) benefits. (European Commission, 2003, p. 15)

Goals and targets – general definitions

Generally speaking, it is possible to distinguish between *qualitative* intentions and *quantitative* targets in diversity management (Kreikebaum, 1997). Note: The terms goal and target are used synonymously.

Figure 3.4 Business benefits of diversity
Source: CSES (2003, p. 16).

Qualitative intentions can be defined as strategic positions, which are used to quantify targets. Only *quantified targets* can be measured and evaluated, while qualitative intentions are usually formulated rather vaguely and thus evade economic evaluation.

The relationship between these quantitative targets and qualitative intentions can best be illustrated in a pyramid (see Figure 3.5).

At the pyramid apex we see that general intentions are usually expressed in a company mission statement, a diversity statement or a code of conduct. Specific intentions, derived from these general intentions and including more detail, are still more qualitative in nature than quantifiable. Finally, at the pyramid base, intentions are broken down into concrete quantifiable targets.

For example, a mission statement can promote the general value of diversity within the organization (to employees) or outside of it (to customers, suppliers and other stakeholders). One particular intention derived from the statement could be to reflect a diverse customer base in a diverse workforce. A quantifiable goal could then be, for instance, to increase the number of minorities and women at all organizational levels by 30 per cent.

A hierarchical relationship exists between:

1. economically coercive goals;
2. disposable goals.

Disposable targets are those that will only be pursued if no economically coercive goals stand in the way (Gladen, 2003), and thus the goal of increasing the workforce ratio of women or minorities is disposable unless linked directly to economic rationales. This emphasizes the importance of providing supporting facts and figures in order to anchor diversity management as a sustainable and strategic management concept within organizations.

Figure 3.5 Diversity management within a pyramid of organizational goals
Sources: Adapted from Gladen (2003), and Mensi-Klarbach (2010).

Goals of diversity management

Diversity management is a highly contextual concept, and therefore goals, strategies and resulting diversity practices will vary from organization to organization. Table 3.1 gives an overview of various (quantifiable or qualitative) goals that can be pursued by diversity initiatives:

Table 3.1 Goals of diversity management

1. Content-related goals		
Economic goals		**Social goals**
Marketing goals: matching workforce diversity with market diversity; opening up new markets (minorities); good diversity reputation with customers and suppliers		Avoiding discrimination in the workplace
Personnel marketing: exploit current workforce diversity and increase diversity through targeted recruitment		Increasing employee loyalty and commitment
Cost savings: lower absenteeism and fluctuation due to higher motivation and employee happiness; better conflict management due to better communication, internally and externally		
2. Goals according to outreach		
Operative goals	**Strategic goals**	
Better problem-solving	Gaining sustainable competitive advantages through heterogeneous and uniquely diverse human capital	
Increasing resource flexibility		
3. Goals according to organizational levels		
Individual goals	**Group goals**	**Organizational goals**
Benefiting from individual career goals	Using group potential for problem-solving, creativity, innovation and learning	Enhancing system flexibility by reacting more quickly to changing environments
	Enhancing productivity through interpersonal skills	Gaining sustainable competitive advantages
		Lowering conflict potential between individuals and groups
		Positive business rivalry among individuals and groups
Source: Adapted from Becker (2006, p. 27f).		

The table shows that goals can be formulated in terms of their content, their outreach or organizational level. We can see that moral and business targets do not have to be opposing goals, but can rather supplement one another; for example, the social goal of 'increasing employee loyalty and commitment' goes hand in hand with the cost savings from 'lower absenteeism and fluctuation due to higher motivation and employee happiness'.

Detailed information about the goals companies pursue with regard to diversity can often be found on their websites.

Example 3.3: *Diversity at Nokia*

Let's agree to disagree.

At the last count, the Nokia Group employed approximately 139,000 people around the world: not bad for a company that started life as a small riverside paper mill in Finland.

In 2010, the devices and services business alone employed approximately 60,000 people from around 115 different nationalities. And approximately 41 per cent of them were women.

Such diversity is crucial to our success so far – and to our continued success in the future. We're operating in more markets than ever before, and employees from diverse backgrounds can give us invaluable insights into our customer bases. Just as important, a mix of cultures, genders, age groups, beliefs, interests and opinions in the workplace helps foster debate, discussion, ideas and innovation. Not to mention making Nokia a more enjoyable, stimulating and rewarding place to spend your working day.

Source: NOKIA Home page, 2012.

Which company goals with regard to diversity does this statement reveal? Are they financial or non-financial, qualitative intentions or quantified targets? How can they be measured?

The formulation of goals is just one step towards building a business case. When it comes to quantifying and evaluating the goals, several challenges have first to be overcome.

THE BUSINESS CASE: CHALLENGES IN EVALUATING DIVERSITY MANAGEMENT

'Unfortunately, in almost all aspects of organizational operations, what is most easily measurable and what is important are often only loosely related' (Pfeffer, 1997, p. 360). As stated earlier, the impact of diversity management on perfor-mance is very rarely measured by organizations (European Commission, 2008). This can be attributed, amongst other factors, to a lack of quantified goals, as many organizations do not break down their qualitative intentions into con-crete targets. Another difficulty in evaluating diversity management in terms of efficiency gains becomes clear when looking more closely at the targets formulated in Table 3.1. It can be seen that diversity management primarily affects human and organizational capital, the so-called intangible assets (CSES, 2003).

> *Intangible assets* can be defined as assets other than material and financial assets, which bring value to an organization (Stoi, 2004, citing Lev, 2001).

Intangibles embrace three forms of capital (Stoi, 2004):

1. Human capital, such as the knowledge and skills of employees;
2. Customer capital, for example strong relationships with customers;
3. Structural capital, which can include the effectiveness of internal procedures and practices or a positive organizational image.

Intangible assets display two important characteristics (Lev, 2003). First, they are themselves inactive, so that certain structures and systems are needed to exploit them. Second, intangibles are fluid; they can be easily lost, for example, if skilled employees leave the company. Diversity management and the fostering of inclusion influence the structural capital by enabling a diverse workforce. It should be clear that there are pitfalls to be avoided when attempting to measure or evaluate such intangibles.

Traditional evaluation tools that make use of relevant facts and figures are mainly *past*-oriented (Lev, 2003). However, when evaluating the costs and benefits of diversity management it is necessary to focus on the *future*, as the impact which diversity initiatives have on human or structural capital will become most apparent on the medium to long term, while costs are incurred immediately.

The causal relations of these medium- and long-term effects cannot be analysed precisely, but must be assigned a degree of probability. There is no generally agreed method how to measure the impact of human capital or changes to human capital (as under diversity management) on the economic performance of an organization (Schellinger, 2004). However, several approaches can be suggested. In order to capture the short- and long-term effects of diversity management and give a holistic picture of its organizational effects, *financial* and *non-financial* data can be pooled to allow intangible assets to be considered in the business rationale, which is traditionally oriented towards tangibles (Mensi-Klarbach, 2010).

Cause and effect relations are posited in order to estimate the likely future impact of diversity management. These relations can be either based on empirical findings (for example when a manager observes that training initiatives enhance employee satisfaction) or derived theoretically (Crössmann, 2004). One well-known model that creates a chain of cause and effect relationships by combining financial and non-financial strategic drivers is the *balanced scorecard* (Kaplan and Norton, 1996). This concept has been further refined to create the so-called *diversity scorecard* (Hubbard, 2004).

The diversity scorecard

The balanced scorecard was devised by Kaplan and Norton in the 1990s to translate an organization's strategy and vision into measurable goals (Rieger, 2006). In a similar fashion, the diversity scorecard quantifies the value-added which a diversity initiative brings to the overall business performance, while also supporting continued efforts to improve diversity. Hubbard (2004) has proposed that the diversity scorecard should encompass six key categories: Financial Impact, Diverse Customer/Community Partnerships, Workforce Profile, Workplace Climate/Culture, Diversity Leadership Commitment as well as Learning and Growth (see Figure 3.6).

Hubbard (2004) suggests that these categories can be adapted for particular companies or products, and indeed emphasizes that it is crucial to refine the diversity scorecard (and define relevant categories) for specific contexts. In order to be able to build a scorecard it is necessary that the members of an organization share a common understanding of diversity, including its values and norms, as well as a common culture regarding issues of diversity (Rieger, 2006).

Based on this shared understanding of the meaning of diversity, value chains are created in order to depict the impact of diversity activities on products and services provided by the company.

When enterprises build a diversity scorecard they are forced to consider which relevant diversity activities and processes are likely to add value. In turn,

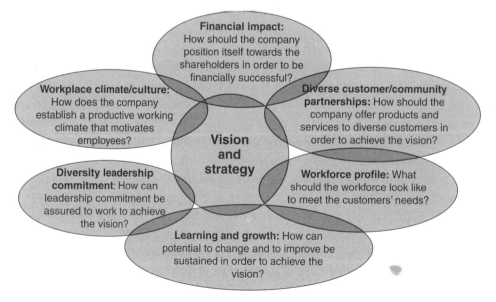

Figure 3.6 Perspectives of the diversity scorecard
Sources: Adapted from Hubbard (2004); and Rieger (2006).

Table 3.2 Examples of typical value chains

Activity/process	Outcome	Impact	Value-added
Increase diverse talent recruitment resources	Shorter time-to-fill rates; lower agency rates	Jobs filled faster; lower hiring costs	Reduced operating expenses
Improve diverse work team problem-solving processes	Reduced time to solve	Increase in reasons given in survey for long service by diverse members	Retention savings as compared to rolling average of previous years
Source: Hubbard (2004, p. 301).			

these value chains already comprise implicit goals that should be achieved by these activities (see Table 3.2).

Try to devise possible value chains concerning diversity management practices and their potential impact. In your opinion does there exist general agreement on causal relations regarding the introduction and impact of diversity initiatives? What is required to establish convincing cause and effect chains?

Diversity perspectives should be specified by measureable indicators, so that goals are made explicit and a framework is set up for the evaluation of diversity activities. Indicators and ratios can be based on cause and effect chains.

Business ratios are concentrated economic information, preferably quantitative in nature, while indicators are employed when subjects can only be depicted incompletely (Gladen, 2003).

Table 3.3 shows two example indicators: the *proportion of employees of a certain age* and the the *proportion of women in management*. Clearly these indicators are derived from a specific diversity strategy (and resulting targets), namely to address age within the workforce and gender in management.

Table 3.3 Example indicator: workforce demographics

Indicator	Definition/ formula
Proportion of employees of a certain age	$\dfrac{\textit{Number of employees of certain age}}{\textit{Total number of employees}}$
Proportion of women in management	$\dfrac{\textit{Number of women in management}}{\textit{Total number of management positions}}$
Source: Adopted from Rieger (2006, p. 269).	

Table 3.4 Example indicator: financial impact

Indicator	Definition/ definition/formula
Financial savings due to diversity activities	*Costs before implementation of diversity activities minus costs after implementation of diversity activities*
Diversity return on investment	$$\frac{Diversity\ benefits\ minus\ Diversity\ costs}{Diversity\ costs}$$

Source: Adapted from Rieger (2006, p. 271).

It may be concluded that indicators are always based on previously defined goals; here these are the proportion of women in management positions as well as the age of those recruited. Activities, which address these goals, can be evaluated by tracking the indicators as they change over time.

Regarding the business case of diversity management, financial impact is frequently the most important variable. An example indicator for such considerations of profit and loss is given in Table 3.4.

It may be seen that financial savings constitute a goal, which can be measured by applying these indicators, either in terms of absolute numbers (savings due to diversity activities) or a ratio (diversity return on investment).

Let us sum up our brief discussion of the diversity scorecard by outlining the main advantages of this management tool:

1. the enterprise is forced to define a common understanding of diversity;
2. devising value chains for diversity activities reveals underlying assumptions about the impact of certain activities;
3. it is a business truism that 'what gets measured gets done'. In this sense, introducing indicators to measure the achievement of goals can in itself be a driving force.

However, it should be noted that the practical relevance of this tool is restricted by the highly complex and time-consuming processes involved in setting up and updating a diversity scorecard.

Another similar framework has been established by the European Commission (2003).

Methods and indicators to measure the cost-effectiveness of diversity policies in enterprises

The European Commission (2003) proposed an extensive measurement framework consisting of several indicators and corresponding measurement methods to evaluate the 'Cost-Effectiveness of Diversity Policies in Enterprises'. The cause and effect relation is based on the assumption that diversity management, and the way in which activities are implemented, will influence the composition of the workforce (representation) and the diversity climate within the working environment. This in turn is expected to generate business benefits.

The framework developed by the European Commission (2003) embraces the indicators presented in Table 3.5.

While there are various ways to measure these principal indicators, the framework suggests some methods of measurement (see Figure 3.7). Of course, the indicators can be evaluated by means of value chains like those discussed in connection with the diversity scorecard. However, in contrast to the diversity scorecard, the EC framework presents a large number of indicators and offers

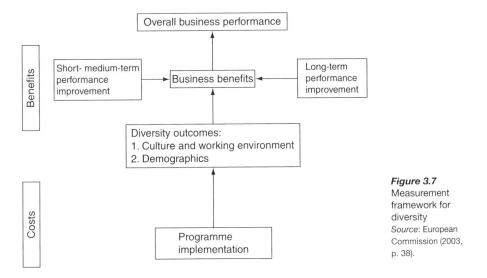

Figure 3.7 Measurement framework for diversity
Source: European Commission (2003, p. 38).

Table 3.5 Indicators to calculate costs and benefits of diversity management

Programme implementation	Diversity outcomes	Business benefits
• top management commitment • diversity strategy and plan • organizational policies • employment benefits • managerial incentives • organizational structures • reporting process (monitoring and evaluation) • communication support networks • education and training • productivity losses	• workforce demographics (representation) • employment culture/working environment	• cost reductions • reduced labour shortages • access to new markets • improved performance in existing markets • access to talent • global management capacity • innovation and creativity • reputation with governments and other stakeholders • marketing image • culture value
Source: CSES (2003, p. 39f).		

Table 3.6   Example indicator: cost reductions

Indicator	Methods of Measurement
Cost reductions	Labour turnover by specific groups (e.g. age, gender, ethnic groups, disabled, gay/lesbian, different religious groups) compared to the company average
	Absenteeism by specific groups (e.g. age, gender, ethnic groups, disabled, gay/lesbian, different religious groups) compared to company average
	Direct recruitment costs – changes over time
	Expenditure on discrimination – related litigation cases – legal costs (changes over time)
	Expenditure on discrimination – related litigation cases – settlement costs (changes over time)
Source: European Commission (2003, p. 46).	

Table 3.7   Example indicator: labour shortages

Indicator	Methods of measurement
Labour shortages	Number of unfilled vacancies (internal and external) – absolute and changes over time
	Number of applicants for job vacancies (internal and external) – absolute and changes over time
	Time taken to fill vacancies (internal and external)
Source: European Commission (2003, p. 46).	

several methods to measure each indicator, as can be seen in the example of Table 3.6.

As with the indicator examples for the diversity scorecard, the goal here is clearly set. Certain assumptions on how to reduce costs by implementing diversity management are made explicit, namely by reducing turnover and absenteeism rates and thereby lowering direct recruitment costs. Further it is assumed that litigation costs can be reduced.

Let us look at another example indicator, namely 'labour shortages' (Table 3.7).

WEBLINK

For more detailed information on indicators and methods of measurement see http://www.diversityatwork.net/NL/Docs/CostsBenefExSum.pdf.

Again the selected indicator points to a goal (here reducing labour shortages) that can be achieved through diversity management. The impact of diversity activities can be constantly evaluated by tracking the changes in labour shortages over time.

Summarizing, we can say that the strategic integration of diversity management into the core business of organizations requires the careful planning and evaluation of measures. It is crucially important to show the financial impact of diversity management, yet this is not an easy process. Indicators and measures such as those presented by the European Commission (2003) show how the costs and benefits of diversity practices can be quantified. This aids the sustainability of diversity management by establishing good practice examples for other companies, as well as supporting the continual improvement of diversity programmes by monitoring their impact.

CONCLUSION

In this chapter we have traced the historical roots of diversity management in the USA and Europe in order to outline the close relationship between the business and the moral case for diversity. We have pointed out that there generally exists a hierarchical relationship between coercive (mainly financially based) goals and disposable goals, and thus it is essential to set and evaluate economically relevant diversity goals when attempting to anchor diversity management both strategically and sustainably. If equal opportunities are a primary goal in diversity management then we see that the business rationale is a prerequisite when aiming for equity in the workforce through sustainable diversity management. Some concepts and concrete indicators have been presented to encourage debate on the likely impact of diversity management.

Through various examples we have shown that the moral and business rationales are generally interwoven, implying that an organization can derive considerable moral *and* financial benefits by reducing discrimination, creating a climate of inclusion and establishing a more diverse workforce.

Several additional examples have been presented in order to indicate how diversity management goals can be formulated and how best to measure progress towards achieving these goals. The 'diversity scorecard' and the CSES framework were introduced in order to provide examples of value chains, indicators and methods of measuring diversity outcomes.

Chapter Review Questions

- Which business arguments are typically given in support of affirmative action programmes?
- What are some possible goals of diversity management?
- Why is it important to evaluate diversity management in financial terms?
- How can the costs and benefits of diversity management be measured?
- What is the difference between the business case for diversity and the business case for diversity management?

Case Study

Diversity management: a useful tool for solving all problems?

An Austrian non-profit social services organization has an increasingly diverse workforce. Nearly 35 per cent of employees in its health care department have a migration background; within the organization as a whole the figure is 75 per cent of staff (770 persons) and volunteers (660 persons). Some 95 per cent of staff in the health care department are female, aged between 35 and 45. No fewer than 23 different languages are spoken by employees. In general, health care work is characterized by highly stressful working conditions, low wages and inconvenient hours due to the necessity of working shifts. Women and men in the health service department of the organization mainly work as mobile nurses looking after patients in their homes. Twenty-four hour shifts are not uncommon as many of the patients need round-the-clock care. The staff of the health care department are organized into teams of 60 members, each responsible for a specific geographic region. Team leaders organize the shifts, draw up work schedules for holidays and organize 'emergency' staff replacement when a worker becomes ill or suddenly quits.

In previous years a major problem for the CEO of this organization was the rather high rate of fluctuation and absenteeism (15 per cent). The deterioration in working conditions and excessive workload for the 'remaining' employees created a vicious circle in which the rate of fluctuation continued to grow. In addition to this difficult situation, more and more employees complained of discrimination within the organization and in their dealings with patients.

In an attempt to resolve these problems, the CEO decided to introduce diversity management. Initially a diversity statement was developed and presented on the corporate homepage, promoting toleration and valuing differences in terms of religion, culture and language. The statement also called for openness and respect of the individual, while rejecting discrimination of any kind. It stressed the belief that: 'Diversity makes us stronger. We acknowledge the diversity of our employees, members and customers.'

The CEO then organized focus groups among health service department employees in order to discover the current role of diversity and determine a basis for future action. These focus groups revealed several culturally and religiously-motivated sources of conflict. For example, Turkish female employees felt they were unfairly treated by being required to work undesirable shifts (beginning at 6 am or after 7 pm) more frequently than Austrian employees. On the other hand, the latter complained of discrimination in holiday scheduling by not being given time off during school holidays in contrast to the 'non-Austrians' who were allowed four or five weeks off in order to take their children to their 'home countries'. Employees also reported that they did not have a strong sense of 'belonging' or loyalty to the company; they believed that their work was undervalued and perceived as non-essential.

For the CEO, who herself took on the position of diversity agent, it became clear that these issues were driven by intercultural conflict, which could be greatly reduced by raising the awareness of diversity. She therefore set up a diversity training programme, including awareness-raising activities to teach the value of diversity. As the budget was limited (in fact very nearly non-existent), the courses were held in the organization's main office before the beginning, or at the end, of shifts. Even though the courses were offered free of charge, the CEO wondered why most employees refused to participate in the training programme, in some cases even claiming that they had no need of diversity management. As the problems of fluctuation, absenteeism and claims of discrimination continued, the CEO became more determined to find a solution, but started questioning whether diversity management was the right approach for her organization.

When an external group of consultants analysed the company, they identified several aspects that may have hindered the positive impact of diversity management: First, employees were expected to attend the diversity awareness courses in a central building *in addition* to their normal work schedule. For many this meant an extra two or more hours 'at work' after a long shift, and frequently entailed travelling long distances from their normal workplace to the course location. The diversity manager stated that as there was no additional money to invest in the awareness training, these courses had to take place outside normal working hours, and in a central company building so as to avoid paying for rented premises.

Second, after analysing the problematic working conditions with focus groups, it became clear that conflicts in holiday and shift planning occurred because of a lack of management transparency. Usually the team leader had the responsibility of drawing up work schedules and granting holiday applications. Employees perceived this process as arbitrary, so that resulting conflicts were attributed to intercultural friction rather than to decision-making processes within the team. An important first step in resolving the situation would have been to investigate and re-design team processes, while awareness-raising activities could have highlighted employees' unconscious use of stereotypes. However, without sufficient funding, any diversity training programme was bound to fail.

Test Your Understanding

1. What was the motivation for introducing diversity management?
2. What concrete measures were implemented to promote diversity?
3. What was the goal of these measures?
4. How could the impact of these diversity measures be evaluated in financial terms?
5. Can you think of potential cause and effect chains?
6. What are the potential costs and benefits of a diversity programme for this company?

REFERENCES

P. Ahonen and J. Tienari (2009) 'United in Diversity? Disciplinary Normalization in an EU Project', *Organization*, 16 (5), 655–79.

M. Becker (2006) 'Wissenschaftstheoretische Grundlagen des Diversity Management' in M. Becker and A. Seidel (eds) *Diversity Management. Unternehmens- und Personalpolitik der Vielfalt* (Stuttgart: Schäffer-Poeschel), pp. 5–50.

R. Bendl, H. Eberherr and H. Mensi-Klarbach (2011) 'Vertiefende Betrachtungen zu ausgewählten Diversitätsdimensionen' in R. Bendl, E. Hanappi-Egger and R. Hofmann (eds) *Diversität und Diversitätsmanagement* (Wien: UTB), pp. 79–135.

*N. M. Carter and H. M. Wagner (2011) 'The Bottom Line: Corporate Performance and Women's Representation on Boards (2004-2008)', *Catalyst*, http://www.catalyst.org/publication/479/tho-bottom-line-corporate-performance-and-womens-representation-on-boards-20042008, date accessed 12 July 2011.

A. H. Chayes (1974) 'Make your Equal Opportunity Program Court-proof.', *Harvard Business Review*, 52, 81–9.

J. Crössmann (2004) 'Möglichkeiten und Grenzen von Kennzahlensystemen', *IS Reports: Betriebswirtschaft*, 8 (5), 40–45.

European Commission (2003) *Methods and Indicators to Measure the Cost-Effectiveness of Diversity Policies in Enterprises*. October, catalogue no. KE-55-03-399-EN-N.

F. Dobbin, J. Sutton, J. Meyer and R. Scott (1993) 'Equal Opportunity Law and the Construction of Internal Labor Markets', *American Journal of Sociology*, 99 (2), 396–427.

L. Edelman (1990) 'Legal Environments and Organizational Governance: The Expansion of Due Process in the American Workplace', *American Journal of Sociology*, 95, 1401–40.

*European Commission (2008) *Continuing the Diversity Journey. Business Practices, Perspectives and Benefits* (Luxembourg: Office for Official Publications of the European Communities).

For Diversity. Against Discrimination (2011), http://www.ec.europa.eu/justice/fdad/cms/stopdiscrimination/fighting_discrimination/Rights_and_Responsibilities/?langid=en, date accessed 12 July 2011.

W. Gladen (2003) *Kennzahlen- und Berichtssysteme. Grundlagen zum Performance Measurement* (Wiesbaden: Gabler).

J. A. Gonzales and A. S. Denisi (2009) 'Cross-level Effects of Demography and Diversity Climate and Firm Effectiveness', *Journal of Organizational Behavior,* 30, 21–40.

E. Hanappi-Egger, T. Köllen and H. Mensi-Klarbach (2007) 'Diversity Management: Economically Reasonable or "only" Ethically Mandatory?', *The International Journal of Diversity in Organizations, Communities and Nations,* 7 (3), 153–67.

*F. Hansen (2003) 'Diversity's Business Case doesn't Add up', *Workforce,* 28–32.

C. Herring (2009) 'Does Diversity Pay?: Race, Gender, and the Business Case for Diversity', *American Sociological Review,* 74 (2), 208–24.

Hewlett-Packard home page (2011) Diversity and Inclusion, http://www.hp.com/hpinfo/globalcitizenship/society/diversity_and_inclusion.html, date accessed 11 July 2011.

E. E. Hubbard (2004) *The Diversity Scorecard: Evaluating the Impact of Diversity on Organizational Performance.* (Oxford: Elsevier).

W. B. Johnston and A. E. Packer (1987) *Workforce 2000: Work and Workers for the 21st Century* (Indianapolis: Hudson Institute Inc.).

R. S. Kaplan and D. P. Norton (1996) *The Balanced Scorecard. Translating strategy into Action.* (Boston: Harvard Business School Press).

*E. Kelly and F. Dobbin (1998) 'How Affirmative Action Became Diversity Management', *American Behavioral Scientist,* 4 (7), 960–84.

*E. E. Kossek, S. A. Lobel and J. Brown (2006) 'Human Resource Strategies to Manage Workforce Diversity' in A. M. Konrad, P. Prasad and J. K. Pringle (eds) *Handbook of Workplace Diversity.* (London, Thousand Oaks and New Dehli: Sage), pp. 53–74.

H. Kreikebaum (1997) *Strategische Unternehmensplanung,* 6th edn (Stuttgart: Kohlkammer).

H. E. Krishnan and D. Park (2005) 'A Few Good Women – On Top Management Teams', *Journal of Business Research,* 58, 1712–20.

B. Lev (2001) *Intangibles: Management Measurement and Reporting* (Washington, DC: Brookings Institution Press).

B. Lev (2003) 'Intangibles at a Crossboard', *Controlling,* 3 (4), 121–7.

*D. Litvin (2006) 'Diverslty: Making Space for a Better Case' in A. M. Konrad, P. Prasad and J. K. Pringle (eds) Handbook of Workplace Diversity (London, Thousand Oaks and New Dehli: Sage), pp. 75–94.

N. R. Lockwood (2005) 'Workplace Diversity: Leveraging the Power of Differences for Competitive Advantage', *Strategic Human Resource Management Research Quarterly,* 2–10.

H. Mensi-Klarbach (2010) *Diversity und Diversity Management – die Business Case Perspektive. Eine kritische Analyse* (Hamburg: Verlag Dr. Kovac).

H. Mensi-Klarbach (2011) 'Der Business Case für Diversität und Diversitätsmanagement' in R. Bendl, E. Hanappi-Egger and R. Hofmann (eds) *Diversität und Diversitätsmanagemen'* (Wien: UTB), pp. 301–28.

S. Meriläinen, J. Tienari, S. Katila and Y. Benschop (2009) 'Diversity Management versus Gender Equality: The Finnish Case', *Canadian Journal of Administrative Sciences,* 26, 230–43.

Nestlé home page (2011), Diversity at Nestlé, http://www.nestlecareers.co.uk/html/diversity-nestle-careers.html, date accessed 11 July 2011.

NOKIA home page (2012) Nokia: Our People and Culture, http://www.nokia.com/global/about-nokia/company/about-us/culture/our-people-and-culture/, date accessed 4 January 2012.

NUTEK (2011) Extract from Gender and Profit. Stockholm, http://www.women2top.net/download/employer/key/genderandprofit.pdf, date accessed 5 October 2011.

*J. Pfeffer (1997) 'Pitfalls on the Road to Measurement: The dangerous Liaison of Human Resources with the Ideas of Accounting and Finance', *Human Resource Management*, 36 (3), 357–65.

C. Rieger (2006) 'Die Diversity Scorecard als Instrument zur Bestimmung der Erfolges von Diversity-Maßnahmen' in M. Becker and A. Seidel (eds) *Diversity Management. Unternehmens- und Personalpolitik der Vielfalt.* (Stuttgart: Schäffer-Poeschel), pp. 258–77.

*Q. M. Roberson and H. J. Park (2007) 'Examining the Link between Diversity and Firm Performance', *Group and Organization Management,* 32 (5), 548–68.

*G. Robinson and K. Dechant (1997) 'Building a Business Case for Diversity' in *The Academy of Management Executive*, 11 (3), 21–9.

J. Schellinger (2004) *Konzeption eines wertorientierten strategischen Personalmanagements.* (Frankfurt/Main and Wien: Lang).

V. Singh and S. Point (2004) 'Strategic Responses by European Companies to the Diversity Challenges: An Online Comparison', *Long Range Planning*, 37, 295–318.

R. Stoi (2004) 'Management und Controlling von Intangibles auf der Basis der immateriellen Wertreiber des Unternehmens' in P. H. Horvath (ed.) *Intangibles in der Unternehmenssteuerung* (München: Vahlen).

*R. R. Thomas, Jr. (1990) 'From Affirmative Action to Affirming Diversity', *Harvard Business Review,* March–April, 107–17.

G. Vedder (2006) 'Die historische Entwicklung von Diversity Management in den USA und in Deutschland' in G. Krell and G. Vedder (eds) *Diversity Management. Impulse aus der Personalforschung* (München and Mering: Rainer Hampp Verlag), pp. 1–24.

R. D. Wheeler (1997) 'Managing Workforce Diversity', *Tax Executive*, 49 (6), 493–5.

PART TWO

INDIVIDUAL AND CROSS-CULTURAL DIVERSITY

Contents

CHAPTER 4

GENDER AND DIVERSITY ACROSS CULTURES

Marie-Thérèse Claes, Edeltraud Hanappi-Egger and Henriett Primecz

Chapter Objectives

After completing this chapter, you should be able to:
- define what is meant by 'culture';
- explain the different levels at which cultural differences in gender and diversity relations can be analysed;
- critically discuss methods of cross-cultural research on diversity;
- apply methods of deconstruction in order to unmask diversity biases in organizational texts;
- detect hidden diversity inequalities in seemingly neutral texts;
- explain the nature of cultural diversity biases and discuss ethical dilemmas in business contexts.

Chapter Outline

- Introduction
- The concept of culture: approaches, definitions and contradictions
- Gender and diversity across cultures: a three-level approach
- Gender and diversity across cultures: a summary
- Chapter review questions
- References

INTRODUCTION

It is often pointed out that one basic difference between human beings and animals is that we are self-aware. Another alternative definition of humanity says that our unique characteristic is to have developed various forms culture that we pass on down the generations.

But what do we mean by 'culture'? And how do we isolate 'a culture'? First we should note that from a cross-cultural perspective, the 'borders' of any culture are not necessarily consistent with those of individual countries. Sometimes a culture can cover a large *supra*-national area, for example Asian, northern European or Mediterranean cultures. However, on a much smaller scale, the focus can turn to *sub*-national cultural entities, for example that of the German or French-speaking minorities in Switzerland, the Sami in Finland, Norway and Sweden, or the Aborigines in Australia. Clearly the term 'culture' is highly ambiguous. Over the past decades various approaches to defining the term have been adopted. In business schools culture is defined in terms of cross-cultural management; students are taught how to behave 'correctly' in unfamiliar cultures by knowing and respecting various forms of behaviour. For example, most business students know that in Japan business cards must be presented and received with two hands.

There is no doubt that knowledge of customs and societal norms is vital to be able to fit into unfamiliar cultural contexts. However, the objective of this chapter is not to focus on the individual psychological and behavioural level of intercultural communication, as most of these codes of behaviour can be found in standard guides to the 'dos and don'ts' of foreign travel. Instead, we intend to highlight the role of cultural settings, in particular the cultural contextualization of diversity relations in a business context. The discussion opens with a case intended to illustrate the role and meaning of 'culture' and 'cross-culture' in regard to gender and diversity.

A Clash Of Cultures? A German–Thai Dilemma

'Have you ever been on a plane full of German males on their way to Thailand?'

Adam Becker, the Chief Executive Officer (CEO) of Toras, a German engineering company, sat back in his chair and pondered the question which his sales director Frank Klein had just posed upon leaving the room. What was he supposed to do now?

He picked up the document which the director of his company's Thai subsidiary had sent two days previously. It was an employment contract for a sales manager in Thailand, signed by the local Thai human resources manager, the local German director and the applicant, indicating the monthly salary of the new sales manager. It was a standard contract, and in his role as human resource director at the German headquarters, Adam had not noticed anything unusual at first glance. He was glad that the Thai subsidiary seemed to have identified an experienced salesperson for their highly specialised biotechnology and weighing devices. Reviewing the documents attached, including a copy of the passport and driving licence, he remembered how surprised he had been to discover that the identification of sex was noted as 'M' for male, and yet the face shown on the documentation was that of a woman. Only then had he noticed that the applicant's signature on the contract was preceded by 'Mr'.

The first thing he had done the morning before was to call his director in Thailand, Detlef Mueller, for clarification.

He had been somewhat taken aback by the explanation:
- She's a Kathoey.
- A what?
- A transgender. A ladyboy, if you like.
A ladyboy! Images flashed through his mind: Thailand, the sex industry, ladyboys, prostitution...
- It isn't what you think, added Detlef. Kathoeys are everywhere in Thailand, in entertainment of course, but also in sales, in medicine, in legal professions. They are a part of everyday life. She's the right person for the job, and so we gave her the contract.
Adam had scheduled an appointment with the sales director for the afternoon, but Frank had come in just after the conversation with Thailand, obviously very upset, and brandishing the contract for the Thai sales manager.
- Have you seen this? Have you noticed that he has recruited a ladyboy?
- Yes, I've just been talking to him. He says that it's no big deal in Thailand.
A long discussion had ensued, with Frank explaining that they were in a serious business, and that clients elsewhere would not be so understanding. There would be all kinds of jokes about Toras employing a ladyboy in Thailand. Adam had argued that rejecting a transgender individual was against the law; that such action would put them at risk of being sued for

discrimination, and furthermore, it was against the diversity policy of the company.

But Frank had been adamant. The reputation of the company was at stake. Until now the name of Toras stood for excellence in the field. It was a highly regarded engineering company with an international customer base, collaborating with pharmaceutical and other research laboratories, as well as production facilities, around the world. Maybe the Thai salesperson was good in her field – he could see that from the curriculum vitae – but how would customers from different countries react to this individual? And what would be the impact on company business? It was not their role, after all, to change the world.

Adam explained that public opinion in Thailand was quite different, that people were used to doing business with transgender persons, and that there was a much higher degree of tolerance. And besides, the contract had been signed.
- Well, said Frank, we will just have to cancel it. I know the world of sales, and in our business we cannot afford to come over as being involved with ladyboys in Thailand.
They had decided to call Bangkok again. Detlef, somewhat annoyed, tried to understand the dilemma of the two directors at headquarters, but repeated that this was a complete non-issue in Thailand. Furthermore, he emphasized that discrimination was against Thai law, and that cancelling the contract now would be regarded as grounds for legal action. He added that this topic was frequently brought up on the many talk shows on Thai television, and so they had to step carefully. There could be serious repercussions on the company's image in Thailand, making it very difficult for them to find a new sales manager. He added that headquarters should be sensitive to the local environment and culture.

Frank retorted that they had to consider the global environment, and what the reaction would be from customers elsewhere. Maintaining the overall global image and strategy was more important than accommodating this one case in Thailand. They simply could not take the risk.

After the conversation with Bangkok, Frank insisted on Adam cancelling the contract, even if it meant giving the candidate a month's salary in compensation. As Adam still showed signs of hesitation, Frank walked to the door, saying:

– Have you ever been on a plane full of German males on their way to Thailand?

This case highlights a rather common problem for companies who have to take the cultural contexts of subsidiaries into account. One important consideration is the local employment law, as such legislation clearly influences the decision-making processes of managers. Thus in some countries the right to parental leave is rather restricted (such as the USA), while in others maternity or paternity leave is granted for extended periods. Of course, custom will also dictate how these rights are then used. For example, although Hungarian fathers have the right to take parental leave, less than 2 per cent do so, while mothers spend an average of 4.7 years at home with children (Blaskó 2010, p. 100).

The rights of same-sex partnerships also vary from country to country. In Austria a recently established 'partnership law' allows gay or lesbian couples to be formally registered as couples, although several distinctions to heterosexual marriages have been maintained. Thus such same-sex partnerships can only be registered at municipal offices rather than the civil registrar, which is reserved for heterosexuals. Also the legal documents of registered partners are changed from having the category 'family name' to 'surname', which in effect discloses their sexual orientation in documents such as passports and driving licences. Some other legal inequalities also still exist, concerning for instance the rights of a partner in a rainbow family to be officially recognized as a parent (Bendl, Hanappi-Egger and Hofmann, 2010).

Returning to our original case, we note that it brings to light various aspects of the cultural contextualization of business with respect to diversity.

What are the main problems raised by this case?

Which cultural issues are involved?

Is this a case of:

• Discrimination by Frank Klein?
• Culture clash between Germany and Thailand?
• Conflict regarding organizational culture, in view of the fact that Toras is an engineering company?
• Ignorance about aspects of Thai culture?
• German corporate values being imposed on Thai subsidiaries?
• Global strategy versus local management?
• Different interpretations of sexuality?

Finally, what would you do if you were the CEO of Toras?

The rest of the chapter will take the following structure. First, we attempt to give a definition of 'culture'. Then a three-level approach to the analysis of cross-cultural gender and diversity differences is introduced, known as the 'Gherardi approach' (Gherardi, 2003). This approach is then extended and adapted with respect to gender and diversity across cultures. Our discussion closes with a detailed exploration of each of the three levels These are the *body level*, including bodily assignments and the meaning they have in various cultural contexts; the (*organizational*) *culture level*, which relates to norm settings in organizations with respect to gender and diversity; and finally the *language level*, relating to the meaning of linguistically constructed norms and values in terms of gender and diversity.

THE CONCEPT OF CULTURE: APPROACHES, DEFINITIONS AND CONTRADICTIONS

There is no one single generally accepted definition of culture; instead we find overlapping and sometimes contradictory approaches. For example, Allaire and Firsirotu (1984) identified various definitions of 'culture' across eight main schools of thought. Also Kroeber and Kluckhohn (1952) reviewed more than

100 different definitions of culture before creating their own definition – widely acknowledged as the most comprehensive formulation (Adler and Gundersen, 2008). This definition will therefore be used as a working reference throughout this chapter.

> *Culture* consists of explicit and implicit patterns of behaviour (knowledge, language, values and customs) and the complex interaction of symbols, values and behaviours of distinct human groups.

The essential core of culture consists of traditional (for example, historically derived and selected) ideas and especially their attached values and culture systems, which may be considered as products of action as well as conditioning elements of future action (adapted from Kroeber and Kluckhohn, 1952, p. 181).

As Adler and Gundersen (2008) have pointed out, culture is therefore something:

- shared by all, or almost all, members of a given social group;
- which older members of a group pass on to younger members;
- that shapes behaviour, or structures one's perception of the world, as in the case of morals, laws and customs.

In other words, it is assumed that culture serves to shape (and is in turn shaped by) numerous societal phenomena and processes. First, culture is learned through socialization, with the most active phase taking place in childhood. At this time we constantly learn new forms of culture by becoming members of different groups such as schools, circles of friends, sport clubs, workplaces, intellectual communities, bands and so on. Second, members of a cultural group are socialized along specific norm systems, thereby developing an understanding of which behaviour is desirable and which actions are condemned either socially or legally. Hence, culture serves as an orientation and as a guide for the social co-existence of groups (Triandis, 1996). Although there exists a huge mass of scholarly work on how to measure culture (Hofstede, 1980), as yet no satisfying model has been developed which can grasp its complexity and multi-faceted nature (Heine, Lehmann, Peng and Greenholtz, 2002).

As Thomas (1996, p. 114) states, 'culture is a system of orientation providing norms for cognition, action, and behaviour to its members'. The definition given above emphasizes that culture does not bind, but rather orientates its members.

These orientation systems and behavioural codes shape people's understanding of their world and their social interactions, including of course their attitudes to issues of diversity. One aspect of particular interest to us here is gender, particularly gender role expectations, that is, what it means to be a 'man' or a 'woman', which norms are generalized and what is perceived as 'abnormal'. Clearly, these issues play a crucial role in organizations. For example, a strong 'hetero-normativity' at the societal level (defining heterosexuality as the societal norm and all other kind of sexual desire as abnormal) will strongly influence the organizational definition of the 'norm'. Even when organizations are regarded as asexual or gender-neutral units (Chapter 1), this view often masks underlying tensions regarding the issue of gender. Hanappi-Egger (2011) has highlighted how the issue of gender is neglected in SET-organizations (science, engineering and technology) and shown that 'objectivity' is equalized with asexuality.

Therefore it is important to bear in mind that 'culture' encompasses not only societal values and norm systems, but also organizational and professional aspects (Mead, 1994).

GENDER AND DIVERSITY ACROSS CULTURES: A THREE-LEVEL APPROACH

Let us return to the case which opened this chapter to discuss in a German–Thai context the three levels at which gender (and diversity) differences are constructed. Note that while *Kathoeys* are regarded as 'normal' by the majority of Thais, in Germany such an ambiguous gender classification (neither male nor female, but transgender) can quickly lead to problems with officialdom and in daily life. This will be discussed in more detail in the following sections. But first, let us start with a small exercise:

Exercise 4.1

How would you describe yourself? Write down some attributes you think worth mentioning.

Cross-cultural gender and diversity analysis: the *body level*

Transgender is an umbrella term used to designate any group of people whose lifestyle appears to conflict with the gender norms of society.

In its broadest application, transgender persons cross conventional boundaries of gender by presenting themselves contrary to general expectations regarding their biological sex, even in some cases undergoing multiple surgical procedures in order to be fully reassigned in their preferred gender role. Whittle, Turner and Al-Alami (2007) have found that trans-people have complex, shifting gender identities, often moving from one 'trans' category to another over time. Some definitions of gender-related terms can be found in the LGBT glossary on the website of the Swedish Federation for Lesbian, Gay, Bisexual and Transgender Rights (RFSL, 2011).

In order to understand the prominence of Kathoeys in Thai society, it is necessary to investigate the religious and cultural background. In Thailand, as in other South East Asian societies, non-normative gender and sexual categories form part of the indigenous cultural tradition (ten Brummelhuis, 1999). Until today there is a widespread belief amongst Thais of the existence of three distinct sexes (Jackson, 1995), the third being male–female. The western Judaeo-Christian bipolar categories male/female, man/woman or heterosexual/homosexual cannot be applied to a society in which 'the biological makeup of the individual, the gender of that individual and the sexual preferences of the individual must be treated as three separate, albeit interrelated, areas' (Totman, 2003, p. 34). The concept of more than two genders is encapsulated in the Thai expression for Kathoey: *phet this sam*, or 'the third sex'. It is the generally held view that maleness is not merely defined by anatomy, but in terms of what you do with that anatomy, a sentiment echoed in some Buddhist scriptures. For example, Jackson (1996; 1998) notes that the Buddhist *Vinaya* text, which is a code of conduct for monks, identifies four main sex/gender categories: males, females, *ubhatobyanjanaka* (hermaphrodites) and *pandaka* (those displaying a variety of other anatomies or sexual preference) (Claes, 2011).

Hence it becomes clear that in our case study, two societal cultures are colliding with respect to sex/gender categories: a dualistic sex category concept at the German headquarters and a multi-faceted sex/gender category concept represented by the Kathoey at the Thai subsidiary.

A similar range of cultural norms can be observed in respect to other elements of diversity. To discuss these in more detail, let us turn back to the questions given in Exercise 4.1. Look at your description and consider the following:

- Did you mention your sex? Remarkably, more women do so in such cases than men. The explanation is perhaps because men more frequently see themselves as constituting the 'norm', and thus their sex is nothing 'special' to be recorded. In contrast, women feel the need to mention their gender as being an 'extra-ordinary' aspect of their identity.
- Did you mention your age? Usually, age is not consciously recognized *within* certain group or generations (such as students) if the group is homogenously constituted. Furthermore, in western Europe the term 'age' is not entirely neutral in its associations, but often linked to the concept of 'anti-ageing'. This emphasizes both the desirability of staying young and the negative perceptions of growing old. In a rather different culture, Hanappi-Egger and Ukur (2011) have shown that in Kenya the diversity element 'age' is not related to some

highly positive conception of 'youth', but rather to the concept of 'elderly'. There, older people enjoy high status due to their longer experience, and thus most organizations give tasks and roles requiring a degree of trust to this age group.

- Did you mention your skin colour? It has been frequently observed that people belonging to the majority group in any society (regardless of which shade of skin colour) take this for granted and thus do not see it as worth mentioning.

This *body level*, referring to visible diversity categories or to normative bodily assignments, is a crucial element in the generation of social discrimination and exclusion. It affects both societies and organizations – as demonstrated by the case we have described.

Visit the following weblink: 'Michael Kimmel: On Gender (Clip)', http://www.youtube.com/watch?v=JgaOK74HqiA&feature=related (Kimmel, 2011). Reflect on Michael Kimmel's account: Are you able to confirm from your own experience that 'privileges are invisible for those who have them'? What does this mean for organizational practices?

Cross-cultural gender and diversity analysis: the *level of organizational culture*

Let us again review the introductory case to discuss how gender and diversity differences are constructed and reproduced in organizations. We read about the German engineering company Toras, which has subsidiaries in Thailand. The hiring of a Kathoey presented the managers with a problem, and thus proved to be an issue of concern for the CEO, by challenging the organizational value systems at the company's German headquarters. In order to understand the dilemma, one has to consider the relevant issues in terms of organizational culture. The professional codes of conduct of western (and thus German) engineering companies were devised back in the early days of industrialization, a period in which 'objectivity' became a major argument in rationalization (Hanappi-Egger, 2011). One important aspect of such a culture is that the organization intentionally ignores social dynamics and hierarchies of power, instead placing the focus on objective, rational processes and practices. This goes hand in hand with the claim that science, engineering and technology companies are asexual and gender neutral (Chapter 1). Several scholars (Schein, 1995; Wilson, 2000; Rutherford, 2001; Martin, 2002) have identified this organizational culture based on *apparently* objective norms, which are in fact male-coded, as a source of indirect and subtle exclusion mechanisms. In our case the belief system of a CEO was challenged when forced to deal with an unfamiliar cultural phenomenon. Arguments presented by management, that the recruitment of a Kathoey would negatively impact productivity and badly damage the company's reputation are evidence of discrimination absent from the Thai cultural setting. Since organizational culture is shaped by daily practices as well as history (Chapter 5), it can be assumed that such a decision will also have an impact on Thai culture.

Let us discuss the topics of organizational culture and cross-cultural phenomena by reflecting on the questions which followed the case study.

Which cultural issues are involved?

The case study shows the relevance of the cultural context of business operations on 'both sides'; that is the cultural context in the headquarters in Germany as well as the local subsidiary in Thailand.

Culture is a holistic concept referring to different kinds of value systems and beliefs at various levels: individual, team, national/societal, functional, identity group and organizational.

Each person has his or her own culture, shaped by specific forms of socialization, by experiences and settings. Your values and beliefs were acquired in childhood from your family, school and friends. Your culture helps you to distinguish right from wrong, to decide what constitutes fairness, and even determines your aesthetic preferences (for example, what you regard as beautiful).

The team or group in which you work consists of other individuals, each with their own cultural background. Any similarities and differences in these backgrounds are reflections of the norms and values of the societal/national environment, which are also embodied in laws and customs. The professional culture is determined by expert knowledge and the 'language' of technical jargon. Of course, we can belong to many other groups, whether ethnic, religious or demographic in nature. These groups influence our ways of thinking and our interpretation of the world, in addition to supplying their own behavioural norms and values. What is deemed acceptable behaviour in one group may be unacceptable in another.

Last but not least, we have to look at the role of organizational culture. The culture of the engineering company in our case study will certainly be different from the culture of an IT firm or that of a marketing company. These differences are expressed in the way offices are organized, in equipments, in dress codes and the like (Schein, 2010).

We can examine these different levels of culture for each party involved in our case, including the Kathoey. What was their original cultural context, and in which context do they now reside? How does this context influence their reactions and behaviours? Let us examine these issues using the set of sub-questions listed previously:

- *Is this a case of discrimination by Frank Klein?*
  Frank Klein is profoundly loyal to his company. He is mainly concerned with keeping the good reputation of Toras intact, while other considerations are of secondary importance.

Are you able to 'put yourself in his shoes' and judge the situation from his perspective? How could you help him to change his perspective and see the situation through Detlef Mueller's eyes?

- *Is this a case of culture clash between Germany and Thailand?*
The cultures of these two countries are different not only in terms of ways of thinking (different philosophies and education systems) but also in terms of their contrasting traditions and customs – as varied, perhaps, as the climate and food. One important fact to remember is that bosses generally enjoy great authority in Thailand. As people in higher positions (and indeed older people generally) are held in such respect, subordinates would not consider contradicting their bosses in public. In our case this means that the opinions and decisions of management at the Thai headquarters will be supported even if other Thai employees see the hiring of a Kathoey as a bad decision (Niratpattanasai, 2001; Claes and Gerritsen, 2011).

- *Is this a case of conflict regarding organizational culture, in view of the fact that Toras is an engineering company?*
In general engineering professions have a very high status in Germany, and Toras is no different. It is a widely respected company in its specialized field. Naturally the reputation of the firm is of crucial importance to its management. In such an organizational culture, quality and accuracy are more important than speed (Schein, 2010).

- *Is this a case of ignorance about aspects of Thai culture?*
Knowledge of Kathoeys is not particularly widespread, even among expatriates living in Thailand. People very often incorrectly assume that all Kathoeys are ladyboys working in the sex industry. Although it may appear from various websites that Kathoeys are indeed strongly involved in prostitution, in fact this is simply not the case. In order to obtain in depth knowledge of a society's culture, it is necessary to spend time there, absorbing a great deal of background information regarding the local customs, values and beliefs. Similarly, in commercial decision-making it is vital to make a serious attempt at cultural contextualization, so as to eliminate as far as possible common prejudices and stereotypes. In our case study, the reaction from Toras's headquarters can be attributed to the employees' limited knowledge of Thai culture.

- *Is this a case of German corporate values being imposed in Thailand?*
As a successful international company, it is highly likely that Toras will have a strong organizational culture, one which promotes clear values and a code of conduct. Governed by EU and national employment legislation, the company is obliged to eradicate discrimination from the workplace. Yet having subsidiaries in Thailand, it must also pay attention to the relevant Thai laws. The interesting grey area is our readiness to accommodate and respect unfamiliar

cultural habits and customs. We have to ask ourselves how far we are willing to go to accept alien cultures. Do we set limits regarding that which is acceptable? When an organization delocalizes, it is important that the original vision, mission and values are transmitted and acknowledged by the subsidiaries. However, this does not mean that a code of conduct should never be interpreted differently by a subsidiary, but rather that *basic* norms and values must be maintained.

Consequently an organization always 'imposes' its values on the subsidiary, and even on involved stakeholders in another country.

- *Is this a case of global strategy versus local management?*
The challenge for leaders is to manage the tension between the global values and strategy of the organization, and the need to adapt locally. Which facets of business have to remain at the global level and which have to focus on local conditions? Do you think, for example, that human resource (HR) management has to function at a local level, or that some aspects should be local and others global?

For Frank Klein the reputation of the company in Germany, and perhaps even globally, is at stake. But what about the company's standing in Thailand? What about the repercussions which Toras's conduct will have on the recruitment of potential candidates? Do Thai people understand the reasoning behind the decision at the German headquarters? How far can the company go in adapting locally without damaging its reputation on both sides?

- *Is this a case of different interpretations of sexuality?*
It is clear that the concept of 'being Kathoey' is different from that of 'being a ladyboy'; in fact most people will never even have heard of the term Kathoey. The difference lies in the terminology, in the language, and in the interpretations attached to the words. We will discuss these aspects in more detail when we consider the third level of analysis: the language level.

This is only one, rather extreme, example of differences in interpretation of terminology which so commonly occur in the field of management. Although much business terminology is generally of Anglo-Saxon (and mainly North American) origin, even a simple word like 'boss' may have a range of connotations in different cultural contexts. Can you think of any other English words that have a different connotation – or even meaning – when transposed into another language?

Hopefully it has become clear that the (organizational) cultural level deals with different layers of overlapping cultures. Managers must therefore use great care, thought and knowledge to deal successfully with gender and diversity across cultures. Critical self-reflection on one's own cultural biases is as vital as expertise in local contexts.

Review Questions

- Can you imagine what would be the reaction if this case of discrimination against a Kathoey were published in Thai newspapers?
- What impact would the case have on Thai managers in subsidiaries of international organizations (bearing in mind that they have a culture of respecting authority)?

- How could this affect the attitudes of Thai authorities who are looking to attract foreign direct investment to Thailand, as well as those of holidaymakers from Europe not engaged in sex tourism?
- What impact could this have on the behaviour and self-representation of Kathoeys?
- What might be the effect on the reputation of Toras in Thailand?

Cross-cultural gender and diversity analysis: the *language level*

Our case study also lends itself to a discussion on the role of language, from a multicultural perspective, in producing and reproducing gender and diversity hierarchies. As previously mentioned, outside Thailand the word 'kathoey' is sometimes used as a synonym for 'ladyboy', which is clearly associated with the sex industry. Thus 'kathoey' is linked in the minds of foreigners to prostitution (a legal profession in some countries and strictly prohibited in others), thus blurring the original Thai connotation and its specific cultural background.

Language does not always mirror reality in a truly objective or 'neutral' way, but can instead function as a distorting medium to convey power inequalities in a 'taken-for-granted' way. Often seemingly neutral language may disguise power imbalances, which can only be revealed with the help of discourse analysis (Foucault, 1972) and techniques of deconstruction (Derrida, 1976). Discourse does not merely describe the status quo; it is an important channel in the social construction of reality, shaping knowledge, social identity and relationships between people (Hardy, Palmer and Philips, 2000). Some have argued that deconstruction is simply a kind of discourse analysis (Kelemen and Rumens, 2008), but in fact these constitute two different methods. Quite simply, the object of discourse analysis is to investigate written, spoken or signed language, while deconstruction seeks to analyse written text.

Deconstruction is a specific method of discourse analysis which is designed to reveal subtexts, power relations and unspoken ideologies in written text.

Although it was Jacques Derrida (1976) who coined the term 'deconstruction', he never precisely explained its meaning or indicated how the technique should be applied. In fact he argued against using his concept as a specific method. As it applies to management studies, Joanne Martin (1990) has given an excellent summary of the methods of deconstruction, providing a short text for illustrative purposes.

The basic assumption behind deconstructionism is that texts can be read in different ways. Deconstructionists, who believe that we can always elaborate several interpretations of a text, deny the existence of one 'true' interpretation. Their methods can help reveal power inequalities and hidden ideologies, conflicts and contradictions. By deconstructing seemingly 'neutral' texts it should be possible to determine the interests of marginalized groups and identify dominant voices. Generally speaking, deconstruction starts with a straightforward exercise: readers should pinpoint words (that is verbs, adjectives, subjects and so on) for which opposites exist (for example men/women, black/white, open/closed, home/work, adult/child, European/non-European, equal/unequal, and so forth).

When several such pairings have been found, the reader then chooses one of these and exchanges the original term in the text with its antonym. These 'small' changes in wording will of course radically alter the meaning of the text, which may then become strange, irritating, ridiculous, unbelievable, unnatural or pointless. The irritation of the reader will increase as more and more basic hidden assumptions (that is ideologies) are challenged. This method has the power to reveal dominant voices and ways of sense-making, and hence bring to light underlying power inequalities.

As Fougère and Moulettes (2011) have shown, textbooks on international business (IB) and international management (IM) can be deconstructed from a post-colonial perspective. By examining 17 IB/IM textbooks they tried (a) to identify contradictions between initial disclaimers and the actual discussion of culture; (b) to search for essentialist, uncritical western-centred descriptions of the 'other'; and (c) to spot a lack of any discussion of colonial history in cases where colonialism obviously shaped the current business environment. We will quote an example from a textbook examined by Fougère and Moulettes (2011) in order to show how essentialist and western-centred assumptions become visible after deconstructing and reconstructing a text. The final version can be read as a mirror image of the original.

Exercise 4.2

Just as there is no totally homogeneous thought in other religions of the world, such as Europe and South America, there is no totally homogeneous thought in Africa. There is in fact a diverse sociocultural, linguistic, and historical composition among the African nations. However, as is the case in other regions throughout the globe, there is an underlying pan-African character that results from a unique geographical, historical, cultural, and political experience.

Therefore, Africans can be identified by certain characteristics in their daily lives. Just as there is an Asian thought system – Confucianism, for example, there is an African thought system – *Ubuntu*. One important characteristic of Ubuntu is a high degree of harmony – unity of the whole rather than the parts is emphasized. Thus, similar to Confucianism, the individual is strongly connected to the group. Hence, *Ubuntu*, too, emphasises suppression of self-interest for the sake of the group's needs [...] Therefore, in general, managing people in organizations in Africa is likely to require a substantially different managerial approach from that used in many of the organizations in the United States, Sweden, and Denmark, for example. This means that, in many organizational situations in Africa, a reward system emphasizing group achievement is often more effective than a reward system emphasising individual achievement. (Rodrigues, 2009, p. 21)

And now the same text *mirrored*:

Just as there is no totally homogeneous thought in other religions of the world, such as *Africa* and *South Asia*, there is no totally homogeneous thought in *Europe*. There is in fact a diverse sociocultural, linguistic, and historical composition among the *European* nations. However, as is the case in other regions throughout the globe, there is an underlying pan-*European* character that results from a unique geographical, historical and cultural, and political experience. Therefore, *Europeans* can be identified by certain characteristics in their daily lives. Just as there is an *American* thought system (*Self-actualizationism*), there is a *European* thought system – Egoism. One important characteristic of egoism is a high degree of *individualism* – unity of the *parts* rather than the *whole* is emphasized. Thus, similar to *Self-actualizationism*, the individual is strongly *disconnected from* the group. Hence, egoism, emphasizes suppression of the *group's* interest for the sake of the individual's needs ... therefore, in general, managing people in organizations in *Europe* is likely to require a substantially different managerial approach to that used in many of the organizations in China, Swaziland, and Lesotho, for example. This means in many organizational situations in *Europe*, a reward system emphasizing *individual* achievement is often more effective than a reward system emphasizing *group* achievement.' (Fougère and Moulettes, 2011, p. 11)

Examined side by side, the deconstructed and reconstructed texts reveal not only an oversimplification of the unknown 'other' (in this case Africa), but also the imposition of an essentialist picture of African society. This becomes clear when Europe is described in the same basic terms as those used for Africa. The strangeness of the second text points to the dangers of an overly simplistic generalization, which takes no account of cultural complexity. Thus we see that deconstruction can illuminate our 'taken-for-granted' knowledge of culture, revealing where we place our points of reference and which facts we assume as natural and self-evident.

GENDER AND DIVERSITY ACROSS CULTURES: A SUMMARY

In this chapter we have tried to show how cultural contextualization, in terms of gender and diversity, has a huge impact on doing business. Complex decisions and problems often prove insoluble using a simplistic approach; instead it is necessary to take account of context- and culture-sensitive perspectives regarding the organizational culture, its gender and diversity content and its embeddedness in broader contexts.

We have also explored the ambiguity of the concept of 'culture', pointing out how hard it is to provide a satisfactory definition. Difficulties can also arise when simple 'cross-cultural-comparisons' are attempted using quantitative methods and indicators. The focus of this chapter has been on the 'doing' approach

(Chapter 5), referring to different ways and practices of cultural norm-setting. We have highlighted examples of how specific values are introduced or even unconsciously imposed. The three levels of analyses – the body level, the organizational level and the language level – allow for a structured discussion on how to address, reflect on and eliminate cultural biases and prejudices. Of course, no one single 'objective' or 'neutral' approach exists; instead we are influenced (also as scholars) by our own cultural socialization. Consequently, in order to contribute to the establishment of inclusive organizations, particularly in international and cross-cultural settings, it is necessary to carefully examine the local and de-localized cultural context.

Chapter Review Questions

- What is culture? Which aspects of culture have an impact on diversity relations?
- What is meant by the body, organizational and language levels of analysis with respect to diversity and cultural contextualization?
- How is deconstruction defined? What kinds of things can this method reveal in texts dealing with gender and diversity?

REFERENCES

*N. Adler and A. Gundersen (2008) *International Dimensions of Organizational Behaviour*, 5th edn (Mason: Thomson).

Y. Allaire and M. E. Firsirotu (1984) 'Theories of Organizational Culture', *Organization Studies*, 5 (3), 193–226.

R. Bendl, E. Hanappi-Egger and R. Hofmann, R. (2010) 'Austrian Perspectives on Diversity Management and Equal Treatment: Regulations, Debates, Practices and Trends.' in A. Klarsfeld (ed.) *International Handbook on Diversity Management at Work. Country Perspectives on Diversity and Equal Treatment* (Cheltenham, Northampton: Edward Elgar), pp. 27–44.

Z. Blaskó (2010) 'Meddig maradjon otthon az anya? – gyermekfejlődés szempontjai.', *Esély*, 2010/3, 89–116

M. T. Claes (2011) 'Kathoeys of Thailand: A Diversity Case in International Business', *The International Journal of Diversity in Organisations, Communities and Nations*, 10 (5), 183–98.

M. T. Claes and M. Gerritsen (2011) *Interculturele communicatie in international perspectief* (Bussum: Coutinho).

J. Derrida (1976) *Of Grammatology* (Baltimore, Ireland: The John Hopkins University Press).

M. Foucault (1972) *The Archeology of Knowledge* (New York: Pantheon).

*M. Fougère and A. Moulettes (2011) 'Disclaimers, Dichotomies and Disappearances in International Textbooks: A Postcolonial Deconstruction', *Management Learning*, 2011, 1–20.

*S. Gherardi (2003) 'Feminist Theory and Organization Theory: A Dialogue on New Bases' in H. Tsoukas and C. Knudsen (eds) *The Oxford Handbook of Organization Theory* (Oxford: Oxford University Press): 210–36.

*E. Hanappi-Egger (2011) *The Triple M of Organizations: Man, Management and Myth* (Vienna and New York: Springer).

E. Hanappi-Egger and G. Ukur (2011) 'Challenging Diversity Management: On the Meaning of Cultural Context: The Case of Kenya', Proceedings at the 7th Critical Management Studies Conference, Naples, Italy, 11–13 July 2011.

*C. Hardy, I. Palmer and N. Philips (2000) 'Discourse as a Strategic Resource', *Human Relations*, 53 (9), 1227–48.

*S. Heine, D. Lehman, K. Peng and J. Greenholtz (2002) 'What is Wrong with Cross-cultural Comparison of Subjective Likert Scales? The Reference-group Effect', *Journal of Personality and Social Psychology*, 82 (6), 903–18.

G. Hofstede (1980) *Culture's Consequences: International Differences in Work-related Values* (Beverly Hills, CA: Sage).

P. Jackson (1995) 'Kathoey: The Third Sex' in P. Jackson (ed.) *Dear Uncle Go: Male homosexuality in Thailand* (Bangkok, Thailand: Bua Luang Books).

P. Jackson (1996) 'Non-normative Sex/Gender Categories', *Theravada Buddhist Scriptures*, http://www.buddhistlinks.org/Homosexual.htm, date accessed 29 March 2009.

P. Jackson (1998) 'Male Homosexuality and Transgenderism in the Thai Buddhist Tradition' in W. Leyland (ed.) *Queer Dharma: Voices of Gay Buddhists* (San Francisco, CA: Gay Sunshine Press).

*M. Kelemen and N. Rumens (2008) *An Introduction to Critical Management Theory* (London: Sage), pp. 84–102.

M. Kimmel (2011) *On Gender*, Youtube-Video, http://www.youtube.com/ watch?v= JgaOK74HqiA&feature=related, date accessed 31 October 2011.

A. Kroeber and C. Kluckhohn. (1952) *Culture* (New York: Meridian Books).

J. Martin (1990) 'Deconstructing Organizational Taboos: The Suppression of Gender Conflict in Organizations', *Organizational Science*, 1, 339–59.

*J. Martin (2002) *Organizational Culture: Mapping the Terrain* (Thousand Oaks, CA: Sage).

R. Mead (1994) *International Management* (Malden, MA: Blackwell Publishing).

K. Niratpattanasai (2001) *Bridging the Gap*. (Bangkok: A.R. Business Press).

RFSL (2011) LGBT Glossary, http://www.rfsl.se/?p=3307, date accessed 18 October 2011.

C. Rodrigues (2009) *International Management. A Cultural Approach* (Thousand Oaks, CA: Sage).

S. Rutherford (2001) 'Organizational Cultures, Women Managers and Exclusion', *Women In Management Review*, 16 (8), 371–82.

E. Schein (1995) 'The Role of the Founder in Creating Organizational Culture', *Family Business Review*, 8 (3), Fall 1995, 221–38.

*E. Schein (2010) *Organizational Culture and Leadership*, 4th ed. (San Francisco, CA: Jossey-Bass).

H. ten Brummelhuis (1999) 'Transformations of Transgender: The Case of the Thai Kathoey' in P. Jackson and G. Sullivan (eds) *Lady Boys, Tom Boys, Rent Boys: Male and Female Homosexualities in Contemporary Thailand* (New York: The Haworth Press).

A. Thomas (1996) *Psychologie interkulturellen Handelns* (Göttingen: Hogrefe).

R. Totman (2003) *The Third Sex Kathoey: Thailand's Ladyboys* (London: Souvenir Press).

H. C. Triandis (1996) 'The Psychological Measurement of Cultural Syndromes', *American Psychologist*, 51, 407–15.

S. Whittle, L. Turner and M. Al-Alami (2007) Transgender and Transsexual People's Experiences of Inequality and Discrimination, http://www.theequalitiesreview.org.uk, date accessed 29 March 2009.

*E. Wilson (2000) 'Inclusion, Exclusion and Ambiguity – The Role of Organisational Culture', *Personnel Review*, 29 (3), 274–303.

CHAPTER 5

THE 'DOING' PERSPECTIVE ON GENDER AND DIVERSITY

Janne Tienari and Julia Nentwich

INTRODUCTION

Diversity in organizations can be looked at from various perspectives. We suggest that it is useful to view diversity as something that is actively created or 'done' in social practice, rather than merely an assemblage of essential traits or fixed characteristics of individuals. This 'doing' perspective treats diversity as a social accomplishment. Focusing on social practices offers scope to valorize and question the ways in which differences and inequalities (arising from our taken-for-granted assumptions and routines) based on gender, race or ethnicity, class, age, (dis)ability and sexuality are maintained and reproduced through everyday actions and activities.

In Europe the primary focus of diversity initiatives and discussions has thus far been on gender. Although our particular concern here is to examine how gender is 'done,' we also provide examples that consider other dimensions of diversity. Throughout the chapter we intend to highlight the impact of different socio-cultural contexts across Europe on the 'doing' of gender, and on diversity in general.

The issue of gender can be used to exemplify the dangers of categorizations and labelling. While our own experiences and common sense tell us that no two women, or indeed two men, show an identical range of characteristics, it is easy to talk as if this were the case, evoking stereotypes of female traits and male traits as if they were universally shared and applicable. The same holds true for stereotypes of ethnic groups and different age groups. In contrast, the 'doing' perspective enables us to move beyond such misleading generalizations, forcing us to take our complex and sometimes ambiguous experiences of social inter-action between individuals seriously by zooming in on local settings. In so doing we expose assumptions and stereotyping that too often pass unnoticed in our everyday lives.

> The *'doing' perspective* brings into sharp relief the range of common daily practices that contribute to the (re)construction of differences and inequalities in certain socio-cultural conditions. This perspective avoids the rigid and artificial categorization of individuals as women/men, black/white, young/old and the assignment of a dubious list of characteristics.

In this chapter we first provide an outline of the 'doing' perspective, with a particular focus on gender. We then offer examples of management engaged in the process of 'doing' gender, and pinpoint why this perspective is helpful in understanding how contemporary organizations function. We also reflect on how it may be possible to 'undo' gender and thus to work for change in terms of equality, diversity and inclusion. Although our discussion begins with theories and examples of '(un)doing' gender in the workplace, we also intend to investigate what this means for other dimensions of diversity, as well as for managing diversity in organizations.

'DOING' GENDER

The notion of 'doing' gender was first proposed by Candace West and Don Zimmerman (1987) in an article discussing Harold Garfinkel's (1967) study of a transsexual, Agnes, who took on a female gender identity at the age of 17 after being raised as a boy. Garfinkel's groundbreaking work explains succinctly the process of 'doing' gender. He studied how Agnes developed various skills and techniques in order to pass as a young woman while still trapped in a male body (she later underwent gender reassignment treatment). The analysis showed that a great deal of interactional work was necessary to accomplish this. For example, Agnes had to learn how to dress appropriately, how to use make-up, and how to walk and talk in order to meet the expectations of others regarding the 'right' behaviour for a young woman. She had to be careful not to use too much make-up or talk with an overly high pitch, as this would have been perceived as unnatural and thus raised suspicions.

The case of Agnes shows in great detail what kind of daily work is necessary to 'do' something which we usually take for granted: to pass as a woman or a man in social interaction. In this respect, 'doing' gender can be understood as the 'activity of managing situated conduct, in the light of normative conceptions of attitudes and activities appropriate for one's sex category' (West and Zimmerman, 1987, p. 127).

'Doing' gender is a routine accomplishment. As human beings in society, we automatically assign a gender categorization to all those we meet, while in turn we ourselves are similarly categorized. Thus we all lead lives under constant gender assessment. According to the 'doing' perspective, gender does not simply reflect biological differences between women and men, but is created through practices of social interaction, for example at the workplace. Both women and men contribute to the establishment and perpetuation of gender differences.

Because gender is such an integral part of an individual's identity, as well as of social interactions, organizational practices and societal structures, one can never *not* 'do' gender. Throughout our lives we are socialized into holding specific beliefs of what it means to be a woman or a man. When interacting with others, we constantly encounter situations where gender plays a role, whether we like it or not. We are members of schools, friendship groups and organizations which expose us to particular practices that differentiate between men and women, ascribing particular traits and qualities to these gender categories. Such practices often lead to gender-based inequalities, in which men and the masculine are more highly valued than women and the feminine.

Last but not least, we live in societies that impose cultural conventions on us as women and men, prescribing how we can, and should, combine work with other areas of our lives. Societal structures and conventions that force women to make choices between having children and pursuing a career while forcing men to spend their days at work and not with their children are a case in point.

> What kind of situations have you encountered in your life where the relevance of gender has been apparent? Why do you think gender was relevant in those cases? Try to describe gender as something that was 'done' in the specific situations!

Our particular focus in this chapter is on *practices* through which gender and diversity are 'done' in organizations. Theodore Schatzki (2001) defines practices as arrays of human activity organized around shared practical understandings. For our purposes we will think of practices as recurring activities, carried out as common everyday interactions in different kinds of organizations and through inter-organizational fora such as the media. They provide both the resources and the mundane scripts for how gender can be 'done' – and how our gendered identities are produced and reproduced.

In short, the 'doing' perspective views organizational practices and societal structures, on the one hand, and individual agency, on the other, to be in a mutu-ally constitutive relationship (Martin, 2003). When we 'do' gender, our activities are constituted by practices and structures, while at the same time we take part in reproducing those same practices and structures.

Just as organizational practices such as recruitment and leadership training are not gender-neutral, more mundane activities also contribute to the 'doing' of gender, such as how meetings are conducted or male/female behaviour patterns seen during after-work activities (for example in a bar or at office parties). They provide the resources which serve, through interaction, to establish and main-tain gender differences. In other words, such activities create and recreate what we perceive as differences between women and men. A fundamental point to bear in mind here is that such practices develop in organizations slowly over time, and are usually difficult to modify. Any attempt to change the status quo requires, first, that actors highlight and scrutinize established ways of 'doing' gender, and second, that meaningful alternatives to the status quo are proposed and negotiated.

In the following section, examples are given of practices that contribute to gender differences. As power relations are (re)produced in and through these differences, gendered practices tend to lead to inequalities. We begin by focusing on how gender identity is constructed within particular occupations, and continue with examples from management.

GENDER IDENTITY AT WORK

A basic assumption in the 'doing' perspective is that an individual's gender identity is created through the mundane interactions required for carrying out particular *jobs and tasks*. For example, the job of flight attendant typically enacts a female gender identity. Flight attendants are expected to be friendly to passengers and take care of them; they are expected to engage in behaviour that is closely linked in society with femininity. As the job requires 'doing' femininity in a certain way, a particular gender identity is enacted while doing the job (Hochschild, 1983).

Gender, identity and performing in the job become intertwined in practices: in order to perform well as a flight attendant, it is crucial to practice femininity. Conversely, being a competent flight attendant stabilizes a female gender identity. In other words, it is not possible to 'do' a job without 'doing' gender identity at the same time. The gendered job is thus reflexively produced and stabilized through the performance of individual gender identity, while at the same time the gender identity is produced and stabilized through performing the job.

However, if women in a female-dominated occupation 'do' femininity, what about men working as flight attendants, nurses or kindergarten teachers? Do they succeed in enacting a male gender identity while performing their jobs? Research on men in female-dominated occupations shows that, for example, male nurses are said to engage more frequently in physical tasks such as lifting or moving patients (Heintz, Nadai, Fischer and Ummel, 1997). Men working in childcare, for example, may try to avoid interactions that can be interpreted as nurturing behaviour associated with femininity. In general, studies show the importance of 'boundary work' for men in female-dominated occupations: in order to be able to enact masculinity, men differentiate between female and male aspects of the job, that is they draw boundaries, in order to engage more actively in activities associated with masculinity (Cross and Bagilhole, 2002).

> Select an occupation and decide what qualities are needed to perform it. Which of the qualities could be designated as masculine, which as feminine? How is gender 'done' while carrying out this job?

The 'doing' perspective draws our attention to established ways of interacting and accomplishing differences within particular jobs and tasks. This usually takes place in various kinds of *organizations*, for example, airlines, hospitals or kindergartens. Gendered practices such as men engaging in activities regarded as masculine, develop slowly over time, until they are taken-for-granted and considered 'natural'. It is difficult to break such patterns and to act contrary to one's assigned gender position and identity.

Crucially, the 'doing' perspective highlights the fact that both men and women actively (re)produce these kinds of gendered practices in their everyday working lives, thereby maintaining not only gendered identities, but also gendered hierarchies and structures. Thus we see that a great deal of societal inequality originates in organizations (Acker, 2006). In general, gendered hierarchy means that men and the masculine are routinely favoured over women and the feminine. Outcomes of this hierarchy are, for example, persistent wage disparities between men and women, and the lack of women in organizational positions of power. We will illustrate this point in the next section by discussing the case of management.

> Gendered identities, structures and hierarchies are 'done' while carrying out particular jobs in organizations. This 'doing' perspective emphasizes the importance of taking into account not only the biological sex of individuals at work, but also their gender as incorporated in perceptions of specific jobs and tasks, as well as the hierarchical differences that are constructed through them.

MANAGEMENT, MASCULINITY AND THE DOUBLE BIND

Let us dig deeper into the phenomenon of 'doing' gender by examining the following question: what is the gender of management? Schein and Davidson (1993) have provided a pithy answer: 'Think manager, think male.' And indeed, two major indicators for the dominance of men and masculinity in management positions are working time conventions and career paths, culminating in the image of the 'ideal' manager, who in practice is generally male (Acker, 1990). A subtext of the male breadwinner is subtly evoked by expectations that managers should dedicate their body and soul to the organization and to their managerial position. They have to be constantly available and constantly on the go.

This means that in order to 'do' management as expected, the manager must in practice be free of responsibilities outside the workplace. This is only possible if someone else is willing to take care of the 'ideal' manager's home (Kelan, 2008). In other words, the taken-for-granted qualities necessary to perform well in a managerial job in Europe rely on traditional bourgeois notions of gender relations in nuclear families: while men are seen as providing the family's main income, women are conceived as the primary care-takers (Nentwich, 2008). Under these conditions, women can only perform well as managers if they do not have family responsibilities. Thus what appears to be a gender neutral formulation of the dedicated manager proves to incorporate highly gendered conventions of how management is 'done'.

(Re)constructions of the 'ideal' manager can be found in all organizations. Management consulting is a case in point. Kumra and Vinnicombe (2008) studied promotion processes to top management in consultancies in the United Kingdom (UK), and argue that these processes are sex biased. They found two areas in which women are disadvantaged: the need to proactively demonstrate an individual contribution, and the need to 'fit' a prevailing masculine model of success within the firm. In a similar vein, Meriläinen, Tienari, Thomas and Davies (2004) studied management consultants in the UK and in Finland, focusing on the (re)construction of the 'ideal' consultant. Those interviewed portrayed themselves as driven, self-assertive and hard-working individuals, both perpetuating the masculine 'ideal' and measuring themselves against it. They argued that this is unavoidable when seeking to rise to a managerial position in the consultancy. Thus, the upper echelons in such firms are dominated by men because it is easier in practice for them to live up to this 'ideal'. In brief, these examples from the field of management consulting show that male dominance In management is not about men and women per se, but about demonstrating masculinity.

Assumptions about masculinity, and why it matters

'Doing' management is equivalent to 'doing' masculinity. Being a manager is associated with strength, rationality and competitiveness, and it is thus congruent with masculine *stereotype* in society. Being a woman, in turn, implies a different set of stereotypes, such as softness, emotion and care, not readily associated with management. Consequently, we can describe management as a job with masculine connotations. Performing a managerial job means engaging in behaviour that is consistent with general a stereotype of masculinity, with the result that women are regarded as exceptions in management.

Stereotypes are popular beliefs about social groups or types of individuals: for example men and women, particular ethnic groups, or people of a particular age. They are standardized and simplified conceptions based on prior, often deeply held, assumptions. Gender stereotypes abound in relation to management. For example, men are stereotypically assumed to be competitive and active, while women are regarded as empathetic and caring.

Because the relationship between gendered organizational practices and the practising of gender while 'doing' the job is mutually constitutive (as previously discussed), stereotypes not only *describe* what we tend to believe about women and men, but also *prescribe* what counts as feminine or masculine, and what are appropriate masculinities and femininities in 'doing' management. When men and women in specific interactions behave according to stereotypical prescriptions, they stabilize what counts as 'good' management, and thereby keep these beliefs and assumptions alive and powerful. Any violation of the gendered prescriptions relating to particular jobs, such as flight attendant or manager tends to be perceived as the individual's incompetent behaviour, and only rarely as a justified challenge to the prescription itself.

Even if we do not consciously wish to foster inequality or discriminate against groups of people, this is the result when we act according to gender (or other) stereotypes. For example, by privileging white men when shortlisting for managerial position we exclude women and members from ethnic groups or class backgrounds other than the dominant, under the assumption that these individuals lack particular positive traits or qualities associated with management. However, what we are actually 'doing' is to perceive them as lacking white, middle class, heterosexual masculinity.

Perceived lack of fit with this 'ideal' explains, for example, why women find it hard to make it to the top in consultancy firms in the UK (Kumra and Vinnicombe, 2008), why young adults with a family name that is not German or French find it significantly harder to obtain an apprenticeship position in Switzerland (Fibbi, Lerch and Wanner, 2006), and why openly gay managers are few and far between. Stereotyping leads to inequality.

> As management positions are imbued with male connotations, being a man is seldom considered an obstacle to a managerial position, whereas being a woman is. The same applies to ethnicity. In western countries, being white rarely hinders managerial career development, whereas being non-white does. The stability of these constructions is due to stereotypes that not only describe, but also prescribe, how a competent manager should act.

Stereotypical assumptions of how men and women should behave in managerial positions are played out in everyday activities and practices in organizations. A telling example is the ways in which members of the management team in a company (in most cases white, heterosexual men) are used to acting during meetings. 'Doing' gender may mean that the men feel comfortable taking time to make their viewpoints known, while the women, according to the general stereotype of femininity, are used to staying quiet. Also, while men may refer to ideas as 'theirs' (demonstrating competitive masculine individualism), women prefer to describe ideas as originating in the 'team' (demonstrating cooperative feminine togetherness). The same pattern can be discerned in other recurring activities such as interaction with clients.

Double bind

Against the backdrop of western conceptions of management, stereotypically masculine behaviour is commonly perceived as more competent. As a consequence, 'doing' masculinity enhances men's opportunities for further career progression within the organization, while forcing women in management into a double bind. According to the definition by Bateson, Jackson, Haley and Weakland (1956), a double bind in communication is an emotionally distressing dilemma in which an individual (or group) receives mutually conflicting messages. This creates a situation in which a successful response to one message results in a failed response to the other, and vice versa, so that the individual is automatically wrong in his or her answer.

'Doing' femininity, on the one hand, and engaging in what counts as competent management behaviour, on the other, are commonly perceived as mutually exclusive. Not only may this double bind experienced by women in management result in a false estimation of their potential and actual performance as managers, it is also likely to reduce their chances of being hired or promoted in the first place (Eagly and Sczesny, 2009).

However, as masculinity is a set of attributes not necessarily tied to the male body, it can be 'done' by both men and women (Fournier and Smith, 2006). This has been confirmed by a social psychological study on stereotyped perceptions of masculinity and femininity conducted by Sczesny, Spreemann and Stahlberg (2006) in Germany. In a series of personnel selection experiments, the researchers tested the influence of the physical appearance, styling and scent of candidates on how their competence was assessed. While masculine styling and scent led to higher perceptions of competence for individuals presumed to be in managerial positions, feminine styling and perfume produced lower scores for equivalent positions. This effect held for both women and men. However, men with masculine styling or perfume scored slightly higher than women showing the same attributes.

This study suggests that both women and men are required to practice a certain kind of masculinity in order to be perceived as competent managers. Hence, by engaging in the 'doing' of masculinity, women (as well as men) help perpetuate the inherent masculinity of management positions. In other words, the gender associated with the position does not necessarily change according to the gender of its occupant. As managers of both sexes engage in 'doing' masculinity, they contribute to the dominant stereotypical belief that masculinity = strong and active, while femininity = soft and passive. The binary difference between women and men is (re)constructed and gender is 'done' through activating powerful stereotypical images of masculinity and femininity that are not directly linked to the bodies that perform them.

Look in some business newspapers or magazines for advertisements or articles dealing with high profile female managers. What kind of gendered images are they expected to live up to? How is gender 'done' when these female managers are portrayed in the media? What kind of a double bind do they face?

A common practice of female managers 'doing' masculinity is to renounce motherhood, thus conforming to the stereotype of the 'ideal' manager. However, at the same time female managers are expected to engage in 'doing' femininity; otherwise they would fail to be perceived as women. It seems a difficult balancing act for any woman to pursue a career as a successful manager when she is expected to practice two things that appear to be mutually exclusive: 'doing' femininity (and thus being perceived as a woman) and 'doing' masculinity (thus being perceived as a competent manager).

In order to be seen as competent and successful managers, women have to become masters in manoeuvring their individual ('doing' femininity) and their professional ('doing' masculinity) identities. They are simultaneously expected to be different from, and similar to, men in management (Gherardi, 1994; Tienari, Holgersson, Meriläinen and Hook, 2009). They have to engage in 'doing' femininity and masculinity in such a carefully balanced way as not to cause unease or discomfort in their professional environment. Social psychological research on women in managerial positions shows that if they do not act according to the normative prescriptions of 'proper' feminine behaviour then they risk being perceived as 'bitchy' or even hostile, and are evaluated by others as less likeable and competent managers than men (Eagly and Johannesen-Schmidt, 2001; Heilman, 2001).

This double bind explains why, for example, female senators in the United States Congress have been found to use conciliatory, people-focused, consensus-building language when engaging in power games (Bligh and Kohles, 2008). Although political wheeling and dealing is generally depicted as a masculine activity, female senators risk being perceived negatively if they attempt to copy their male colleagues in 'doing' masculinity. In contrast, adopting a communication style viewed as feminine can be a strategic way of 'doing' femininity, with the aim of minimizing the negative effects for a woman in a powerful position stereotypically framed as masculine. In other words, female senators attempt to minimize the risk of being unfairly labelled as arrogant and domineering when they are simply doing the same as their male colleagues, namely striving for influence.

> Women in management face a *double bind*. They have to simultaneously engage in 'doing' masculinity and 'doing' femininity. Being a successful female manager means coping with the prominence that comes with belonging to the minority. Depending on the situation, this can entail the adoption of masculine practices in order to become 'one of the boys', or emphasizing femininity to compensate for the disturbance caused by these practices.

In addition to companies and other similar organizations, another crucial forum for (re)constructing management as masculine is the media. Anna-Maija Lämsä and Tanja Tiensuu (2002) studied how the Finnish business media portray female managers. They observed that when the media in that country investigate the subject of gender, it is generally only in regard to female managers. Thus male managers (in contrast to their female colleagues) are never asked whether they feel their sex to be an advantage or disadvantage, or whether they have suffered discrimination because of it. Similarly, Linda Krefting's (2002) study of front page coverage in *The Wall Street Journal (WSJ)* shows how women and men are portrayed differently by the media. According to Krefting, the *WSJ* frequently presents negative perceptions of executive women in terms of their competence and likeability. These issues are not raised in the same way in the coverage of male executives.

Day in day out, journalists therefore reinforce stereotypical images of men and women, perpetuating the male norm in management even though many of them probably do so unintentionally (Tienari et al., 2009). Since women are usually treated as exceptions and curiosities, it is difficult to resist or counteract this 'doing' of management. In general, the media promote particular versions of social reality (men as the norm in management) while marginalizing and excluding others. They highlight gendered differences and fix meanings. Media texts and visual images are a key site for 'doing' gender, and serve to perpetuate the double bind for women in management.

A story appeared in the Danish newspaper *Berlingske Tidende* (12 August 2011) with the title 'Women simply do not have the competition gene'. How is gender 'done' when such titles are published in media texts? The article was a guest column written by a female corporate director. What does this suggest about the 'doing' of gender in management?

HOMOSOCIALITY AND COMPETENCE

Apart from everyday activities at work and in the media, the masculinity of management is confirmed by organizational practices such as recruitment and promotion. While the 'ideal' is privileged, those not fitting in are excluded. This brings us to the practising of what researchers have termed *homosociality* and the socially constructed nature of competence.

Homosociality in practice

Charlotte Holgersson (2003) studied recruitment processes by investigating two Swedish firms each wishing to hire a new managing director. Holgersson shows how 'doing' gender relates to defining and (re)constructing competence in ways that explain, and justify, specific recruitment decisions. In brief, competence becomes a magic word that can be unconsciously – although more often than not purposefully – used by decision-makers to dismiss criticism of their decisions.

> *Homosociality* can be defined as the seeking and preference for the company of people who are perceived as similar in some significant way, for example, in terms of gender. In management, homosociality means that managers tend to feel more comfortable when working with people whom they think resemble themselves. Obviously this can have a considerable impact on recruitment and promotion decisions in organizations.

Relying on such a discourse of competence (or on that of meritocracy, which is based on individual achievement and qualifications) to legitimize recruitment decisions is well accepted and rarely questioned in western societies. Any meritocratic system assumes the existence of fair and free competition between individuals in the labour market, with a firm belief that the most able individual will prevail.

However, as Holgersson shows, in practice questions of competence and merit are reduced to that of mere suitability. In the case of recruitment to top management in the Swedish companies, suitability was about decision-makers' (that is board members') estimation of the likelihood that the newcomer would fit in and become 'one of the boys'. Holgersson interprets the logic in the selection process to be a form of homosociality; the only characteristic of the newcomers distinguishing them from the men on the selection board was age. This underlying preferential tendency was accentuated by the fact that the search processes were carried out under a veil of strict secrecy, with only a small number of key actors involved in the decision-making. This is typical of the recruitment procedure of top managers.

What Rosabeth Moss Kanter (1977) demonstrated with her groundbreaking research in the 1970s holds today: homosociality tends to reproduce itself and remains a major obstacle to diversity in organizations. Women, of course, can also 'do' homosociality, while other dimensions of diversity, for example race and ethnicity, age or social class, can alternatively form the shared group characteristic.

Examples abound of how homosociality shapes organizations. In a study of Finnish call centres, Tuija Koivunen (2011) found strong evidence of gender segregation. A call centre is a communications platform through which companies deliver and market products and services via remote real-time contact. Koivunen revealed how homosocial patterns structured the ways in which call centre employees interacted with each other and with clients. Thus we see that homosocial bonding between top managers is merely the tip of the iceberg.

Check out a job advertisement in a business newspaper or magazine for a particular management position. What 'competences' are indicated as necessary for the position? Are these gender-neutral? What repercussions do the valuing of particular 'competences' have on recruitment? Are these the same for men and women?

In general, the discourse of meritocracy is a powerful means to hide the benefits that such a system generates for the dominant group (Riley, 2002). As notions of merit are devised by those in positions of power, these will reflect such individuals' own interests and achievements (MacKinnon, 1987; McNamee and Miller, 2004). Seemingly neutral merit-based performance evaluations are thus underpinned by gendered differences, while also serving to reproduce them, as men and women may in practice be evaluated differently (Jonnergård, Stafsudd and Elg, 2010).

This was the case in the recruitment processes investigated by Charlotte Holgersson. She noticed, for example, the unbalanced treatment of the qualities of male candidates: their strengths were highlighted and the 'competence' needs of the position moulded to fit the preferred candidate's specific qualities. In turn, the top male candidates' weaknesses were dismissed or framed as development opportunities rather than as flaws. The outcome was that women were not seriously considered as candidates in the recruitment processes.

The key issue here is not that the men in charge – in this case, the board members – deliberately discriminated against women. Rather, they acted as they had always done, feeling comfortable with both the process and its outcome. In other words, they found what they were looking for, and found it where they looked for it.

Van den Brink and Benschop's (2012) study of recruitment practices in Dutch universities exemplifies the same phenomenon. Equal opportunity policies veil practices of inequality because such policies are not in fact put into practice, but only used to make the decision-making process *appear* transparent and objective. Van den Brink and Benschop examined recruitment processes for professorships, finding that the 'ideal' professor, although an evasive construct, is inherently gendered. The qualification and competence criteria favour men, who are also more frequently perceived to have the right personality and potential for the job, and are believed to have the best network connections. This was found to be a self-fulfilling process, because the system preferentially assists up-and-coming male academics over their female colleagues to obtain the credentials needed to take the next crucial career step. Once again, a practice which seems gender-neutral on the surface turns out to be inherently gendered.

In brief, when the organizational policy of gender equality (established for example in recruitment procedures) is taken to imply equality of outcome (who is eventually chosen), then the frequent failure to achieve such an outcome is glossed over by the discourse of merit. Competence, that magic word, can be used to justify the decisions made: 'the most competent candidate was chosen, period'. More often than not women are either disregarded or quickly deselected during the recruitment process, so that the most 'competent' candidate turns out to be a particular type of man.

Can you identify homosocial practices in organizations where you have worked or studied? How would you go about challenging such homosocial patterns at the workplace? What are the benefits and drawbacks for individuals who challenge homosociality? Are they the same for men and women? Consider also how homosociality can affect different ethnic groups, age groups or GLBT individuals.

'Doing' competence

Competence can be conceived of as something that is 'done'; it is a socially constructed and elusive characteristic, based on criteria laid down and used by those in positions of authority. Rather than being constituted rationally and objectively, competence is really another form of 'doing' gender. As qualities associated with men and masculinity are emphasized and rewarded, it comes as no surprise that 'desirable' competences often turn out to be male competences. Thus women are (re)constructed as deficient in terms of individual competence when applying for top jobs, although the process may be masked by ostensibly objective and gender-neutral language under a specious system of meritocracy.

The catch is that this system ignores the true qualities and skills of individual women and men, as only one particular type of man is accorded a privileged position. More often than not this is an unconscious process, which passes unnoticed in everyday organizational life. However, the consequences are serious if we consider the inequalities that are produced.

When revealed, the unstated but relevant criteria defining the 'ideal' manager can appear to be somewhat absurd. On the basis of Charlotte Holgersson's (2003) study, for example, it can be concluded that a new managing director in a Swedish company should:

- be male;
- be between 40 and 50 years of age;
- have a degree from a prestigious university;
- keep a low profile (this is important in Swedish culture);
- be in very good physical condition and able to work 15 hours a day;
- be heterosexual and unlikely to be perceived by others as 'odd' in any way;
- be cultivated and able to master different cultures and situations;
- be in his first marriage, and have a wife who is presentable and has a high tolerance level.

Although such assumptions related to the 'ideal' manager are not objectively defined or clearly stated in company policy documents, they nevertheless serve as the basis for decision-making. In brief, the example of recruitment to top management shows that gender is not merely an issue of individual stereotyped beliefs; it is at the heart of organizational practices. Once any homosocial group is established, it tends to reproduce itself. Although competence (as defined by this group) is treated as an objective criterion, its function in practice is to legitimate decisions based on other criteria, such as 'fitting in'.

'DOING' GENDER IN DIFFERENT SOCIETAL SETTINGS

Throughout the world, management is dominated by men (Thornton, 2009). The form of such domination, however, varies between societies, reflected in how gendered notions of management are realized. This is due to differences in the ways in which societies have developed and in how gender relations are structured and organized.

Researchers talk about *gender orders*, which refer to culturally and historically constructed patterns of the gendered division of labour and power relations between men and women, as these are institutionalized in society (Connell, 1987). Such orders will determine how gender is 'done' in organizations, thus hugely affecting the outcomes for men and women in management, as shown by Tienari, Quack and Theobald (2002) in their study of female bank managers and their careers in Germany and Finland.

A *gender order* comprises the ways in which a particular society organizes the roles and responsibilities of men and women. Gender orders frame and condition practices in organizations. Although based on cultural conventions, they are reflected in legislation, for example, concerning maternity and parental leave and the availability of childcare. Religion can also contribute to a gender order. Societal gender orders are not monolithic; rather they display inconsistencies and even conflicting elements. Furthermore, they are not static, but are susceptible to change when challenged.

In Germany, the gender order is strongly oriented towards the male breadwinner model, which governs normative assumptions about successful management. This is important when trying to understand the dominant logic of managerial careers. In order to enjoy regular promotion in a German bank, workers of both sexes are expected to make choices that prioritize work over family life (Tienari et al., 2002). However, while this accords with normative assumptions about heterosexual gender relations for men (who can simultaneously be managers, husbands and fathers because their wives will, it is assumed, take care of their homes), the breadwinner model conflicts with women's familial obligations. The gender order prescribes that women cannot be wives or mothers *and* prioritize their career. Gender is 'done' differently in relation to being a father as opposed to being a mother: fathers are perceived to perform well through being successful in their jobs, while mothers are assumed to perform well when they prioritize their children and caring responsibilities (Nentwich, 2008).

In Finland, in contrast, women as well as men are expected to perform both at work and at home. A double-earner family model is prevalent in Finnish society, supported by public childcare arrangements which enable mothers (as well as fathers) to combine a career and family. Female bank managers in the study by Tienari et al. (2002) are able to balance and juggle different spheres of their lives. In principle it is possible for women with children to advance in the organization in the same way as their childless (male or female) colleagues. Thus in Finland, gender is 'done' in similar ways by fathers and mothers, at least in terms of consequences for their careers. The different gender orders in German and Finnish societies are therefore seen to affect the ways in which gender is 'done' in organizations in these two countries.

In their study of management consultants, Meriläinen et al. (2004) argue that while the image of the 'ideal' consultant regulates identities and elicits desired behaviours from employees in the UK and Finland, marked differences come to the fore in terms of the possibilities to integrate work with other life areas. In the UK it is considered a 'badge of honour' to work long hours at the office. Thus under a gender order which defines women as the primary care-takers in families, it is difficult for mothers to advance in their careers if they have to reject this organizational culture of unpaid overtime. In Finland, however, a discourse which promotes the notion of 'balanced individuals' (also evident in the previously mentioned bank manager study) encourages both men and women to excel at work and at home. Finnish male and female consultants feel comfortable in balancing different areas of their lives because this is what is expected in society.

In the end, then, it is impossible to understand how gender is 'done' in organizations without considering the underlying societal gender order. This gender order will determine how hierarchies and structures are formed in any society, and indeed how differences between men and women are (re)constructed.

Find out how your country is represented in an international management textbook, and try to describe the reigning gender order. How does work impact on family obligations, and vice versa? Are the career opportunities of fathers and mothers identical, or can you detect differences? How does the gender order affect management?

GENDER 'UNDONE'?

Some of the examples already given in the chapter may have given the impression that gender orders and gendered practices are immutable. However, the 'doing' approach to gender not only alerts us to taken-for-granted expressions of difference (that appear natural, but are not) and to the dynamic maintenance of stability in terms of inequalities; it also offers the potential to work for change. The philosopher Judith Butler (1990) has pointed out that that every 'doing' of gender also bears the potential for 'troubling' it. She argues that binary gender differences can be subverted and 'undone'. Further, Francine Deutsch (2007) has shown how they may be downplayed, set aside or ignored in interactions. By focusing on the 'troubled' aspects of gender (or other relevant forms of identity), we can reveal the paradoxes and dilemmas of the all too simplistic categorization in terms of 'men' and 'women'.

Bearing in mind that every interaction carries the potential to 'undo' as well as 'do' gender, we return to our example of women in management. In attempting to overcome the double bind they face, we ask: How can women 'undo' gender? To provide an answer, we will consider the example of a management team consisting of six men and one woman. At a team meeting it is discovered that no secretary is available to take the minutes, and so the woman is asked to stand in. How will she react? She could 'do' gender by accepting the invitation and perform what is expected of a female member of staff. This would, of course, serve to stabilize taken-for-granted beliefs about women and their place in the organizational hierarchy. Or she could also decide to 'undo' gender by refusing the invitation. In so doing there are at least two tactics she could adopt.

The first would be to smile and provide good reasons why this did not indicate a general rejection to such a task, but merely a one-time decision under these specific circumstances. As her refusal to function as secretary is an inherent challenge to the gender binary, she would have to reframe the issue as a matter of workload or timing. In other words, she would have to try to find rational reasons to legitimize the 'no' without negative consequences for her personally, for example, being perceived as arrogant or uncooperative because her reaction violates common beliefs about femininity.

Alternatively, she could react as described by Chris Mathieu (2009): refuse briefly, sit silently and wait for someone else to be selected. Now she disrupts the gender order by consciously confounding the expectations of male colleagues. However, such a challenge could have adverse consequences for the individual, as she is held accountable for not performing a proper (female) gender identity. In our example, the best path for the woman to follow would be to stay silent; all arguments put forward in such a gendered situation will tend to 'do' rather than 'undo' gender. Thus, by engaging with the ambivalences of masculinity and femininity at work, female managers can find ways to cope with the double bind discussed earlier.

Our example makes clear that 'undoing' is a rather fragile endeavour. Gender is omnirelevant, which means that it is perceived as a valid interpretative frame in any social situation. 'Masculinity' and 'femininity' can be posited from almost any type of social interaction. Hence, attempts to disrupt or change stereotypical assumptions about correct male or female behaviour, traits and tasks are always at risk of being domesticated by the dominant logic of gender difference (Nentwich, 2008).

This means that every attempt to 'undo' gender opens up the possibility of 'doing' gender; attempts at 'undoing' always bear the risk of backfiring, so that gender orders are confirmed instead of challenged. In our example, the female manager's attempt at 'undoing' may be interpreted as masculine behaviour. In this way, the gender order is kept intact. This example shows, first, how the gender order is ultimately made up of daily interactions, and second, how difficult it is to change the order. In such mundane interactions the challenger is always at risk of being labelled deviant.

Considering Mathieu's (2009) example, how could gender be 'undone' in other ways? If one of the male managers volunteered to take the minutes, how would he have to frame his offer in order to 'undo' gender? Would he still be perceived as a competent manager? Would the repercussions be different than for a female manager?

Gender can best be 'undone' by systematically focusing on organizational practices. Here, too, the first step toward change is to reveal and question established ways of doing things. In recruitment to top management positions, as exemplified by Charlotte Holgersson's (2003) study, this would entail more transparency throughout the process and a reconsideration of the competence criteria used to evaluate male and female candidates. 'Undoing' would require the establishment of organizational practices that challenge the link between masculinity and competence (and, conversely, femininity and incompetence) and thus contribute to equality instead of inequality.

The gender of candidates could be deliberately concealed in the initial search and shortlisting, enabling an estimation of their qualifications and competences without the inevitable gender bias. Companies in the hospitality sector, for example, have established such practices where those directly involved in assessing job applications are not given information about the sex of candidates. The first round of assessment is carried out as a blind review.

The criteria against which competence is measured are often already biased along gendered dimensions, and therefore must be critically analysed. Companies in financial services in the Nordic countries, for example, have introduced policies whereby decision-makers are expected to ensure that both sexes are represented in the last three candidates for a managerial position. This guarantees that the evaluation criteria do not exclude relevant candidates by favouring either men or women.

Organizational practices and their gendered consequences can also be scrutinized more generally. While an employee's willingness to work long hours is highly valued, women's success in simultaneously managing their jobs and family obligations is not sufficiently appreciated as a value-added for the job. 'Undoing' could thus mean not only adopting more impersonal recruitment practices and re-evaluating performance criteria, but also emphasizing men's responsibilities in non-work activities such as raising children. A Finnish law firm, for example, has developed its employer brand by promising all employees that they are not expected to work unreasonable hours. This serves to 'undo' gender while also helping the firm to distinguish itself in the legal profession, where working long hours – a gendered practice – is usually an unspoken precondition for career development.

'DOING' DIFFERENCE AND DIVERSITY

The examples presented so far in this chapter have largely focused on the issue of gender, primarily because the main body of research on the 'doing' approach to diversity is related to gendered practices. This does not imply that gender is our primary form of identification as human beings, or that this is the only significant source of inequality in organizations. In fact, the 'doing' approach can be successfully applied to other dimensions of diversity and identity-relevant categories such as race, ethnicity, sexuality, age or class.

Differences

Assuming that identity-relevant categories are reproduced and stabilized in social practices, Candace West and Sarah Fenstermaker (1995) talk about *'doing' difference*. They maintain that gender, race, and class are comparable as mechanisms for (re)producing social inequalities, despite significant differences in their characteristics and outcomes. These dimensions all organize identities in a binary and hierarchical way, establishing and maintaining 'differences that make a difference' in terms of privilege and power.

In other words, being male is not the only characteristic of the 'ideal' manager. In western societies we can add white, heterosexual, able-bodied and (upper) middle class to the list, all being identity-relevant dimensions of diversity that function in a binary way to privilege one side while devaluing the other: white over non-white, heterosexual over homosexual, able-bodied over disabled, (upper) middle class over working class. What complicates the issue is that no individual can be assigned to one single category.

Identities are formed by the intersection of various diversity dimensions. Hence, the double bind (as experienced by women in management) is likely to be perceived and performed differently by a woman with an upper middle class as opposed to a working class background, or by an expatriate new to the socio-cultural context as opposed to someone who has made her entire professional career in one organization.

However, such generalizations made from the outside are always suspect. Identities are relational constructs that are negotiated in context. Patricia Hill Collins (1995) criticizes the 'doing' perspective for its inability to reveal how the social contexts in which interactions between people take place are shaped by 'messy' intersections of various systems of oppression, especially gender and race (or ethnicity). Nikki Jones (2009), in turn, shows how others' expectations of gender, race, class and sexuality are manipulated. She presents a study of Kiara, a 22-year-old woman with multiracial heritage living in the inner-city of San Francisco. Kiara has learned to manage her interactions with others differently in different situations, and 'undoes' gender in her own life by violating and manipulating the normative expectations associated with categorical understandings of identity. She defies being categorized and labelled, and shows that the significance of 'doing' is always context specific. However, evidence regarding gender and race is strong enough across multiple contexts to conclude that as markers of difference, they serve to legitimize practices that produce inequalities on a global scale (Calás, Smircich, Tienari and Ellehave, 2010).

Managing diversity

The considerations above have consequences for making sense of diversity and its management in organizations. First, we must bear in mind that diversity is in itself a social construction: there is no 'diversity' outside the discourses (ways of representing) from which it is constituted, only individuals with various characteristics that become categorized in relation to each other – in particular ways at particular times and in particular places. The crux of the matter is how this diversity labelling is applied, as such acts of labelling always constitute the norm against which the 'diverse' is measured (Prasad and Mills, 1997; Omanović, 2011).

Second, power relations are crucial in determining what is constructed as the majority group, on the one hand, and the minority (the 'diverse'), on the other. Anja Ostendorp and Chris Steyaert (2009) have shown in a study of diversity management discourses in Switzerland that diversity management (DM) as an organizational activity assists in (re)constructing the form of diversity it is attempting to manage. Paradoxically, their study confirms that not all notions of diversity management contribute towards creating a more equal workplace, but may in some cases serve to strengthen the image of the 'ideal' manager, and thus also those who are considered to deviate from this ideal.

Ostendorp and Steyaert point out that from a 'doing' perspective, diversity management should serve to tackle power and privilege in the organization (to pinpoint and challenge practices that create inequalities), and not create additional programmes for the marginalized. This means that those advantaged in the present system must relinquish some of their privileges. Alas, this rarely happens without pressure from outside the organization, for example, through legislative means.

Despite their good intentions, diversity management programmes have a tendency to maintain the status quo. Annette Risberg's (2010) study of the Swedish city of Malmö provides an illustration of this. Malmö Stad (the municipality) implemented diversity management programmes with the intention of creating more inclusive organizational structures. In practice, however, the experience of such managed diversity was ambiguous. 'Diversity' became equated with ethnicity, so that immigrants and refugees were labelled as the 'diverse'. Through the DM programmes, ethnicity was 'done' in such a way that differences between ethnic groups and 'Swedes' were accentuated. The majority group and their practices were, of course, not the target of the diversity initiative.

In a similar vein, on the basis of her studies of Finnish organizations, Jonna Louvrier (2011) argues that ethnic minorities are typically viewed in terms of some deficiency. A frame of 'lack' is introduced: a lack of Finnish language skills and lack of Finnish attitudes and cultural competence. This frame distracts attention away from the benefits which ethnic minorities could bring to Finnish organizations and society. Again, a more useful approach would be to shift the focus away from the 'diverse' to the majority; the target for change would be the mundane practices of this majority that contribute to the (re)construction of privilege and inequality in everyday organizational life. 'Undoing' these will better serve to increase equality and inclusion, rather than introducing haphazard programmes which ignore taken-for-granted assumptions and recurring activities in the organization.

If 'doing' diversity stands for the (re)construction of differences, creating and maintaining mechanisms of inclusion and exclusion, and hence power and privilege in organizations, 'undoing' diversity should offer a way forward in terms of change. As we have argued throughout this chapter, inequality is produced by organizational practices that differentiate between those who fit in and the 'others' who are left outside. 'Undoing' any specific identity category – whether gender, ethnicity, sexuality, age or class – should bring to light the underlying organizational power structures. Thus we see how differences are constructed along identity categories governed by a binary system, and not in terms of merit, competence, or other more objective and factual criteria. Such a process of 'undoing' requires a great deal of courage from those privileged by the current state of affairs.

Applying the 'doing' perspective to various identity-relevant dimensions of diversity in organizations emphasizes the social construction of difference, as well as the connections between (re)constructions of differences and power relations (that is domination and subordination, privilege and exclusion). Diversity interventions in organizations should therefore tackle these power issues, question whatever stereotypical assumptions and practices are the cause of inequality, and 'undo' differences.

SUMMARY

In this chapter we have argued the theoretical and practical benefits of regarding gender and other relevant identities as things that are 'done' and potentially 'undone' in social practices, rather than essential traits or qualities of individuals. In this way the 'doing' perspective serves to highlight and question the ways in which inequalities in organizations are maintained and reproduced in, and through, everyday activities and practices.

In effect, inequalities arise from our taken-for-granted assumptions and activities that are inherent to organizational practices and societal structures. The 'doing perspective' of diversity shifts the focus away from the individual to the particular actions that create and maintain inequalities. Simultaneously we shift the attribution of blame for such inequalities in organizations and society away from individuals (usually women and non-whites, seen as 'deficient' in some way) and groups (usually white men accused of discriminating against women and non-whites). Instead we try to uncover taken-for-granted understandings and practices, which can then be challenged in order to foster change.

Chapter Review Questions

- What does it mean to describe gender and diversity as things that are 'done'?
- How can the 'doing' perspective be used to make sense of organizational practices?
- How can the 'doing' perspective be used to identify and challenge stereotypes related to particular groups of people, for example, women in management?
- How can the 'doing' perspective be used to scrutinize and question arguments regarding 'competence' in organizations?
- How can the 'doing' perspective be used to work for change in organizational practices related to recruitment and promotion?

Case Study

The Nordic countries – Denmark, Finland, Iceland, Norway and Sweden – take pride in their efforts to achieve gender equality. Year after year, they demonstrate the greatest equality between men and women according to the World Economic Forum's Global Gender Gap Reports (World Economic Forum, 2012). The common understanding in these countries is that equality has already been achieved (Korvajärvi, 2002), and that it is up to women to take advantage of their equal position in relation to men (Tienari et al., 2009). This is the societal setting for our case study.

In its annual report, a multinational company based in the Nordic region, which we mask here as IDEA, declares that it adheres to a Nordic heritage of freedom, equal opportunity, care for the environment and good citizenship. Apart from this one reference, however, the question of equal opportunities does not appear elsewhere in the annual report, while care for the environment and good citizenship are discussed at length.

In the section on 'human resources', a table shows the distribution of men and women in IDEA's management team, but with no explicit distinctions made between different layers of managerial responsibility. While it is evident that plenty of women hold supervisory and middle management positions, it can be concluded from the list of senior executives (provided in the last pages of the annual report) that the top echelons of the company consist exclusively of men.

The dearth of women in top management at IDEA is not something that can be merely swept under the carpet. In the staff newsletter, a column was published entitled 'More Women in Managerial Jobs', accompanied by the smiling face of the author of the text, a male executive. The message was that 'there are simply too few women who seek vacant managerial positions'. The full text, provided below, declares that 'we want to change this':

> More Women into Managerial Jobs
>
> The demands on management grow year by year. Therefore we shall make sure that we have the right number of qualified candidates when selecting managers in the future.
>
> Currently the distribution of managerial positions between the sexes is unfavourable: while more than half of the employees of IDEA are women, only one in seven managers above the level of team leader is female. There are simply too few women applying for vacant managerial positions.
>
> We want to change this, as currently IDEA is failing to exploit the managerial potential of female employees. That is why we are now launching a process that will create a more equal gender division in managerial positions in IDEA.
>
> There may be many reasons why women do not apply for vacant managerial positions. One is the tradition-bound attitude that the

> manager is the first to arrive in the morning and the last to leave – an expectation that is difficult to live up to when one has small children.
>
> The executive management's opinion is that it should be possible to combine an attractive managerial job with a well-functioning family life. As we require 'whole' managers of both sexes, individual needs should be better accommodated, along with the possibility of devising work schedules which are more in line with modern patterns of family life.
>
> We have asked IDEA's human resources experts and directors to point out potential female managers. If they do not apply for vacant managerial positions then we will find out the reasons why, pinpointing whether these are due to barriers which IDEA can influence, and perhaps break down.
>
> In the future we must have more women in managerial positions. Not as a contribution to gender politics, but to ensure that such positions will always be filled by the best qualified employees.

Based on your reading of this newsletter column, and drawing from insights on the 'doing' perspective presented in this chapter, please consider the following questions:

Test Your Understanding

1. In what ways is gender 'done' in the newsletter column?
2. What counts as 'good' management in this case? What stereotypical assumptions about men and women are reproduced? What does this tell you about IDEA?
3. How is competence in management defined? What is the 'double bind' for women in management at IDEA?
4. Consider different organizational measures that could be introduced to improve the current situation (for example, in terms of recruitment, rewards and training). What are the pros and cons of each measure with respect to 'doing' gender?
5. What opportunities do men and women at IDEA have for 'undoing' gender?

REFERENCES

*J. Acker (1990) 'Hierarchies, Jobs, Bodies: A Theory of Gendered Organizations', *Gender and Society*, 4 (2), 139–58.

J. Acker (2006) 'Inequality Regimes: Gender, Class, and Race in Organizations', *Gender & Society, 20* (4), 441–64.

G. Bateson, D. Jackson, J. Haley and J.H. Weakland (1956) 'Towards a Theory of Schizophrenia', *Behavioral Science*, 1, 251–64.

M. C. Bligh and J. C. Kohles (2008) 'Negotiating Gender Role Expectations: Rhetorical Leadership and Women in the US Senate', *Leadership*, 4 (4), 381–402.

J. Butler (1990) *Gender Trouble: Feminism and the Subversion of Identity* (New York: Routledge).

M. Calás, L. Smircich, J. Tienari and C. Ellehave (2010) 'Editorial: Observing Globalized Capitalism: Gender and Ethnicity as an Entry Point', *Gender, Work and Organization,* 17 (3), 244–5.

*P. H. Collins (1995) 'Symposium: On West and Fenstermaker's "Doing Difference"', *Gender & Society*, 9, 491–4.

R. W. Connell (1987) *Gender and Power* (Stanford, CA: Stanford University Press).

S. Cross and B. Bagilhole (2002) 'Girls' Jobs for the Boys? Men, Masculinity and Non-traditional Occupations', *Gender, Work and Organization*, 9 (2), 204–26.

F. M. Deutsch (2007) 'Undoing Gender', *Gender & Society* 21 (1), 106–27.

A. H. Eagly and M. C. Johannesen-Schmidt (2001) 'The Leadership Styles of Women and Men', *Journal of Social Issues*, 57 (4), 781–97.

A. H. Eagly and S. Sczesny (2009) 'Stereotypes About Women, Men and Leaders: Have Times Changed?' in M. Barreto, M. K. Ryan and M. T. Schmitt (eds) *The Glass ceiling in the 21st Century: Understanding Barriers to Gender Equality*, Psychology of women book series (Washington, D.C.: American Psychological Association), pp. 21–47.

R. Fibbi, M. Lerch and P. Wanner (2006) 'Unemployment and Discrimination Against Youth of Immigrant Origin in Switzerland: When the Name Makes the Difference', *Journal of International Migration and Integration*, 7 (3), 351–66.

V. Fournier and W. Smith (2006) 'Scripting Masculinity', *Ephemera*, 6 (2), 141–62.

H. Garfinkel (1967) 'Passing and the Managed Achievement of Sex Status in an "Intersexed" Person', *Studies in Ethnomethodology* (Englewood Cliffs, NJ: Prentice-Hall), pp. 116–85.

*S. Gherardi (1994) 'The Gender We Think, the Gender We Do in Our Everyday Organizational Lives', *Human Relations,* 47 (11), 591–610.

M. E. Heilman (2001) 'Description and Prescription: How Gender Stereotypes Prevent Women's Ascent Up the Organizational Ladder', *Journal of Social Issues*, 57 (4), 657–74.

B. Heintz, E. Nadai, R. Fischer and H. Ummel (1997) *Ungleich unter Gleichen. Studien zur geschlechtsspezifischen Segregation des Arbeitsmarktes* (Frankfurt a.M.: Campus).

A. R. Hochschild (1983) *The Managed Heart. Commercialization of Human Feeling* (Berkeley, CA: University of California Press).

C. Holgersson (2003) *Rekrytering av företagsledare. En studie i homosocialitet* (Stockholm: EFI). [Recruitment of Business Executives: A Study in Homosociality]

N. Jones (2009) ' "I was Aggressive for the Streets, Pretty for the Pictures": Gender, Difference, and the Inner-city Girl', *Gender & Society*, 23 (1), 89–93.

K. Jonnergård, A. Stafsudd and U. Elg (2010) 'Performance Evaluations as Gender Barriers in Professional Organizations: A Study of Auditing Firms', *Gender, Work and Organization*, 17 (6), 721–47.

R. M. Kanter (1977) *Men and Women of the Corporation* (New York: Basic Books).

*E. Kelan (2008) 'Gender, Risk and Employment Insecurity: The Masculine Breadwinner Subtext', *Human Relations*, 61 (9), 1171–202.

T. Koivunen (2011) *Gender in Call Centre Work*, Acta Universitatis Tamperensis 1680 (Tampere: University of Tampere Press).

P. Korvajärvi (2002) 'Gender-neutral Gender and Denial of Difference' in B. Czarniawska and H. Höpfl (eds) *Casting the Other. The Production and Maintenance of Inequalities in Work Organizations* (London: Routledge), pp. 119–37.

L. Krefting (2002) 'Re-presenting Women Executives: Valorization and Devalorization in US Business Press', *Women in Management Review*, 17 (3/4), 104–19.

S. Kumra and S. Vinnicombe (2008) 'A Study of the Promotion to Partner process in a Professional Services Firm: How Women are Disadvantaged', *British Journal of Management*, 19, 65–74.

A. M. Lämsä and T. Tiensuu (2002) 'Representations of the Woman Leader in Finnish Business Media Articles', *Business Ethics: A European Review,* 11 (4), 363–74.

J. Louvrier (2011) 'Finnish Multicultural Work Organizations and Diversity Management. Providing Solutions or Increasing Challenges?' in P. Lappalainen (ed.) *It's Just PEOPLE WITH PEOPLE: Views of Corporate Social Responsibility* (Helsinki: Aalto Print), pp. 26–38.

C. A. MacKinnon (1987) Feminism Unmodified: Discourses on Life and Law (Cambridge: Harvard University Press).

P. Y. Martin (2003) ' "Said and Done" versus "Saying and Doing" Gendering Practices, Practicing Gender at Work', *Sociologists for Women in Society Feminist Lecture*, 17 (3), 342–66.

C. Mathieu (2009) 'Practising Gender in Organizations: The Critical Gap Between Practical and Discursive Consciousness', *Management Learning*, 40 (2), 177–93.

S. J. McNamee and R. K. Miller (2004) *The Meritocracy Myth* (Lanham, MD: Rowan and Littlefield).

*S. Meriläinen, J. Tienari, R. Thomas and A. Davies (2004) 'Management Consultant Talk: A Cross-Cultural Comparison of Normalising Discourse and Resistance', *Organization*, 11 (4), 539–64.

*J. C. Nentwich (2008) 'New Fathers and Mothers as Gender Trouble Makers? Exploring Discursive Constructions of Heterosexual Parenthood and their Subversive Potential', *Feminism and Psychology*, 18 (2), 207–30.

V. Omanović (2011) 'Diversity in Organizations: A Critical Examination of the Assumptions about Diversity and Organizations in 21st Century Management Literature' in E. Jeanes, D. Knights and P. Yancey Martin (eds) *The Handbook of Gender, Work and Organization* (London: Wiley-VCH), pp. 315–32.

A. Ostendorp and C. Steyaert (2009) 'How Different Can Differences Be(come)? Interpretive Repertoires of Diversity Concepts in Swiss-based Organizations', *Scandinavian Journal of Management,* 25 (4), 374–84.

*P. Prasad and A. J. Mills (1997) 'Showcase to Shadow. Understanding the Dilemmas of Managing Workplace Diversity' in P. Prasad, A. J. Mills, M. Elmes and A. Prasad (eds) *Managing The Organizational Melting Pot: Dilemmas of Workplace Diversity* (Thousand Oaks, CA: Sage), pp. 3–27.

S. C. E. Riley (2002) 'Constructions of Equality and Discrimination in Professional Men's Talk', *British Journal of Social Psychology*, 41, 443–61.

A. Risberg (2010) *Diversity Management in Practice – The Case of Diversity Work in a Swedish Municipality*, Proceedings of the International Conference on Intercultural Collaboration (ICIC10) Conference, Copenhagen, Denmark, 19–20 August 2010.

T. R. Schatzki (2001) 'Introduction: Practice Theory' in T. R. Schatzki, K. Knorr Cetina and E. von Savigny (eds) *The Practice Turn in Contemporary Theory* (New York: Routledge): 1–14.

V. E. Schein and M. J. Davidson (1993) 'Think Manager, Think Male', *Management Development Review*, 6 (3), 24–8.

S. Sczesny, S. Spreemann and D. Stahlberg (2006) 'Masculine = Competent? The Different Impact of Biological Sex and Physical Appearance on the Attribution of Leadership Competence', *Swiss Journal of Psychology*, 65 (1), 15–23.

G. Thornton (2009) Global Survey: Women Still Hold Less Than a Quarter of Senior Management Positions in Privately Held Businesses, http://www.grantthornton.com/portal/site/gtcom/menuitem.550794734a67d883a5f2ba40633841ca/?vgnextoid=83c4c21cd49c0210VgnVCM1000003a8314acRCRD&vgnextfmt=default, date accessed 1 January 2012.

*J. Tienari, S. Quack and H. Theobald (2002) 'Organizational Reforms, "Ideal Workers" and Gender Orders: A Cross-Societal Comparison', *Organization Studies*, 23 (2), 249–79.

J. Tienari, C. Holgersson, S. Meriläinen and P. Höök (2009) 'Gender, Management and Market Discourse: The Case of Gender Quotas in the Swedish and Finnish Media', *Gender, Work and Organization*, 16 (4), 501–21.

M. Van den Brink and Y. Benschop (2012) 'Gender Practices in the Construction of Academic Excellence: Sheep With Five Legs', *Organization*, in press.

*C. West and S. Fenstermaker (1995) 'Doing Difference', *Gender & Society,* 9 (1), 8–37.

*C. West and D. H. Zimmerman (1987) 'Doing Gender' *Gender & Society*, 1 (2), 125–51.

World Economic Forum (2011), Global Gender Gap, http://www.weforum.org/issues/global-gender-gap, date accessed 23 January 2012.

PART THREE

ORGANIZATIONAL PRACTICES INCLUSIVE DIVERSITY

Contents

CHAPTER

DIVERSITY AS STRATEGY

Mary Ann Danowitz and Edeltraud Hanappi-Egger

Chapter Objectives

After completing this chapter, you should be able to:
- describe diversity management as a strategic and evolutionary process;
- compare and contrast diversity management and equal opportunity;
- describe the different kinds of diversity management models;
- explain the differences between organizational culture and diversity climate;
- outline steps for a successful diversity initiative.

Chapter Outline

- Introduction
- Differences between diversity management and equal opportunities
- Organizational approaches to diversity management
- Specifying diversity strategies with a focus on inclusion
- Diversity management as dynamic evolving strategy
- A good practice example
- Chapter review questions
- Case study
- References

INTRODUCTION

Diversity management can be seen as a top-down (senior) management function combined with bottom-up (employee) activities, which requires the commitment of the whole organization in order to foster inclusion. Of course, any organization wishing to implement diversity management must first decide: what is the best way to initiate the process? This chapter attempts to provide an answer by exploring the various elements and structure of a well-designed diversity strategy. Hence, key concepts and practices associated with strategies for organizational diversity are presented and linked to the development of specific diversity initiatives. Since the chapter introduces diversity as strategy, it will serve as a framework for Chapter 7, which focuses on incremental organizational analyses, Chapter 8, which addresses implementation, and also Chapter 9, which examines the work-life equilibrium as a core dimension of diversity strategies.

Building blocks for diversity as strategy

In order to change existing organizational structures and organizational cultures to be less discriminatory and more inclusive, it is necessary to revise (at least some) organizational rules and practices.

We have learnt that diversity management requires us to question routine practices in organizations in order to identify hidden and subtle discriminatory or exclusion mechanisms. This presupposes a deep understanding of organizational structures, processes and power relations; furthermore, it entails a long-term project of continuous learning, as well as of analysis, reflection, decision-making and the evaluation of these decisions. Thus we are often required to alter our given notions of organizational functioning and employee relationships when engaging in diversity management.

Diversity management is an evolutionary, and more importantly, a *strategic* process; in other words, it is a dynamic series of steps and decisions that are continuously being reviewed and refined. Diversity management concepts should be developed on a case-by-case basis for each organization (see Chapter 1). There is no 'one fits all' model of how to establish diversity management, and thus the first step should always be to develop a *diversity strategy*.

A *diversity strategy*, based on its defining vision, specifies not only goals and objectives to foster inclusion, but also the most appropriate courses of action and the allocation of resources necessary to achieve those goals.

Diversity as strategy implies an integrated and evolving process of change, in which initiatives are incorporated into management and organizational practices, thereby transforming the basic functioning of the organization in its treatment of diversity.

Table 6.1   The different foci of managing diversity and equal opportunities

MANAGING DIVERSITY
• ensures all employees maximize their potential and their contribution to the organization • embraces a broad range of people; no one is excluded • concentrates on movement within an organization, the culture of the organization and the meeting of business objectives • is the concern of all employees, especially managers • may include but does not rely only on positive action/affirmative action
EQUAL OPPORTUNITIES
• concentrates on discrimination • is perceived as an issue for ethnic minorities, people with disabilities and other protected groups • concentrates on the numbers of different groups employed • is seen as an issue for personnel and human resource professionals • relies on positive action
Source: Adapted from Kandola and Fullerton (2004, p. 167).

DIFFERENCES BETWEEN DIVERSITY MANAGEMENT AND EQUAL OPPORTUNITIES

Some scholars have proposed that it is impossible to make a clear practical distinction between the two concepts (Maxwell, Blair and McDougall, 2001). For example, Kirton and Greene (2009, p. 160) have observed that a growing number of UK organizations use the diversity management label for their equality policy, and that diversity management can only be understood in reference to a prior equal opportunities programme. This is also the case in other parts of Europe. Meriläinen, Tienari, Katila and Benschop's research (2009) explains why there exist multiple meanings of diversity management, showing how diversity and diversity management are influenced by the reigning social values, the dominant discourse and the social political context (including the social mix of minority groups). By analysing the websites of the 20 largest companies in Finland, they show how diversity management is generally linked to discourses on gender equality, and how the gender egalitarian context of that country affects the manifestation of diversity by largely focusing on the equality of white women and men in the workplace. Other recent cross-national work has shown that the legal, cultural and social context has an impact on diversity management; for example, companies operating in the following countries have to comply with anti-discriminatory and positive legislation to institutionalize employee equality: Germany (Bruchhagen, Grieger, Koall, Meuser, Ortlieb and Sieben, 2010), the Netherlands (Bleijenbergh, van Engen and Terlouw, 2010), France (Bender, Klarsfeld and Laufer, 2010) and Sweden (Kalonaityte, Prasad and Tedros, 2010). Therefore, an approach to diversity in many organizations and nation states which is sensitive to local conditions is likely to combine diversity management

Figure 6.1 The Hewlett-Packard diversity value chain
Source: Hewlett-Packard, 2012.

with equality initiatives. The distinctions that have emerged from the USA may, therefore, be very different to those in other countries. For example, the historical value chain of the American technology giant Hewlett-Packard, a leader in diversity, reveals the company's various overlapping priorities and approaches which, over the years, have created a diverse and inclusive organization (see Figure 6.1).

Each link in the chain represents a new orientation of corporate policy. While the first two links correspond to the changing legal requirements in the USA, the last two reflect changing demographics and the increasing impact of global markets. The chain can also be taken as an illustration of the idealistic aims of diversity and equality in some US-based organizations, although of course the reality on the ground was, and is, somewhat different. However, when used with caution, and bearing in mind that an organization may function simultaneously across all links, this chain can be a useful visual aid to describe the kind of diversity work an organization may undertake and/or be preparing to undertake. Distinctions between the categories are seldom clear cut, and it is not uncommon for organizations to implement several kinds of initiative at the same time, especially when targeting different groups.

Successful diversity management means, first, understanding the differences and similarities between individuals and social groups, as well as the impact of these differences and similarities, and second, implementing policies and work practices to change behaviour and thereby increase work efficiency. Thus diversity management goes beyond equal opportunities by transforming pre-existing practices and the culture of the organization to enhance performance.

Organizational culture refers to values, artefacts (office design, logos and websites), norms (guiding principles and shared implicit and explicit expectations and roles, behaviour and practices) that influence social interaction.

ORGANIZATIONAL APPROACHES TO DIVERSITY MANAGEMENT

Various models of diversity management have been developed, reflecting different policy approaches to the implementation and impact of diversity efforts in organizations. To understand the many ways in which diversity management can be approached, particularly in terms of strategy, we draw upon the work of Agars and Kottke (2004) to outline some models describing the phases of organizational response to changing demographics and legal requirements, including activities and processes at the individual, group and organizational level.

Table 6.2 shows three basic models of diversity management, each addressing a slightly different strategic approach.

Stage and process models

The early models of diversity management from the 1990s are stage models, meaning that they describe how the functions and structures of organizations change in distinct stages in response to external factors such as demographic transformation, labour market changes, policy shifts and rising globalization. These models have three features in common: they take an organizational policy perspective; they identify distinct phases of equality and associated processes; and they link these with improved approaches to addressing diversity. Such stage models, however, provide little information about how change can occur internally to move an organization from one level to another. The models of Taylor Cox (1991), Roosevelt Thomas (1991; 1996), Robert Golembiewski (1995) and more recently, Gary Powell (2011) show how organizations can and should take advantage of increased workforce diversity. These models emerged in part as a response to affirmative action legislation in the United States. For example, Gary Powell's proposed model (2011) classifies organizations in one of three stages by the types of actions they take. The first two of these are *promote*

Table 6.2 Models of diversity management from a strategy point of view

	Stage and process models	**Change models**	**Organizational learning models**
Perspective	Reactive to environmental changes	Proactive change strategy	Learning orientation
Focus	Phases of equality (non-discrimination, diversity, inclusion)	Structural functions and processes to change organizational cultures	Individual and group receptivity, accommodation of diversity
Features	Organizational policy to improve equality stages	Multiple and broad activities	Moving to inclusive organizations
Most important references	Cox (1991); Thomas (1991); Golembiewski (1995), Powell (2011)	Cox (2001); Allen and Montgomery (2001); Friday and Friday (2003)	Thomas and Ely (1996); Dass and Parker (1999); Agars and Kottke (2004)

non-discrimination, namely encourage compliance by all employees with equal opportunity and anti-discrimination laws so as not to discriminate on the basis of non-relevant personal characteristics, and *promote diversity*, namely increase the numbers of minority employees holding specific positions across various levels of the organization, so that improved workforce diversity will improve business performance. The third category, *promote inclusion*, dealing with the nature and quality of work relationships, aims to respect the norms and values of different groups, so that all employees feel accepted and are given the opportunity to make meaningful contributions (Powell, 2011, p. 214). This last aspect is closely aligned to Taylor Cox's notion of a 'multicultural organization'. The three stages of response in the model devised by Roosevelt Thomas (1996) are described as: *affirmative action* (include, deny, assimilate, suppress and isolate), *valuing differences* (tolerate and build relationships) and *accepting and managing diversity* (foster mutual adaptation).

Change models

These models build on the stage models by incorporating change strategies, meaning that organizations adopt a more proactive and engaged approach to equality and diversity. To varying degrees they look at those structural functions and internal processes of the organization that can serve to increase diversity and inclusion, while stressing the need for multiple, broad activities. Taylor Cox's 'Change Model for Work on Diversity' (2001) extends his earlier model by adding five central components: *leadership, research and measurement, education (enhancing the learning process), alignment of management systems* and *follow-up*. Each component is associated with specific processes. For example, the leadership component entails personal commitment to a new management philosophy and vision, organizational design and communications strategy, as well as the strategic integration of all measures.

Allen and Montgomery's model for creating diversity (2001) builds on Taylor Cox's (1991, 2001) models and the Lewin-Schein change model (Schein, 1996) by providing a framework for planned organizational change to build cohesive and diverse multicultural organizations. Allen and Montgomery's approach to change is organized around three processes necessary for a transformation of organizational culture. The first is termed *unfreezing*, namely overcoming those forces that resist change, followed by *moving*, which means translating the diversity vision and symbolic actions of top management into concrete activities throughout the organization, such as training and education, as well as the recruitment and advancement of underrepresented groups (Allen and Montgomery, 2001, p. 156). The last change process in this model is called *refreezing*, namely the securing and aligning of organizational policies, procedures and the incentive system to perpetuate the new culture.

Elaborating on the idea of organizational change to manage diversity, Friday and Friday (2003) place greater emphasis than Allen and Montgomery (2001) on the dimension of planned change to implement corporate diversity strategy. Their proposed stages of the diversity continuum include *acknowledging diversity*, *valuing diversity* and *managing diversity*. They too rely on the Lewin-Schein change model (Schein, 1996) to articulate the phases an organization must pass through when attempting to manage diversity as a strategic planning process. Friday and Friday see cultural reengineering as essential to shift individuals and the organizational culture along the diversity continuum.

Organizational learning models

We can point to three models of diversity management – those of Thomas and Ely (1996), Agars and Kottke (2004) and Dass and Parker (1999) – which adopt a learning orientation, and thus emphasize the importance of group and individual receptivity and accommodation to diversity (Agars and Kottke, 2004). Thomas and Ely incorporate a learning dimension into their three organizational paradigms, believing that organizations should encourage employees 'to bring the entire sum of their demographic and cultural knowledge to bear on organizational problems' (Yang and Konrad, 2011, p. 7).

Agars and Kottke's (2004) full integration model stresses the psychological dimension (cognitive and emotional) within a three-stage model framework. *Issue identification* denotes the initial stage, when organizations prioritize diversity management. This is followed by *implementation*, during which existing practices are adapted and new policies implemented. The final stage, *maintenance*, sees the establishment of formal and informal processes to promote a culture that values diversity (Agars and Kottke, 2004, p. 67). The major advantage of this model in understanding how organizations fully integrate diversity – or as Cox (1991; 2001) describes it, 'become multicultural' – is that it recognizes the importance of the individual and group levels. Agars and Kottke (2004, p. 69) have pointed out that social identities, which develop along demographic lines, can be a significant source of resistance and group conflict unless social perceptions, as well as perceptions of threat and justice, are successfully managed during implementation.

SPECIFYING DIVERSITY STRATEGIES WITH A FOCUS ON INCLUSION

In order to investigate in detail how organizational change strategies lead to the achievement of an inclusive organization, we will look more closely at the model proposed by Dass and Parker (1999), which gives added value to the aforementioned stage and change models by operationally defining dimensions and processes of these models while taking into account the external environment.

We believe that this model is a useful tool in helping managers (a) better understand the dynamics of implementing diversity, in particular the different repercussions which measures can have at each organizational level (top to middle management, or lower echelons); and (b) identify alternative strategies that organizations can adopt to address diversity issues under a range of conditions.

Dass and Parker (1999) state that the specific approach chosen to manage diversity within an organization will depend on the external and internal pressures for or against diversity, as well as management's perspectives and priorities. Together, these factors influence the strategic and practical response (Dass and Parker, 1999, p. 69). In the model devised by Dass and Parker, the three diversity perspectives of Thomas and Ely's (1996) approach are supplemented by a fourth: *resistance*.

Organizations holding a *resistance perspective* either disregard diversity as a relevant issue or see it as a threat. In the latter case their aim is to maintain the status quo, which usually includes a homogenous workforce. Under the *discrimination and fairness perspective*, protected groups (those enjoying some form of legal protection) are defined in response to unfair or discriminatory treatment that they have suffered in the past. However, this approach is aimed at assimilating these 'others' rather than challenging the characteristics and perceptions of dominant groups. The *access and legitimacy* perspective describes the situation that exists when organizations have recognized the potential benefits of diversity, such as the exploitation of unfamiliar markets or improved service to 'new' consumers. Although here diversity is celebrated for the benefits it provides in certain business areas, such diversity initiatives are then often restricted to those specific areas rather than being allowed to spread throughout the entire organization. The fourth approach, the *learning perspective*, describes the case in which an organization perceives both the opportunities which diversity can bring as well as the accompanying costs, especially when measures towards inclusion are fully implemented throughout all organizational levels and activities. The idea is to learn from diversity while promoting pluralism in the long term.

Find examples from your own country of companies that are attempting to manage diversity. Try to position these efforts within the discussed models. What are the advantages and drawbacks of the specific approaches?

An analysis by Dass and Parker (1999, p. 72) (see Figure 6.2) of how organizations go about integrating diversity initiatives into their core processes

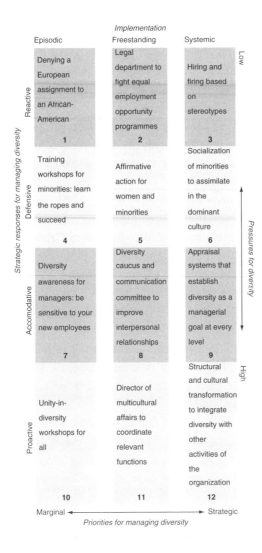

Figure 6.2 Strategic responses for managing diversity and their implementation
Source: Republished with permission of Academy of Management Executive, from Dass and Parker (1999, p. 74), permission conveyed through Copyright Clearance Center, Inc.

provides us with a useful orientation when investigating various strategic approaches.

At the top of the table we find three approaches to implementation. The first, the *episodic approach*, is usually followed by organizations with low or no pressure for diversity, so that diversity initiatives are introduced only sporadically and not integrated into the core business activities. The second, the *freestanding approach*, describes the situation where moderate pressure exists for managing diversity. Here we find more initiatives than in the episodic approach, yet these are still not integrated into the core activities of an organization. For example, several unconnected programmes and measures may have been implemented (such as a 'take a daughter to work' day) to promote the organization's image rather than contribute to core change. Finally, the *systemic approach* describes the situation where diversity initiatives and programmes are closely linked to the core activities of the organization. This approach is usually found when a strong pressure to foster and exploit diversity exists, so that the management of diversity becomes a strategically relevant topic.

Underlying this analysis of implementation is the implicit assumption that diversity management is not an isolated activity of companies, but rather is linked to changes in the external environment or to internal organizational problems (described as 'pressures' in Figure 6.2).

Scholars of diversity and diversity management outside the United States have placed a greater emphasis on the nature of the external context. For example, Jackson (2002), Sippola and Smale (2007), Syed and Özbilgin (2009) and Klarsfeld (2010) have explored the mutual dependencies that exist between organizations and the socio-cultural or political context in which they are embedded.

Recognizing the importance of congruency between company 'values' and the reigning societal culture, Schulz (2009) has linked an organization's internal diversity strategy to its sense of environmental and social responsibility, labelling this the 'strategic socially responsible and sensitive perspective'. It is clear that this perspective emphasizes the issue of corporate social responsibility, thus highlighting the role of organizations as social actors, and not just business actors (Hanappi-Egger, 2011).

Scholars in Europe, such as Syed and Özbilgin (2009), have departed from models developed in the USA to examine more closely the relational features of diversity management and the social embeddedness of organizations. They believe that various aspects of the societal context must be taken into account when constructing diversity strategies to foster inclusion. Context is seen as crucial in the tailoring of models, definitions, strategies and actions for diversity initiatives; and indeed when dealing with resistance to diversity.

DIVERSITY MANAGEMENT AS DYNAMIC EVOLVING STRATEGY

Our review of models and approaches to managing diversity gives some idea of the many approaches and practices that organizations can adopt to promote inclusion. However, managers often fail to recognize a vital point: that individual diversity initiatives must take account of both the *organizational* and the *individual* level in order to ensure systemic, holistic change towards inclusion.

Next we present a model that views diversity management as a contextualized system by drawing together insights and principles from the stage and change models (as well as from other writings on organizational topics). Diversity is conceptualized as a dimension of strategic management within a particular context.

We start with a basic question: if an organization's path to inclusion is as complex as the other models imply, then how are managers supposed to proceed? Our approach, rooted in the learning school of strategic management, suggests that organizations learn over time (Mintzberg, Ahlstrand and Lampel, 2009). This implies that diversity management is an *evolving* and *intentional* process of planning and implementation. A prerequisite for this process is the construction of an integrated organizational-specific framework for diversity initiatives, aimed at fostering trust, commitment and diversity-friendly learning environments (Cox and Blake 1991; Kandola and Fullerton 2004; Thomas, 2004b; Bassett-Jones, 2005; Konrad, Prasad and Pringle, 2006). This framework supports all intermediate phases towards the establishment of inclusion, but is especially crucial in the initial phase when access barriers are identified and discriminatory structures eliminated. Of course, most individuals and organizations will experience some discontinuity as behaviours are changed and an inclusive working environment is proactively created; they will have to adapt to a new perception of the working environment, and will encounter systematic organizational changes of which they have no prior experience (Reese and Overton, 1970).

Figure 6.3 gives an overview of our proposed model. Influenced by institutional theory (Martinez and Dacin, 1999) and various writings on organizational change (Burns, 1996; Rajagopalan and Spreitzer, 1996), it adopts a relational framework (Syed and Özbilgin, 2009) to propose that an organization's structures and actions regarding diversity are legitimized by conforming to the rules and belief systems of the external context in which it is embedded. Thus the process of change is greatly influenced by the interaction between the organization and its context.

The contextual levels that impact on each organization are the *macro-environment*, representing the societal, national and even supra-national influences, and the *micro-environment*, that is the particular regional circumstances. These contexts have a strong influence on the culture and diversity climate at the organizational level; they are relevant factors for a company's diversity management, more specifically its diversity strategy.

Organizational climate refers to employees' perceptions, attitudes and expectations of the work environment including the atmosphere, practices, procedures and rewards.

Diversity climate is a shared understanding among organization members of an organization's diversity related structures and actions. It comprises the perception of fairness regarding inclusion and exclusion of people from diverse backgrounds.

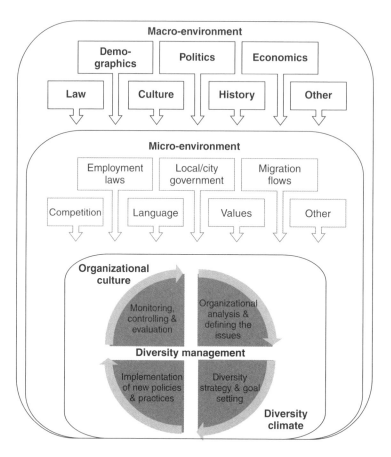

Figure 6.3 Diversity management as a contextualized system
Note: This model extends the work of Hanappi-Egger and Walenta (2007) and of Danowitz, Hanappi-Egger and Hofmann (2009).

Instances of macro level contextual factors are EU regulations regarding anti-discrimination, or national employment legislation that regulates the actions of companies, in particular the recruitment of employees. To give a more concrete example, the promotion of women in technological fields by the municipal authorities of Vienna is also a macro level contextual factor. In this case companies receive additional funding if they are willing to initiate programmes to promote women. Of course, the way in which these programmes are implemented will influence – and be influenced by – the diversity climate in the company.

At the *organizational level*, diversity management should be incorporated into the *organization's mission statement, main objectives, strategies, structures and processes* (Belinszki, Hansen and Müller, 2003). As a strategic management concept, diversity management simultaneously considers and influences the organizational culture *and* climate. Therefore, the specific definition of diversity, the issues tackled, the choice of diversity goals and strategies, as well as the implementation of new policies and practices, are always closely related to the organizational culture and climate. Thus an analysis of the underlying organizational culture and climate is necessary in order to ensure a *sustainable* implementation of diversity management. When undertaking this analysis we must bear in mind that diversity issues in organizations are defined and constructed by common sense, reflected in basic assumptions and implicit expectations. Employees transform their experiences of organizational culture into meanings, which in turn influence the *organizational climate*.

Diversity climate can also be seen as reflecting the depth of trust engendered within staff members, as well as the structure of power relations. Various contextual aspects of diversity climate, as described by Cox (1993), are individual-level factors (identity structures, prejudice, stereotyping and personality), group and intergroup factors (cultural differences, ethnocentrism and intergroup conflict) and organizational-level factors (culture and acculturation processes, structural integration, informal integration and bias in human resource systems).

In a discussion of the three-layer scheme of Schein (2004), Thomas (1991) has pointed out that to successfully tackle diversity, organizations must do more than simply formulate diversity mission statements; the commitment to creating an inclusive organisation has to be 'lived'. This acknowledges that culture is both a product and a process. Thus, for example, in addition to the symbolic rewarding or sanctioning of behaviour, the underlying attitudes of employees and managers should be considered as part of diversity management.

These ideas support the case for treating diversity management as a process of strategic management and organizational change. In this context Flood's (1995) work helps to describe and identify four different types of change, namely *process* change (flows and their steering), *structural* change (functions, rules), *cultural* change (values, beliefs, social rules, relationships, work climates) and *political* change (power relations, group interests).

One example of process change is the re-distribution of work roles, tasks and responsibilities in order to strengthen teamwork. Structural change, on the other hand, could entail a re-orientation of what counts as 'success' within an organization. A typical example of cultural change is when a company's code of conduct is revised. Finally, political change could be achieved by establishing task forces involving senior managers and various interest groups.

Think about these kinds of changes. How could they be used as activities and processes for diversity management?

Although much of the literature on diversity management considers only cultural aspects of organizational change, we believe it is necessary for organizations to follow an integrative approach to diversity management, one which takes account of all organizational levels and their interactions with the macro- and micro-environment (Cao, Clarke and Lehaney, 2003; Syed and Özbilgin, 2009). This allows diversity to be fully incorporated into strategic management.

Defining the issues

Figure 6.3 makes clear that organizations are embedded in a specific environmental context, and consequently are highly shaped by societal pressures regarding diversity.

It is not difficult to find examples of the societal context having a direct effect on organizational diversity issues: a wide-ranging political discussion on securing equal rights for gays, lesbians and bisexuals, or on the pros and cons of introducing a women's quota on corporate boards, can clearly have an impact on organizations expected to follow laws and adhere to public policy positions (Hanappi-Egger, 2012). These external dynamics may also raise managers' awareness of diversity issues and their willingness to engage in diversity, as has been the case following the introduction of diversity charters in several European countries. Other factors in the external environment, such as the state of the labour market and the general business climate may also influence dealings with diversity, for example, when a company hires more international employees or the press decries the absence of women in top management.

Internal problems can also act as catalysts for organizations to engage in diversity management and become more inclusive. High job turnover, low job satisfaction, low motivation and employee complaints or even lawsuits may be signs that employees are suffering under a negative diversity climate.

Review Questions

An organization's first step in the diversity management process is to define relevant diversity issues by answering the following questions:
- What is the socio-demographic composition of our staff?
- Are there specific problems related to diversity that require further investigation to determine root causes?
- Are there any external factors that indicate the need to engage in diversity management?
- Do we have the necessary knowledge and diversity competences to tackle these issues?

It is important to note that, because we are dealing here with *values*, any discussion of diversity issues may lead to divergent opinions, insights and responses, or indeed conflict and resistance (see Chapter 8). Nonetheless, it is vital that the topic of diversity and diversity management be explicitly discussed with more than just a casual degree of commitment. In order to avoid a superficial attachment to diversity, it is necessary that an organization develop both an awareness of the problem and a willingness to implement change. This implies that organizational analysis must play a crucial role in building a diversity strategy, a subject which is addressed in Chapter 7.

Diversity strategy and goal setting

In order to become part of an organization's strategy, diversity issues should be addressed and incorporated in a mission statement (Cox, 2001). But the story does not end there: a high level of commitment can only be assured when mission statements are clearly communicated and backed-up by an inspiring vision shared by stakeholders (Hayes, 2007). The outcome of this initial phase of defining diversity issues should be to pinpoint strategically relevant areas and adopt specific goals.

Review Questions

Diversity strategy and goal setting should include a critical review of an organization's most crucial long-term goals and objectives. The following are typical questions that must be answered in this review process:

- What are our main strategic goals across all functional areas (products, services, markets, marketing and human resource)?

- How do these goals relate to diversity?
- How can diversity management contribute to these strategic goals?
- What is our strategy concerning diversity?
- What should a corresponding diversity mission statement look like?
- Whom should we involve in the early phases of developing a diversity mission statement?
- How could diversity goals affect power relations and dominant values?

Of course, there will be multiple, possibly divergent, answers to these questions. Thus the next step involves a determination of preferences and priorities: what is the most salient strategic goal, and how can diversity contribute to achieving it?

After an organization has developed a context-sensitive diversity strategy, Figure 6.4 shows that it must then turn to the question of implementation (see Chapter 8), followed by monitoring and evaluation (see Chapters 7 and 8).

A strategic perspective to establishing inclusion

It is important to bear in mind that both top-down and bottom-up activities are necessary to establish an inclusive organization, requiring the involvement of various stakeholders. Anwander (2002, p. 382) has argued that different groups are responsible for specific tasks pertaining to diversity management, with the various areas of responsibility summarized in Table 6.3. Each circle represents the particular level of involvement, ranging from no circles to signify a complete lack of involvement, to five circles indicating extensive involvement and responsibility. The levels of involvement and responsibility are important aspects of power relations and a means of generating trust and 'buy in' from members of the organization. With respect to our model of 'diversity management as a contextualized system' (Figures 6.3 and 6.4), this means that each cycle of action (defining the issues, formulating diversity goals, implementation, monitoring

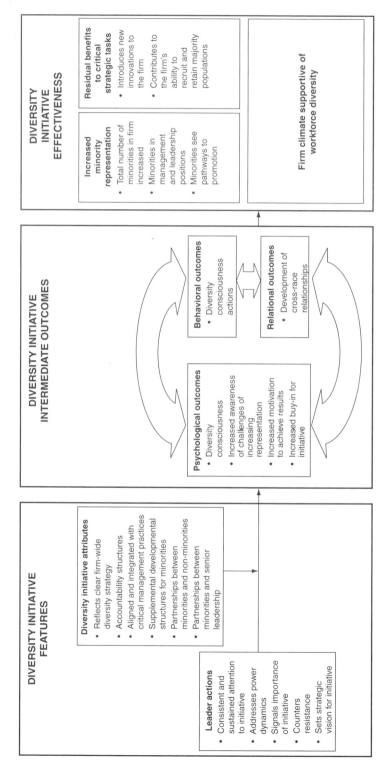

Figure 6.4 Factors influencing the effectiveness of organizational diversity activities

Source: Akinola and Thomas (2008).

Table 6.3 Fields of action of different organizational stakeholders

	Provide orientation	Initiate change	Intensify action	Normalize
Top management	OOOOO	OOO	O	O
Middle management	OO	OOO	OOO	OO
Employees		OO	OOO	OOOOO

Source: Adapted from Anwander (2002, p. 382).

and evaluating) requires the involvement of different stakeholders with varying degrees of intensity and responsibility.

Table 6.3 also indicates the various strategic levels. Long-term strategies (usually lasting several years and concerning the organization as a whole) are mainly devised by top management to provide a general orientation. While the translation of these strategies into policy (and thus initiating change) is also the responsibility of top management, they share this responsibility with middle management and, to a lesser extent, other employees. The actual implementation and normalization of activities issuing from the strategy is carried out through daily practices that more directly involve non-managerial employees, accompanied by more limited top management responsibility. In daily practices this rather hierarchical approach will not be fully realized, as there is a continuous 'feedback' of discussion and negotiation regarding the continued relevance of certain issues and how best to proceed. Nevertheless, with appropriate adaptations for the nature of the organization and its social context, this model is a helpful reminder that the involvement and commitment of both management and subordinate employees is required to establish an inclusive organization.

From diversity management to effective diversity initiatives

Diversity management may be described as the totality of an organization's efforts to become inclusive. Once an overall diversity strategy has been developed, the next step is to investigate how best to implement specific diversity activities. For example, how can an organization improve its structure and practices to include under-represented minorities (for example persons with an immigrant background)?

In Akinola and Thomas's (2008) work on diversity initiatives in knowledge intensive firms, the authors identify five core attributes or design features required for any diversity activity to be effective:

1. The activity must relate to a well articulated firm-wide diversity strategy. Its purpose and significance to the organization must be highlighted, thus giving employees a better understanding of the salience of the initiative and contributing to greater employee participation and involvement.

2. The activity must include partnerships between minorities and non-minorities, thereby creating a network of relationships between key stakeholders in the organization and minority constituents, all of whom share the common goal of increasing diversity. Often these networks take the form of task forces, leadership teams or network groups.

3. Supplemental development structures for under-represented minorities must be embedded in the firm to increase retention and advancement. Initiatives such as informal networks, executive mentoring and client assignment monitoring processes offer career resources, create advocacy and become a basis for cross-ethnic relationships.

4. The activity must be well integrated into organizational practices and processes. Incorporating an initiative into core managerial practices connects the activity to fundamental tasks of the organization, thus preventing it from being later discarded.

5. Organizational structures must be in place to assign responsibilities and monitor progress. The activity can be firmly anchored within the organization by appointing key managers and employees to monitor success and by establishing metrics to measure effectiveness and create incentives to achieve goals.

Akinola and Thomas's (2008) model of factors influencing the effectiveness of workforce diversity initiatives is shown in Figure 6.4. The five aforementioned diversity attributes are included in the box on the left.

The middle box shows the intermediate psychological, behavioural or relational outcomes of a diversity initiative. The box on the right summarizes both the direct effects of the diversity initiative and the residual benefits to key organizational tasks.

Diversity management functions on two interrelated levels: (a) the organizational level of strategic diversity management; and (b) the sub-level of a specific initiative or an individual endeavour. The outcomes of diversity measures become clearly visible at the sub-level, as well as the residual benefits (outputs) relating to broader organizational tasks such as increasing innovation or reducing turnover among majority employees. Focusing at this level of individual initiatives also allows organizations to consider whether and when they wish to engage in various kinds of programmes and activities to foster different groups. For example, in a consulting organization that already has a balanced recruitment of staff in terms of gender (about 50 per cent male and female), the management may nonetheless choose to continue its diversity initiatives in order to improve the performance of mixed-gender teams and ensure equal opportunities in promotion and salary. However, additional specific measures might have to be undertaken to increase the number of women from under-represented groups such as Muslims, or those from ethnic minorities.

Example

Relating diversity initiatives to diversity strategy

Let us look at the concrete example of Adecco to examine in more detail the relationship between the mission of an organization and a particular initiative. Adecco is a world leader in human resource services. Headquartered in Zurich, Switzerland, it has a workforce of approximately 33,000 worldwide. Its mission is to inspire individuals and organizations to work more effectively and efficiently, and create greater choice in the domain of work for the benefit of all concerned (Adecco, 2011).

In 1986 Adecco's French subsidiary launched a 'Disability and Skills' initiative to help people with disabilities into employment. Similar initiatives have subsequently been initiated in Italy, Belgium, the Netherlands, Spain, Switzerland, the UK, Argentina and the USA (Adecco, 2011). The programme promotes equality opportunity strictly on the basis of personal skills, qualities and experience. The objective is to identify and provide work opportunities for disabled candidates, whilst also helping to develop additional skills to ensure sustainable employment. Thus Adecco works with companies, as well as individuals with disabilities and their families, to cover all aspects of training and entry into employment (Business and Disability: A European Network, 2011).

A dedicated international 'Business and Disability' coordination team was put together in 2004 to manage the programme's implementation and investigate its results across the group. This team is headed by a 'Corporate Social Responsibility/Disability and Skills' project director at group level, working in collaboration with a team of project leaders responsible for programme implementation at national and local levels. The coordination team ensures the transfer of know-how and the mainstreaming of disability inclusion throughout Adecco's major business units. Adecco is also a founding member of 'Business and Disability: A European Network', which works to raise awareness of the business case for disabled workers, thereby promoting disability inclusion in the private and public sectors as well as within communities.

Internally Adecco has introduced compulsory induction training courses on non-discrimination and disability inclusion for managers and staff. The aim is to ensure that all employees understand the company's corporate diversity values, while fostering commitment to the policy's implementation and helping staff deal with any cases of discrimination. Evaluation of the diversity programme includes monthly, quarterly and yearly status reports of Adecco's achievements in this field, including the number of disabled individuals who have joined the workforce.

Outcomes

Adecco sets targets and objectives relating to the work placement and employment of people with disabilities. In 2004 it facilitated access to work to 9578 disabled persons across Europe, an increase of 9 per cent compared to 2003, and thus exceeding its own targets. The 'Disability and Skills' initiative has, through demystification of disability in the workplace, transformed a previously hostile organizational climate. The programme benefits from the support of both permanent and temporary staff, as well as disabled and non-disabled staff, to create enhanced satisfaction amongst staff and clients. The commitment to disability inclusion has been a key factor in Adecco winning calls for tenders from some clients.

Source: Europa (2005) with updated information from the Adecco website.

A GOOD PRACTICE EXAMPLE

Examples of good practice are activities and measures that companies have suc- cessfully undertaken towards achieving optimal diversity management. Most of these activities adopt a process-oriented, long-term approach, and adhere to a top-down management strategy involving managers and employees as partners in all functional areas of the organization. While all staff members, regardless of position, can function as advocates for diversity, the following checklist identifies the crucial actors and activities required to implement and maintain diversity management in any company wishing to foster inclusion (Danowitz et al., 2009, pp. 86–7):

- The top management initiates and/or champions a change process by developing a strong and clearly formulated company strategy and vision. The approach and definitions are broad, inclusive and contextually appropriate, with diversity viewed as a long-term economic resource (Keil et al., 2007).
- The top management commits itself to diversity management by communicating the diversity strategy internally and externally, allocating resources in ways that are consistent with the organization's strategy (Thomas, 2004a).
- Diversity goals and objectives are anchored within the organization's mission statement and strategy. This includes implementing measures to reduce barriers to diversity management and establishing a set of indicators and feedback loops as part of the monitoring system to continually evaluate progress and suggest improvements (Kandola and Fullerton, 2004).
- Information and training are provided to all members of the organization in order to develop diversity awareness and competencies, thereby ensuring a transformative shift in the organizational culture. Practical and positive steps are undertaken to help employees manage this transition.
- A 'diversity audit' is carried out to investigate staff demographics and turnover, the organizational culture and employee attitudes and perceptions, as well as all systems and procedures relevant to diversity.
- Responsibilities and accountability are determined for all levels, functional areas and activities, along with the necessary coordination steps. Diversity management is incorporated into transparent performance and evaluation reviews.
- Outward-facing activities are undertaken to help raise the organization's external standing and corporate image, thereby contributing to its success. Such activities include the development of partnerships with academic institutions and NGOs; the support of education and training for socially excluded groups; participation in external networks; and the achievement of wider recognition, in particular through positive media attention and the winning of relevant awards (Keil et al., 2007).

These points confirm that for an organization to become an example of good practice, its members must be encouraged to see diversity as a context-sensitive strategy. They must be willing to question established norms, structures and processes. In other words, staff commitment and competence is required to initiate the change that, in the end, becomes good practice. These internal organizational processes have to be seen in the context of both the macro- and micro-environment. It must be borne in mind that the organizational diversity climate and culture are influenced by the political, societal and economic circumstances, as well as by the narrower regional context in terms of policy, cultural values and attitudes towards diversity. Clearly these factors must be incorporated into a context-sensitive diversity strategy and implementation plan.

Chapter Review Questions

- What is a diversity strategy?
- Which models of diversity management can you list and describe?
- How is diversity climate defined?
- What is the relationship between organizational culture and diversity climate?

- What is meant by *diversity management as a contextualized system*?
- What determines the effectiveness of diversity initiatives?
- Can you name some characteristics of 'good practice' in diversity management?

Case Study

IKEA is a Swedish multinational retailer of furniture and home products. It has a commercial network of 186 stores in 31 countries and employs 70,000 workers. The company has a long experience of diversity management, reflected in its declared value of 'plurality', or workforce diversity, in terms of gender, culture, ethnicity and religion. This goal of inclusion is also pursued at the 13 sales outlets in Italy, where managers have introduced a plurality project to ensure that IKEA Italia (total staff: 5,500) can adapt to different contexts and markets, as well as to enhance the workforce. The project focuses on three main factors: customer diversification, workforce diversification and raising awareness of diversity as a crucially important factor of innovation (Mapelli and Scarpaleggia, 2004, in Murgia and Poggio, 2010). When opening a new store in Florence, IKEA Italia decided to implement a pilot project on ethnic diversity. The specific aims of the project were to enhance workforce diversity, seen as a source of creativity; to create a body of staff representative of the local social context; and to foster intercultural integration between Italian and immigrant employees.

The initial phase involved identifying the largest ethnic communities in the local area. After an unsuccessful attempt to involve the Chinese community, careful analyses were made of other ethnic groups residing in Florence. Some of these communities became involved in the project, and contacts were established to various organizations working with immigrants. Some 350 résumés were then collected, from which 125 suitable candidates were identified after screening. Following a process of evaluation by assessment committees, 25 people from non-EU countries and 12 EU citizens were hired by IKEA Italia. Specific training courses were offered to majority employees to foster the integration of minority workers. In particular these aimed at improving the intercultural skills and cultural awareness of group leaders, department heads and human resource professionals.

In collaboration with a trade union, IKEA also opened an information desk on matters of interest to immigrant employees. And for good measure it organized a film festival on the subject of integration.

Source: 'Working for Good Practices across Nation States', Murgia and Poggio (2010, pp. 174–5).

Test Your Understanding

1. Drawing on material from this chapter, decide which model(s) could be used to describe IKEA Italia's approach to diversity management when opening their Florence

store. Then develop more complete scenarios about factors not mentioned in the case that would explain the situation at IKEA Italia.

2. Would you describe the various activities in the case as examples of equal opportunities, positive action or mainstreaming (see Chapter 2)?

3. What is the relationship between IKEA Italia's overall organizational diversity strategy and the local community context? How important is the local culture?

4. How might the adopted strategies differ in regard to other underrepresented groups?

5. What forces of resistance do you think IKEA Italia's top management might face, and how should they deal with such forces?

REFERENCES

Adecco (2011), Adecco website, http://www.adecco.com/SocialResponsibility/OurPriorities/Integration/Pages/Disabled.aspx, date accessed 11 September 2011.

*M. D. Agars and J. L. Kottke (2004) 'Models and Practice of Diversity Management: A Historical Review and Presentation of a New Integration Theory' in M. S. Stockdale and F. J. Crosby (eds) *The Psychology and Management of Workplace Diversity* (Oxford: Blackwell), pp. 55–77.

M. N. Akinola and D. A. Thomas (2008) 'Defining the Attributes and Processes that Enhance the Effectiveness of Workforce Diversity Initiatives in Knowledge Intensive Firms', HBS Working paper 07–019.

R. Allen and K. Montgomery (2001) 'Applying an Organizational Development Approach to Creating Diversity' *Organizational Dynamics,* 30, 149–61.

A. Anwander (2002) *Strategien erfolgreich verwirklichen. Wie aus Strategien echte Wettbewerbsvorteile werden* (Heidelberg: Springer).

N. Bassett-Jones (2005) 'The Paradox of Diversity Management. Creativity and Innovation', *Innovation Management*, 14 (2), 169–75.

E. Belinszki, K. Hansen and U. Müller (eds) (2003) *Diversity Management. Best practices im internationalen Feld* (Münster: LIT).

A. F. Bender, A. Klarsfeld and J. Laufer (2010) 'Equality and Diversity in the French Context' in A. Klarsfeld (ed.) *International Handbook on Diversity Management at Work* (Cheltenham and Northampton: Edward Elgar), pp. 83–108.

I. Bleijenbergh, M. van Engen and A. Terlouw (2010) 'Laws, Policies and Practices of Diversity Management in the Netherlands' in A. Klarsfeld (ed.) *International Handbook on Diversity Management at Work* (Cheltenham and Northampton: Edward Elgar), pp. 179–97.

V. Bruchhagen, J. Grieger, I. Koall, M. Meuser, R. Ortlieb and B. Sieben (2010) 'Social Inequality, Diversity and Equal Treatment at Work: The German Case' in A. Klarsfeld (ed.) *International Handbook on Diversity Management at Work* (Cheltenham and Northampton: Edward Elgar), pp. 109–38.

B. Burns (1996) *Managing Change: A strategic Approach to Organizational Dynamics* (London: Pittman).

Business and Disability: A European Network (2011), Business and Disability: European Case Studies, http://www.businessanddisability.org/case_studies/publication.html, date accessed 11 September 2011.

G. Cao, S. Clarke and B. Lehaney (2003) 'Diversity Management in Organizational Change: Towards a Systemic Framework', *Systems Research and Behavioral Science,* 20 (3), 231–42.

T. Cox (1991) 'The Multicultural Organization', *Academy of Management Executive*, 5, 34–47.

T. Cox (1993) *Cultural Diversity in Organizations. Theory, Research & Practice* (San Francisco: Berrett-Koehler).

*T. Cox (2001) *Creating the Multicultural Organization* (San Francisco: Jossey-Bass).

T. Cox and S. Blake (1991) 'Managing Cultural Diversity: Implications for Organizational Competitiveness', *Academy of Management Executive*, 5 (3), 45–56.

*M. A. Danowitz, E. Hanappi-Egger and R. Hofmann (2009) 'Managing Gender and Diversity in Organizations' in L. Zsolnai and A. Tencati (eds) *The Future International Manager. A Vision of the Roles and Duties of Management* (Houndmills: Palgrave Macmillan), pp. 70–93.

*P. Dass and B. Parker (1999) 'Strategies for Managing Human Resource Diversity: From Resistance to Learning', *Academy of Management Executive*, 13 (2), 68–80.

Europa (2005) *The Business Case for Diversity – Good Practices in the Workplace* (Brussels: Directorate-General for Employment, Social Affairs and Equal Opportunities).

R. Flood (1995) *Solving Problem Solving* (Chichester: Wiley).

E. Friday and S. S. Friday (2003) 'Managing Diversity Using a Strategic Planned Change Approach', *Journal of Management Development*, 22 (10), 863–80.

R.T. Golembiewski (1995) *Managing Diversity in Organizations* (Tuscoloosa: University of Alabama Press).

E. Hanappi-Egger (2011) 'Diversitätsmanagement und CSR: One size fits it all?' in R. Schmidpeter and A. Schneider (eds) *Corporate Social Responsibility – Theoretische Grundlagen und Praktische Anwendung einer verantwortungsvollen Unternehmensführung.* (Vienna: Austrian Chamber of Commerce).

E. Hanappi-Egger (2012) 'Die Rolle von Gender und Diversität in Organisationen: Eine organisationstheoretische Einführung' in R. Bendl, E. Hanappi-Egger and R. Hofmann (eds) *Diversität und Diversitätsmanagemet* (Wien: Facultas), pp. 175–201.

E. Hanappi-Egger and C. Walenta (2007) 'An Integrative Multidisciplinary Model of Diversity Management', Paper presentation, *13th European Congress of Work and Organizational Psychology*, Stockholm, Sweden.

Hewlett-Packard (2011) The Diversity Value Chain, http://www8.hp.com/us/en/hp-information/about-hp/diversity/value.html?jumpid=reg_R1002_USEN, date accessed 27 July 2011.

J. Hayes (2007) *The Theory and Practice of Change Management*, 2nd edn (New York: Palgrave Macmillan).

T. Jackson (2002) 'Reframing Human Resource Management in Africa: A cross-Cultural Perspective', *International Journal of HRM*, 13 (7), 998–1018.

V. Kalonaityte, P. Prasad and A. Tedros (2010) 'A Possible Brain Drain: Workplace Diversity and Equal Treatment in Sweden' in A. Klarsfeld (ed.) *International Handbook on Diversity Management at Work* (Cheltenham and Northampton: Edward Elgar), pp. 244–62.

*R. Kandola and J. Fullerton (2004) *Diversity in Action: Managing the Mosaic* (London: CIPD).

M. Keil, B. Amershi, S. Holmes, H. Jablonski, E. Lüthi, K. Matoba, A. Plett and K. von Unruh (2007) Training manual for diversity management, http://ec.europa.eu/employment_social/fundamental_rights/pdf/train/traisem_en.pdf, date accessed 3 October 2008.

G. Kirton and A-m.Greene (2009) *The Dynamics of Managing Diversity: A Critical Approach* 3rd ed (Oxford: Elsevier-Butterworth Heinemann).

A. Klarsfeld (2010) *International Handbook on Diversity Management at Work* (Cheltenham and Northampton: Edward Elgar).

*A. Konrad, P. Prasad and J. Pringle (2006) *Handbook of Workplace Diversity* (London: Sage).

S. Liff (1999) 'Diversity and Equal Opportunities: Room for a Constructive Compromise?', *Human Resource Management Journal*, 9 (1), 65–75.

R. Martinez and M. Dacin (1999) 'Efficiency Motives and Normative Forces: Combining Transactions Costs and Institutional Logic'. *Journal of Management*, 25, 75–96.

G. Maxwell, S. Blair and M. McDougall (2001) 'Edging Towards Managing Diversity in Practice', *Employee Relations*, 23 (5), 468–82.

S. Meriläinen, J. Tienari, S. Katila and Y. Benschop (2009) 'Diversity Management Versus Gender Equality: The Finnish Case', *Canadian Journal of Administrative Sciences*, 26 (3), 230–43.

*H. Mintzberg, B. Ahlstrand and J. Lampel (2009) *Stategy Safari,* 2nd edn (London and New York: Prentice Hall Financial Times).

A. Murgia and B. Poggio (2010) 'The Development of Diversity Management in the Italian Context: A Slow Process' in A. Klarsfeld (ed.) *International Handbook on Diversity Management at Work* (Cheltenham and Northampton: Edward Elgar), pp. 160–78.

G. Powell (2011) *Women & Men in Management,* 4th edn (London and Thousand Oaks: Sage).

N. Rajogopalan and G. Spreitzer (1996) 'Toward a Theory of Strategic Change: A Multi-lens Perspective and Integrated Framework', *Academy of Management Review*, 22 (1), 48–79.

H. Reese and W. Overton (1970) 'Models of Development and Theories of Development' in L. R. Goulet and P. B. Baltes (eds), *Life-span Developmental Psychology* (New York: Academic Press).

E. H. Schein (1996) 'Culture: The Missing Conception in Organization Studies', *Administrative Science Quarterly,* 41 (2), 229–40.

E. H. Schein (2004) *Organizational Culture and Leadership* (San Francisco: Jossey-Bass).

A. Schulz (2009) 'Strategisches Diversitätsmanagement. Unternehmensführung im Zeitalter der kulturellen Vielfalt' in D. Wagner and B.-F. Voigt (eds) *Beiträge zum Diversity-Management* (Wiesbaden: Gabler).

A. Sippola and A. Smale (2007) 'The Global Integration of Diversity Management: A longitudinal Case Study', *International Journal of HRM*, 18 (11), 1895–916.

J. Syed and M. Özbilgin (2009) 'Relational Frameworks for International Transfer of Diversity Management Practices', *International Journal of Human Resource Management,* 20 (12), 2435–53.

*D. Thomas (2004a) 'Diversity as Strategy', *Harvard Business Review*, 82 (9), 98–108.

D. Thomas (2004b) 'IBM finds profit in diversity', Harvard Business School working knowledge, http://hbswk.hbs.edu/cgi-bin/print?id=4389, date accessed 25 January 2012.

*D. Thomas and R. Ely (1996) 'Making Differences Matter: A New Paradigm for Managing Diversity', *Harvard Business Review,* September-October, 79–90.

R. Thomas, Jr. (1991) *Beyond Race and Gender. Unleashing the Power of Your Total Work Force by Managing Diversity* (New York: Amacom).

R. Thomas, Jr. (1996) *Redefining Diversity* (New York: Amacom).

*Y. Yang and A. Konrad (2011) 'Understanding Diversity Management Practices: Implications of Institutional Theory and Resource-Based Theory', *Group & Organization Management,* 36 (1), 6–38.

CHAPTER

7

ORGANIZATIONAL ANALYSIS

Heike Mensi-Klarbach and
Edeltraud Hanappi-Egger

Chapter Objectives

After completing this chapter you should be able to:
- explain various concepts and approaches concerning organizational analysis;
- undertake an organizational analysis with respect to diversity;
- choose and apply appropriate methods for organizational analysis;
- apply selected approaches and tools in individual cases;

Chapter Outline

- Introduction
- Organizational analysis: taking relevant steps towards strategic diversity management management
- Tools for organizational analysis
- Conclusion
- Chapter review questions
- Case study
- Sources and further reading
- References

INTRODUCTION

As discussed in previous chapters, diversity management should be understood as a holistic and strategic process encompassing all areas of an organization's activities and business. Several steps are required to implement diversity management, the first of which is an *organizational analysis* to investigate the characteristics of a company wishing to introduce a diversity management initiative. Clearly it is impossible to adopt a 'standard' framework into which all companies must be squeezed. Rather one must take account of varying contextual factors such as the environment, the particular business sector, the company size and ownership structure, to name only a few. All of these factors greatly influence the type and scope of diversity initiatives. Furthermore, there is no one *single* optimal approach that organizations can employ to foster diversity. According to Dass and Parker (1999), organizations and managers can adopt a range of different strategies in order to address the issue of diversity (Chapter 6). The authors state that the path followed by an organization in managing diversity depends on external and internal pressures in favour of, or against, diversity, as well as management perspectives and priorities which influence the strategic response and the implementation of diversity management practices (Dass and Parker, 1999, p. 69).

According to Gilbert, Stead and Ivancevich (1999) diversity management comprises all measures that have a fundamental impact on organizational culture; the value of diversity is not just passively acknowledged, but actively exploited to benefit the organization. However, as Dass and Parker (1999) have indicated, organizations may follow different paths to achieve the same goal. According to the level of integration into core organizational processes, the authors differentiate between three approaches: the *episodic*, the *freestanding* and the *systemic* approach (Dass and Parker, 1999, p. 72).

> *Diversity management* may be defined as a management concept which, acknowledging the value of difference, strategically and systemically strives to promote equity among its workforce in order to create added value.

It is clear that the long-term goals of diversity management can only be achieved by initiating a transformation of organizational culture. This requires, as a first step, an organizational analysis to identify the status quo as well as the current approach to diversity and diversity management. Such an analysis then forms the basis for systemic and strategic change (see Figure 7.1).

In this chapter we stress the importance of adopting a strategic perspective within diversity management, specified as a 'systemic approach' (Chapter 6). Furthermore, we claim that a learning perspective offers the greatest chance of benefitting from diversity in the long-term. In this sense the chapter will propose

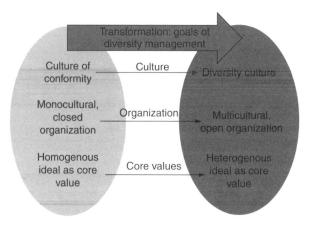

Figure 7.1   Paradigmatic shifts within the transformation process of diversity management
Source: Adapted from Schulz (2009, p. 89).

an 'ideal' model of diversity management that is rooted in systemic, strategic and learning concepts.

The main assumptions are as follows:

1. context specificity: every organization will require its own unique form of diversity management depending on the individual contextual framework;
2. systemic-strategic approach: diversity management must be integrated into the core business activities of an organization;
3. learning perspective: diversity management means engaging in a long-term learning process at the individual, group and organizational levels (Hanappi-Egger and Hofmann, 2012).

In order to determine the *context specificity*, that is the context-relevant issues with respect to diversity management, it is necessary to undertake an organizational analysis. Within the *systemic-strategic approach*, diversity management is viewed as a holistic and recursive process. The *learning perspective* implies that the success of diversity management is largely dependent on the degree of organizational and individual awareness and understanding (which must be learned).

Based on these principles, the various steps and sub-tasks of an organizational analysis are presented in the following, along with the necessary tools and their application. The discussion will be exemplified by several concrete examples.

ORGANIZATIONAL ANALYSIS: TAKING RELEVANT STEPS TOWARDS STRATEGIC DIVERSITY MANAGEMENT

As already pointed out in previous chapters, diversity management should be understood as a holistic and strategic project. The model shown in Figure 7.2 depicts the implementation process of diversity management from beginning to end; in this process organizational analysis is located in phase two.

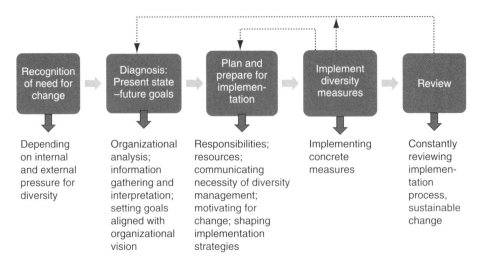

Figure 7.2 Implementation process
Source: Adapted from Hayes (2007, p. 88).

In this model *diagnosis* comes directly after the *recognition of need for change*, as such recognition is clearly the pre-condition of any further activity to foster diversity within an organization. However, as Aretz and Hansen (2003) have pointed out, diversity is a flexible term: It may not always be understood in a concrete sense (for example, gender diversity) but can be rather freely defined by the collective norms reigning within the organization. Therefore any diagnosis has to be guided by the question: what is understood by diversity, and in which context? As shown in Chapter 5, the first step in strategic diversity management is to define the diversity issues at stake. Of course, when an organizational analysis is undertaken, the principal decision to introduce diversity management has already been made. This means that a conscious and explicit discussion on diversity and diversity management has been previously initiated, indicating an awareness of the problem and a readiness to implement change. Nonetheless, the basic problem of defining the relevance of diversity accompanies the whole phase of organizational analysis.

Such analysis can provide a useful framework for discussing context-specific forms of diversity management in different organizations. When analysing the current situation, the following questions must be answered internally:

- How do we currently deal with diversity (internally and externally) and how should we progress from here?
- What are our concrete goals for 20 years hence?

Aretz and Hansen (2003) have proposed the notion of a 'diversity continuum' (Figure 7.3) along which organizations can locate their current attitude to diversity.

Figure 7.3 Diversity management
continuum
Source: Adapted from Aretz and Hansen
(2003, p. 19).

As can be seen, the continuum begins on the left with 'combating diversity', denoting organizations characterized by strict and uniform selection procedures, the assimilation of minorities and strict normation. In the middle Aretz and Hansen (2003) have introduced the term 'isolation', meaning that diversity is not uniformly tolerated, but only accepted in specific isolated organizational areas. On the right, 'promotion of diversity' indicates the situation in which individual diversity is valued and structurally relevant, so that diversity comes to permeate the organization.

Returning to the model of an ideal implementation process of diversity management, the steps following *diagnosis* are *plan and prepare for implementation*, *implement diversity measures* and *review*.

Of course, none of these stages and phases exists in isolation; rather they are interconnected, with the implementation phase, in particular, closely tied to the planning and evaluation phases. The measures must be continually reviewed and evaluated to monitor how they are contributing to the achievement of the diversity goals. Analytical tools are, of course, applied throughout the implementation process to assess and evaluate the impact of measures. Thus the review phase is closely linked to the diagnosis phase, although reviewing means detecting changes over time rather than clarifying the original situation (as in the diagnosis phase). Time is an important factor, as we know that diversity measures usually have a delayed impact on organizational processes (Robinson and Dechant, 1997). Evaluation is only possible if the goals of management initiatives are clearly defined at the outset. Otherwise it is impossible to determine whether the implemented measures are effective, useful or appropriate for an organization.

Note that the implementation process as described above is both dynamic and evolutionary. It is important to construct some sort of *ideal* process (following change management models such as Hayes, 2007; or Senge, 2000), even if such a process will hardly ever be found in practice. Yet having this 'prototype' in mind makes it easier to evaluate previously implemented diversity measures by examining which steps have been taken and what is still to be done. This provides a useful learning effect by pinpointing the reasons for the failure of previous initiatives.

TOOLS FOR ORGANIZATIONAL ANALYSIS

In order to create a 'tailor-made' diversity management programme, it is important to first analyse the organization, to gather and interpret relevant information, and thus determine how diversity is currently regarded and handled. Of course, the analysis and interpretation of such data is a highly specialized and selective task, requiring a great deal of background knowledge and context sensitivity. For example, as Hanappi-Egger states in the opening chapter of this book, feminist researchers have pointed out that organizational theory and analyses are gender-blind rather than gender-neutral (Acker, 1992; Gherardi, 2003). The same may be said for other dimensions of diversity such as ethnicity, age, disability, religion and sexual orientation (Brotherton, 2003; Hall, 1990; Prasad, 2003; Smith, 1996). Sexual orientation, for example, is often treated as a non-issue by relegating it to the private sphere, thereby denying its relevance for the organization (Hall, 1990). However, when examining the interrelation between work and leisure, for example at firm gatherings, celebrations or excursions, sexual orientation can very well become a relevant issue. Religion can also affect organizational practice in regard to celebrations: in western Europe company celebrations are often scheduled around traditional Christian festivals, such as Christmas parties or events at Easter and New Year, while the festivals and calendars of other religions are rarely considered. These are just a few examples to show that some individual sensitivity and knowledge is required when analysing an organization in regard to diversity issues. It is necessary to investigate the *actual* degree of diversity while also looking at the *perceived* relevance of diversity, as the actual degree of diversity (according to a headcount of the workforce, for example) might not accord with the general perception (Aretz and Hansen, 2003). Thus a combination of *quantitative* organizational analysis methods (such as headcounts) and *qualitative* methods (such as qualitative interviews, focus group interviews) are required. Traditional methods of analysis include interviews, questionnaires and direct observation, as well as unobtrusive measures such as the gathering of statistical information (Hayes, 2007).

Note: Qualitative methods of analysis generally make use of freely available or openly collected information. The process of analysis is oriented towards data collection and interpretation, while acknowledging that different data collection methods may lead to different interpretations. Examples of qualitative analysis methods are: observation, artefact analysis, analysis of protocols, analysis of structural data, qualitative interviews in the form of focused interviews, narrative interviews and problem-centred interviews (Diekmann, 2003; Lueger, 2000). For further information on methods see Glaser and Strauss (1979), Cassell (2006), Swift and Piff (2010), as well as Creswell and Plaro (2011).

Quantitative analysis, on the other hand, makes use of statistical techniques to analyse standardized datasets, such as surveys.

The primary difference between these two approaches is that qualitative methods constitute an attempt to obtain 'in depth' information from a small field of investigation. Often such methods are used to gain an initial overview, to formulate an idea or hypothesis. By contrast, quantitative methods provide a large swathe of information on a specific and well-defined topic. In short, 'qualitative = in-depth, but restricted in extent; quantitative = extensive datasets, but conclusions generally superficial'.

Diversity analysis

The roots of diversity analysis can be traced to the attempt to investigate gender relations within organizations, so-called 'gender analysis' (Blickhäuser and von Bargen, 2005; Lange, 2006; Warmuth, 2012). Such analyses generally comprise a catalogue of questions designed to investigate the current state of diversity. These are largely formulated as 'open' questions, encouraging the responder to engage in storytelling as a standard feature of qualitative interviews. Lange (2006, p. 161) has proposed a framework of eight different levels of analysis.

In the following each of these levels of analysis (see also Table 7.1) will be described in more detail, with example questions and practical examples provided (questions adapted from Lange, 2006; Blickhäuser and von Bargen, 2005).

Table 7.1   Levels of organizational analysis

Level of analysis
<ul><li>institutional history and organizational goals</li><li>ideologies, values, rules and strategic orientation</li><li>organizational culture and structure</li><li>hierarchy, management and personnel policy</li><li>products, services offered</li><li>time, place, work-life balance and other issues</li><li>sexuality in the organization</li><li>performance measurement.</li></ul>
Source: Adapted from Lange (2006, p. 162ff).

Institutional history and organizational goals

- When, how and by whom was the organization founded?
- What myths and legends are communicated concerning the organization's history?
- What were the primary goals at the time of foundation? Who were the main actors, and whose interests did they serve?
- Which groups are targeted by the organization's business?
- What is the primary vision and mission vocalized both internally and externally (image, brand, and corporate identity)?
- What services and products affect or influence the public?
- In what ways are diversity issues explicitly mentioned in institutional goals/missions?

It is clear that we require a variety of techniques to answer these questions. While qualitative interviews with employees will uncover myths and legends, the history of the company's foundation as well as its primary vision can only be deduced from secondary data, such as inter- or intranet files, PR texts and so on. The formulation of individual questions depends on the current state and goals of the potential diversity strategy, on the one hand, and on financial restrictions on the other, as qualitative surveys are more time- and cost-intensive.

Example 7.1

Accenture is a global player in management consulting, technology services and outsourcing, operating in more than 120 countries. It currently has a workforce of around 236,000 employees. Combining unparalleled experience, comprehensive expertise in all industrial and commercial sectors, as well as extensive research into the world's most successful companies, Accenture collaborates with clients (enterprises and governmental agencies) to help boost their performance.

Thus Accenture is a truly international company, and as such is strongly supportive of inclusion and diversity management. To better communicate this international profile, Accenture has produced an advert highlighting the importance of diversity.

Weblink

Accenture homepage, 2011 http://www. accenture.com/us-en/company/people/ diversity/, date 24.1. 2012.

Ideologies, values, rules and strategic orientation

- What are the organization's main values and principles (for example future-oriented, market-oriented, ecological, environmentally aware, family-oriented, innovative and so on). How do these affect attitudes to diversity?
- What goals does the organization have concerning diversity? Are power inequalities relevant and a feature of internal discussion?
- In which ways are the various interests and needs of employees respected in regard to diversity?
- Are diversity policies in place, and if so, in which way do they relate to the organization's strategic management?
- Are there specific goals for diversity at management level, such as quotas?
- How is individual performance measured and valued, and how is it tied to organizational performance?
- Who embodies the organization's values and norms? What is the implication for diversity?
- What specific diversity measures has the organization implemented?
- What rules, strategies and procedures has the organization introduced to deal with resistance and conflict relating to diversity?

Example 7.2

A traditional Austrian retail company (the country's largest private employer) can be characterized as highly family-oriented. This business philosophy is reflected in its handling of diversity issues. The company has its own publicly accredited academy, where apprentices aged 15 to 19 are taught retailing skills. The ethnic backgrounds of these youngsters are highly diverse. Conflicts that arise within the academy are dealt with 'as you deal with problems in your own family'. The apprentices are seen as joining the company 'family'; they are treated with respect, are valued and supported in all their problems, even those of a purely private nature. For example, an 'emergency hotline' has been introduced for all apprentices in need of urgent help.

Organizational culture and structure

- What traditions, habits, preferences or rites are found in the organization? Are diversity issues part of the culture? Are they seen as relevant or even honoured?
- Are there any examples of diversity (for example, diversity in top management) and how does this impact the organization?
- What degree of diversity exists within the organization (nationality, gender, ethnicity, religion, sexual orientation, age, disability and so on) and in what way does such diversity influence the organizational culture and climate? Is diversity perceived as a strength or weakness?
- In which ways are employees and managers skilled in dealing with diversity issues?
- In which ways are learning processes concerning diversity institutionalized and knowledge accumulated? Is there a system of knowledge management in place?

Example 7.3

PannonJob is a medium-sized Hungarian human resource firm with 91 employees, of whom 18 are women over the age of 50. The top management team consists of three men and five women. Besides having four disabled persons among their employees, Pannonjob cooperates actively with organisations that specialise in finding employment for people with disabilities. The main areas of activity are recruitment, staffing, payroll outsourcing and training. PannonJob maintains strong links with higher education institutions throughout Hungary both for internment purposes and for careers advice. Pannonjob encourages mothers with young children to come back to work by offering them full-time and part-time employment, which is not very usual in Hungary. Additionally, the company holds an annual family day for all employees and their partners and children, to cook and play together, and emphasize that Pannonjob believes in the importance of the family.

Weblink

http://www.pannonjob.hu/

Hierarchy, management and personnel policy

- Which form does the organizational hierarchy take (formal hierarchical system)?
- Which formal and informal networks exist, and what influence do they exert within the organization (informal networks, micro-political processes)?
- Do internal networks show aspects of diversity (vertical and horizontal segregation)?
- Which aspects of diversity are revealed by the distribution of power (age, gender, sexuality, ability, religion, ethnicity and so on)?
- Which strategies are in place to reduce possible power imbalances?
- How is diversity manifested in different departments (also in regard to voluntary and paid work)?
- Which diversity dimensions are not represented in the organization, and what are the repercussions both internally and externally?
- How does the current composition concerning diversity (vertical and horizontal) influence work relationships and performance?
- How is performance measured and remunerated? Is the ethos 'equal pay for equal work' followed?
- What measures are in place to increase the representation of minority groups in key positions (affirmative action, gender mainstreaming, mentoring)?
- How are these diversity measures managed, executed and evaluated?
- What principles and instruments are in place to recruit and develop personnel? In which ways are diversity issues respected?
- What is the reaction of hegemonic groups within the organization who face a loss of power due to diversity measures? And how does the organization deal with this?

Example 7.4

BACA is an Austrian bank belonging to the Italian Unicredit group. It maintains branches in 22 European countries, with a strong presence in Central and Eastern Europe. A long-time supporter of the promotion of women, BACA is committed to achieving a quota of 40 per cent female staff in all management positions.
In recent years the bank has also begun to look at other social dimensions such as age, ethnicity, religion, sexual orientation and disability.
In general, there is a high commitment to diversity management: BACA established the position of Diversity Manager in 2000, followed by Disability Manager in 2010 to give disabled workers a stronger voice. The company also offers a special bankcard for visually handicapped clients has set up an internal network for disabled individuals and maintains barrier-free communication structures.

Weblink

http://www.bankaustria.at/de/open.html#/de/28098.html, 21.12.2011

By answering the questions listed above we will be able to paint a wide-ranging picture of an organization's values, norms and culture, as well as its attitude to diversity. The following questions go into more detail, focusing on potential applications and fields of action in diversity management.

Products, services offered

- What are the core competences of the organization/department/unit?
- In what way can, or should, the organization develop (narrow-mindedness)?
- How did these core competences evolve and which employees were involved (diversity dimensions)? Were the interests of marginalized groups taken into account?
- What diversity-related considerations have hitherto influenced the organization's design of products and services?
- How has knowledge and experience of diversity been utilized (analysing potentials and resources)?
- Which diversity dimensions are relevant for the improvement and sustainability of performance in different departments/units?
- In which ways is diversity management integrated into day-to-day business (planning, execution and monitoring of work processes)?
- Which resources are available to integrate diversity management into daily business (expertise, time, space, consulting, skills and so forth)? Are they perceived as being sufficient?

Example 7.5

Several airlines believe that food and beverages provided during their flights should reflect the diversity of passengers. Air Berlin, for example, offers upon request the following special menus for long-haul flights: vegetarian, gluten-free, lactose-free, vegan, kosher, halal and meals for diabetics.

Weblink

http://www.airberlin.com/site/flug_service_an_bord.php?LANG=eng&checkNavi=1, 21.12.2011.

Time, place, work-life balance and other issues

- What working-time model(s) does the organization employ?
- How are these models perceived by employees? Do they take account of diversity in some way?
- How intensive is the workload and other pressures in departments/units, and how do employees cope?
- Are staff members required to do overtime? If so, how often and for how many hours? In what way are private obligations respected?
- Who in the organization schedules overtime, and what reasons are given for the requirement to work overtime?

- What practices are in place to support a healthy work-life balance (such as flexi-time, part-time contracts, job sharing, parental leave and so on)?
- In which ways are different biographies, backgrounds and individual needs respected? What are the repercussions of discontinuities[1] in the individual career path?
- Are staff members offered some kind of training in diversity, and if so, how is this linked to the work process? Are these courses subject to quality control?
- How is the management of personnel incorporated into the overall organizational strategy, and what role do diversity issues play?
- In what way does the organization, specifically the personnel department, see the issue of diversity in terms of the needs of individual employees?

Example 7.6

A small Austrian company, active in the field of video games, employed a staff of nine men (including two native English-speakers) and one woman. The average age of these employees was 32. The organizational culture with respect to time and work pressure was described as 'rather tough'. A 60-hour working week was standard, as were weekend and night shifts. Problems quickly arose when many of the employees (around two-thirds) began having children, and consequently felt their work-life balance to be inadequate and unacceptable. The management, forced to negotiate new working conditions, subsequently came to appreciate the advantages of an inter-generational workforce.

Sexuality in the organization

- Is sexuality and sexual orientation relevant to the organization, and if so in which context?
- Is hetero-normativity visible, and if so how?
- Are diverse forms of sexuality accepted and integrated (such as bisexuality, homosexuality or transsexuality)?
- Are social sanctions imposed on individuals acting outside the dominant sexual norm (open or subtle forms of discrimination)?
- Have there been any cases of sexual harassment, and what was the reaction within the organization?

Example 7.7

VW Financial Services is an active proponent of diversity measures regarding 'sexual orientation'. In 2002 it began supporting a 'Christopher Street Day' parade in the German city of Braunschweig, and subsequently established an internal network for gay and lesbian employees called 'QUEERdirect'. In 2006, the company was awarded the Max-Spohr Management Prize for

---

[1] Discontinuities are typically due to periods of parental leave, sabbaticals or further education courses. What is regarded as a discontinuity depends on how the norms are defined within an organization, industry, region or country.

its efforts in supporting gays, lesbians, bisexual and transgender people at work.

Weblink

http://www.vwfsag.de/content/sites/

vwcorporate/vwfsag_de/en/home/einstieg_ und_karriere/wir_als_arbeitgeber/our_ diversity_management.html, 21.12.2011

Performance measurement

- What kind of individual, group and team outputs is rewarded?
- In what way is performance acknowledged, and does it result in promotion?
- Are similar standards applied to all employees regardless of age, gender, ethnicity, and so forth?
- Are all individuals valued similarly according to their training and qualifications?
- Is the financial and social acknowledgement of performance the same for all employees?

Example 7.8

Microsoft is an information technology company based in the USA with many subsidiaries all over the world. It has a total workforce of over 90,000. Diversity management has been integrated into the company's structures and processes from its earliest days, recognized by several awards that Microsoft has won as a 'good employer' regarding positive workplace conditions. The performance contracts of managers now require them to gain skills in diversity management,

monitored by means of evaluation questionnaires to assess knowledge, skills and qualifications on diversity issues. Negative feedback not only leads to a recommendation from the manager's supervisor that s/he attend further training courses, but also the loss of bonus payments. Continual negative feedback could even severely restrict an employee's career opportunities.

Weblink

http://www.microsoft.com/about/diversity/en/us/ default.aspx, 21.12.2011

Of course, the questions presented above merely offer a general framework which requires contextual adaptation. The eight levels of analysis can be restructured to better fit the particular context, while the individual questions can be selected or discarded to ensure that all the most important issues are covered.

The diversity analysis questions we have been discussing are mainly open and qualitative questions in nature. In the following section we will offer a number of quantitative indicators to assess an organization's current attitudes to, and treatment of, diversity.

European Commission indicators to evaluate programme implementation

The European Commission (EC) (2003) study has already been presented in Chapter 3 in a discussion of indicators to measure the business benefits of diversity management. Now indicators (see Tables 7.2–7.5) will be described that can be used to evaluate the implementation of measures and analyse diversity outcomes, thus enabling an assessment of an organization's current treatment of diversity. The concept proposes the following principal indicators (EC, 2003, p. 39 ff.):

- workforce demographics;
- employment culture and working environment;
- top management commitment;
- diversity strategy and plan;
- organizational policies;
- employment benefits;
- managerial incentives;
- organizational structures;
- reporting process (monitoring and evaluation);
- communication;
- support networks;
- education and training;
- productivity losses.

The indicator 'workforce demographics' (generally calculated by simple 'head counting') offers a picture of the specific composition of the workforce. However, after determining the size of diversity groups, it is vital to ascertain what aspect of diversity is perceived as relevant to the organizational context (Aretz and Hansen,

Table 7.2   Example indicator: workforce demographics

Indicator	Methods of measurement
Workforce demographics	• number of people from various diversity groups in the workforce as a whole (gender, age, ethnicity, ability, and so on); • number of people from various diversity groups compared to external benchmarks; • number of people from various diversity groups in specific departments/units/functions (at management level, vertical and horizontal segregation); • pay levels of people from various diversity groups compared to pay levels of other equivalently graded employees; • trends in diversity groups' representation in workforce – year by year comparison; • number of people recruited into the organization from different diversity groups; • number of people promoted within the organization from different diversity groups; • number of people from various diversity groups leaving the organization, compared to average.
Source: Adapted from European Commission (2003, p. 44).	

2003). For example, although the demographic indicator might reveal a highly heterogeneous workforce in terms of age, it could still be true that this is not a relevant factor for most employees. Additional investigation using qualitative questions must be undertaken in order to determine which dimension of diversity is crucial for the organization.

Exercise 7.1

Go back to the questions under 'diversity analysis' and choose those which could elicit further information on the relevance of specific diversity dimensions in the organization.

The indicator 'employment culture and working environment' clearly looks at the 'overall climate' (as it is termed in diversity analysis). While here the focus is on formal complaints, which can easily be researched by going back to secondary data, the diversity analysis presented earlier collects data directly by reviewing formal and informal cases of harassment and complaints related to discriminatory behaviour. Clearly the difference lies in the complexity and effort of data collection. Qualitative interviews and their evaluation are far more time-consuming than the process of gathering and interpreting quantitative data on formal diversity-related complaints. Nevertheless, it is clear that quantitative data has a major drawback: relevant information may get overlooked, especially in terms of diversity-related issues about which people are often reluctant to make an official complaint.

Further, the indicator points to the relevance of employee surveys. These are standardized questionnaires designed to collect representative and quantitative information on staff attitudes towards diversity.

Note that the term 'representative' refers to studies that cover a multitude of different characteristics, and which are thus able to 'represent' the population.

Table 7.3   Example indicator: employment culture/working environment

Indicator	Methods of measurement
Employment culture/ working environment	• number of formal, company-internal complaints related to diversity; • number of formal, company-external complaints related to diversity; • employee attitudes on issues related to diversity – responses to opinion questions in employee surveys (differences between various diversity groups) and changes over time; • employee attitudes to diversity issues compared to other companies (for example via a benchmark study).

Source: Adapted from European Commission (2003, p. 45).

Representative samples usually consist of a random sample or proportional sample. Analysing a randomly selected sample with a multitude of characteristics increases the probability that a reliable picture of the population is captured (Diekmann, 2003).

Consider the differences between qualitative and quantitative data collection. Name some diversity topics that are best investigated using qualitative measures and some for which quantitative measures are more suitable. Discuss the option of using mixed methods.

The indicator 'Top management commitment' offers quantitative information on this topic. The diversity strategy and plan already call for the interpretation of what is meant by 'good quality' diversity strategy and annual goals.

Exercise 7.2

Try to find diversity strategies published on company home pages, or contact diversity departments directly for information. Consider how you could assess their quality.

Note: Questions that investigate the indicator 'organizational policies' will elicit simple 'yes/no' replies. They merely determine whether or not organizational policies have been amended, and do not analyse the quality of any amendments.

How could the quality of amendments to organizational policy be assessed?

Table 7.4   Example indicators 1

Indicator	Methods of measurement
Top management commitment	• management time spent on diversity issues; • communication of diversity issues (such as number of references in formal speeches); • inclusion of diversity outcome targets in performance contract? If yes, what is the nature of the diversity outcome target? • commitment to diversity management structures (for example number of senior managers on diversity councils or equivalent).
Diversity strategy and plan	• diversity strategy in place; • 'quality' of diversity strategy; integration into overall corporate strategy; • annual diversity goals derived from that strategy; • 'quality' of these annual diversity goals.
Organizational policies	• Has recruitment policy been amended to take account of diversity strategy? • Has staff development policy been amended to take account of diversity strategy? • Have policies governing staff behaviour been amended to take account of diversity strategy?
Source: European Commission (2003, p. 39f).	

Table 7.5   Example indicators 2

Employment benefits	• diversity-related employment benefits in place (for example recognition of same-sex partners, retirement age and pension changes equal for men and women, adopted health care and holiday arrangements, childcare facilities, job-sharing, flexi-time, telecommuting, better access to facilities and the like); • uptake of diversity-related employment benefits (proportion of people from diversity groups using specific offers);
Managerial incentives	• managerial incentives included in performance contract; • measurement processes in place to assess management performance on diversity-related issues (for example 'upward feedback'); • incentives and processes – assessment of their nature and appropriateness.
Organizational structures	• structures in place to support diversity management (for example diversity council); • membership of these structures (for example number of senior managers involved); • diversity units in place (for example diversity teams or task forces) to monitor and support the process; • role and importance of diversity units, resources they can draw on.
Reporting process (monitoring and evaluation)	• systems in place to monitor diversity performance; • effectiveness of process (timeliness, penetration).
Communication	• number of positive and negative references to diversity-related issues in external media (TV, general press, specialist press); • assessment of the relevance and quality of these references; • number of positive and negative references to diversity in internal media (like intranet, company newsletter); • number of references (or minutes) in key speeches which deal with diversity-related issues.
Support networks	• existence of diversity support networks (such as gay, lesbian and transgender networks, women in management networks and other); • number of members in these networks; • the activity of networks (for instance number of meetings per year).
Education and training	• participation in diversity training (absolute numbers, proportion of specific groups; proportion of 'new' and 'existing' employees); • perceived value of such training measures amongst 'existing' and 'new' employees (for example via post-training assessment form); • impact of training on future development (link between attendance on training courses and retention or development of diversity groups).

Source: European Commission (2003, 40ff).

These indicators assess the quality of diversity measures which are already in place, and therefore cannot be employed in organizations where such initiatives are lacking. However, all of these indicators can be used to monitor the implementation process by assessing the progress of measures and evaluating their effectiveness.

The following 4-R method can be used to analyse the relevance of diversity issues in an organization. It provides a structured framework which can easily accommodate the CSES indicators and various questions previously proposed for diversity analysis.

The 4-R method

4-R is a refinement of the 3-R method developed in Sweden to assess the relevance of gender measures and projects implemented at the municipal level (Döge, 2002). The method can easily be transferred and applied to other contexts and diversity dimensions (Bendl, Hanappi-Egger and Hofmann, 2004; Warmuth, 2012). Here the gender focus will be expanded to include all relevant diversity dimensions. The original 3 Rs stand for *Representation*, *Resources* and *Realization*, to which Lange (2006) added a fourth, *Rights*.

Representation

Here 'representation' describes the proportion of employees belonging to a minority group who hold specific positions (such as in management) within an organization. This relates to the quantitative description and analysis of horizontal and vertical segregation (Lange, 2006). In the past two sections (diversity analysis and CSES indicators) we have looked at several concrete methods of obtaining relevant data which allow us to describe and evaluate the specific representation of members of diversity groups (defined by gender, ethnicity, age, disability, religion and so forth) in relevant positions, as well as in projects.

Resources

'Resources' refers to the distribution of scarce resources such as *money* (income, subsidies, and so on), *time* (time autonomy, time control and the like), *power* (formal and informal leadership), *knowledge* (access to expertise, experience, and so on), *space* (individual and collective space) and *personnel* and other (Lange, 2006, p. 167). This can be used to assess the 'importance' of projects according to the dedication of resources. Analysing the degree of importance of a project and the composition of project members in terms of diversity can reveal something about how diversity is dealt with. However, the dimension 'resources' can also be used to assess units or departments in a similar fashion, and thus is a useful tool to reveal hidden practices of devaluation and discrimination.

Realization

'Realization' refers to the qualitative survey of an organization's norms, values and principles which relate to diversity issues. The focus lies on potential reasons for inequalities in organizations, based on taken-for-granted, collective norms that produce inequalities. Likely fields of action and improvement can be derived from the realization analysis.

Some possible questions are (Lange, 2006, p. 168):

- What values, norms and principles relating to diversity help to mould action?
- What reasons can be found for the distribution of representation and resources as previously assessed?
- What specific barriers and disadvantages do people face due to their diversity characteristics?
- What action is needed to improve equality?

The basic goal of these questions of 'realization' is the achievement of equality, which also underlines the dimensions 'representation' and 'resources'. This is rather unsurprising, as the 3-R method was originally devised as a public sector tool. Diversity measures deduced from these questions target the equal opportunities of all employees.

Rights

'Rights' is the supplementary fourth dimension added to the method by Lange (2006). Here the object of concern is the external and environmental context in terms of legislation, instructions, rules and mission statements. It is crucial to take account of this framework of 'rights' in which an organization operates when designing a holistic diversity management programme. As the legal and normative context will vary from country to country, it is necessary to adapt such diversity initiatives to the requirements of subsidiary organizations operating abroad. Two useful questions to investigate the dimension 'rights' are (Lange, 2006):

- Do individuals displaying diversity in terms of gender, age, ethnicity, religion, disability and so on, have similar rights?
- Do there exist specific rules, laws or normative instructions which have an impact on diversity?

The 4-R method can be used to structure an organizational analysis using the four dimensions *Representation*, *Resources*, *Realization* and *Rights*. At the same time the questions presented previously – diversity analysis and the CSES indicators – can help suggest further lines of questioning to gain information about each of the four Rs.

Exercise 7.3

Adapt the questions listed under diversity analysis and CSES indicators to create ones more suitable for an investigation of the four Rs. Find at least 5 indicators and/or questions for the dimensions: Representation, Resources, Realization and Rights.

CONCLUSION

Organizational analysis is the first step in determining an organization's specific needs and potential forms of diversity management. Such analysis requires the gathering of basic information such as statistical data on the socio-demographics of employees and structural data relevant for diversity.

Workforce data should be supplemented by qualitative perception data obtained internally (from staff) or externally (from customers and rating agencies). An organizational analysis should enable the pinpointing of awareness-building measures and top-down activities, such as training events and communication campaigns, necessary to improve the situation in regard to diversity. Also the analysis should produce some information about bottom-up involvement programmes, such as employee networks, mentoring and support structures for specific groups, as well as analysis of the external outreach (diversity-specific external engagement, sponsoring and so on).

In general terms, the analysis phase of diversity management tackles the following four Ws: *Why* should we deal with diversity; *Where* do we get the relevant information; *Who* should be involved; and, *Which* first steps do we have to undertake? This chapter has taken a close look at tools used to conduct an organizational analysis. In our examples we have shown how these tools can be applied, while emphasizing that every company is uniquely embedded in its own context, and thus requires analytical tools specially adapted to the task at hand.

Chapter Review Questions

- Which tools of organizational analysis can you describe?
- In which stage(s) of the implementation process is organizational analysis relevant?
- What are the main differences between qualitative and quantitative methods of

analysis? Give a concrete example.
- Imagine a company which has had no experience of diversity management. How would you go about implementing an organizational analysis? Outline the processes and describe concrete methods of analysis.

Case Study

Diversity at L'Oréal

With €19.5 billion in consolidated sales in 2010, L'Oréal Group is the world's leading cosmetics and beauty products company. Established and headquartered in France, the group currently owns 23 brands such as *Garnier*, *The Body Shop*, *Maybelline*, *Ralph Lauren* and *Lancôme*. L'Oréal operates in 130 countries, and its staff of 66,000 encompasses 113 nationalities. Diversity is one

of the core values espoused by the managing board, and is seen as vital to the business strategy. Thus the company has placed diversity at the heart of all its activities. L'Oréal's website provides extensive information on diversity management, including the following ambitious goals:

1. To reflect the diversity of its customers in its sales teams, recruitment policies and every level of the company's operations;

2. to promote gender equity within its teams by promoting women to positions of responsibility and, for example, ensuring equal salaries;

3. to be recognized as a company which hires and promotes the disabled;

4. to valorise the work experience in anticipation of a longer working life by building up know-how and capitalizing on employees' experience; and

5. last but not least, to develop a managerial culture which fosters the inclusion of all and capitalizes on team diversity.

In order better to accomplish its ambitions regarding diversity, L'Oréal has decided to focus on six priority dimensions: nationality, ethnic origin, social promotion, gender, disability and age.

The aim of these six diversity dimensions is to reflect the composition of its customers and the countries in which the company operates. This is based on the notion that an enterprise will benefit from having a workforce that mirrors the demographics of the community in which it resides and does business (Heffes, 2009). In markets where diversity is either publically suppressed or even prohibited, L'Oréal can promote the values of diversity within its own community of workers, and hence influence general attitudes in society.

L'Oréal's commitment to diversity has been widely recognized and praised. The company has received several awards for its ethical business operations, and statistics show that L'Oréal really does promote women to top positions and keenly recruits staff of diverse nationalities and from various minority groups. One of the reasons why the company has succeeded in its diversity programme is that a link has been forged to the wider organizational strategy and mission. No successful diversity programme can be created and implemented in isolation; it has to be embedded within the general business goals of the enterprise (HR Focus, 2010).

There is no doubt that L'Oréal is committed to the active promotion of diversity. Yet the group acknowledges that certain gaps still exist in their six priority points, as can be seen in a diversity overview report that the company commissioned to examine its French operations.

The gaps which the report identified, as well as the recommendations it made, are largely based on data provided by L'Oréal France. Here our case study will focus on the dimensions *age* and *disability* (for other dimensions see the relevant chapters in this book).

Age

With regard to tackling ageism, L'Oréal's ambition is to promote a global human resource management policy that helps it retain all employees, particularly senior employees. One initiative in this context was an 'Agreement for the Employment of Senior Employees', signed by French subsidiary companies in December 2009, which provided for a career stage review and measures for tutorship and transmission of knowledge, as well as introducing end-of-career arrangements. Furthermore, in 2008 L'Oréal France also co-organized a public forum together with recruitment agencies entitled 'Employment and Diversity for Seniors'. The forum looked at how to optimize the 'second stage' of an employee's career, aiming to encourage other companies (in addition to L'Oréal's own business partners) to recognize senior employees as a valuable source of talent. In Canada, L'Oréal also recognises the differing work perspectives of younger (so-called 'Generation Y') and older staff members, implementing a training programme for all employees in 2006 entitled 'Creating Value for Intergenerational Differences'. The goal of this training programme is to 'demystify Generation Y', that is remove prejudices and taboos concerning these younger members of staff by encouraging open discussion between the three generations of employees within the company. At the same time it is hoped that these open discussions will create value through greater understanding, enhanced cooperation and improved work effectiveness. As a result of these initiatives to promote the recruitment of older staff, the company reported that at the end of 2009 the average age of workers employed by L'Oréal France was 42.5 years. A breakdown revealed that 33.4 per cent were aged over 45 years, and 24.4 per cent over 50 years, seen by L'Oréal France as an indication of success.

However, due to a lack of comparable data from other companies it is difficult to evaluate these results objectively. Moreover, while L'Oréal France seems to be achieving the goals it has set itself in this area, it would be interesting to know if the French subsidiaries who also signed the agreement, as well as other local and regional offices, have also seen progress in reducing the discrimination of older staff.

Disability

Another aim of L'Oréal is to promote the recruitment of disabled workers. To this end it has implemented numerous initiatives, some of which can be highlighted. As a basic step the company has participated in special diversity and disability forums (for example in France in 2006, Spain in 2009 and Italy in 2008 and 2009) and career fairs, helping to boost the recruitment of disabled people. Recognizing the value of young talent, L'Oréal has conducted a training scheme for young disabled persons in France and Spain. Every year 12 disabled apprentices are offered professional training contracts lasting six months, during which time tutors help them to develop their skills in a professional environment. L'Oréal also makes sure that its employees are fully aware of the company's positive stance towards the disabled, as well as measures to integrate them into the workplace. In France one step aimed at raising awareness of this issue was the organization of special events for both handicapped and able-bodied employees, such as demonstrations of wheelchair basketball by professional players at which those attending could also take part in team matches. The reaction to these events was reported to be positive, viewed by the disabled employees as an original way for the able-bodied to become better aware of the obstacles and potentials which disability brings.

Through these initiatives L'Oréal was able to report in 2009 that the proportion of disabled employees in the company's French operations had risen from 3.94 per cent to 4.71 per cent in the previous year, although the latter figure is still under the legal mandated level of 6 per cent. In other countries the figures for 2008 varied greatly: at L'Oréal Austria the rate of employment of handicapped persons was 0.5 per cent (below the legal obligation of 4 per cent), at L'Oréal Italy 7 per cent (in line with the legally mandated level), 0.5 per cent in Spain (under the legal obligation of 2 per cent) and 1 per cent in Greece (where the legal obligation is 8 per cent).

Thus, despite the extensive efforts by L'Oréal to raise awareness of the problems and prejudices which disabled people face at the workplace and on the job market, the striking disparities between L'Oréal's rates of employment of disabled staff and current legal requirements show that there is still much work to be done – even if the basic objective of promoting the issue of disabled persons at work has been achieved.

While L'Oréal is well on the way, through their own initiatives, to reconciling the gaps identified in each of their six priority points, a lot still needs to be done in order to achieve the organizational objectives which have been set.

Note: Marie-Thérèse Claes is the author of this case study.

Test Your Understanding

1. Try to identify the 4 Rs of the 4-R method in this example.
2. If you had to expand the diversity management programme at L'Oréal concerning age and disability, what further information would you need?
3. What methods could you use to get the missing information?

SOURCES AND FURTHER READING

L'Oréal Global websites

Diversity at L'Oréal (2010) L'Oréal Diversity Report, March 2010.

L'Oréal website (2011) Diversity Policy http://www.lOréal.com/_en/_ww/html/our-company/our-policy.aspx, date accessed 25 November 2011.

L'Oréal website (2011a), Diversity Statement, http://www.lOréal.com/_en/_ww/html/our-company/diversity-is-a-priority.aspx, date accessed 26 November 2011.

L'Oréal website (2011b),Diversity Involvement, http://www.lOréal.com/_en/_ww/html/our-company/our-involvments.aspx, date accessed 26 November 2011.

REFERENCES

Accenture (2011) Inclusion & Diversity at Accenture, http://www.accenture.com/us-en/company/people/diversity/, date accessed 24 January 2012.

*Acker, J. (1992) 'Gendering Organizational Theory' in A. Mills and P. Tranced (eds) *Gendering Organizational Analysis* (Newbury Park: Sage): 248–60.

Air Berlin (2011) Service on Board, http://www.airberlin.com/site/flug_service_an_bord.php?LANG=eng&checkNavi=1, date accessed 21 December 2011.

H.-J. Aretz and K. Hansen (2003) 'Erfolgreiches Management von Diversity. Die multikulturelle Organisation als Strategie zur Verbesserung einer nachhaltigen Wettbewerbsfähigkeit', *Zeitschrift für Personalforschung*, 17 (1), 9–36.

BACA (2011) Unser Engagement für die Nachhaltigkeit, http://www.bankaustria.at/de/open.html#/de/28098.html, date accessed 21 December 2011.

R. Bendl, E. Hanappi-Egger and R. Hofmann (2004) 'Spezielle Methoden der Organisationsstudien' in R. Bendl, E. Hanappi-Egger and R. Hofmann (eds) *Interdisziplinäres Gender- und Diversitätsmanagement* (Wien: Linde Verlag), pp. 73–101.

*A. Blickhäuser and H. von Bargen (2005) 'Gender- Mainstreaming- Praxis Arbeitshilfe zur Anwendung der Analysekategorie "Gender" in Gender- Mainstreaming- Prozessen', *Schriftenreihe zur Geschlechterdemokratie*, 12 (Berlin: Heinrich Böll Stiftung).

C. Brotherton (2003) 'Is Diversity Inevitable? Age and Ageism in the Future of Employment' in M. Davidson and S. Fielden (eds) *Individual Diversity and Psychology in Organisations* (Hoboken: John Wiley).

*C. Cassell (2006) *Essential Guide to Qualitative Methods in Organization Research* (London: Sage).

J. W. Creswell and C. V. Plaro (2011) *Designing and Conducting Mixed Methods Research* (Los Angeles: Sage).

European Commission (2003) *Methods and Indicators to Measure the Cost-Effectiveness of Diversity Policies in Enterprises*, October, catalogue no. KE-55-03-899-EN-N.

*P. Dass and B. Parker (1999) 'Strategies for Managing Human Resource Diversity: From Resistance to Learning', *Academy of Management Executive*, 13 (2), 68–80.

A. Diekmann (2003) *Empirische Sozialforschung. Grundlagen, Methoden, Anwendungen* (Reinbek/Hamburg: Rowohlt).

Diversity at L'Oréal (2010) *L'Oréal Diversity Report*, March 2010.

P. Döge (2002) 'Gender Mainstreaming als Modernisierung von Organisationen. Ein Leitfaden für Frauen und Männer', *IAIZ – Schriften*, 2 (Berlin).

S. Gherardi (2003) 'Feminist Theory and Organizational Theory. A Dialogue on New Ideas' in H. Tsoukas and C. Knudsen (eds) *Oxford Handbook of Organization Theory* (Oxford: University Press): 210–36.

*J. Gilbert, B. A. Stead and J. M. Ivancevich (1999) 'Diversity Management: A New Organizational Paradigm', *Journal of Business Ethics*, 21, 61–76.

*B. G. Glaser and A. L. Strauss (1979) 'Die Entdeckung gegenstandsbezogener Theorie: Eine Grundstrategie qualitativer Sozialforschung', in C. Hopf and E. Weingarten (eds) *Qualitative Sozialforschung* (Stuttgart: Klett), pp. 91–111.

M. 89) 'Private Experiences in the Public Domain: Lesbians in Organizations' in J. Hearn, D. Sheppard, P. Tancred-Sheriff and G. Burrell (eds) *The Sexuality of Organization* (London: Sage): 125–38.

E. Hanappi-Egger and R. Hofmann (2012) 'Diversitätsmanagement unter der Perspektive organisationalen Lernens: Wissens- und Kompetenzentwicklung für inklusive Organisationen' in R. Bendl, E. Hanappi-Egger and R. Hofmann (eds) *Diversität und Diversitätsmanagement* (Wien: Facultas WUV), pp. 327–50.

*J. Hayes (2007) *The Theory and Practice of Change Management,* 2nd edn (Basingstoke and New York: Palgrave Macmillan).

E. M. Heffes (2009) 'Diversity & Inclusion', *Financial Executive.* 25 (1), 52–5.

HR Focus (2010) 'Link Diversity to Business Goals for Best Results', *HR Focus*, 87 (1), 5–10.

*R. Lange (2006) *Gender Kompetenz für das Change Management* (Bern, Stuttgart and Vienna: Haupt Verlag).

M. Lueger (2000) *Grundlagen qualitativer Sozialforschung* (Wien: WUV).

Microsoft (2011) Microsoft Diversity and Inclusion, http://www.microsoft.com/about/diversity/en/us/default.aspx, date accessed 21 December 2011.

Pannonjob (2012) Kiemelt állásajánlataink, http://www.pannonjob.hu/, date accessed 24 January 2012.

*A. Prasad (2003) 'The Gaze of the Other: Postcolonial Theory and Organizational Analysis' in A. Prasad (ed.) *Postcolonial Theory and Organizational Analysis. A Critical Engagement* (New York: Palgrave Macmillan): 3–43.

G. Robinson and K. Dechant (1997) 'Building a Business Case for Diversity', *Academy of Management Executive,* 11 (3), 21–30.

*A. Schulz (2009) *Strategisches Diversitätsmanagement* (Wiesbaden: Gabler).

P. Senge (2000) *The Dance of Change* (Wien and Hamburg: Signum Verlag).

B. Smith (1996) 'Working choices' in G. Hales (ed.) *Beyond Disability. Towards an Enabling Society* (London: Sage): 145–61.

L. Swift and S. Piff (2010) *Quantitative Methods for Business, Management* and Finance (Basingstoke: Palgrave Macmillan).

Volkswagen Financial Services (2011) Diversity Management, http://www.vwfsag.de/content/sites/vwcorporate/vwfsag_de/en/home/einstieg_und_karriere/wir_als_arbeitgeber/our_diversity_management.html, date accessed 21 December 2011

G. S. Warmuth (2012) 'Die strategische Implementierung von Diversitätsmanagement in Organisationen' in R. Bendl, E. Hanappi-Egger and R. Hofmann (eds) *Diversität und Diversitätsmanagement* (Wien: Facultas. WUV), pp. 203–36.

CHAPTER 8

ORGANIZATIONAL IMPLEMENTATION: DIVERSITY PRACTICES AND TOOLS

Annette Risberg, Alexandra Beauregard and Gudrun Sander

Chapter Objectives

After completing this chapter, you should be able to:
- understand the challenges in implementing diversity management in companies;
- understand the interplay between structures, cultures and practices that lead to more (or less) diversity in an organization;
- identify key processes in HR management that must be improved in order to reach a culture of diversity and inclusion;
- describe, compare and discuss various diversity practices;
- analyse the positive and negative aspects of various diversity practices;
- review the roles of different 'players' in top and middle management (including HR management) as well as diversity officers, diversity committees, network groups and so on;
- identify and describe various forms of resistance to diversity;
- discuss why resistance occurs;
- explain how to overcome resistance to diversity.

Chapter Outline

- Introduction
- Organizing and positioning diversity work
- Changing discriminatory structures
- The role of strategies, planning and budgeting – mainstreaming gender and diversity
- Diversity practices as a function of human resources
- Diversity practices as a leadership task and management responsibility
- Dealing with resistance to diversity
- Conclusion
- Chapter review questions
- Case study
- References

INTRODUCTION

There can be a range of reasons why organizations decide to engage in diversity work, but in most cases such work will begin with an internal organizational assessment, a written policy and the implementation of a programme of awareness training. However, in order to reduce discrimination, foster inclusion and have a *lasting* impact, these efforts must be backed up by systemic and structural change, accompanied by genuine support and understanding from management. Furthermore, if diversity is simply pigeonholed as a 'human resources issue', then the full benefits will not be felt outside the HR department. It is clear that all levels of an organization must be engaged in diversity work, and that the active support of senior management is essential.

This chapter begins with a description of how diversity work can be organized and positioned within the organization. Thereafter we outline the various steps that organizations can take in order to change potentially discriminatory structures and improve the treatment of diversity, followed by a discussion of gender and diversity policies and missions (which often constitute the initial stage of any diversity work). After describing how existing structures and practices can be analysed in order to detect discrimination and bias, we examine the role of training, recruitment, networking and mentoring programmes in creating a diverse workplace. As many discriminatory structures can be found lurking within an organization's strategic processes, the areas of budgeting and planning are addressed as crucial for gender and diversity management. HR practices and tools to create an inclusive workplace are discussed. We then look at measures that individual managers and other staff members can take to create a more inclusive workplace, while reviewing various conceptions of effective and successful practices in diversity management. The chapter closes with a discussion of resistance to diversity within organizations, and how this phenomenon can be reduced.

ORGANIZING AND POSITIONING DIVERSITY WORK

It is true that diversity practices are part of the daily work of an HR department such as recruitment, training, remuneration and the improvement of working conditions. Yet the issue of diversity must not be defined as a topic relevant only to human resources: if diversity management is to have an impact on daily organizational life, then it must be incorporated into all existing levels and practices (Risberg, 2010). Later in the chapter we will argue that diversity must be the responsibility of managers at every level (Foster and Harris, 2005). Indeed, every single employee must be encouraged to think, behave and act in ways which promote a culture of diversity and inclusion.

Diversity work will vary depending on where it is located in the organizational hierarchy. At the highest level it takes the form of organizational policies and inclusion in the mission statement, fixing guidelines for diversity management. A dedicated committee made up of representatives of different departments and units of the organization is often convened in order to implement diversity initiatives at the various organizational levels on behalf of senior management. The members of diversity committees are often called 'diversity champions' (Omanović, 2006) or 'diversity ambassadors' (Subeliani and Tsogas, 2005). Such committees, which ideally should include representatives from different hierarchical levels of the organization, are typically charged with overseeing diversity initiatives, identifying potential remedies and monitoring progress (Kalev, Kelly and Dobbin, 2006).

The committees may be made up of specially selected employees or open to all staff members. The HSBC in Canada, for example, operates a programme in which employees at all hierarchical levels can become a diversity ambassador, thereby fostering diversity work throughout the workforce and the customer base (HSBC, 2010). In the Netherlands, the diversity manager for Rabobank has created a diversity network of employees – the 'ambassadors of diversity' – of different ethnic backgrounds selected from various local branches, departments and hierarchical levels (Subeliani and Tsogas, 2005). This network meets twice a year to discuss problems, achievements, ongoing projects and future plans related to diversity. Members receive regular newsletters and training, so that the network functions as an important tool to disseminate information about diversity and to raise awareness in the organization for this issue (Subeliani and Tsogas, 2005).

Diversity committees in Switzerland, for example, are often supported in their work by a dedicated diversity manager or an equal opportunity service centre that implements individual diversity measures. This form of organization is very similar to that of other work fields with a multi-functional impact such as accounting, marketing, legal or environmental services.

Furthermore, diversity work must be an integral part of all organizational activities (whether group or individual tasks) at all levels, that is from 'top to bottom'. In addition, adequate resources must be made available: 'If managers are to be expected to be responsible for a new function – managing diversity – then they should be given time and resources to make that effort useful' (Pitts, 2007, p. 1581). Managing diversity should not just be one more task pencilled onto an existing 'to do' list, in which case there is little chance of diversity work being taken seriously.

Let us turn to a concrete example: in Sweden all organizations with more than 25 employees are obliged to present a newly revised equality plan every three years. In one particular municipality (the subject of a study by Annette

Risberg) the local politicians decided that each administrative service should write an update and follow-up to a diversity plan on an annual basis. A range of plans was drawn up for each administrative service; in one city district sub-plans were produced for each separate operative area, namely a school and childcare plan, a health and social care plan, a social welfare plan, a social work plan and so on. Only a few selected line managers were active participants in the writing of these plans, in which various diversity goals were set for each year. Almost all of these goals (for example an increase in the number of male staff working in childcare facilities) were quantitative in nature, making it easy to determine whether the goal had been achieved by the end of the year. In general, the plans changed little from year to year. After observing the treatment of diversity plans, the researcher had the impression that goals were monitored to see if they had been achieved, and then 'cut and pasted' from one year to the next with only minor amendments. When the plan was updated, the responsible manager ticked the task as 'completed', thus regarding the diversity work for the entire year as finished. One possible explanation of such behaviour could have been lack of time on the part of the line managers to tackle the additional responsibility of diversity work. Or perhaps the managers had little idea how to implement diversity work into their daily operations: 'New programs decoupled from everyday practice often have no impact' (Kalev, Kelly and Dobbin, 2006, p. 591). One way of remedying this problem is to link diversity achievements to remuneration. For example, the multinational pharmaceutical company, Novartis, has tied its bonus system to the reaching of diversity targets. A manager can only receive the maximum bonus if s/he has fully contributed to the diversity goals of the company. Of course, for such a system to be effective, key performance indicators must be established for these goals. Procter & Gamble, for instance, bases its management pay on specific diversity indicators. The managers there are in part judged on how their teams respond to a staff survey on diversity. Workers are asked questions about how well their manager is driving diversity efforts, and how comfortable they feel expressing concerns about diversity (Personnel Today, 2008).

As part of their diversity work some organizations may decide to appoint a *diversity manager* (Tatli and Özbilgin, 2009) or a *chief diversity officer* (Thomas, 2004). Although the role of such a dedicated manager may vary from organization to organization, this position is generally charged with identifying diversity needs, developing diversity plans and strategies, and implementing these with the support of line managers. Indeed, Tatli and Özbilgin (2009) emphasize the importance of diversity managers by labelling them 'change agents'. Kalev, Kelly and Dobbin (2006) write that diversity-related change is likely to be more effective if such a diversity manager, or a diversity committee, is appointed. They claim that dedicated managers and committees are more effective than annual diversity training sessions, periodic evaluations or decentralized networking and mentoring programmes. Certainly it is vital that accountability and responsibility for diversity work and organizational change be clearly assigned. 'In organizations that do not assign responsibility for diversity goals to a specific office, person, or group, these goals may fall by the wayside' (Kalev, Kelly and Dobbin, 2006, p. 591).

> A *diversity manager* or *chief diversity officer* is responsible for guiding efforts to define, assess, nurture and cultivate diversity as an organizational resource. Following the organization's diversity policy, the diversity manager works to promote a culture of diversity and inclusion through the support and coaching of managers and employees, while monitoring cultural diversity within the organization. Diversity officers support line managers in achieving the designated diversity goals.

Diversity management in large companies is usually structured so that diversity managers are obliged to report to more than one manager (so-called 'dotted-line' reporting structure – that is, when a person reports to one manager while also underlying the authority of another) (see Figure 8.1). At the top of the organizational chart there is an appointed head of diversity, who may be part of the management board or who may function as an advisor to the chief executive officer (CEO). At the next level we find diversity managers, who are responsible for business units or subsidiaries. Although these diversity managers report to the head of diversity regarding diversity issues, at the same time they belong to their

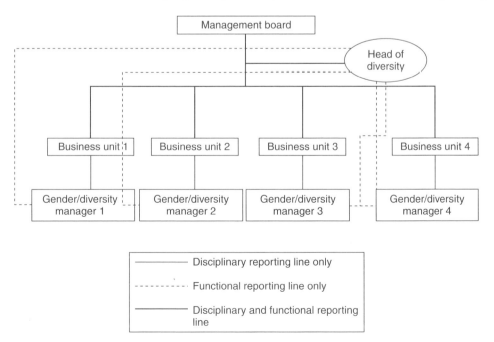

Figure 8.1   Organizational integration of diversity management in large companies
Source: Adapted from Müller and Sander (2009, p. 153).

respective units and thus report to the line manager. Organizing diversity work in this way ensures that there exists a person responsible for promoting diversity work at all levels and in every unit of the enterprise. This means, in turn, that the central diversity policy is implemented locally and with regard to the various challenges at the level of the business unit.

After this discussion of how diversity work can be organized, we will now examine the wide range of measures and tools available for diversity management. In particular, we intend to look at various measures and tools that can transform discriminatory structures into ones that contribute to a more inclusive environment.

CHANGING DISCRIMINATORY STRUCTURES

Müller and Sander have pointed out some key factors that they believe can contribute to the successful transformation of an organization by fostering diversity and developing a culture of inclusion (Müller and Sander, 2005; 2009). They mention the need for resources (expertise, money and personnel), support from senior management, diversity policies, measurable goals, transparency, clearly identified processes and responsibilities, as well as endurance on the part of the primary actors. A first milestone on the path towards increased diversity is usually a declaration in the company's mission statement regarding the importance of diversity. The next step tends to be the establishment of a diversity management policy, developed by a diversity manager together with the managing director and the head of human resources. Of course, it is a long road from a declared intention to a daily routine, and so the question arises: how can we breathe life into this paperwork? To try to find an answer, let us first turn to diversity management policies and mission statements.

> *Positive action* refers to proportionate measures intended to foster full and effective equality for members of groups that are socially or economically disadvantaged, or otherwise suffer the consequences of past or present discrimination.

> *Equal opportunities* (EO) refers to an equal distribution of opportunities for education, training, employment, career development and the exercise of power, so that individuals are not disadvantaged on the basis of their sex, race, language, religion, economic or family situation, or any other factor.

Diversity management policies and mission statements

There is some debate in academic circles as to whether diversity should be broadly or narrowly defined (Subeliani and Tsogas, 2005). When defined broadly, diversity may encompass all types of difference. For example, Friday and Friday (2003, p. 863) define diversity as 'any attribute that happens to be salient to an individual that makes him/her perceive that he/she is different from another individual'. A narrow definition tends to focus on characteristics stemming from anti-discrimination issues, for example, gender, ethnicity or sexual orientation. This discussion on definition has its origin in differing viewpoints: should diversity mainly focus on anti-discrimination measures (equal opportunities, positive action) or on managing diversity to maximize the utilization of employee potential? This debate is reflected in organizations' policies and mission statements. In fact, most organizations incorporate both anti-discrimination and diversity management policies into their official policy statements (Risberg and Søderberg, 2008). For example, the Danish pharmaceutical company Novo Nordisk A/S sees diversity as an organizational resource, while simultaneously seeking to ensure that no employee suffers discrimination.

Example

From Novo Nordisk's annual report on diversity (2010)

Diversity

Diversity is important to Novo Nordisk; it allows us to better understand customer needs, attract and retain talented people, and operate more effectively in a global business environment. Diversity fosters an international mindset that enhances innovation as well as our ability to work cross-culturally and expand into new markets. It also gives us a better understanding of the societies in which we operate.

We have had a diversity strategy since 2009, which includes the aspiration that within five years all senior management teams must be diverse in terms of gender and nationality.

Approach

Developing a diverse organization at all managerial levels enables the globalisation of the company, reflects our social responsibility, and ensures future business success. It is our firm belief that a diverse organization produces better business results.

In recruitment, we select the best individual for a particular position while ensuring equal opportunities and non-discrimination as part of our values-based framework.

The foundation of Novo Nordisk's approach to diversity is guided by the United Nations Universal Declaration of Human Rights. People seeking employment with Novo Nordisk, or those already employed with the company, have the right not to be discriminated against because of their background in respect of gender, sexual orientation, age, disability, marital status, religion, colour, race, ethnic origin or political orientation. Novo Nordisk works to ensure equal opportunities with regard to recruitment, conditions at work, remuneration, training and promotion, and termination of employment.

Performance

Diversity in the organization stimulates engagement and innovation. Novo Nordisk puts great emphasis on enhancing opportunities for current and future employees and creating an inclusive environment where individual differences are valued and respected.

Source: Novo Nordisk, 2011.

IBM is well known for adopting a business case approach to diversity in its operations. For example, it attempts to bridge the gap between the workplace and the marketplace by using internal diversity to learn more about existing and potential customers:

> By deliberately seeking ways to more effectively reach a broader range of customers IBM has seen significant bottom-line results. For example, the work of the women's task force and other constituencies led IBM to establish its Market Development organization, a group focused on growing the market of multicultural and women-owned businesses in the United States. (Thomas, 2004, p. 99)

In general, a statement of diversity policy is an important document in serving to guide managers and other staff in their diversity work. It must be specific and coherent (Pitts, 2007). A good start is to invite senior management, together with the diversity manager, to determine the main goals regarding diversity (Keil, Amershi, Holmes, Jablonski, Lüthi, Matoba, Plett and von Unruh, 2007). The following questions should be answered when formulating such goals:

* How will the organization benefit from implementing diversity work?
* What orientation of our diversity work are we aiming for (EO or the business case for diversity, or both)?
* What forms of diversity do we wish to focus on?
* Which main processes and functional areas of the organization will be affected by diversity work?

The resulting objectives must then be specified and addressed in the mission statement and policy documents. Managers and employees must be given specific guidelines on how to fulfil these objectives (Pitts, 2007). One may discern that the vague policies and statements often posted on company websites are not always designed to be read by employees, but are rather intended to demonstrate to external stakeholders that the organization is addressing the issue of diversity. Any working policy document which is intended to initiate internal change must, of course, include detailed steps and measurable goals.

Review Questions

Read through the diversity policies of Novo Nordisk again and consider the following questions:
* Is the policy mainly oriented towards EO or the business case for diversity?
* Who is affected by the policy (employees, customers, owners, managers or anyone else), and who will benefit from the diversity work? In which ways will they benefit?
* What are the goals of diversity work?
* Could the diversity policy function as a concrete guideline for diversity work?

Analysing existing structures and practices

Another important early step in diversity work is to determine which areas of the organization show a lack of diversity, and whether actions are required to remedy this. It may be necessary to analyse existing data on personnel (Cox and Blake, 1991), for example in terms of the representation of majority as well as minority women at various levels, the representation of employees with different ethnic backgrounds, as well as the salary levels of minority groups. Much of this information will already by captured by existing HR systems. However, we should note that many countries forbid the keeping of records on employees' ethnicity, religion or other personal characteristics. In Sweden and Denmark, for example, an organization may only hold records of the sex and age of their employees. If an organization wants to find out how many of its employees have an immigrant background, they may have to send personnel files to the national bureau of statistics for cross-tabulation.

Analyses such as these are not always sufficient to address inequalities and foster diversity. Often one discovers hidden discriminatory practices lurking within the structures of the organization, from where they act to prevent an organization from achieving its diversity goals. In this case it is necessary to conduct an analysis of these structures in order to uncover, and change, their discriminatory nature (Kalev, Kelly and Dobbin, 2006). One could, for example, begin by analysing whether *occupational segregation* is a feature of the organization. This requires an investigation of the backgrounds of employees at all levels and in various departments, units and groups. It may, for instance, become clear that staff in one unit is largely low-educated minority women while in another they are white middle-aged men with an engineering degree. Or perhaps the organization has no disabled staff. When such patterns have been detected, the next step is to analyse and understand how they have emerged. This can be achieved by performing a critical analysis of current HR practices such as recruitment and selection procedures, criteria for job entry, selection tools, performance appraisals and rates of compensation (Shen, Chanda, D'Netto and Monga, 2009). Thus, for example, if the skills stipulated as necessary for a certain position are investigated, it may turn out that these have not been critically reviewed for some time, and indeed may no longer be necessary to carry out the advertised job. Thus it is not uncommon to read that a firm is seeking a candidate fluent in a particular language, even though the job neither requires the writing of formal letters nor close contact with customers. Other stipulated skills may be possible to learn on the job. Consider this example: a company wishes to advertise for a caretaker to look after a number of rental properties. Previously it has always been considered necessary that caretakers should be skilled in pruning trees. This is, however, a task that they are seldom called upon to perform. In fact, the stipulated skill has discouraged many competent caretakers from applying for the job. After carefully analysing the skills actually needed for the position, the company's management decides not to include pruning as a requirement in the job advertisement. The result is that they receive many applications from highly competent people. The person who gets the job is then sent on a training course to learn how to prune trees.

Some job descriptions and job ads are gender or culture biased, even though the manager drawing up the list may be unconscious of this. For example, Gaucher, Friesen and Kay (2011, p. 109) have demonstrated that 'gendered wording commonly employed in job recruitment materials can maintain gender inequality in traditionally male-dominated occupations'. When a job advertisement contains stereotypically masculine wording such as 'leader', 'competitive' or 'dominant', Gaucher, Friesen and Kay (2011) have found that these words can discourage female candidates. The women in their study did not refrain from applying because they saw themselves as lacking skills required for the job; rather they did not apply because the choice of words signalled to them that 'women do not belong'. It is thus imperative that job descriptions and job advertisements use gender and culturally *neutral* language as well as expressions which explicitly embrace diversity.

Occupational segregation is the tendency of particular social groups (for example men, women and immigrants) to be overly represented in certain kinds of jobs at different hierarchical levels in the organization. For example, immigrant women are often employed in low level, low paid jobs such as in the fields of caring and cleaning, while majority men are overly represented in technically-oriented fields, such as construction or engineering jobs.

Promotion is another practice which often displays bias for majority men. The 'glass (or concrete) ceiling' is a term used to describe the well-established phenomenon that the higher one goes up the hierarchical ladder, the fewer majority women and minority employees one finds (Liff, 1997; D'Netto and Sohal, 1999; Kirton and Greene, 2010). Each organization must investigate the reasons for such bias. Instead of relying on the dubious argument that 'there are no competent women or people with an immigrant background available to promote', management must seek to understand the nature of the structures and mechanisms underlying promotion decisions that lead to *homosocial reproduction* (Chapter 5). Which stipulated competencies lead to the appointment of white middle-aged men with a certain educational background to management positions? And how are the candidates for promotion identified? Is it necessary to belong to informal networks (such as golf clubs or after-work drinking parties), or are certain types of gendered or culture-specific behaviour favoured over others (for example some forms of aggressive or assertive behaviour)? Vinkenburg, van Engen, Eagly and Johannesen-Schmidt (2011) have found, for instance, that women and men were expected to perform *different* kinds of leadership styles in order to be promoted to managerial positions: 'Inspirational motivation was perceived as more important for men than women and especially important for promotion to CEO. In contrast, individualized consideration was perceived as more important for women than men and especially important for promotion to senior management.' (Vinkenburg et al., 2011, p. 18f.) Organizations must dare to ask questions about such practices in order to reveal underlying patterns that inhibit a culture of diversity. Such in-depth analysis will provide a firm basis from which to fix clear goals when attempting to transform discriminatory structures.

Homosocial reproduction refers to the phenomenon that individuals involved in the recruitment or promotion process select candidates who most closely resemble themselves.

Diversity training

Diversity training is one of the most visible and, to some extent, do-able aspects of diversity work. Although the importance of such training has been recognized by both practitioners and researchers, the focus of efforts varies (Hite and McDonald, 2006). Training initiatives can be aimed at developing an *awareness* of diversity at an individual level, in particular an awareness of what diversity is and which benefits it can bring to the organization; or the aim can be to disseminate diversity-related legal issues (often anti-discrimination); or to develop *skills* for a diverse work environment, and to apply those skills to improve and change the organization (Hite and McDonald, 2006). Research has found that the goals of diversity training generally look to:

> (a) improve the work environment among all employees by making employees aware of bias and discrimination, (b) improve the nature of work relationships by helping trainees acknowledge their own biases and prejudices, and generate coping strategies for dealing with these biases, and (c) improve employee performance and, consequently, the organization's performance by helping everyone understand how diversity can be an asset and developing skills to capitalize on this asset. (Cocchiara, Connerley and Bell, 2010, p. 1096)

While the first two goals are addressed by awareness training, the latter goal is achieved through skills training.

The impact of diversity training is difficult to predict and control. One reason for this is that when an organization becomes more diverse, its structures and culture must also change (Cox and Blake, 1991). Another reason is that training concerns the attitudes, values and experiences of individuals, all of which are difficult, if not impossible, to control. Training alone may not have a lasting impact on the individual and his or her behaviour. Even if the primary message has been absorbed, it is difficult to integrate the newly acquired experiences and knowledge into daily operations and workplace routines if not all co-workers receive similar training, or if the organizational structures, values and culture are not aligned with the content of the training sessions. Thus it is vital that training forms only one link in a chain of diversity work, and that such training measures be constantly reinforced and reiterated. Unfortunately, some organizations see diversity training as a one-time effort. This runs contrary to research which has found that change is unlikely to follow from a single diversity training event, but rather that such training must take place continuously throughout a person's career (Roberson, Kulik and Pepper, 2001). In addition, diversity training must be adapted to the organization in order to be effective. Cocchiara, Connerley and Bell (2010) have examined some factors that should be taken into consideration when designing training measures, including:

- The need for diversity – the design of training measures will depend on how diverse and inclusive the organization currently is.
- The company's perception of diversity – do staff embrace or resist diversity? (see also the end of this chapter).
- Company objectives for diversity training – as with any diversity work, management must decide why they feel that such training is necessary, and what the goal of training should be.

Of course, it is an impossible task to describe and list all types of diversity training. Therefore, we focus here on two common generic goals in diversity training: to raise awareness and to develop skills and competences.

Awareness training is the kind of training most organizations first adopt (Wiethoff, 2004). It is a standard form of diversity training, useful for trainees with limited experience of diversity. The training aims to increase an awareness of diversity and to sensitize workers to different kinds of values and norms, behaviours and interaction patterns (Wiethoff, 2004) that may impede daily interaction between individuals. The training is often designed so that staff can 'experience' diversity directly and share their experiences with each other. It is therefore beneficial if awareness training takes place in heterogeneous groups in order to foster interaction between people of different backgrounds (Roberson, Kulik and Pepper, 2001). Awareness training programmes should encourage employees to explore their feelings about diversity, to increase tolerance and understanding among diverse work groups, and to build an appreciation of the value of diversity. Awareness training may also aim to create an organizational consensus about the value of diversity in order to improve individual and organizational outcomes (Shen et al., 2009). The content of an awareness programme typically includes problems of discrimination in the workplace, the role of stereotypes in discrimination, the provision of equal employment opportunity or anti-discrimination laws, and an examination of the cultures of various minority groups. Techniques such as self-awareness exercises and role-playing are frequently employed (Bendick, Egan and Lofhjelm, 2001). However, awareness training alone is not sufficient to change an organization. Employees must also learn the skills necessary to implement all that they have learned during training measures (Hite and McDonald, 2006).

Skills training is another form of training that aims to teach participants how to handle diversity in the workplace. The focus here is on building skills and competencies to enable each employee to utilize the diversity and differences among co-workers to make better business decisions (Anand and Winters, 2008). One aim is to change the behaviour of staff members in order to foster a more inclusive organization. Research suggests that initiatives that focus on developing and practising new ways of acting and speaking are more likely to have a lasting effect on post-training behaviour (Bendick, Egan, and Lofhjelm, 2001). The content and methods of a skills training programme can typically include exercises on how to make different groups feel welcome in the workplace, an analysis of the organization's diversity policies, tips on how to recruit without discriminating, how to conduct non-discriminatory employee evaluations and promotions, and how to retain and develop minority groups (Bendick, Egan, and Lofhjelm, 2001).

One company with experience in diversity training is IBM Netherlands (IBM Netherlands, 2012). A strong believer that the key to managing diversity is inclusive leadership, IBM defines such leadership as 'creating a corporate culture where people feel respected and rewarded, regardless of differences and similarities'. In order to foster this, IBM provides international leadership training in diversity. Several executives from the Dutch subsidiary (and their local diversity coordinator) who participated in this training programme claim that they were made aware of the fact that diversity implies the inclusion of all employees. One exercise, in particular, was mentioned because it clearly showed how every individual sometimes feels excluded from a group, and that this experience is almost universally experienced as negative. The participants of the training initiative came to understand that diversity is something that concerns all employees, and not just those belonging to a minority. IBM strongly believes that this greater understanding forms the basis for inclusive leadership (IBM Netherlands, 2012).

Bendick, Egan, and Lofhjelm (2001) have identified nine benchmarks for effective diversity training. They state that the most common type of training, which focuses on individual attitudes, has only modest results. Effectiveness increases when training is more comprehensive, addressing individual behaviour, organizational systems and employer performance goals. The criteria are as follows:

1. the training must have strong support from senior management;
2. it must be tailored to the company;
3. it must link diversity to central operational goals;
4. the trainers should be managerial or organizational development professionals;
5. all employees at all organizational levels must participate;
6. discrimination should be discussed as a general process, and not one which affects only certain minority groups;
7. the training should explicitly address individual behaviour;
8. it must be complemented by changes in human resource practices;
9. it should impact the corporate culture.

These nine benchmarks indicate that training alone is insufficient to make an organization more diverse and inclusive, but constitutes only one part of a programme of diversity management.

Networking programmes

It is common for larger companies to organize networks programmes. These programmes are established to assist majority women and minority group men and women. The networks provide an opportunity for community building and the exchange of information and experiences, as well as to obtain career advice and support. Some networks may be more active in proposing policy changes or even diversity programmes to senior management (Kalev, Kelly and Dobbin, 2006), while others may meet simply for discussion in order to share experiences. The structure of these networks can vary, taking the form of regular meetings, informal after-work get-togethers, large annual conferences or virtual networks that operate list servers across multinational companies. Networks may be initiated by any employee from senior management down.

Lesbian, gay, bisexual and transgendered (LGBT) individuals at the Danish railroad company DSB initiated a network for mutual support (DSB, 2012a; 2012b; 2012c). In Sweden a similar network was set up by municipality employees of the city of Malmö, later sanctioned by senior management (field observations by Annette Risberg). The Swedish Volvo group has for many years operated a programme called 'employee networks', serving to support various minority groups. Volvo's management believes that such networks not only foster the career development of underrepresented groups, but also provide valuable employee feedback on individual programmes and policies (Volvo, 2011). Thus the networks are understood to provide benefits to both minority employees as well as the company itself. In addition to these employee networks,

Volvo maintains networks for people who work actively with diversity issues, so-called Regional Diversity Networks. These networks serve as platforms for the exchange of experiences and ideas on how to manage diversity.

Example

Volvo networks

Employee Networks

In addition to the organization-based networks, Volvo management supports the creation of Employee Network Groups, which are based on an element of diversity. The Volvo Group believes that networks such as these enhance our ability to provide the needed career development and support opportunities for various groups within the company, as well as providing valuable feedback on various company programs and policies.

Regional Diversity Networks

Regional Diversity Networks have been created within several countries. The members of the networks are individuals who work actively with diversity initiatives and programmes within the Group. The networks create an opportunity for sharing new ideas and informing other Volvo entities within the same country of ongoing programmes within each other's business areas. This internal sharing of best practices will enable Volvo to create a comprehensive and innovative diversity program within each country. In addition, it will facilitate collaboration for development and implementation of programmes.

Source: Volvo, 2012.

Mentoring programmes

Mentoring programmes are organized as a means to help majority women and minority group men and women advance to the upper echelons of the organizational hierarchy. For example, research undertaken in the United States of America (USA) has found that 'women and African Americans are crowded in the lowest ranks of management' (Kalev, Kelly and Dobbin, 2006, p. 590). Advocates for formal mentoring programmes argue that these provide majority women and certain minorities with the kind of relationships that majority men forge through 'old boy networks'. The idea behind mentoring is to match aspiring managers with a senior mentor, who already enjoys a successful career. The mentee and mentor meet regularly for career counselling and advice. However, while such efforts may help members of minority groups to become higher ranking managers, they do not change the underlying organizational structures, which act to prevent minority employees from reaching the first rung of the managerial career ladder. Mentoring programmes are thus unlikely to succeed on their own, but must be supplemented by other diversity efforts.

IBM Denmark is an active proponent of mentoring programmes. In this case the programmes are rather broad, targeting a wide array of minority and majority group men and women. Also included are cross-generational as well as cross-cultural matching programmes in order to transfer and harness knowledge across generations and cultures. The programmes are aimed at all employees. No less than 70 per cent of female staff at IBM Denmark are currently being mentored (IBM Denmark, 2012).

Price Waterhouse Cooper US (PwC) is another company working with mentoring programmes (Human Capital Institute, 2008). With the aim of improving the company's culture of inclusion for women and minorities, PwC created a customized approach called 'Targeted Coaching'. This is a set of programmes specially designed for different needs (Human Capital Institute, 2008). One programme, entitled 'The Firm', is a series of lighthearted video clips dealing with various topics such as careers and diversity (the clips can be found at http://www.careertv.com, search for PwC The Firm). Another programme, 'Mentor Moms', is aimed at employees about to become mothers. These are matched with other PwC employees who already have children, and thus are experienced in juggling work and parenthood. The mentorship starts before a woman goes on maternity leave and continues after she has returned to work. The 'Full Circle' programme is designed for staff that wish to 'off ramp' (Hewlett and Luce, 2005) their careers for family reasons, whether to look after children or elderly relatives. Participant are able to stay connected to their careers, and to return to the company when their private obligations become less onerous. Finally PwC has a programme to help female partners become company leaders called 'Partner Advocates', in which the woman is mentored by a male regional leader to sponsor her career advancement. An outcome of the programme is that when male leaders meet to make leadership decisions, the female partners who have been mentored are much more likely to come under consideration. (Human Capital Institute, 2008).

THE ROLE OF STRATEGIES, PLANNING AND BUDGETING – MAINSTREAMING GENDER AND DIVERSITY

Company mission statements often declare a general intention to foster and exploit diversity in the workforce. Frequently an explicit commitment to equal opportunity regardless of gender, class, age, nationality or religion is given. Diversity management and gender equality objectives, however, are rarely anchored in the business strategy of a company. Common management processes, for example strategy development, mid-term financial planning and annual budgeting, or human resource planning, are crucial for the implementation of gender *mainstreaming* and the management of diversity. The missing link between a company's diversity policy and its HR practices is often just these management processes.

> *Diversity and gender mainstreaming* seeks to promote equality at all levels and in all areas by taking equality issues into account during policy formation, implementation and evaluation.

Although it is not difficult to find company mission statements which extol the benefits of a diverse workforce or a diverse customer base, the relevance for company strategy is often underestimated. In a McKinsey and Company study from 2010 that looked at the issue of gender diversity, only 28 per cent of 763 companies selected from of all business sectors and regions of the world believed it to be of strategic relevance (Desvaux, Devillard and Sancier-Sultan, 2010). The Corporate Gender Gap Report 2010 of the World Economic Forum (Zahidi and Ibarra, 2010), which encompassed data from 20 countries and 16 different industries, gave similar results. For example, 60 per cent of all Swiss companies have no specific goals, quotas or other diversity measures to increase the representation of female employees at management level or below. If we consider that gender is the main focus of diversity management in Switzerland, then it is very unlikely that other dimensions of diversity such as culture, age or disability will be regarded as in any way relevant to the business strategy of companies. At the same time, it is possible to point to some other companies in Switzerland that treat diversity as a strategic issue. For example Raiffeisen, the third biggest banking group in Switzerland, includes in its corporate strategy the explicit strategic goal of being an attractive employer for current and future employees. This strategic goal is to be met through the group-wide development and implementation of diversity management, and the promotion of a so-called 'life domain balance'. Corresponding measurable indicators (key performance indicators) have been defined, such as ensuring that at least 30 per cent of middle and upper management positions are held by women, and increasing the number of part-time employees in upper management and in the organization as a whole. Thus measurable objectives are in place for the different levels of the organization's hierarchy and integrated into the group's management information system. Special measures such as incentives to fill full-time positions with several part-time employees, a mentoring programme and a special training programme for women returning to the job market, called 'Women Back to Business', are all designed to assist in the achievement of these objectives (Raiffeisen, 2007; 2008).

Switzerland's biggest travel and transport company, SBB, offers another example of the importance of adapting management routines. The SBB Corporation follows a gender strategy that is implemented from the top down. One goal in this strategy is to increase the proportion of part-time staff, both managers and general staff, which should also boost the number of female employees as most Swiss women prefer to work part-time (especially when they have a family). The HR management decided to advertise all open positions as available at 80 per cent, 90 per cent or full-time. It turned out, however, that the human resource planning process and the budgeting process were not set up to implement this objective. Managers are required to project their personnel requirements a year in advance, and budgets are constructed on this planning, making it difficult for part-time employees to be accommodated. If managers do decide to take on a part-time member of staff in the middle of the financial year, then they will lose a portion of their resources. Thus if the measure to employ more part-time employees is to succeed, the human resource planning process must first be changed. To solve this problem, managers must be accorded some leeway in their planning and budgeting requirements. Perhaps managers could be provided with an overall budget, which they are then free to allocate according to their needs. This would allow, for example, the hiring of an older person on an 80 per cent contract, or two younger persons in a job-sharing-arrangement at no extra cost (SBB, 2010).

Two management processes that generally take no account of diversity are product development and innovation. This may result in a great waste of resources when product designs do not meet diverse customer expectations and needs. For example, the first voice recognition systems to be released onto the market were unable to recognize the speech of many female users. The reason: the design team simply neglected to include women in their development and testing processes. Unsurprisingly, the costs incurred by the company to rectify this defect were considerable (Bührer and Schraudner, 2006).

A highly positive example of how diversity drives innovation is the experience of the German supermarket chain, Edeka, which made improvements in their shops to benefit a wide range of customers, for example families with children, the elderly, handicapped individuals and so on. Supermarkets now feature extra large parking spaces, clear guidance for the disabled to appropriate entrances as well as floor markings for better orientation, the provision of walking frames, large print price tags for the elderly, talking scanners and scales, magnifiers, recovery zones as well as play areas and buggies for children. The company enjoyed a good return on its investment as turnover subsequently increased. This confirms how diversity can also serve as a business driver (Edeka, 2012).

Another positive example for innovation based on the recognition of diversity is the latest generation of urban trams. Today these are built to offer easy access to wheelchairs and prams (no steps and automatic 'kneeling' of the tram at stops).

Of course, it is a long path from diversity goal setting to the reality of daily working life and routine. On the way, many large and small processes must be adapted, tasks reorganized and skills enhanced. Lived diversity management is found in concrete decision-making situations, and is therefore a leadership task that cannot be delegated. It is the manager who decides about a vacancy, a promotion, a pay rise, an opportunity for further training or education, or a new customer project. Managers must implement diversity and equal opportunity goals themselves, while relying on the support of external experts and diversity officers in the company.

Without continuous reflection and clear goals, managers will tend to fall back on old habits when trying to fill a vacant position. Thus a 'young male' from the dominant group will be chosen instead of, for example, a woman, a foreigner, a man who wants to work part-time, or a mother re-entering the workforce. A critical reflection of management's own attitudes is an important first step toward mainstreaming gender and diversity.

DIVERSITY PRACTICES AS A FUNCTION OF HUMAN RESOURCES

As mentioned earlier, a great deal of the diversity work in any organization is done by the HR department. This makes sense as many of the discriminatory structures that can inhibit an organization from becoming more diverse traditionally lie within this department and its functions. In this section we will identify workforce planning, recruiting, remuneration, performance appraisal, promotion and professional development as important functions that can be utilized to foster diversity.

Workforce planning

The first step in the selection of employees is workforce planning, also called talent management (Stewart and Harte, 2010). This is an ongoing process of analysing the skills, turnover, retention and retirement of current employees in order to identify future needs. It is vital that diversity policies are incorporated into this planning process (Mathews, 1998).

Adding diversity to the workforce planning will require an approach rather different from traditional workforce planning 'because the "talent pool" identified is coming from within a managed diverse workforce where everyone is managed and developed "differently" according to their backgrounds, beliefs, religions, etc.' (Stewart and Harte, 2010, p. 511). Companies must therefore develop their functions and skills in this matter. The question is: how? Stewart and Harte

(2010) have found that diversity connected to workforce planning is a topic virtually ignored by researchers, and that few companies and organizations make the link between talent management and diversity.

Recruitment and selection practices

One business case argument for managing diversity is that it helps to attract the best talent (Kelly and Dobbin, 1998). Without such an awareness of diversity, many applicants are often consciously or unconsciously rejected during the selection process (Shen et al., 2009). This is not due to any consideration of their professional qualities, but because they have a strange name, are the wrong sex, possess foreign educational qualifications, or are labelled 'different' in some other way irrelevant to the position at hand. There are two approaches to diversity recruitment. One is to consider how to avoid discrimination during the recruitment process. The other is to actively try to attract minority applicants. Both approaches are discussed below.

A first step in the recruitment process is to write a job description and list of requirements that deal specifically with relevant qualifications (D'Netto and Sohal, 1999) while ignoring all other considerations. Stated requirements for vacant positions are frequently redundant in that they are either unrelated to the open position or can be learned on the job.

A carefully written job description and job specification should incorporate the following dimensions (Frost-Danielsen, Fröberg, and Jonsson, 2002, p. 7):

- *Professional competencies*, which are the skills and knowledge required to perform all vocational tasks correctly. These include knowledge of specific work fields, as well as theories, models, tools and regulations.
- *Personal competences*, which refer to individuals' creative capabilities, ethics, respect for others and sense of responsibility.
- *Social competencies*, which describe the ability to cooperate with others in both a friendly and professional manner. Such competencies are especially important if the job requires an employee to engage in teamwork, to take part in company meetings and to have frequent dealings with customers.
- *Strategic competencies*, which refer to a high degree of business intelligence. This requires a continual updating of knowledge regarding the external and internal environment, and the ability to analyse relevant information. Employees must be familiar with the organization's aims, mission and values.
- *Functional competencies*, which constitute a so-called 'hub dimension', link together several skills from different areas. Functional competencies are probably those which require the greatest degree of experience. Typical examples are good problem-solving skills and the ability to explain difficult topics to others.

It is useful to bear these dimensions in mind when writing a job specification. Dimensions where bias and discrimination are most likely to creep in are personal and social competences, as these may be gendered or cultural biased. However, the stipulated professional competence must also be carefully drawn up to exclude any skills *not* required to perform the job. Knouse (2009) has pointed out that the requirements expressed for skills and competencies will also affect the retention of employees. If, during the recruitment process, the company emphasizes that it values skills, abilities and competences above age, gender or any particular social, ethnic or educational background, the newly hired individual is more likely to have realistic expectations of the new job. As Knouse puts it (2009, p. 145):

> If recruiting using impressive management promotion techniques focuses upon these aspects of diversity (skills, abilities and knowledge), employees will develop realistic expectations, higher job satisfaction, and stay with the organization. On the other hand, if the recruiting process emphasizes only background diversity (race, gender and age), unrealistic expectations may occur.

At the same time one should remember that some jobs require only a specific competency or selection of competencies. Strategic competencies, for example, are generally only required in management jobs, while social competencies can be largely ignored if the position does not involve much interaction with other people. As an illustration, consider the following example:

Example

Jane, a woman with Asperger's syndrome, is employed in the accounts department of the United Kingdom (UK) based TGM Construction Firm. She is very good at her job, being extremely skilled in dealing with numbers and in keeping everything in perfect order. Due to her disorder, however, she has problems socializing with other people. Sufferers of Asperger's syndrome generally have significant difficulties in social interaction and in interpreting social situations. In this case Jane participates in meetings when required and meets the demands placed on her. She refrains, however, from participating in staff coffee breaks. This is due to one particular incident which occurred when, asked if she could make coffee, Jane replied 'Yes', in the literal sense of 'Yes, I know how to make coffee', before returning to her office. After a couple of similar incidents, she starts to be regarded by her colleagues as not only strange, but even incompetent. Then, when the firm is forced to make some redundancies, Jane is chosen as one of those who must go.

Questions
- What competencies does Jane possess?
- What competencies and skills were important for her job?
- How important are social competencies generally in the workplace?
- Choose a couple of jobs you are familiar with, and identify the required dimensions of competency.
- Take a look at some job advertisements and decide if the stipulated skills and experience required are in fact relevant for the job at hand.

Attention must also be paid to a job advertisement's design and placement. If the organization wants to attract applicants from specific groups, then it must determine which sources of information these people use to locate vacancies. For example, when trying to reach a particular ethnic group, it is important to advertise in websites, newspapers or journals dedicated to this group. If a company wants to encourage minority group applicants for a job, then the relevant advertisements should include images of minority workers (Avery, 2003). It is important that minority workers also be shown in managerial positions, as this is likely to increase the attractiveness of the workplace for the job seeker. Today many vacant positions are advertised on the Internet, and therefore companies must ensure that information presented on their websites is diversity sensitive. While studying the effect of recruiting adverts on black applicants, Avery (2003, p. 167) found that 'ads containing Blacks in high-status positions are likely to convey to Black applicants that advancement opportunities will not be hindered by institutional racism'. In order to attract majority women and minority group job seekers, a company must signal through its advertising that diversity is valued. This can be done by placing specially designed job adverts in targeted media, by including diversity policy statements in the adverts, or by using female or minority recruiters (Avery and McKay, 2006).

This technique of using images and stories of minority employees to attract applicants from minority groups is a form of targeted recruitment (Knouse, 2009). Knouse discusses various media that can help in targeting specific minority groups, pointing to career fairs, community centres or specialized professional organizations. Two-way communication is, according to Knouse, the most effective way to produce realistic images of what the workplace and the job will be like. In such situations it is vital that company representatives are also members of targeted groups. Thus, if a company wishes to target minority women, its representatives should not be white males. One way to get around this problem, Knouse suggests, is to exploit the Internet. Many companies already make use of online advertising to attract applicants from minority groups. One common form is to use film clips featuring minority workers. For example, Ericsson has created a short video in which a number of majority and minority workers present their view of the company, and explain why they enjoying working there (Ericsson, 2012). Other enterprises which have also adopted this technique are L'Oréal and Maersk. Watch the aforementioned clips under:

WEBLINK

http://www.ericsson.com/article/employee_video_20100331154235
http://www.careertv.se (search for L'Oréal, Maersk or PwC The Firm)

As recruitment processes will differ from organization to organization, there does not exist one simply solution to the problem of fostering diversity in recruitment. Yet it is possible to draw up some guidelines. The International Organization for Diversity Management (IDM) (2007) suggests the following steps to build a recruitment process which embraces diversity:

Example

How to recruit for diversity:

- decide on the skills, knowledge and experience that the business needs to fill a specific job or role;
- produce a 'job description' and a personal specification that outlines the skills and experience needed for the role;
- check that the job description does not exclude anyone from applying because of racial or ethnic origin, religious belief, gender, sexual orientation, age or disability;
- adapt your methods to allow (and encourage) disabled people to apply;
- avoid 'word of mouth' recruitment processes. Consider a range of advertising methods (such as job centres, national local or community newspapers; schools, colleges or universities; community organizations; commercial recruitment agencies; news boards in retail outlets; websites or the internet);
- state that you welcome applications from all sections of the community;
- do not give age limits or ranges in job advertisements;
- talk informally about the job to potential candidates. This will help to include people that may be worried about their age, gender and/or impairment, and so on.

Source: Keil et al. (2007).

The HR staff doing the initial selection of candidates should be trained to avoid bias towards a specific group in the selection process, so that individuals are not rejected on the basis of the aforementioned factors. One way to avoid bias is to use anonymous job applications (Hausman, 2012). This means that those who read and select the applications do not know the name of the applicant, and can therefore not discriminate on the basis of name or sex.

Many orchestras, for example, conduct blind auditions in which the sex of applicants is hidden (they are required to play behind a screen). Historically, women were long banned from playing in orchestras, and indeed the Vienna Philharmonic Orchestra only hired its first female player in 1997 (http://www. german-way.com/women.html, date accessed 2012-01-17).

Training is necessary to eradicate discrimination in the recruitment process and establish a diverse workforce. The manager responsible for hiring must, for example, be aware of his or her own prejudices and stereotypical beliefs regarding minority groups (Frost-Danielsen et al., 2002). One measure to avoid bias in the selection process is to establish a selection committee (D'Netto and Sohal, 1999) made up of representatives of various minority groups. This ensures that a range of viewpoints is heard. Job interviews must also take place in such a manner that certain groups are not excluded due to the working language used, or topics discussed. Interviews should focus primarily on the vacant position and its requirements; the interviewer should not ask questions about the applicant's private life unless he or she brings the topic up voluntarily. Let us give an example of an interview in which irrelevant issues are a feature of the discussion.

Example

Maria Abreu Melo, who holds an engineering degree from the top university in Portugal, came to Denmark 15 years ago. At first she continued her studies, successfully taking a Master's degree in computer engineering. She quickly became fluent in Danish, having understood the importance of speaking the local language, and thus working hard to master it. Now she is looking for a new position. Online she finds the following job advert:

> Comp Company is looking for a junior-level IT employee proficient in SQL and Java programming to join our Maximo technical support team. We are looking for a self-starter with strong logic skills who is eager to learn. He or she will be instructed in various aspects of implementing, operating and supporting the IBM/Tivoli Enterprise Asset Management system, Maximo.

Maria decides to apply and is asked to come for a job interview in December. During this meeting she is not asked any questions about her skills, how she can contribute to the organization, or what her career ambitions are. Instead, the recruiter asks about her reasons for coming to Denmark; whether she has any Danish friends; and what she thinks about Danish Christmas food. The interviewer also starts to talk about the lovely coastline of Portugal, where he once spent his summer holidays. Later Maria feels dejected about the interview because she was not given the opportunity to discuss her skills, knowledge or professional experience. She strongly suspects that she will not be offered the job.

Even though the example above is fictitious, similar situations occur frequently in job interviews. Recruiters should be aware of what kinds of questions are relevant when a minority (or majority) person applies for a job. Is it relevant to ask a candidate about his or her sexuality, or when they are planning to have a baby, or about the traditional food of their home country? Of course, asking cultural or minority specific questions at the beginning of an interview may be a valid ice-breaking technique. This, however, should not overshadow the more important issue of the candidate's relevant competencies.

Put yourself in the position of the recruiter. Based on the dimensions of competency described above (professional, personal, social, strategic and functional), make a list of relevant competencies and skills that should have been the focus of the interview with Maria Abreu Melo.

Performance appraisal and employee evaluation

Performance appraisal and other types of employee evaluation are methods to assess an employee's performance, which, by identifying weaknesses and strengths, should also help to improve that performance. Such appraisals may have a direct effect on an employee's career advancements and pay (Igbaria and Shayo, 1997; Igbaria and Baroudi, 1995; Terpstra, 1997). However, appraisal and evaluations often display bias. For example, in some cases we can discern gender bias (Rubery, 1995): Women's performance is generally rated lower than men's, especially if the evaluator is male (Hennessey and Bernardin, 2003; Igbaria and

Baroudi, 1995; Feild and Holley, 1982). Other researchers claim that members of minority groups tend to be given lower ratings (Shen et al., 2009) and that older or younger workers will get lower job performance evaluations (Saks and Waldman, 1998). Igbaria and Shayo (1997) found, for example, that if women or black people enjoy high ratings, their success is attributed to luck, easy job tasks or help, whereas if men are highly rated, their success is attributed to ability and skills.

The particular design of the performance appraisal may influence the degree of such bias. Hennessey and Bernardin (2003, p. 145) note that 'it is not unreasonable to assume that a racist, sexist, or ageist rater is more likely to manifest these tendencies in personnel decisions when the performance criteria that are supposed to be the basis of these decisions are relatively more ambiguous'. According to them, research has frequently revealed performance appraisals to be not only ambiguous, but also subjective and imprecise in the formulation of performance criteria.

Unfortunately, Hennessey and Bernardin's study showed that minority employees still get lower ratings when criteria are more specific and objective. In fact, they found that 'Females actually fared better with the more subjective system' (Hennessey and Bernardin, 2003, p. 155). Their conclusion was that greater objectivity in the appraisal does not necessarily translate into less discrimination and bias.

Various steps can, however, be successfully taken to avoid bias (Shen et al., 2009), depending on the specific type of appraisal system and the size of the organization. If an appraisal committee is in charge of the evaluation, then it must contain representatives from all the different groups within the organization, and not only the majority group. How this is realized depends, of course, on the size of the organization and the number of minority employees. Smaller companies tend to dispense with such committees, while in companies with few minority workers it may become very burdensome and time consuming to carry out such a service. Clearly the evaluation criteria should be closely examined for any sign of bias. The competencies listed above can be of use here, together with objective measures of performance. Another step could be to ensure that the performance appraisal focuses only on the employee's performance, and not on his or her personality (Shen et al., 2009).

Based on the work of Igbaria and Shayo (1997, p. 21) the following recommendations can be made to human resource managers regarding performance evaluations:

1. Organizations should initiate strategies with clearly defined and communicated hiring/promotion policies and practices for all employees.
2. Organizations need open and frank discussion on how differences can be exploited as sources of individual and organizational effectiveness.

3. The quality of first line supervision is critical to the success or failure of all employees, but especially to minorities and women. Therefore organizations should:

- help supervisors recognize their own subjectivity, and take steps to ensure that rewards and promotions are delivered in as fair a manner as possible;
- develop training programmes to give supervisors effective and bias-free tools to better evaluate employees' performance potential and to support them in their career planning and development needs;
- be encouraged to include majority women and minorities in their informal job-related social interactions, where important information is exchanged regarding the organization's activities.
- develop concrete performance measurement criteria to objectively evaluate all employees.

Performance appraisals can also serve to promote diversity within an organization. If managers at various levels are evaluated according to how well they have implemented diversity initiatives, then diversity will be viewed internally as a real priority.

Promotion and career opportunities

One aim of diversity management is, of course, to provide all employees with the same opportunities for promotion and career opportunities. Regardless of background, each individual should have the same opportunities for professional development as members of more privileged groups. As mentioned earlier, the glass ceiling is a well-known phenomenon referring to the fact that in most countries few women and people from minority groups occupy leading positions within organizations (Bjerk, 2008; Kirton and Greene, 2010). Research has found that due to the experience of discrimination, majority women and minority workers tend to be less satisfied with promotional opportunities (Hau Siu Chow and Crawford, 2004). It is often argued that the reason these groups do not reach the upper organizational echelons is not explicit discrimination or barriers to promotion, but simply a lack of suitably qualified applicants. Bjerk (2008), amongst others, has shown this argument to be implausible. And in fact by simply looking at the numbers of women and minority groups in higher education, and at their representation at lower levels in organizations, we can confirm that the pool of qualified individuals from these underrepresented groups is sufficiently large. Indeed, statistics from 2009 show that in European institutions of higher education, female graduates outnumbered male graduates by a ratio of approximately three to two (Eurostat, 2011).

In a study of career advancement in one UK firm, Hau Siu Chow and Crawford (2004) determined that majority women and minority group men and women consistently suffered poor career advancement in comparison to majority men. The researchers found that 'whites were less educated with slightly better professional qualifications and longer organizational tenure. Ethnic minorities had higher educational attainment to compensate for their low-status group identity. The number of promotions was significantly higher for males and whites' (Hau Siu Chow and Crawford, 2004, p. 26). The study attempted to measure how well the company exploited its workforce's pool of diverse skills, abilities and knowledge by looking at membership in committees and taskforces as one indicator. They found that majority women and minority workers were underrepresented, showing that their competencies were not fully valued. Of course, the lack of women and minority workers in such positions will affect decision-making processes in the company. It also means that these groups of workers are left out of important networks and information streams, diminishing their possibilities for career advancement. When turning to the question of promotion, Hau Siu Chow and Crawford (2004) found that women were more than twice as likely to fail in their promotion applications as their male counterparts, while no minority ethnic group worker in the sample had ever been promoted despite having the same qualifications as their white colleagues. The result of such overt or covert discrimination is that an organization is deprived of the valuable contribution of a diverse workforce.

Many different ways have been proposed to eliminate bias and discrimination in promotion processes. Just as in performance appraisal, there is a risk in any organization dominated by a majority group that women and underrepresented minorities will be evaluated for promotion using criteria valid mainly for this majority (Rubery, 1995; Shen et al., 2009). To correct such bias the organization must take measures similar to those discussed above for recruitment and appraisal systems. Underlying discriminatory structures must be uncovered and eliminated in order to ensure that promotion is based on an unbiased view of merit and performance. For example, after suspecting structural discrimination in their promotion process, one department at the University of Minnesota developed a promotion process that would ensure unbiased opportunities for promotion and career development for all faculty members, regardless of background (Duranczyk, Madyun, Jehangir and Higbee, 2011). A component of this process was the creation of a committee of faculty members to participate in the evaluation process.

Even if an organization has developed a non-biased promotion process, it may still not ensure equal opportunities for career advancement if majority women and minority group men and women are not given the same opportunities to develop and gain experience as majority men (Hau Siu Chow and Crawford,

2004). It is therefore vital that these employees be allowed to participate in orga-nizational activities under the same conditions as majority men, so that they can be appropriately evaluated by senior management.

Pay and remuneration

Pay inequality is one of the most common causes of job dissatisfaction. It is a per-sistent problem for many European countries as evidenced by the gender pay gap (Eurostat, 2010). Remuneration systems are designed to reward those who have contributed to organizational performance and to encourage even better individ-ual performance (D'Netto and Sohal, 1999). If, however, the pay or remuneration system has built-in discriminatory structures which favour certain groups, then it is likely that some valuable employees will be motivated in the long or short term to resign. Research has found that despite efforts to close the gap, women consistently earn less than men (Blau and Kahn, 2007; Ng, Eby, Sorensen and Feldman, 2005). Discriminatory practices in performance-based compensation will occur if measures to evaluate work performance are biased towards infor-mal requirements such as working long hours, attending weekend meetings or high verbal fluency. Often the criteria for merit- or performance-based pay are not directly discussed within an organization, allowing hidden discriminatory structures to persist (Rubery, 1995). In order to detect such bias, an organiza-tion must analyse whether women and minority groups are paid less on average than the majority group. Alkadry and Tower (2011), for example, have claimed that women are always paid less than men. They acknowledge that compensa-tion for women tends to be higher than normal in male-dominated occupations, but argue that regardless of whether the occupation is male-dominated, gender-mixed or female-dominated, men persistently earn more than women. Similarly, Ng et al. (2005) have found that socio-demographic variables such as being male, white, older and married have a positive effect on salary.

Continuing our analysis of bias in pay, the next step is to compare different kinds of jobs and pay systems in order to reveal basic inconsistencies. Surpris-ingly, research has found that merit-based systems can make payment struc-tures less transparent, and therefore serve to mask and maintain discriminatory practices (Rubery, 1995), if the categories for merit are vaguely or subjectively defined. One sensible first step, therefore, is to analyse the organizational his-tory of compensation to determine which criteria were used for decision-making, and which category of employee received the highest compensation. Objective criteria are not, however, a guarantee for unbiased compensation. One exam-ple of gender bias in an apparently objective criterion is compensation based on the number of employees which a manager supervises. This would appear to be a rather objective criterion. Nonetheless, Alkadry and Tower (2011) have determined that the number of people reporting to a manager, as well as the economic value of his or her area of operations, are factors related to the manager's sex. In the study men were found to be accorded more authority than women, and hence the number of employees in their department or work group turned out to be a covert form of gender-based pay discrimination. Consequently, any analysis of biased and discriminatory structures must carefully scrutinize seemingly objective and fair organizational structures or behaviours.

Sweden's 'Discrimination Ombudsman' has developed a model to analyse pay in relation to job description and job content, which has been adopted by a number of municipal and government organizations as well as companies (Rosenberg, 2003). One such company, Inlandsbanan AB, conducted an analysis in two steps. It began by undertaking a salary survey of the relative compensation of men and women, revealing that for any two jobs of equal status, a male worker was paid more than a female worker. The analysis continued by investigating different job descriptions, comparing these with the actual job content in order to ensure equal pay for equal work (Rosenberg, 2003). Through this analysis it became possible to classify jobs that were essentially equivalent, and thus determine any inequalities in rates of payment. Although such investigative work takes time and money, it furnishes a strong framework for the implementation of equal pay.

WEBLINK

More good examples of equal pay can be found at http://lonelotsarna.se/equalpay/index.html

Another very useful tool, available in Germany and Switzerland, is 'logib' (http://www.logib.de and www.logib.ch). Offered free of charge, it can help SMEs (small and medium-sized enterprises) to discover whether they have a problem with wage or occupational discrimination. However, it is a first step only; a deeper analysis must be undertaken if any sign of discrimination is uncovered.

Compensation and pay inequalities not only affect individual employees; they also have repercussions on the organization. As already noted, pay inequality is a leading cause of job dissatisfaction and de-motivation among minority workers (Shen et al., 2009); if female employees and those from other underrepresented groups perceive that their salaries are lower than those of white, male colleagues (Rubery, 1995), then they are likely to seek a position elsewhere. A discriminatory pay system can therefore lead an organization to lose valuable employees. Perfectly fair and objective systems of remuneration rarely exist, and thus it is vital that organizations continuously strive to uncover discriminatory mechanisms, which, in the end, are damaging to both morale and business.

DIVERSITY PRACTICES AS A LEADERSHIP TASK
AND MANAGEMENT RESPONSIBILITY

Ideally, an organization's diversity policy, diversity management programme and diversity initiatives should issue from the very top in order to be perceived as credible and worthwhile (Pitts, 2007; Müller and Sander, 2005). In addition, line and middle managers must be directly involved in diversity programmes; they should be encouraged to feel that they have something to gain from these initiatives, rather than viewing them as just another obligation (Foster and Harris, 2005; Müller and Sander, 2009). Paul-Emile (2006, p.16) writes that:

> the interests of top executives and that of middle managers are often quite different. Top executives see the introduction of diversity programs as policy making or part of their overall corporate institutional strategy. Middle managers, however, deal directly with employees, with day-to-day implementation and are responsible for outcomes. They are concerned about how diversity will impact work performance and their authority in their departments.

Middle managers must be involved in all parts of diversity programmes in order to secure their commitment, while additional resources and economic incentives must be provided to ensure that diversity initiatives are fully implemented. If the commitment of middle managers to diversity is not won then discrepancies will arise in their view of the importance of this issue for the organization. In a study of diversity management amongst British retailers, Foster and Harris (2005) found that line managers did not have a clear conception of diversity, and differed in their views as to how diversity initiatives should be implemented.

One way to give clear evidence that diversity programmes have strong support at the top is to have the lines of reporting lead directly to the managing director or the president of the organization, as well as to the vice president of human resources: 'The higher the level of the reporting relationship and the more visibility this relationship has, the more the programme is seen to be important and central to the workings of the organization.' (Paul-Emile, 2006, p. 17) An example of this is IBM's adoption of diversity as strategy (Thomas, 2004), in which the company used workforce diversity to better understand its markets. This initiative came from the very top, namely IBM's Chief Executive Officer, Louis V. Gerstner, Jr. Eight task forces were created to promote diversity: Asians, Blacks, People with Disabilities, White Men, Women, LGBT Individuals, Hispanic, Native Americans. Senior managers were appointed to these task forces to ensure that diversity was supported and respected by executive managers throughout the organization.

Another way for the executive team to manifest their commitment to diversity is to allocate sufficient resources (Pitts, 2007). This refers not only to financial support, but also to time and decision-making authority. If senior management has decided that a diversity programme should be implemented, then it must also allocate a portion of the annual budget to attain the stipulated goals. The diversity manager or the diversity committee will soon lose enthusiasm and commitment if forced to make a formal application for funds for each individual initiative. Moreover, any employee who is asked to take part in the diversity programme must be allowed to arrange their work schedule accordingly. If staff are invited to participate in a diversity committee, senior management must give clear directives to the unit and middle managers that these employees should be permitted to take time off from their regular duties. Likewise, all staff members should be given the time to participate in diversity training measures. Those with the responsibility for implementing the diversity programme should also be given the authority to make decisions regarding individual diversity initiatives. If the diversity manager or the diversity committee is required to seek approval from higher ranking managers for each decision they must take, employees will quickly perceive that senior management does not support the initiatives sufficiently to grant decision-making power to the responsible parties. Assigning responsibilities without the requisite authority for implementation is a recipe for disaster. It brings frustration for those responsible for a diversity programme, and in the end failure for the programme itself.

Senior managers can also indicate their support of diversity by actually participating in diversity training (Bendick, Egan and Lofhjelm, 2001). Hite and McDonald (2006, p.372) have confirmed the huge impact on a programme's acceptance if leaders take part in diversity training classes. One of the employees they interviewed noted that company leaders made a point of addressing every training session as a visible means of supporting the programme: 'From the time I went to the first train-the-trainer [class], and I've been through a couple, [the CEO] walks in and when he finishes you are so geared up and motivated . . . he not only talks the talk, he walks the walk.'

Ultimately, however, the best way for senior management to show that they are fully committed to a diversity programme is to foster diversity in management at all levels, including the leadership team.

To conclude, senior managers have a pivotal role in initiating and legitimizing diversity work in an organization. In particular, middle managers and the human resource department play a key role in implementing diversity policy and strategies on a day-to-day basis. The commitment of all these actors is essential to successfully establish a culture of diversity and inclusion.

Despite all the approaches to creating a more diverse, inclusive and non-discriminating organization which we have outlined so far in this chapter, it is a sad fact that diversity is not always accepted and valued by organizations. Indeed, it is not uncommon to find managers as well as other employees who actively resist diversity in various ways. To complete our discussion, therefore, we must turn to strategies which attempt to deal with such resistance to diversity.

DEALING WITH RESISTANCE TO DIVERSITY

Thorough organizational planning, together with the best intentions in the world, may still not be enough to ensure that a supportive culture for diversity goes uncontested in organizations. Some degree of resistance to diversity is to be expected, and managers must be prepared to recognize and address this force in order to safeguard the benefits that diversity work can bring to an organization.

What is resistance to diversity?

Resistance to diversity has been defined as 'a range of practices and behaviours within and by organizations that interfere, intentionally or unintentionally, with the use of diversity as an opportunity for learning and effectiveness' (Thomas and Plaut, 2008, p. 5). Resistance can be shown to diversity itself (the presence of 'different' people in the organization), or to specific diversity initiatives. This resistance can arise at either the individual or the organizational level, and it can be either overt or subtle (see Table 8.1).

Overt resistance to diversity consists of behaviours or attitudes that are performed or displayed openly, and that are plainly apparent to observers. For instance, using racist language to belittle a co-worker can be considered overt resistance to diversity.

Subtle resistance to diversity is much less obvious than overt resistance; it is frequently concealed and can therefore be difficult for observers to accurately perceive or describe. For example, choosing to remain silent after witnessing acts of overt discrimination or harassment can be considered subtle resistance to diversity, as can forming exclusive friendship groups with members of one's own social category, while avoiding members of other social categories.

Individual resistance to diversity is displayed by individual workers within an organization. This resistance may include instances of overt prejudice, discrimination and harassment, as well as more subtle forms of exclusion, avoidance, distancing or even silence in the face of acts of discrimination and harassment by others.

Organizational resistance to diversity manifests itself in organizational policies and practices. For instance, holding training sessions after normal working hours or on weekends, when workers with childcare responsibilities may not be able to attend, is a relatively overt form of organizational resistance to diversity. Another, more subtle, example of organizational resistance is refusing to acknowledge diversity as an issue of relevance to the organization, and thus generating a culture of silence around the topics of diversity and discrimination.

Table 8.1 Symptoms of resistance to diversity

Subtle ← Manifestations → Overt	
• intentional and hostile forms of discrimination; • verbal, physical harassment; • graffiti.	• discriminatory HR management policies and practices; • victimization of workers who report instances of discrimination.
Individual ← Level of resistance → Organizational	
• avoidance and exclusion of others based on differences; • silence regarding inequalities; • discrediting of ideas and individuals who are different from the mainstream.	• cultures of silence around diversity and discrimination; • mixed messages on diversity; • diversity portrayed as too time-consuming or complex; • diversity as a 'non-issue'.

Source: Thomas and Plaut (2008).

Cases of overt resistance to diversity are usually easy to identify, and can be dealt with by revising organizational policies. As discussed earlier in this chapter, analysis and adjustment of potentially discriminatory recruitment and selection practices or performance appraisal processes can serve to foster a greater sense of inclusion for all workers. Subtle forms of diversity resistance, as one can imagine, are more difficult to recognize and manage. For instance, silence in the face of acts of discrimination, harassment or mistreatment serves to reinforce that mistreatment by failing to challenge it. Social distancing from employees who are 'different' from the dominant majority can reduce the opportunities of such minorities for career development and mobility (Combs, 2003). Dominant group members distance themselves from individuals belonging to more marginalized groups for a variety of reasons. For example, potential male mentors might avoid working with female employees because they are afraid that the professional relationship could be perceived as romantic in nature (Elsesser and Peplau, 2006; Morgan and Davidson, 2008), or because they assume that female staff will be distracted by family responsibilities, rendering them unsuitable for promotion (Hoobler, Wayne and Lemmon, 2009). These stereotypes and assumptions often prevent women from receiving the valuable career boost of mentoring, especially in industries or workplaces that are male-dominated and where senior female mentors are in short supply. Research conducted among Master of Business Administration (MBA) graduates shows that men tend to have mentors who are higher ranking, better compensated, and wield more influence in the organization; this is significant, because having a mentor who is high up the company hierarchy will generally result in a greater number of promotions and higher compensation for the mentee (Carter and Silva, 2010).

Covert forms of diversity resistance can also be passive, as in the case of 'ethnic drift'. This is the phenomenon that arises when organizations assign new workers to supervisors of the same ethnicity in order (it is hoped) to capitalize on their expected similarities. Yet such artificial 'grouping' may inadvertently restrict minority workers' opportunities for career development (James, 2000). Basing job assignments on ethnicity helps to ensure that ethnic minority workers continue in the same career paths as those who have come before them. As many ethnic minority groups are concentrated in lower status, lower paid jobs than the white majority, this practice perpetuates job segregation and pay inequalities (Brief, Butz and Deitch, 2005). At the same time, organizations are prevented from utilizing minority workers' abilities in a wide variety of departments or divisions, potentially hindering organizational performance.

Seemingly benign organizational attitudes toward diversity may conceal an underlying resistance. Firms adopting what Thomas and Ely (1996) refer to as an 'access and legitimacy' perspective towards diversity, view ethnic and gender diversity among their workers almost exclusively as a means to expanding into new markets. A form of subtle organizational resistance to diversity underlies this apparently 'positive' attitude to difference: although women and minority employees may be welcomed into an organization in order to tap a more diverse consumer base, such employees generally find themselves limited to one function, and eventually may end up feeling exploited. Valuing women and ethnic minority workers only for their niche knowledge may thus engender a sense of alienation and exclusion, resulting in higher levels of staff turnover. Ely and Thomas's (2001) research has demonstrated that when ethnic minority staff are matched with a particular market segment, this can establish the perception that positions held by these minority workers are lower in status than those held by ethnic majority workers. Thus 'ethnic drift' creates segregated career opportunities, leading ethnic minority workers to doubt the extent to which the organization respects and values them.

Another way to conceptualize resistance to diversity is to compare it to support for diversity. Avery (2011) posits that an individual's level of support or opposition to any particular idea will vary in terms of both endorsement and activism (see Table 8.2). Endorsement refers to the extent to which an individual concurs with an idea, while activism refers to the degree of personal action an individual is willing to take in order to support (or oppose) that idea. Thus an organizational member who highly endorses diversity, but is low in activism, can be said to passively support diversity. Although she or he may value diversity, this attitude is not reflected in positive action. By contrast, an organizational member who is low in endorsement of diversity, and high in activism, is likely to engage in overt discrimination. This individual's negative attitude toward diversity is accompanied by negative behaviour, such as openly challenging organizational diversity initiatives and engaging in discriminatory practices such as harassment.

Table 8.2   Typology of organizational support/resistance regarding diversity

Opposition ← ENDORSEMENT → *Support*	
Quadrant I: Silence • bystander during diversity discussions or incidents; • untapped diversity resource.	*Quadrant II*: Championing • actively leads or promotes diversity initiatives; • intervenes and interjects to promote diversity.
Passive ← ACTIVISM → *Active*	
Quadrant III: Subtle resistance • potential source of diversity resistance; • tolerates discrimination and disregards ideas from marginalized groups.	*Quadrant IV*: Overt discrimination • openly challenges and undermines diversity initiatives; • perpetuates and supports discriminatory practices (for example harassment and hostility).
Source: Adapted from Avery (2011).	

Outcomes of resistance to diversity

As resistance to diversity can be manifested at both the organizational and individual level, it is clear that the repercussions of such resistance will also impact these two levels. For organizations, resistance to diversity can incur financial, productivity and emotional costs. Significant financial costs are, for example, the settlement of employment tribunal cases and compensation payouts, including fees paid to legal representation. For example, the average compensation payout awarded by employment tribunals in the UK for cases of age discrimination grew from £10,931 in 2009/10 to £30,289 in 2011; the average awards in 2011 for discrimination based on other social categories ranged from £8,515 for religious discrimination to £14,137 for disability discrimination (Chamberlain, 2011). Typical productivity costs are those caused by high employee turnover and absenteeism, as well as disengagement arising from mistreatment at work (Ragins and Cornwell, 2001; Sims, Drasgow and Fitzgerald, 2005; Willness, Steel and Lee, 2007). Emotional costs can be a loss of organizational reputation and workplace morale due to high profile discrimination cases at tribunal (James and Wooten, 2006; Kath, Swody, Magley, Bunk and Gallus, 2009).

For individual workers who belong to underrepresented groups, resistance to diversity can have a negative impact on career development as well as mental and physical well-being. Overt discrimination, social distancing, exclusion and avoidance create glass ceilings for women and members of minority groups by denying them access to informal lines of communication, social support, developmental opportunities and relationships, as well as financial benefits. Psychological costs are often experienced as reduced self-esteem, decreased job performance and high stress levels (Miller and Major, 2000; Sekaquaptewa and Thompson, 2003; Williams and Williams-Morris, 2000). Costs to health are typically stress-related diseases, such as hypertension or heart disease, provoked by constant, long-term workplace discrimination (Din-Dzietham, Nembhard, Collins and Davis, 2004).

What generates resistance to diversity?

There are a number of potential motivating factors behind resistance to diversity. At the individual level, workers may apply stereotypes to categorize others on the basis of rigid social group membership. This is particularly the case when employees from different social groups have only limited contact with one another. With increased exposure, stereotypical preconceptions are replaced with a more sympathetic understanding, while personal characteristics other than membership of a minority group become more salient (Locksley, Hepburn and Ortiz, 1982; Kunda and Thagard, 1996).

According to social identity theory, our reaction to others is driven by our social identity needs, such as the need to reduce uncertainty and the need to maintain or increase self-esteem (Hogg and Terry, 2000; Tajfel and Turner, 1986). Self-esteem can be enhanced by attributing positive characteristics to one's own social group(s) and negative characteristics to others. Thus workers come to perceive dissimilarity in others as inherently negative, a kind of deficiency. This bolsters resistance to diversity in the workplace.

Personality traits also play a role in determining resistance to diversity at the individual level. Right-wing authoritarianism, for instance, is a trait characterized by a high degree of submissiveness to established authority and strong adherence to tradition and social norms. Workers displaying such traits are more likely to hold conventional belief systems; they are strong defenders of the status quo and tend to have negative attitudes toward individuals who are 'different' or who belong to a minority group (Parkins, Fishbein and Ritchey, 2006). Another relevant personality trait is social dominance orientation, which describes an individual's preference for hierarchy within social systems. Those who adhere to such hierarchical systems view inequality of employment outcomes as a clear reflection of natural social hierarchies, and tend to hold strong prejudices against a range of other groups. Both right-wing authoritarianism and social dominance orientation have been found to be predictive of discrimination in the workplace (Parkins, Fishbein and Ritchey, 2006).

Subtle forms of racism, or indeed sexism or homophobia, can also serve to weaken support for diversity initiatives. For example, aversive racists (those who avoid interaction with other racial groups) generally view themselves as low in prejudice; they take care not to engage in acts of overt discrimination. In situations fraught with ambiguity, however, aversive racism may lead to discriminatory decision-making, motivated by an underlying discomfort when dealing with ethnic minorities, women or LGBT individuals (Dovidio and Gaertner,

2000). The individualistic values of modern racists, meanwhile, lead to the perspective that inequality of employment outcomes is due to the efforts – or lack thereof – of minority group members, as equal opportunity legisla- tion and anti-discrimination policies have already established a 'level playing field' (McConahay, 1986). This is similar to the notion of 'natural' social hier- archies, discussed in the preceding paragraph, held by individuals high in social dominance orientation.

Another motivation for resistance to diversity, or to diversity initiatives, may be rooted in the desire to maintain the privilege that comes with being a member of the dominant group. While many individuals may acknowledge and decry the disadvantages suffered by members of minority groups, they do not necessarily recognize that they themselves possess unearned advantage, nor do they wish to endorse any programme of action that may reduce that advantage (Acker, 2006).

At the organizational level, resistance to diversity is often due to the influ- ence of senior managers, as these are the employees who establish an organi- zation's values and culture. Such leaders are ultimately responsible for diversity management policies and practices that either support, or fail to support, efforts to create an inclusive climate and equitable outcomes. As discussed earlier in the chapter, diversity initiatives must be supported at the very top of the organization in order to be perceived as credible and worthwhile, while the commitment of middle managers to diversity is required in order to achieve a consensus within the organization on the importance of this issue. The organization's position on diversity is thus clearly shaped in many cases by leaders' values and actions (Herdman and McMillan-Capehart, 2010; Thomas, 2004). For example, a posi- tive diversity climate can signal to organizational members that discriminatory acts are inappropriate, thereby reducing the strength of such discrimination or resistance to diversity initiatives.

Diversity climate is a shared understanding among organization members of an organization's diversity-related structures and actions. It comprises the perception of fairness regarding inclusion and exclusion of people from diverse backgrounds.

The fit between managerial and non-managerial attitudes toward diversity is an important predictor of diversity-related behaviour. Workers further down the organizational hierarchy are more likely to act consistently in their endorsement of, or resistance to, diversity when the management position on equality and diversity is similar to their own (Ziegert and Hanges, 2005). Employees who are prejudiced toward minority groups are more likely to give free rein to their biases when they perceive that their supervisors hold similar prejudices (Brief, Cohen, Dietz, Pugh and Vaslow, 2000).

It has been suggested that managerial resistance to diversity is largely due to the persistence of certain myths (Van Buren, 1996), such as the belief that discrimination is a historical artefact with no relevance to the modern job market; that disparities in the employment outcomes of different social groups are due to merit, rather than bias; that strong diversity initiatives require a heavy outlay of organizational resources; or that many diversity initiatives do not support the business case for diversity.

Organizations often adopt a defensive stance when faced with claims of discrimination or harassment (Wooten and James, 2004). Instead of examining their values and culture to better understand such allegations of bias, organizational leaders may deny claims, blindly defend the organization and justify its practices, while pointing to the existence of anti-discrimination legislation or organizational diversity policies to exclude any possibility that discrimination could have occurred. An example of this is the reaction of clothing retailer Abercrombie & Fitch to numerous allegations of discriminatory behaviour made by current or former employees (see the case study on pp. 225–9). The company has strongly denied any discriminatory action on their part, despite repeatedly losing court cases in the UK and the USA in which they were found to be in violation of both employment law and civil rights legislation (Greenhouse, 2004; Harper, 2011; Topping, 2009).

Clearly, organizations will more or less reflect the reigning values of the societies in which they operate, and thus shift in line with changes in these values. For instance, although the United Kingdom can be described as a reasonably tolerant society, in 2011 the Prime Minister David Cameron spoke out against multiculturalism (referring to the acceptance or promotion of multiple, distinct ethnic communities). Mr Cameron opined that a policy of embracing multiculturalism had contributed to extremism and terrorism in the UK (Wright and Taylor, 2011). This viewpoint has been repeated by other European leaders, including German Chancellor Angela Merkel and French President Nicolas Sarkozy (*Daily Mail*, 2011). Such opinions are, of course, reflected in organizations operating within these societies. Thus companies (and countries) may profess to be meritocracies, in which all members have equal opportunities and the potential for equal outcomes, yet in reality such organizations (and societies) support the assimilation of all individuals to the dominant group. In so doing they perpetuate the status quo and all its inequalities.

Responding to resistance to diversity

Depending on the depth and root cause of resistance, there are a number of steps that organizations can take to reduce opposition to diversity, and to encourage greater levels of support among employees for diversity initiatives.

One option is training in perspective-taking, which can assume a number of different forms. For example, employees may be shown a video of an individual discussing his or her experiences as a member of a minority group, and simply instructed to 'put yourself in his/her shoes', that is, imagine what it is like to be that person. Alternatively, employees may be assigned a partner and instructed to engage in the visual task of copying a diagram from an unusual perspective, namely that of their partner sitting opposite (the diagram can therefore only be viewed upside down). In the ensuing discussion, the task facilitator calls the employees' attention to the importance of considering what a particular situation may look like from another point of view. Research shows that teaching employees to adopt the perspective of out-group members (such as women or ethnic minorities) leads to higher levels of empathy and more positive attitudes towards these groups. Majority workers also then tend to view unequal outcomes experienced by minority workers as due to systemic, external factors, rather than attributing differences in status or pay to personal deficiencies such as a lack of effort or ability (Vescio, Sechrist and Paolucci, 2003).

Organizations that can effectively communicate the business advantages of a diverse workforce may be able to reduce resistance among majority employees. If workers lack faith in the value of diversity initiatives established by senior management, then this discomfort may manifest itself in forms of resistance. Here it is vital to communicate the benefits that diversity can bring to all organizational members by promoting the notion that a diverse workforce and inclusive organizational climate will boost organizational performance. If resistance is founded on myths such as those discussed in the previous section (for example that diversity initiatives are a burden on resources), then framing diversity initiatives as a cost-effective solution to problems of recruitment or talent management can help to alleviate workers' concerns and encourage endorsement of these initiatives.

In some instances members of the majority may come to feel that diversity initiatives are placing them at a disadvantage in terms of performance evaluation or promotion. Managers can prevent the growth of resistance by giving employees honest feedback about such work-related decisions, so that diversity initiatives are not wrongly seen to be the reason why majority employees are passed over for promotion or do not receive highly desirable job assignments (Kidder, Lankau, Chrobot-Mason, Mollica and Friedman, 2004). Similarly, if organizational surveys find that employees view diversity training as unnecessary, managers can supply information about the number of complaints lodged with the organization regarding discriminatory recruitment, retention and promotion practices, or present the latest figures for the advancement of women and minority workers.

Managers who feel threatened by a diversity initiative are unlikely to encourage their subordinates or peers to support it. Lower down the hierarchy, staff are also influenced by their co-workers' beliefs about diversity. One method of reducing resistance to diversity is therefore to use focus groups to identify opinion leaders across all organizational levels. This technique involves selecting a group of employees to take part in a facilitated discussion in order to elicit information about their views and experiences of influential peers in the workplace. These opinion leaders can then be targeted for education regarding the importance of diversity and diversity initiatives, in the hope that they in turn will influence others in a positive manner (Wiethoff, 2004).

In summary, resistance to diversity is a common phenomenon within organizations, which can prove highly damaging if efforts are not made to curb it. Seeking to recognize deep-seated biases and prejudices in individuals is no easy task, and attempting to change these may be just as difficult. Addressing organizational sources of resistance, such as HR management policies and practices and senior management role modeling, may prove more straightforward, and therefore a more fruitful approach to reducing resistance.

CONCLUSION

In this chapter we have shown that diversity work must be a coordinated effort, which permeates the whole organization. Isolated one-off efforts are unlikely to foster lasting diversity and dismantle discriminatory practices. Instead, if a company truly wants to become inclusive, then it must begin by analysing its existing structures and practices in order to locate bias and discrimination.

In describing and discussing various practices, we have emphasized that diversity work must be uniquely designed for each individual organization. As companies will have different requirements and approaches to diversity, it is important that diversity efforts be adapted accordingly.

Nonetheless, we believe that there exist some standard practices that will prove effective for most organizations. Thus diversity work must begin with an identification of specific needs and goals. Based on these, senior management can draw up a diversity policy and mission statement to serve as guidelines for all subsequent work. It is vital that one employee be given the overall responsibility for managing diversity work. Equally, senior managers must give their support to initiatives, and allocate sufficient resources for diversity management.

Of course, an organization may encounter internal resistance to diversity. We have outlined above why such resistance occurs and which strategies can be adopted to curb it.

After finishing this chapter we hope that you will have gained knowledge of some tools and ideas for practical work in diversity management.

Case Study

Abercrombie & Fitch

Background

Abercrombie & Fitch is an American clothing retailer based in New Albany, Ohio. Its products focus on casual wear for consumers aged 18 to 22 years, personifying what the company describes as 'the privileged All-American collegiate lifestyle' (Abercrombie & Fitch, 2007). The company has approximately 85,000 employees and 1,000 outlets in North America, Europe and Asia.

Hiring practices at Abercrombie & Fitch

Abercrombie & Fitch is one of the most recognized names in clothes retailing, due in large part to its strong focus on brand and associated hiring practices. It has been accused of being 'run by marketers who put brand first and everything else second' (Skorupa, 2012). Great emphasis is placed on employing highly attractive sales staff, who fit the retailer's particular brand image. Prospective employees are often approached on the street or while shopping to be told, 'You've got just the right look to come and work for Abercrombie & Fitch' (Cañas and Sorensen, 2011; Carmon, 2010; Mitchelson, 2007). Called 'brand representatives' rather than shop assistants, sales staff also form a pool of potential models used in the firm's advertising campaigns. Some staff are recruited to dance inside the shops rather than serve customers, or to pose shirtless at the shop entrance for passers-by to take photos, thereby further raising awareness of the brand (Lambert, 2011; Mitchelson, 2007).

In a rare interview conducted in 2006, Abercrombie & Fitch's CEO, Michael Jeffries, explained the rationale behind the firm's emphasis on looks: 'we hire good-looking people in our stores ... [b]ecause good-looking people attract other good-looking people, and we want to market to cool, good-looking people. We don't market to anyone other than that.' Jeffries was forthcoming about Abercrombie & Fitch's target customer base: 'In every school there are the cool and popular kids, and then there are the not-so-cool kids,' he said.

> Candidly, we go after the cool kids. We go after the attractive all-American kid with a great attitude and a lot of friends. A lot of people don't belong [in our clothes], and they can't belong. Are we exclusionary? Absolutely. Those companies that are in trouble are trying to target everybody: young, old, fat, skinny. But then you become totally vanilla. You don't alienate anybody, but you don't excite anybody, either. (Denizet-Lewis, 2006)

The company is well known for its racy advertising campaigns featuring scantily dressed models, and has undergone criticism in the past for its now-discontinued magazine and catalogue *A&F Quarterly*, which presented photographs of naked, all-American teenagers in suggestive poses, simulating sex with one another (Denizet-Lewis, 2006; Kazdin, 2003). According to Bruce Weber, the photographer for Abercrombie & Fitch's promotional materials,

Jeffries personally interviews everyone appearing in each photo. He is similarly involved with other aspects of the brand image, approving details of all the company's merchandise down to how the clothes are folded on shop display tables (Berner, 2005).

One might say that Jeffries is the living embodiment of the brand he created after taking over the helm of Abercrombie & Fitch in 1992 (previously an unsuccessful men's clothing retailer). Regardless of the weather, he comes to work each day dressed in flip flops and torn jeans, or shorts. Now in his sixties, Jeffries continues to dye his hair blond 'because it is fun', and photographs suggest that he has undergone cosmetic surgery. According to a former colleague, 'He would like to be a guy with a young body in California' (Berner, 2005).

Diversity and Abercrombie & Fitch

As a result of the focus on youth and beauty amongst its sales staff, which form the majority of its workforce, Abercrombie & Fitch has a youthful employee profile: the average age is 27 years (Skorupa, 2012). Despite the close match in age between its staff and its target audience, however, the company is not always accurate in judging the tastes and values of the younger generation. In 2002 the company launched a range of 'Asian' t-shirts featuring depictions of Chinese men together with stereotypical slogans from the early 1900s such as 'Wong Brothers Laundry Service — Two Wongs Can Make It White'. Members of the Asian-American community were quick to offer reasons why they found the shirts offensive, such as the portrayal of Asian Americans doing menial, low-status work historically forced upon them, and the reproduction of century-old stereotypes of Asians as 'kung-fu fighting, fortune-cookie speaking, slanty-eyed, bucktooth servants' (Kang and Kato, 2002). Such protests took Abercrombie & Fitch by surprise. A public relations representative said that the t-shirts were designed to appeal to young Asian shoppers with a sense of humour: 'We personally thought Asians would love this T-shirt' (Strasburg, 2002).

More controversy came in 2005 when Abercrombie & Fitch launched a series of women's t-shirts with slogans such as 'Who Needs a Brain When You Have These?', 'Gentlemen Prefer Tig Ol' Bitties' and 'Do I Make You Look Fat?'. Protests led to some of the t-shirts being withdrawn from sale. In response, CEO Michael Jeffries claimed that the company has a

> morals committee for t-shirts...Sometimes they're on vacation. Listen, do we go too far sometimes? Absolutely. But we push the envelope, and we try to be funny, and we try to stay authentic and relevant to our target customer. I really don't care what anyone other than our target customer thinks. (Denizet-Lewis, 2006)

Discrimination claims at Abercrombie & Fitch

Race discrimination

In 2003 Abercrombie & Fitch was sued in a class action suit in the United States. Nine former employees accused the firm of discrimination, and specifically of 'engaging in recruiting and hiring practices that exclude minorities and adopting a virtually all-white marketing campaign'. The litigants, all from ethnic minority groups, claimed they were forced to work in stockrooms or take night shifts because they did not fit the 'Abercrombie look'. Day shifts were staffed by white employees, while any minority employees who were hired were assigned to work nights. 'The greeters and the people that worked in the in-season clothing, most, if not all of them, were white', said Anthony Ocampo, one of the litigants. 'The people that worked in the stockroom, where nobody sees them, were mostly Asian-American, Filipino, Mexican, Latino' (Leung, 2003).

> 'I remember how discouraged I felt when I applied for a job at the Santa Clara store and the manager suggested that I work in the stockroom or on the late night crew in a non-sales position', recounted Eduardo Gonzalez, a university student. 'I felt it was because I was a Latino – but there was no one I could report this to at the time.' Ocampo, a recent graduate from Stanford University, was told he could not be hired for a vacant position because there were 'already too many Filipinos'. Another university student, Carla Grubb, was constructively dismissed after having been assigned cleaning and other menial jobs to be performed after the shop had closed.

'I felt demoralized being the only African American employee and being specifically assigned to dust the store, wash the windows and clean the floors.' (Lozano, 2004)

Jennifer Lu, also a university student, worked as a brand representative at Abercrombie & Fitch for over three years. One day a corporate executive visiting the shop pointed to a poster of a white, shirtless male model and told staff, 'This is the Abercrombie & Fitch look – you need to make your store look more like this'. Just under a month later Lu and five other Asian-American sales staff were dismissed, while several African-American staff members were transferred to jobs in the stockroom, out of sight of customers (Lozano, 2004).

Although Abercrombie & Fitch denied any discriminatory action on their part, in 2005 they settled the lawsuit for $40 million. In a statement, CEO Michael Jeffries claimed that: 'We have, and always have had, no tolerance for discrimination. We decided to settle this suit because we felt that a long, drawn out dispute would have been harmful to the company and distracting to management' (Greenhouse, 2004). Tom Lenox, Director of Corporate Communications at Abercrombie & Fitch, also declared that: 'We are an All-American brand with a global reputation and customer base encompassing many national races and ethnic groups. Diversity is essential to our business and our brand' (Esemplare, 2005).

Disability discrimination

In 2009 Abercrombie & Fitch was again the defendant in a lawsuit when Riam Dean, a disabled law student in the United Kingdom, claimed that the company had forced her to work in the stockroom because her prosthetic arm did not fit its brand image. Dean had previously been given permission by the shop manager to wear a cardigan in order to cover the joint of her prosthetic left arm. After a visit from the company's 'visual team', which inspects the appearance of shop staff, Dean was told that she would have to remove the cardigan or work in the stockroom until the company's winter uniform became available later in the year (Pidd, 2009; Topping, 2009).

In her statement to the court, Dean said,
It made me feel as though [the store manager] had picked up on my most personal, sensitive and deeply buried insecurities about being accepted and included. Her words pierced right through the armour of 20 years of building up personal confidence about me as a person, and that I am much more than a girl with only one arm. She brought me back down to earth to a point where I questioned my self worth. My achievements and triumphs in life were brought right down to that moment where I realized that I was unacceptable to my employer because of how I looked. (Pasulka, 2009)

A former Abercrombie & Fitch visual manager, once responsible for hiring and recruiting, attested under condition of anonymity to similar instances of discrimination throughout the company. The former manager stated that an Abercrombie & Fitch regional manager had 'cancelled one of my otherwise-perfectly-good hires when it turned out he had a deformed arm'. A further claim was revealing:

There is a 'style guide' that hiring managers get to see. It contains almost no text – just a few dozen pages, each with a full-sized color photograph of different ethnicities – a male and a female for each. They are supposed to serve as examples of the kind of people you should hire. Presumably so the managers will know what good-looking minorities look like. They're amongst the confidential files that are never meant to leave the office, but I'm surprised none have ever surfaced. And all of the minorities, by the way, are as white looking as a person can be without actually being Caucasian.' (North, 2009)

An employment tribunal awarded Dean £8,000 for unlawful harassment, ruling that Abercrombie & Fitch failed to comply with employment law. The tribunal added that Dean's dismissal was a consequence of unlawful harassment arising 'not from treating the claimant differently from non-disabled associates [in enforcing the 'look policy'], but in treating her the same in circumstances where it should have made an adjustment' (Topping, 2009). In a statement, the company's legal counsel claimed that the findings of the tribunal were based 'on the events of a single day' and that these 'were not at all representative of Ms Dean's overall employment with Abercrombie & Fitch. We continue to believe that these events resulted from a misunderstanding that could have been avoided by better communication on the part of both parties.' (BBC, 2009).

Religious discrimination

Abercrombie & Fitch was also sued in 2009 by Samantha Elauf, an American high school student. Elauf, possessing some previous retail experience, had been interviewed for a position at an Abercrombie Kids shop and was ultimately turned down. During the interview she had worn a black hijab, or headscarf, as is customary among observant Muslim women. Later a friend who worked in the same shop told her that it was the headscarf which had cost her the job. During a subsequent investigation by the Equal Employment Opportunity Commission (EEOC), Abercrombie & Fitch issued an agency policy statement as follows: 'under the Look Policy, associates must wear clothing that is consistent with the Abercrombie brand, cannot wear hats or other coverings, and cannot wear clothes that are the color black' (Gregory, 2009).

In 2011 a federal court ruled that Abercrombie & Fitch had violated Elauf's civil rights, awarding her $20,000 in compensatory damages (Harper, 2011). The court found that the company had failed to show that it would have sustained significant undue hardship if it had accommodated Elauf in allowing her to wear the headscarf on the job. Abercrombie & Fitch's attorneys had argued that 'deviation from even a single element of the Look Policy can distort the desired brand effect and consumer perceptions, resulting in negative customer experiences, damages to the Abercrombie brand and a decline in sales'. The EEOC countered that this was pure conjecture, as there was no existing evidence to suggest that sales would suffer following deviations from the Look Policy. The agency also pointed out that Abercrombie & Fitch had permitted eight or nine other female employees to wear headscarves since 2010, and had also previously allowed female staff members to wear skirts or jewellery for religious reasons (Leblang and Holtzman, 2012). Speaking to journalists after hearing the verdict, Elauf said she had wanted to sue not just for herself, but for other Muslim girls: 'There is no reason why a Muslim girl should go to a job interview worrying about the fact that they wear a headscarf. Stand up for yourself, and don't let anyone tell you you're not

good enough to work somewhere' (Sims, 2011).

A few days before the Elauf ruling, another discrimination lawsuit was filed against Abercrombie & Fitch. Umme-Hani Khan, an American high school student, worked for 4 months at a 'Hollister Co' shop (a clothing chain owned by Abercrombie & Fitch, targeted at young people aged 14–18 years) before being dismissed for refusing to remove her headscarf (Leblang and Holtzman, 2012). Khan, who worked primarily in the stockroom in a 'low-visibility position', had worn the headscarf without incident since being hired. She was told to wear headscarves in Hollister colours, before finally being fired in February 2010 for refusing to remove her headscarf after a visiting district manager told her it violated Abercrombie's employee dress code. A corporate human resources manager also requested that she stop wearing the headscarf. 'When I was asked to remove my scarf after being hired with it on, I was demoralized and felt unwanted', said Khan. 'Growing up in this country where the Bill of Rights guarantees freedom of religion, I have felt let down' (May, 2011). At the time of this book's publication, the case has yet to be resolved. Abercrombie & Fitch has not commented on the lawsuit.

The current picture at Abercrombie & Fitch

Abercrombie & Fitch's website has a page devoted to 'Diversity and Inclusion', where it presents information regarding the composition of its workforce. According to the website, 50 per cent of its shop employees are non-white; 48 per cent of its in-shop models are non-white; and 41 per cent of its shop managers in training are non-white. Some details are also provided concerning the company's diversity leadership, while the three diversity councils charged with providing support for and implementing Abercrombie & Fitch's diversity strategy are listed. The website states that, 'Since launching our initiative, we have made significant strides and embraced the conversation around diversity and inclusion'. The company's diversity and inclusion programme focuses on six key drivers: employee engagement, communication, training and education, measurement and accountability, leadership commitment and policy integration (Babcock, 2011).

Todd Corley, Abercrombie & Fitch's senior vice president, Diversity and Inclusion, says that the company's Look Policy Committee meets on a regular basis to ensure that policy statements 'are mindful of differences, whatever they are'. He describes the company's challenge as being to ensure 'that we are true to our brand because people expect a consistent shopping experience regardless of where our store is located'. According to Corley, CEO Michael Jeffries supports the diversity work undertaken at Abercrombie & Fitch. 'He says to me annually, "Don't take your foot off the pedal. Keep pushing this work because it's important to us".' (Babcock, 2011).

The company has established a partnership with the National Society of High School Scholars to operate the Abercrombie & Fitch Global Diversity Scholarship Program, which awards scholarships to student leaders who champion diversity and equality issues. Internally, the company holds a twice-yearly Diversity Week and an annual Diversity Champion Program. The latter consists of a four-month, metrics-based contest during which the company seeks to discover diversity champions among staff members by assessing hiring statistics and rankings on inclusion surveys, and by conducting a blind vote (Babcock, 2011).

With regard to inclusion of lesbian, gay and bisexual employees, Abercrombie & Fitch has been identified by the Human Resources Campaign in its 2012 Corporate Equality Index as a company that is '100% LGBT friendly'. The rating is only given to organizations that provide 'equal health coverage for all LGBT employees and their families, including full parity for domestic partner benefits not only in the basic medical coverage, but in dependent care, retirement, and other benefits that affect families' financial and medical well-being' (Human Resources Campaign, 2011).

Despite these positive indicators, Abercrombie & Fitch has not managed to avoid further controversy over its diversity-related practices. In 2011 the Centre for Equal Opportunities and Opposition to Racism in Belgium began an investigation into Abercrombie & Fitch's hiring and remuneration policies in that country. The company is suspected of only hiring personnel who are under 25 years of age, or making excessive demands regarding the physical appearance of its staff, and of awarding higher compensation to male models who work shirtless (De Wilde, 2011). It seems that this latter sales tactic is also a standard practice at the UK flagship shop (Mitchelson, 2007).

Abercrombie & Fitch has clearly become a more inclusive employer since the initial discrimination lawsuit in 2003. Notwithstanding the progress made, recent events indicate that there is still some way to go before the company's stated commitment to diversity is fully disseminated throughout its many workplaces. The tension between strict adherence to brand image on the one hand and compliance with discrimination legislation on the other is proving a difficult challenge for Abercrombie & Fitch to manage effectively.

Test Your Understanding

1. Given Abercrombie & Fitch's diversity work, why does the company continue to be sued for discrimination?
2. What are some steps that Abercrombie & Fitch can take to avoid further lawsuits?
3. What role does leadership have to play in establishing Abercrombie & Fitch's perspective on diversity?
4. Go to Abercrombie & Fitch's 'Casting' webpage (http://www.abercrombie.co.uk/webapp/wcs/stores/servlet/Casting?catalogId= 11556&langId= -1&storeId= 19658#) and scroll through all the models. Do they represent the diversity that Abercrombie & Fitch claims characterizes their staff?
5. Do you see evidence of resistance to diversity within Abercrombie & Fitch? Explain your answer.

REFERENCES

Abercrombie & Fitch (2007) Four Iconic Businesses: One 'BRAND', http://www.library.corporate-ir.net/library/61/617/61701/items/249197/Piper_June_2007.pdf, date accessed 17 January 2012.

J. Acker (2006) 'Inequality Regimes: Gender, Class and Race in Organizations', *Gender & Society*, 20, 441–64.

M. G. Alkadry and L. E. Tower (2011) 'Covert Pay Discrimination: How Authority Predicts Pay Differences Between Women and Men', *Public Administration Review*, 71(5), 740–50.

R. Anand and M. F. Winters (2008) 'A Retrospective View of Corporate Diversity Training From 1964 to the Present.' *Academy of Management Learning & Education*, 7(3), 356–72.

D. R. Avery (2003) 'Reactions to Diversity in Recruitment Advertising – Are Differences Black and White?' *Journal of Applied Psychology*, 88 (4), 672–9.

*D. R. Avery (2011) 'Support for Diversity in Organizations: A Theoretical Exploration of its Origins and Offshoots', *Organizational Psychology Review*, 1 (3), 239–56.

D. R. Avery and P. F. McKay (2006). 'Target Practice: An Organizational Impression Management Approach To Attracting Minority And Female Job Applicants', *Personnel Psychology*, 59 (1), 157–87.

P. Babcock (2011) 'Abercrombie & Fitch's Diversity Journey', *We Know Next (Society for Human Resource Management)*, http://www.weknownext.com/workplace/abercrombie-fitchs-diversity-journey, date accessed 17 January 2012.

BBC (2009) 'Woman Wins Clothes Store Tribunal', *BBC News*, http://www.news.bbc.co.uk/1/hi/8200140.stm, date accessed 17 January 2012.

*M. J. Bendick, M. L. Egan and S. M. Lofhjelm (2001) 'Workforce Diversity Training: From Anti-Discrimination Compliance to Organizational Development', *Human Resource Planning*, 24 (2), 10–25.

R. Berner (2005) 'Flip-flops, Torn Jeans – and Control: Abercrombie's Mike Jeffries is quirky and informal, but he sure hates to delegate', *Business Week*, http://www.businessweek.com/magazine/content/05_22/b3935105.htm, date accessed 17 January 2012.

D. Bjerk (2008) 'Glass Ceilings or Sticky Floors? Statistical Discrimination in a Dynamic Model of Hiring and Promotion', *Economic Journal*, 118 (530), 961–82.

F. D. Blau and L. M. Kahn (2007) 'The Gender Pay Gap', *The Economists' Voice*, 4 (4), 1–6.

A. P. Brief, R. M. Butz and E. A. Deitch (2005) 'Organizations as Reflections of their Environments: The Case of Race Composition' in R. L. Dipboye and A. Colella (eds) *Discrimination at Work: The Psychological and Organizational Bases* (Mahwah, NJ: Lawrence Erlbaum), pp. 119–48.

A. P. Brief, R. R. Cohen, J. Dietz, S. D. Pugh and J. B. Vaslow (2000) 'Just Doing Business: Modern Racism and Obedience to Authority as Explanations for Employment Discrimination', *Organizational Behavior and Human Decision Processes*, 81, 72–7.

S. Bührer and M. Schraudner, (2006) *Gender-Aspekte in der Forschung* (Stuttgart, Fraunhofer IRB Verlag).

K. A. Cañas and J. K. Sorensen (2011) 'Case Study: The Classic Look of Discrimination: Abercrombie & Fitch's Struggle to Manage Diversity', in K. A. Cañas & H. Sondak (eds) *Opportunities and Challenges of Workplace Diversity: Theory, Cases and Exercises*, 2nd edn (Upper Saddle River, NJ: Prentice Hall), 109–17.

I. Carmon (2010) 'American Beauty: A Brief history of Abercrombie's Hiring Practices', *Jezebel*, http://www.jezebel.com/5479980/american-beauty-a-brief-history-of-abercrombies-hiring-practices, date accessed 17 January 2012.

N. M. Carter and C. Silva (2010) *Mentoring: Necessary but Insufficient for Advancement* (New York: Catalyst).

L. Chamberlain (2011) 'Tribunal Awards: Which Discrimination Cases Attract the Biggest Payouts?', *Personnel Today*, http://www.personneltoday.com/articles/2011/09/12/57940/tribunal-awards-which-discrimination-cases-attract-the-biggest.html, date accessed 7 October 2011.

F. K. Cocchiara, M. L. Connerley and M. P. Bell (2010) ' "A GEM" for Increasing the Effectiveness of Diversity Training', *Human Resource Management*, 49 (6), 1089–106.

G. M. Combs (2003) 'The Duality of Race and Gender for Managerial African American Women: Implications of Informal Social Networks on Career Advancement', *Human Resource Development Review*, 2 (4), 385–405.

*T. H. J. Cox and S. Blake (1991) 'Managing Cultural Diversity: Implications for Organizational Competitiveness', *Executive*, 5 (3), 45–56.

*B. D'Netto and A. S. Sohal (1999) 'Human Resource Practices and Workforce Diversity: An Empirical Assessment', *International Journal of Manpower*, 20 (8), 530–47.

Daily Mail (2011) 'Nicolas Sarkozy Joins David Cameron and Angela Merkel View that Multiculturalism has Failed', *Daily Mail*, http://www.dailymail.co.uk/news/article-1355961/Nicolas-Sarkozy-joins-David-Cameron-Angela-Merkel-view-multiculturalism-failed.html, date accessed 18 October 2011.

B. Denizet-Lewis (2006) 'The Man Behind Abercrombie & Fitch', *Salon*, http://www.salon.com/2006/01/24/jeffries/, date accessed 17 January, 2012.

G. Desvaux, S. Devillard and S. Sancier-Sultan (2010) *Women Matter 3 – Women Leaders, A Competitive Edge In and After the Crises* (Paris: McKinsey and Company), http://www.mckinsey.com/locations/swiss/news_publications/pdf/Women_Matter_3_English.pdf, date accessed 12 September 2011.

S. De Wilde (2011) 'CGKR opent dossier tegen A&F', *De Standaard*, http://www.standaard.be/artikel/detail.aspx?artikelid= DMF20111209_047, date accessed 17 January 2012.

R. Din-Dzietham, W. N. Nembhard, R. Collins and S. K. Davis (2004) 'Perceived Stress Following Race-Based Discrimination at Work is Associated with Hypertension in African-Americans: The Metro Atlanta Heart Disease Study, 1999–2001', *Social Science and Medicine*, 58 (3), 449–61.

J. F. Dovidio and S. L. Gaertner (2000) 'Aversive Racism and Selection Decisions: 1989 and 1999', *Psychological Science*, 11 (4), 315–19.

DSB (2012a) Mangfoldighed, http://www.dsb.dk/om-dsb/dsbs-csr-politik/medarbejdere/mangfoldighed/, date accessed 4 January 2012.

DSB (2012b) DSB som arbejdsplads, http://www.dsb.dk/om-dsb/job-i-dsb/dsb-som-arbejdsplads/ date accessed 4 January 2012.

DSB (2012c) DSB i Copenhagen Pride 2011, http://www.youtu.be/mbplEwaHwyw, date accessed 4 January 2012;

I. M. Duranczyk, N. Madyun, R. R., Jehangir and J.L. Higbee (2011) 'Toward A Mentoring Model For Promotion And Tenure: Progress And Pitfalls', *Journal of Diversity Management*, 6 (2), 21–30.

Edeka (2012) Supermarkt der Generationen – Konzept erfolgreich, http://www.edeka.de/NORDBAYERN/Content/de/Home/Pressemeldung0148.html), date accessed 20 January 2012.

K. Elsesser, and L. A. Peplau (2006) 'The Glass Partition: Obstacles to Cross-Sex Friendships at Work', *Human Relations*, 59 (8), 1077–100.

*R. J. Ely and D. A. Thomas (2001) 'Cultural Diversity at Work: The Effects of Diversity Perspectives on Work Group Processes and Outcomes', *Administrative Science Quarterly,* 46, 229–73.

Ericsson (2012) Bright Ideas Bright Prospects, http://www.ericsson.com/article/employee_video_20100331154235, date accessed 2012-01-10.

J. Esemplare (2005) 'Abercrombie & Fitch Settles Racial Bias Case', *Black Press USA*, http://www.blackpressusa.com/news/Article.asp?SID= 3&Title= National+News&NewsID= 3703, date accessed 17 January 2012.

Eurostat (2010) Gender Pay Gap Statistics, http://www.epp.eurostat.ec.europa.eu/statistics_explained/index.php/Gender_pay_gap_statistics, date accessed 13 January 2012.

Eurostat (2011) Tertiary Education Statistics, http://www.epp.eurostat.ec.europa.eu/statistics_explained/index.php/Tertiary_education_statistics, date accessed 11 January 2012.

H. S. Feild and W. H. Holley (1982) 'The Relationship of Performance Appraisal System Characteristics to Verdicts in Selected Employment Discrimination Cases', *Academy of Management Journal*, 25 (2), 392–406.

*C. Foster and L. Harris (2005) 'Easy to Say, Difficult to Do: Diversity Management in Retail', *Human Resource Management Journal*, 15 (3), 4–17.

E. Friday and S. S. Friday (2003) 'Managing Diversity Using a Strategic Planned Change Approach', *Journal of Management Development*, 22(10), 863–80.

G. Frost-Danielsen, M. Fröberg and G. Jonsson (2002) *Mångfald som personalidé. Handbok för multikulturell rekrytering* (Stockholm: Svenskt PA Forum AB).

D. Gaucher, J. Friesen and A. C. Kay (2011) 'Evidence that Gendered Wording in Job Advertisements Exists and Sustains Gender Inequality' *Journal of Personality and Social Psychology*, 101 (1), 109–28.

S. Greenhouse (2004) 'Abercombie & Fitch Bias Case is Settled', *The New York Times*, http://www.nytimes.com/2004/11/17/national/17settle.html, date accessed 18 October 2011.

S. Gregory (2009) 'Abercrombie Faces a Muslim-headscarf Lawsuit', *Time*, http://www.time.com/time/business/article/0,8599,1925607,00.html#ixzz1jjwXws2X, date accessed 17 January 2012.

D. Harper (2011) 'Jury Awards $20,000 to Tulsa Woman in Abercrombie & Fitch Lawsuit', *Tulsa World*, http://www.tulsaworld.com/news/article.aspx?subjectid=14&articleid=20110720_14_0_Thefed881279&r=5741, date accessed 18 October 2011.

I. Hau Siu Chow and R. B. Crawford (2004). 'Gender, Ethnic Diversity, and Career Advancement in the Workplace: The Social Identity Perspective'. *SAM Advanced Management Journal*, 69 (3), 22–31.

D. Hausman (forthcoming 2012) 'How Congress Could Reduce Unconscious Job Discrimination by Promoting Anonymous Hiring' *Stanford Law Review*, 64.

*H. W., Hennessey Jr. and H. J. Bernardin (2003) 'The Relationship Between Performance Appraisal Criterion Specificity and Statistical Evidence of Discrimination', *Human Resource Management*, 42 (2), 143–58.

A. Herdman and A. McMillan-Capehart (2010) 'Establishing a Diversity Program is Not Enough: Exploring the Determinants of Diversity Climate', *Journal of Business & Psychology,* 25 (1), 39–53.

S. A. Hewlett and C. B. Luce (2005) 'Off-ramps and On-ramps: Keeping Talented Women on the Road to Success', *Harvard Business Review*, 83 (3), 43–54.

L. M. Hite and K. S. McDonald (2006) 'Diversity Training Pitfalls and Possibilities: An Exploration of Small and Mid-size US Organizations', *Human Resource Development International*, 9 (3), 365–77.

M. A. Hogg and D. J. Terry (2000) 'Social Identity and Self-Categorization Processes in Organizational Contexts', *Academy of Management Review*, 25 (1), 121–40.

J. M. Hoobler, S. J. Wayne and G. Lemmon (2009) 'Bosses' Perceptions of Family-Work Conflict and Women's Promotability: Glass Ceiling Effects', *Academy of Management Journal*, 52 (5), 939–57.

HSBC (2010) 2010 Employment Equity Narrative Report, http://www.hsbc.ca/1/2/en/about-us/careers/valuing-diversity#TrainingAndDevelopment, date accessed 6 September 2011.

Human Capital Institute (2008) 'Award-winning Stories: Mentoring as a Career Development Tool', HCI White Paper, 21 August 2008, http://www.hci.org/files/field_content_file/hciLibraryPaper_79824.pdf, date accessed 9 January 2012.

Human Resources Campaign (2011) Corporate Equality Index 2012: Rating American Workplaces on Lesbian, Gay, Bisexual and Transgender Equality, http://www.sites.hrc.org/documents/CorporateEqualityIndex_2012.pdf, date accessed 17 January 2012.

IBM Denmark (2012), Mentoring as a Business Tool at IBM, http://www.diversitytrainersplus.com/index-41982.html, date accessed 6 January 2012.

IBM Netherlands (2012), Managing Diversity at IBM Nederland, http://www.diversityatwork.net/EN/en_case_004.htm, date accessed 17 January 2012.

M. Igbaria and J. J. Baroudi (1995) 'The Impact of Job Performance Evaluations on Career Advancement Prospects: An Examination of Gender Differences in the IS Workplace', *MIS Quarterly*, 19 (1), 107–23.

M. Igbaria and C. Shayo (1997) 'The Impact of Race and Gender Differences on Job Performance Evaluations and Career Success', *Equal Opportunities International*, 16(8), 12–23.

International Organization for Diversity Management (IDM), http://www.idm-diversity.org/eng/index.html, date accessed 17 January 2012.

E. H. James (2000) 'Race-Related Differences in Promotions and Support: Underlying Effects of Human and Social Capital', *Organization Science*, 11 (5), 493–508.

E. H. James and L. P. Wooten (2006) 'Diversity Crises: How Firms Manage Discrimination Lawsuits', *Academy of Management Journal*, 49 (6), 1103–18.

A. Kalev, E. Kelly and F. Dobbin (2006) 'Best Practices or Best Guesses? Assessing the Efficacy of Corporate Affirmative Action and Diversity Policies', *American Sociological Review*, 71 (4), 589–617.

C. Kang and D. Kato (2002) 'Clothier's New Line of Shirts Backfires', *The San Jose Mercury News*, cited in B. Mikkelson and D. P. Mikkelson (2007, May 3) 'Shirt stop', *snopes.com*, http://www.snopes.com/racial/business/tshirts.asp, date accessed 17 January 2012.

L. M. Kath, C. A. Swody, V. J. Magley, J. A. Bunk and J. A. Gallus (2009) 'Cross-evel, Three-way Interactions Among Work-group Climate, Gender, and Frequency of Harassment on Morale and Withdrawal Outcomes of Sexual Harassment', *Journal of Occupational and Organizational Psychology*, 82, 159–82.

C. Kazdin (2003) 'Have Yourself a Horny Little Christmas', *Salon*, http://www.salon.com/2003/11/26/abercrombie/, date accessed 17 January 2012.

M. Keil, B. Amershi, S. Holmes, H. Jablonski, E. Lüthi, K. Matoba, A. Plett and K von Unruh (2007) 'Training Manual for Diversity Management', International Society for Diversity Management (IDM), http://www.idm-diversity.org/eng/index.html, date accessed 7 January 2012.

E. Kelly and F. Dobbin (1998) 'How Affirmative Action Became Diversity Management', *American Behavioral Scientist*, 41 (7), 960–84.

*D. L. Kidder, M. J. Lankau, D. Chrobot-Mason, K. A. Mollica and R. A. Friedman (2004) 'Backlash Toward Diversity Initiatives: Examining the Impact of Diversity Programme Justification, Personal and Group Outcomes', *International Journal of Conflict Management*, 15 (1), 77–102.

G. Kirton and A. M. Greene (2010) *The Dynamics of Managing Diversity* (Elsevier Butterworth-Heinemann).

S. B. Knouse (2009) 'Targeted Recruiting for Diversity: Strategy, Impression Management, Realistic Expectations, and Diversity Climate', *International Journal of Management*, 26 (3), 347–53.

Z. Kunda and P. Thagard (1996) 'Forming Impressions from Stereotypes, Traits, and Behaviors: A Parallel-Constraint-Satisfaction Theory', *Psychological Review*, 103, 284–308.

E. Lambert (2011) 'Shirtless Models Causing Controversy at Grand Strand Store', *WMBF News*, http://www.wmbfnews.com/story/16387412/shirtless-models-causing-controversy-at-grand-strand-store, date accessed 17 January 2012.

K. B. Leblang and R. N. Holtzman (2012) 'Religious˙Attire at Work: Abercrombie Faces Discrimination Lawsuits', *Lexology*, http://www.lexology.com/library/detail.aspx?g=593bda9f-0cfa-422a-963a-855aa6271c25, date accessed 17 January 2012.

R. Leung (2003) 'The Look of Abercrombie & Fitch', *CBS News*, http://www.cbsnews.com/stories/2003/12/05/60minutes/main587099.shtml, date accessed 17 January 2012.

S. Liff. (1997) 'Two Routes to Managing Diversity: Individual Differences or Social Group Characteristics', *Employee Relations*, 19 (1), 11–26.

A. Locksley, C. Hepburn and V. Ortiz (1982), 'Social Stereotypes and Judgments of Individuals', *Journal of Experimental Social Psychology*, 18, 23–42.

M. Lozano (2004) 'Abercrombie & Fitch Settlement Requires New Diversity Programs', *LegalNewsWatch*, http://www.legalnewswatch.com/496/abercrombie-fitch-settlement-requires-new-diversity-programs, date accessed 17 January 2012.

A. Mathews (1998) 'Diversity: A Principle of Human Resource Management', *Public Personnel Management*, 27 (2), 175–85.

C. May (2011) 'Abercrombie & Fitch Faces Another Diversity Lawsuit', *The Daily Caller*, http://www.dailycaller.com/2011/06/27/abercrombie-fitch-faces-another-diversity-lawsuit/, date accessed 17 January 2012.

J. B. McConahay (1986) 'Modern Racism, Ambivalence, and the Modern Racism Scale' in J. F. Dovidio and S. L. Gaertner (eds) *Prejudice, Discrimination, and Racism* (San Diego: Academic Press), pp. 91–125.

C. T. Miller and B. Major (2000) 'Coping with Stigma and Prejudice' in T. F. Heatherton, R. E. Kleck, M. R. Hebl and J. G. Hull (eds) *The Social Psychology of Stigma* (New York: Guilford), pp. 243–72.

T. Mitchelson (2007) 'Poseurs Paradise! What's it Really Like to Work at the New Abercrombie and Fitch Store?', *Daily Mail*, http://www.dailymail.co.uk/femail/article-447183/Poseurs-Paradise-Whats-really-like-work-new-Abercrombie–Fitch-store.html, date accessed 17 January 2012.

L. M. Morgan and M. J. Davidson (2008) 'Sexual Dynamics in Mentoring Relationships: A Critical Review', *British Journal of Management*, 19, 120–29.

C. Müller and G. Sander (2005) *Gleichstellungs-Controlling. Das Handbuch für die Arbeitswelt* (Zürich: vdf Hochschulverlag AG).

C. Müller and G. Sander (2009) *Innovativ führen mit Diversity-Kompetenz Vielfalt als Chance* (Bern: Haupt Verlag).

T. W. H. Ng, L. T. Eby, K. L. Sorensen and D. C. Feldman (2005) 'Predictors of Objective and Subjective Career Success: A Meta-Analysis', *Personnel Psychology*, 58 (2), 367–408.

A. North (2009) 'Banished Employee, Others Speak Out Against Abercrombie's Awfulness', *Jezebel*, http://www.jezebel.com/5302021/banished-employee-others-speak-out-against-abercrombies-awfulness, date accessed 17 January 2012.

Novo Nordisk (2011) Novo Nordisk Annual Report – Diversity, http://www.annualreport2010.novonordisk.com/social/employees/diversity.aspx, date accessed 2 September 2009.

V. Omanović (2006) *A Production of Diversity. Appearances, Ideas, Interests, Actions, Contradictions and Praxis* (Göteborg: BAS Publishing).

I. S. Parkins, H. D. Fishbein and P. N. Ritchey (2006) 'The Influence of Personality on Workplace Bullying and Discrimination', *Journal of Applied Social Psychology*, 3, 2554–77.

S. Pasulka (2009) 'Riam Dean: "I questioned my self-worth" ', *Zelda Lily*, http://www.zeldalily.com/index.php/2009/09/riam-dean-i-questioned-my-self-worth-zelda-lily-exclusive/, date accessed 17 January 2012.

S. Paul-Emile (2006) 'Diversity Models in Organizations', *International Journal of Diversity in Organisations, Communities and Nations*, 5 (4), 15–19.

Personnel Today (2008) 'Proctor & Gamble Links Manager Pay to Diversity', http://www.personneltoday.com/articles/2008/05/23/45996/proctor.html, date accessed 5 January 2012.

H. Pidd (2009) 'Disabled Student Sues Abercrombie & Fitch for Discrimination', *The Guardian*, http://www.guardian.co.uk/money/2009/jun/24/abercrombie-fitch-tribunal-riam-dean?INTCMP= ILCNETTXT3487, date accessed 17 January 2012.

P. W. Pitts (2007) 'Implementation of Diversity Management Programmes in Public Organizations: Lessons from Policy Implementation Research', *International Journal of Public Administration*, 30 (12–14), 1573–90.

B. R. Ragins and J. M. Cornwell (2001) 'Pink Triangles: Antecedents and Consequences of Perceived Workplace Discrimination Against Gay and Lesbian Employees', *Journal of Applied Psychology*, 84, 529–50.

Raiffeisen (2007) Fachstelle Profil: Strategie 2007–09 [centre profile: strategy 2007–09]. Internal documentation of Gudrun Sander.

Raiffeisen (2008) Projekt Gleichstellungs-Controlling: Kurzprotokoll des Coachings vom 8. Februar 2008 [Project Equality Controlling: Minutes of Coaching from 8 February]. Internal documentation of Gudrun Sander.

A. Risberg (2010) 'Diversity Management in Practice: The Case of Diversity Work in a Swedish Municipality', *Proceedings of the 3rd international conference on Intercultural collaboration,* pp. 1–8.

A. Risberg and A-M. Søderberg (2008) 'Translating a Management Concept: Diversity Management in Denmark', *Gender in Management: An International Journal*, 23 (6), 426–41.

L. Roberson, C. T. Kulik and M. B. Pepper (2001) 'Designing Effective Diversity Training: Influence of Group Composition and Trainee Experience', *Journal of Organizational Behavior*, 22 (8), 871–85.

K. Rosenberg (2003) 'Praktiska exempel. En redovisning av 18 arbetsvärderingsprojekt och några kvalifikationsbedömningsprojekt' *Jämställdhetsombudsmannen,* http://www.do.se/sv/Material/Analys-lonelots/, date accessed 13 January 2012.

J. Rubery (1995) 'Performance-related Pay and the Prospects for Gender Pay Equity', *Journal of Management Studies*, 32 (5), 637–54.

A. M. Saks, and D. A. Waldman (1998) 'The Relationship Between Age and Job Performance Evaluations for Entry-level Professionals', *Journal of Organizational Behavior*, 19 (4), 409.

SBB (2010) Genderkompetenz. Personalgewinnung: Checkliste für HR-Beratung. [Gender competence recruiting: checklist for HR-consulting]. Internal documentation of Gudrun Sander.

D. Sekaquaptewa and M. Thompson (2003) 'Solo Status, Stereotype Threat, and Performance Expectancies: Their Effects on Women's Performance', *Journal of Experimental Social Psychology,* 39 (1), 68–74.

J. Shen, A. Chanda, B. D'Netto and M. Monga (2009) 'Managing Diversity through Human Resource Management: An International Perspective and Conceptual Framework', *International Journal of Human Resource Management*, 20 (2), 235–51.

A. Sims (2011) 'Abercrombie & Fitch Lawsuit Winner Says She Sued for all Muslim Girls', *News on 6*, http://www.newson6.com/story/15119371/winner-in-abercrombie-fitch-lawsuit, date accessed 17 January 2012.

C. S. Sims, F. Drasgow and L. F. Fitzgerald (2005) 'The Effects of Sexual Harassment on Turnover in the Military: Time-Dependent Modelling', *Journal of Applied Psychology*, 90 (6), 1141–52.

D. Skorupa (2012) 'Best and Worst Companies in Retail', *Retail Info Systems News*, http://www.risnews.edgl.com/retail-insight-blog/Best-and-Worst-Companies-in-Retail77668, date accessed 17 January 2012.

J. Stewart and V. Harte (2010) 'The Implications of Talent Management for Diversity Training: An Exploratory Study', *Journal of European Industrial Training*, 34 (6), 506–18.

J. Strasburg (2002) 'Abercrombie & Glitch: Asian Americans Rip Retailer for Stereotypes on T-shirts', *San Francisco Chronicle*, http://www.sfgate.com/cgi-bin/article.cgi?f=/c/a/2002/04/18/MN109646.DTL#ixzz1jiXfljEH, date accessed 17 January 2012.

D. Subeliani and G. Tsogas (2005) 'Managing Diversity in the Netherlands: A Case Study of Rabobank', *The International Journal of Human Resource Management*, 16 (5), 831–51.

H. Tajfel and J. C. Turner (1986), 'The Social Identity Theory of Intergroup Behaviour' in S. Worchel and W. G. Austin (eds) *Psychology of Intergroup Relations* (Chicago: Nelson-Hall), pp. 7–24.

*A. Tatli and M. Özbilgin (2009) 'Understanding Diversity Managers' Role in Organizational Change: Towards a Conceptual Framework', *Canadian Journal of Administrative Sciences / Revue Canadienne des Sciences de l'Administration*, 26 (3), 244–58.

D. E. Terpstra (1997) 'Recommendations for Research on the Effects of Organizational Diversity on Women', *Journal of Business and Psychology*, 11 (4), 485–92.

D. A. Thomas (2004) 'Diversity as Strategy', *Harvard Business Review*, 82 (9), 98–108.

D. A. Thomas and R. J. Ely (1996) 'Making Differences Matter: A New Paradigm for Managing Diversity', *Harvard Business Review*, 74 (5), 79–90.

*K. M. Thomas and V. C. Plaut (2008) 'The Many Faces of Diversity Resistance in the Work-place' in K. M. Thomas (ed.) *Diversity Resistance in Organizations* (Abingdon, Oxfordshire: Lawrence Erlbaum), pp. 1–22.

A. Topping (2009) 'Disabled Worker Wins Case for Wrongful Dismissal Against Abercrombie & Fitch', *The Guardian*, http://www.guardian.co.uk/money/2009/aug/13/abercrombie-fitch-employee-case-damages, date accessed 18 October 2011.

H. J. Van Buren, III (1996) 'Ending the Culture of Corporate Discrimination', *Business and Society Review*, 98, 20–23.

Vattenfall (2012), Mentorprogram för ökad mångfald, http://www.newsroom.vattenfall.se/2012/01/03/mentorprogram-for-okad-mangfald/, date accessed 11 January 2012.

T. K. Vescio, G. B. Sechrist and M. P. Paolucci (2003) 'Perspective Taking and Prejudice Reduction: The Mediational Role of Empathy Arousal and Situational Attributions', *European Journal of Social Psychology*, 33, 455–72.

C. J. Vinkenburg, M. L. van Engen, A. H. Eagly and M. C. Johannesen-Schmidt (2011) 'An Exploration of Stereotypical Beliefs about Leadership Styles: Is Transformational Leadership a Route to Women's Promotion?' *The Leadership Quarterly*, 22 (1), 10–21.

Volvo (2011) *Regionala nätverk för mångfald*, Volvo Group Sverige, http://www.volvogroup.com/group/sweden/sv-se/career/life_at_volvo_group/diversity/resources/pages/resources.aspx, date accessed 8 September 2011.

Volvo (2012) Employee Networks, http://www.volvogroup.com/GROUP/GLOBAL/EN-GB/CAREER/LIFE%20AT%20VOLVO%20GROUP/DIVERSITY/EMPLOYEE%20NETWORKS/PAGES/EMPLOYEE_NETWORKS.ASPX?print=yes?print=yes, date accessed 6 January 2012.

C. Wiethoff (2004) 'Motivation to Learn and Diversity Training: Application of the Theory of Planned Behavior', *Human Resource Development Quarterly*, 15, 263–78.

D. R. Williams and R. Williams-Morris (2000) 'Racism and Mental Health: The African American Experience', *Ethnicity and Health,* 5 (3/4), 243–68.

C. R. Willness, P. Steel and K. Lee (2007) 'A Meta-analysis of the Antecedents and Consequences of Workplace Sexual Harassment', *Personnel Psychology*, 60, 127–62.

L. P. Wooten and E. H. James (2004) 'When Firms Fail to Learn: The Perpetuation of Discrimination in the Workplace', *Journal of Management Inquiry*, 12 (1), 23–33.

O. Wright and J. Taylor (2011) 'Cameron: My War on Multiculturalism', *The Independent*, http://www.independent.co.uk/news/uk/politics/cameron-my-war-on-multiculturalism-2205074.html, dated accessed 18 October 2011.

S. Zahidi and H. Ibarra (2010) The Corporate Gender Gap Report 2010, http://www3.weforum.org/docs/WEF_GenderGap_CorporateReport_2010.pdf, date accessed 20 September 2011.

J. C. Ziegert and P. J. Hanges (2005) 'Employment Discrimination: The Role of Implicit Attitudes, Motivation, and a Climate for Racial Bias', *Journal of Applied Psychology*, 90 (3), 553–62.

CHAPTER 9

WORK, LIFE AND A CULTURE OF CARE

Robyn Remke and Annette Risberg

Chapter Objectives

After completing this chapter, you should be able to:
- describe demographic and other changes in society that affect attitudes towards work;
- understand how demographic and attitudinal changes towards work influence organizations and organizational practices;
- define and explain the different terms used to describe the work-life interface;
- describe how the contemporary workplace is changing to accomodate and encourage greater diversity;
- describe and reflect on ways that organizations can become more inclusive and supportive of worker well-being.

Chapter Outline

- Introduction
- Managing the changing workplace and workforce: the relationship between diversity management and the work-life interface
- A history of the work-life interface
- Organizational practices – manifestations of the work-life interface
- Organizational practices in the changing workplace
- The body at work and the work-life interface
- The work-life interface in the contemporary organization: an organizational culture of care
- Chapter review questions
- Case study
- References

INTRODUCTION

Increasing diversity and the search for a healthy work-life balance are two major forces acting to transform the contemporary workplace in terms of our experience and understanding of work. The first of these is reflected in a continual re-definition of that elusive construct, the 'average worker'. Specifically, the workforce is becoming more inclusive, so that many organizations now display a high degree of diversity in their staff. This trend is being driven by fundamental economic, social and environmental pressures. For example, in advanced economies the double-income or single-parent family has now replaced the traditional male breadwinner model (Edlund 2007; Margherita, O'Dorchai, and Bosch, 2009).

Furthermore, many countries around the world are becoming increasingly reliant on foreign workers (Ehrenreich and Hochschild, 2002; Mohn, 2011), in part due to a dearth of young people within their own ageing societies. Some governments, such as those of the United Kingdom (UK), Denmark and the United States of America (USA) have raised the age of retirement, while older workers are themselves choosing to work past traditional retirement ages in order to supplement their meagre pensions (Brandon, 2010). In regard to the search for a healthy work-life balance (our second transformative force), we see that attitudes and norms regarding workplace behaviour, in particular the relationship between work and private obligations, are changing to reflect a more diverse and globalized workforce. Workers are no longer willing to prioritize organizational values at the expense of their personal values (Sturges and Guest, 2004; Whyte, 1956), and they expect organizations better to accommodate their community and familial needs. In fact, young workers born in Europe and North America during the late 1980s and 1990s, often called 'Generation Me' or 'Generation Y,' increasingly express a strong desire to maintain a healthy balance between work demands and 'life priorities' (Smola and Sutton, 2002; Sturges and Guest, 2004). Even in the midst of a global economic recession, today's highly skilled workers demand to be given the time and resources to care for children and elderly parents, to participate in leisure activities in their communities, sports clubs or religious groups, to enjoy extended holidays, and to look after their mental and physical well-being. And, even in difficult economic times, many companies are willing to sign up to positive work-life policies in order to prevent other companies from poaching their top talent (Knowledge@Wharton, 2011; Needleman, 2011).

Viewed separately, these two forces for change represent great opportunities and major challenges for organizational managers. However, we will argue in this chapter that rather than examining diversity and work-life issues separately, it makes more sense to consider each of these phenomena through the 'lens' of the other. To clarify, we can better manage organizational diversity when we acknowledge that work-life issues have an impact on the pool of potential workers *and* the nature of the work that they are able and willing to carry out. And conversely, we can only fully address work-life challenges when we understand that a diverse workforce will have a different set of needs and expectations than one which is less inclusive.

We begin our discussion by considering the relationship between diversity and the work-life interface, followed by an exploration of the latter concept and its history. Thereafter, we continue by defining various terms related to the work-life interface, discussing their differences and similarities. Towards the end of the chapter we introduce definitions of the family unit, as well as demographic groups that fall outside so-called norms, in order to discuss how these can achieve a work-life equilibrium through a more inclusive workplace. We close the chapter with a discussion of what is required to create an effective and caring workplace, and give a case study example of an unusual yet promising workplace model.

MANAGING THE CHANGING WORKPLACE AND WORKFORCE: THE RELATIONSHIP BETWEEN DIVERSITY MANAGEMENT AND THE WORK-LIFE INTERFACE

We can examine in more detail the relationship between diversity and the work-life interface by considering some of the organizational policies that address these issues. For example, company initiatives regarding flexitime, family leave and workplace adaption are designed to attract and retain a more diverse workforce by meeting the personal and family needs of individual workers. Evidence suggests that these policies are effective first steps in helping organizations, particularly knowledge-based firms, to diversify (Chapter 8). However, the fostering of inclusion and removal of barriers to promotion remain challenges for organizations throughout the world.

Today, many years after affirmative action laws and policies have, at least in theory, produced equal opportunity, women and minorities continue to face glass ceilings to traditional leadership positions. They earn less than white men and are overly represented in certain occupations, such as nursing and teaching (women) or construction work (immigrants) (Shen, Chanda, D'Netto, and Monga, 2009). While equal opportunity, anti-discrimination and affirmative action laws and policies have helped create greater diversity in some organizations, much more needs to be done. If companies wish to attract and retain diverse qualified workers, they must increasingly treat the work-life interface as an integral part of their diversity management strategy.

As mentioned earlier, one response to the changing workforce and workplace is to develop policies that focus on the intersection between professional and private life, such as family leave and flexitime. As they have become widespread, these practices have greatly contributed to the diversification of organizations. Yet policies often fail to adequately address the complexity of the constantly changing work-life interface. For example, although maternity leave policies (whether national or internal) help many women return to work after having or adopting a child, not all countries or organizations support paternity leave. This is a great hindrance to single or same-sex partnered fathers, hetero-sexual couples who both pursue a full-time career, or fathers who choose to be full-time caregivers (Hymowitz, 2012; Morris, Munoz and Neering, 2002). Thus employers and employees continue to search for ways to manage the conflict between professional and private interests. A recent focus on the nature of the workplace culture, or *workplace wellness*, provides evidence of this (Kirby and Harter, 2001).

While there exist various definitions of the term *workplace wellness*, we adopt that of Buck Consultants given in their report 'Working Well: A Global Survey of Health Promotion and Workplace':

'*Workplace wellness* refers to programs designed to improve the health and well-being of employees (and their families), in order to enhance organizational performance and reduce costs. *Wellness programs* typically address specific behaviors and health risk factors, such as poor nutrition, physical inactivity, stress, obesity, and smoking. These factors commonly lead to serious and expensive health problems and have a negative impact on workforce productivity.' (Working Well, 2009)

But are work-life policies really so influential? Do they truly make a difference to the work experience of the average employee? Research suggests that workers who are satisfied with their work-life arrangements demonstrate higher levels of employee loyalty and less workplace stress and conflict (McMillan, Morris and Atchley, 2010; Polach, 2003), indicating that these policies can, at least in part, contribute to a positive work experience. In addition, improved work-life arrangements may help to attract and maintain valuable workers. For exam-ple, women (even fully-employed mothers) continue to perform a greater share of household tasks and caring work than men (Hochschild, 1997; Jayson, 2007; Schiebinger and Gilmartin, 2010). This extra demand on their time and energy leads some female employees to either reduce their working week or to 'opt out' of paid employment entirely (Stone, 2007; Moe and Shandy, 2010). Job sectors in which women are already underrepresented are particularly affected (Eagly and Carli, 2007; Hewlett and Luce, 2005), and this problem can best be remedied by establishing more favourable work-life policies. Similarly, disabled workers can enjoy successful and fulfilling careers while making a valuable contribu-tion to organizational performance if their specific workplace requirements are accommodated (Roulstone, Gradwell, Price and Child, 2003).

In general, we can say that organizations that fail to take account of work-life needs jeopardize the physical, mental and emotional health of their employees, which in turn can have a significant negative impact on the organizational culture and other outcomes. Organizations that fail to introduce creative work-life solutions to the unique needs of current or prospective employees risk losing or discouraging valuable talent, and will find themselves unable to sustain a diverse workplace. The evidence for these policies is significant: Participants in the EU sponsored *Living to Work – Working to Live. Tomorrow's Work-life Balance in Europe* forum held in 2004 provided the following examples of the benefits of various company-sponsored work-life schemes (Eurofound, 2004):

- Stress-related sick leave costs GBP £7.1m each week, while the average cost of an employee leaving is nearly £4,000, rising to £6,000 for a manager.
- Xerox (UK) Ltd estimates it has saved over one million pounds over the last five years through enhanced retention due to better policies, including flexible working and leave schemes.
- BT (UK) reports that 98 per cent of women now return to work after maternity leave, saving the firm three million pounds in recruitment and induction costs. The company also said absenteeism is down to 3.1 per cent compared to the UK average of 8.5 per cent.
- Replacing an employee equates to 50–100 per cent of the annual salary of an employee.

Similarly, a report written for the British secretary of state for business found

> many examples of companies and organizations where performance and profitability have been transformed by employee engagement; we have met many employees who are only too keen to explain how their working lives have been transformed; and we have read many studies which show a clear correlation between engagement and performance – and most importantly between improving engagement and improving performance. (MacLeod and Clarke, 2009, p. 3)

These studies confirm that appropriate and useful work-life measures serve to increase worker loyalty and satisfaction, while decreasing workplace conflict and stress. This constitutes a useful strategy to help organizations attract and retain diverse talents.

Appropriate and useful work-life practices will:
- increase worker loyalty;
- increase satisfaction;
- decrease workplace conflict and stress.

A HISTORY OF THE WORK-LIFE INTERFACE

While many of the issues concerning the work-life interface have arisen in con-nection with the pressures of contemporary lifestyles, their roots can be traced to the worker protection measures and policies sponsored by labour move-ments in western Europe and North America from the late nineteenth century onwards. These labour movements took a rather different form on either side of the Atlantic, and indeed considerable differences could be found between individual European countries. Geary (1972) provides a good overview. The Inter-national Labour Organization (ILO) was set up as one response to the efforts of these labour movements (www.ilo.org). Anti-discrimination laws were designed to tackle the blatant discrimination and exploitation of workers, whether men, women or children, immigrant workers, or those belonging to a specific religion or social class. Employment legislation was put in place to safeguard the fam-ily (for example, introduction of the eight-hour working day) or, more recently, to uphold the right to wear devotional jewellery or religious clothing at work (such as the Christian Cross or the Muslim Hijab). Because most western European economies were industrial or agriculturally based until the mid-twentieth cen-tury, these policies were largely devised to protect factory and manual workers. In time, work-safety agencies and other regulatory bodies were established to attempt to reduce the high risk of occupational injury in such manual and agri-cultural jobs. For example, in the preamble to the ILO constitution (written in 1919), the following areas were listed:

1. regulation of the hours of work including the establishment of a maximum working day and week;
2. regulation of labour supply, prevention of unemployment and provision of an adequate living wage;
3. protection of the worker against sickness, disease and injury arising out of his employment;
4. protection of children, young persons and women;
5. provision for old age and injury, protection of the interests of workers when employed in countries other than their own;
6. recognition of the principle of equal remuneration for work of equal value;
7. recognition of the principle of freedom of association;
8. organization of vocational and technical education, and other measures.
   Source: ILO (2012).

According to the European Centre for the Development of Vocational Training, the nature of work is undergoing considerable change: most new jobs are pro-jected to be in knowledge- or skill-based professions such as management and technical jobs (European Centre for the Development of Vocational Training, 2010). Correspondingly, knowledge-intensive firms and organizations have adapted their workplace policies to take account of the work-life needs of a changing workplace. These policies, which we will discuss later in the chapter, include flexitime and family leave schemes that help workers to manage their work and family demands. Given the predicted shift towards knowledge- and skill-based work, our investigation will focus on the work-life interface as it is constituted in the modern workplace.

Knowledge-intensive firms or *organizations* are those in which the prime commodity is knowledge, in whatever form. Examples are law firms, universities and banking institutions. Of course, even if an organization's primary objective is in manufacturing or some other practical activity, it may still need to maintain a strong knowledge base. For example, large engineering or construction companies will generally have accounting, communication and management departments, which essentially operate as in a knowledge-intensive firm.

To begin let us consider some terms commonly encountered in this context.

The work-life discourse: a definition of terms

Many different terms are used when discussing the relationship between work and private life. Some will be familiar, such as the work-life balance or work-life tension. However, given the inherent complexity of the work-life interface, it is not surprising that some practitioners find it necessary to employ additional terms.

You may wonder why it is important to study and understand the various terms of the work-life discourse because, after all, these seem rather similar. However, each term prioritizes a particular component of the work-life interface, revealing a slightly different understanding of what the work-life interface means. Therefore, we feel it is important to provide a brief overview of key terms, after which you can decide for yourself which terms best match your experience, and meet the goals or objectives you have in mind. What follows is a brief historical overview of some of the most commonly used terms.

The work-family conflict

North American and European psychologists were the first to study the work-life interface in the mid-1960s, when they investigated the societal impact of white middle-class women entering the male-dominated workforce. While immigrant and working-class women have always worked outside the home, researchers assumed that this shift in workplace demographics would have negative repercussions on the family and society at large. Therefore, most studies focused on *work-family stress* or *conflict* (Greenhaus and Beutell, 1985; Misra, Moller and Budig, 2007). The belief was that the workplace was indeed changing, but in ways that were not entirely acceptable or beneficial for all workers. Many researchers, politicians and social commentators alike argued that the influx of middle-class women into the workforce would displace men from their rightful position as family breadwinner, thereby weakening family ties, depriving children of proper care, and allowing women to challenge traditional social and gender roles.

Early definitions of *work-family stress* or *conflict* included any form of discord in the workplace perceived to stem from the conflicting demands of a worker's private and professional lives. Contemporary definitions tend to take a wider view of such discord to look at the effects *beyond* the workplace, namely in the home and in the community, particularly the impact on familial and other relationships.

More positive terms were introduced as organizations and researchers from other disciplines began to focus on work-life interface policies. Thus *work-family accommodation*, *work-family compensation* and *work-family expansion* (Gregory and Milner, 2009) were coined to describe various aspects of the intersection of work and family, all with a decisive shift away from conflict.

Work-family-life balance

Most recently the terms *work-family* or *work-life balance* (often used inter-changeably) have become popular, not only with researchers but also practitioners. The concept of work-life balance is hard to define as it can be understood in various ways (Pitt-Catsouphes, Kossek and Sweet, 2006), but most generally is used to describe the ways in which individuals and organizations manage or negotiate their respective interests. More specifically, Greenhaus and Singh (2003) define work-family balance as 'the extent to which individuals are equally involved in and equally satisfied with their work role and their family role'. Felstead, Jewson, Phizacklea and Walters (2002) define work-life balance as a relationship between the institution, the individual and cultural/social expectations, while noting that workers are constrained by social norms attributed to forces outside the organization, such as familial expectations. Notice in these definitions the shift of emphasis away from the idea of conflict. These terms offer an alternative approach to the work-life interface by highlighting a more positive engagement or *balancing* of multiple interests encompassing diverse aspects of work and family (McMillan et al., 2010). From a traditional viewpoint, balance is achieved and maintained for individual workers through the establishment of workplace policies such as flexitime or the introduction of new technologies, as for example smartphones, laptops and so on.

It is important to note that the term 'work-life balance' does not indicate an *equal* distribution of time and energy between work and family life, but that the individual finds and creates an appropriate *balance* between these two spheres. Therefore, work-life balance occurs when a healthy equilibrium is established in the allocation of time and physical resources, in one's mental attachment to the home and work spheres, and personal satisfaction gained from one's role as worker, family member or community actor (Greenhaus, Collins and Shaw, 2003).

As uncontroversial as this seems, some scholars take issue with the term work-life balance. In fact, Yost (2011) argues in her blog that the use of the word *balance* 'is a major roadblock that stands between us and having true, meaningful flexibility in the way we manage our work, life and careers'. One reason is that by its very nature, *balance* suggests a weighing of two opposing and entirely separate spheres – in this case private life and the field of work – that do not intersect or overlap. *Balance* then becomes the accomplishment of 'role-related expectations that are negotiated and shared between an individual and his/her role-related partners in the work and family domains' (Grzywacz and Carlson, 2007, p. 458). In other words, one must *manage* or *negotiate* conflicting forces in order to achieve the desired balance.

The onus of responsibility for success or failure to achieve balance falls on the individual, while structural or systemic causes and limitations that affect the work-life interface are generally ignored. Recognizing this misalignment, some scholars use the term *work-life management* to describe the work-life interface, thereby emphasizing the active process of managing the various roles which individuals adopt during an average day. This definition differs from work-life balance in focusing on the actual processes that constitute the work-life interface, while the term balance can then be understood to designate the end result that workers strive to achieve.

Review Questions

- Which term do you prefer? Why?
- Are some terms more applicable to particular types of work than others?

Work-life harmony

Alternatively, some scholars prefer to use terms that reflect the more fluid and even harmonious ways in which individuals blend work and life, thereby blurring traditional boundaries (MacDermid, Roy and Zvonkovic, 2005). For example, the terms *work-personal life integration*, *work-life integration*, *work-life articulation* and *work-personal life harmonization* all indicate a more interdependent and even constructive relationship between work and one's personal life (Gregory and Milner, 2009). Thus, work-life harmony is 'an individually pleasing, congruent arrangement of work and life roles that is interwoven into a single narrative of life' (McMillan et al., 2010, p. 15). Just as individual musical notes take on a new and agreeable unity when played as a diatonic chord, so the work-life interface is best understood from the perspective of multiple components operating simultaneously to create a unified and harmonious whole.

While *harmony* may have a more positive connotation than management or negotiation, in its suggested usage the term does not ignore the inherent complexities of the work-life interface. Directly addressing the challenges of work-life balance and allowing for the possibility of conflict, McMillan et al. (2010) suggest that harmony occurs when 'the resources gained through work-life enrichment are successfully aligned with, and serve to, ameliorate, or alleviate the stressors arising from work-life conflict'. Here the idea seems to be that some form of conflict is inevitable; harmony is achieved when such conflict is defused by the application of individual and organizational resources.

In general, the wider public discourse on the work-life interface has focused on the only obvious beneficiary of the desired balance: the individual worker. However, organizations are increasingly realizing that they also stand to gain if their employees are happy both at work and at home. One major benefit is, of course, that organizational practices aimed at helping employees find a good work-life balance will also in many cases foster diversity. By highlighting the importance of the work-life interface, an organization indicates that it has understood the fundamental reality that when an organizational culture functions well, 'work resources meet family demands, and family resources meet work demands such that participation is effective in both domains' (Voydanoff, 2005, p. 825). Workers are no longer required or expected to prioritize work demands over family obligations; moreover, organizations must also provide resources to help workers meet their family's needs because 'organizational survival and economic well-being directly relate to dynamics of the "total job environment" for people' (Kirby and Harter, 2001, p. 121).

This *total job environment* encompasses not only the spheres of work and family life, but also the area of intersection between the two. Therefore, organizations that wish to help their members perform better must provide resources and create policies that address the work-life interface in its entirety. In so doing they establish an organizational culture that is supportive not only of members' official duties, but also their private responsibilities. In the next section we will examine a few of the practices that can be adopted to help foster such a positive culture.

Review Questions

- What is the significance of the alternative terminology described above to describe the work-life equilibrium?
- Do you think the terms that organizations use in their work-life policies have a direct impact?

What do these terms say about our understanding of the workplace and the work-life interface?
- If you were a manager asked to create work-life policies, which terms would you use?

ORGANIZATIONAL PRACTICES – MANIFESTATIONS OF THE WORK-LIFE INTERFACE

We begin with a useful definition: 'Work-life balance practices in the workplace are ... those that, intentionally or otherwise, increase the flexibility and autonomy of the worker in negotiating their attention (time) and presence in the workplace' (Gregory and Milner, 2009, p. 1).

> *Work-life balance practices* let employees determine how and when they work. They help workers create schedules that give them greater autonomy within the workplace.

Practices relating to the work-life interface differ from one organization to the next, and from one country to the next (Abendroth and den Dulk, 2011; Edlund, 2007; Ollier-Malaterre, 2009). A range of family policies can be found across Europe. For example, in the countries of northern Europe, which generally enjoy high levels of female employment, the state (as the dominant caretaker) implements social policy on a nationwide basis. The societal norm is that mothers and fathers both re-enter the workforce after maternity or paternity leave, supported by laws on extensive family leave, subsidized day care and so on.

In other parts of Europe, however, issues related to the work-life interface are dealt with in ways that maintain the family as the dominant caretaker, and there is strong resistance to non-family models of childcare. A report from the European Commission (Commission of the European Communities, 2008) confirms that only five EU member states, namely Denmark, the Netherlands, Sweden, Belgium and Spain, may claim that more than a third of young children (age range 0-3 years) are in some form of daily childcare. In Estonia, Hungary, Malta, Slovakia, Latvia, Austria, the Czech Republic and Poland only 10 per cent of young children are in daily childcare (Commission of the European Communities, 2008). Of course, the supply of daycare for children will dictate the extent to which both parents are able to work full-time.

The two divergent attitudes to the family described above have been termed *de-familialisation* and *familialism*, respectively. Market-driven economies such as those of the United Kingdom and the United States of America tend to leave it up to the individual family and organization to resolve work-life conflicts (Edlund, 2007). Not surprisingly, we find the greatest range and variety of work-life interface policies in these two countries.

Whether at the level of the state, the organization, or indeed the individual worker, many actors around the world are currently attempting to defuse areas of conflict within the work-life interface through the creation and implementation of specific policies and programmes. We begin our discussion of these policies by examining two major concerns of the work-life interface: time management and child/family care.

Time management

Studies show that, for a variety of reasons, workers in all sectors of the economy are working longer hours and taking fewer holidays (Hochschild, 1997; Orr, 2004). Knowledge-based workers often have the luxury of being able to work outside the office, when and where they want, due to the widespread uptake in recent years of new technologies such as laptops and smartphones, and the increased availability of high speed internet connections. While some observers initially expressed concern that such telecommuting could lead to a decrease in efficiency, numerous studies have confirmed that workers actually put in more hours (Kvande, 2009) at the same time as their productivity has increased. It has become common, for example, for employees to answer e-mails or edit reports during the evenings or on weekends. And it is not only the knowledge-based employment sector that shows a lengthening of the working week. Industrial workers and those employed in services also report that they are under pressure to increase their work commitment, including mandatory overtime and double shifts (Kodz, Davis, Lain, Strebler, Rick, Bates, Cummings and Meager, 2003; Tavernise, 2012).

Of course, when individuals are required to put in more hours at work, it means that less time is available to attend to their personal well-being, to look after the family (including in many cases both young children and ageing parents), to attend to community and religious events, and to engage in leisure activities. Yet our families, our religious and civic organizations and our hobbies are essential to maintaining a healthy body and mind. To assist employees in keeping a good work-life balance, some organizations are implementing workplace policies that encourage better time management. These include the introduction of *flexitime*, *part-time contracts*, *working from home* and *job sharing*. There may exist subtle differences in the ways in which organizations implement these policies, but in general the intended result is either to provide greater flexibility in the scheduling of work or to reduce the number of hours in the workplace.

Flexitime (also called flextime or flexible working hours) is a type of flexible work arrangement that allows employees to vary their work schedules, within certain ranges and dimensions, according to their needs (Hyland, 2003).

Job sharing is an employment scheme in which two or more workers share a position. They do not work at the same time, but rather each works a half day, a half week or every second week, for example.

Flexitime and working from home are now commonplace in organizations that employ knowledge workers. In some cases employers are also willing to hire workers on a part-time or reduced-workload basis. The practice of *job sharing* is, however, more difficult to implement with success, although some organizations claim to be satisfied with the results.

While few organizations are will to offer job sharing, Gerri Vopelak and Kathy Tenenbaum, partners at Job Sharing Resources (an employment service company), suggest that there can be some wide-ranging benefits for the employee and employer:

Job sharing

- acts as a benefit that can be worth money and can be used as an attraction and retention mechanism;
- enables a company to reach an untapped pool of highly motivated professionals who are using the services of Job Sharing Resources;
- enables the new employee to get 'up to speed' quicker;
- acts as an incentive for many professionals since time has become as important as money;
- helps to maintain 'diversity' in the workplace;
- rewards talent and increases job satisfaction;
- increases morale and productivity. When an employee has created a more balanced life through job sharing, their anxiety and stress levels are greatly reduced.

Source: Rosenberg McKay (2012).

In general, research indicates that workplace policies for time management are of practical help for all workers in managing the work-life interface (Hayman, 2009; Peters, den Dulk and van der Lippe, 2009; Russell, O'Connell and McGinnity, 2009; Kvande, 2009). In particular, they support women in achieving the balancing act of holding down paid employment *and* meeting their private obligations – which Hochschild (1997) calls the 'Second Shift' – namely the care of children, home and community (Meisenbach, 2010).

Most research into the impact of time management policies confirms that such measures do in fact help workers achieve greater harmony by reducing the conflict between their work and home obligations. Interestingly, however, some individuals who work from home report increased levels of physical and mental stress (Peters et al., 2009; Russell et al., 2009), so that the benefits of improved work-life management seem in these cases overstated. For example, some telecommuters complain that a 'business mindset', with its focus on efficiency and speed, has come to dominate their private lives. The home gradually loses its leisure and family orientation, and thus the potential to relieve stress. Other workers who use flexitime or who work from home have encountered an intensification of the work process (by having to respond to emails at all hours of the day, for example), with negative repercussions on their well-being (Kelliher and Anderson, 2009).

Flexitime and telecommuting are some of the most common work-life schemes offered to employees (Sahadi, 2007). Many kinds of organizations are now drawing up policies to offer workers greater autonomy in choosing how they work. For example, the medium-sized Amerisure Insurance Company allows employees in their Detroit office to schedule their working day as they choose between the hours of 7 am and 10 pm. Or consider the 16-partner Washington D.C. law firm Bailey Law Group, which decided to integrate telecommuting into their workplace culture when two of their top lawyers moved out-of-state. The law firm not only benefited from the worker's increased loyalty, but also in terms of additional business from these new home locations.

Even governments can create a flexible workplace: employees at the Seattle branch of the US Government Accountability Office know that they have to put in 80 hours of work every two weeks. However, they are allowed to schedule those hours as they see fit, with the exception of one day a week when managers require all employees to come into the office at the same time (Sahadi, 2007).

- Have you, or someone you know, used flexitime at work? Was it a positive experience?
- If you had the option, would you choose to telecommute? Do you think it would be a positive experience?
- Why, in your opinion, do some workers have a negative experience of flexitime and telecommuting? Why might they suffer from increased stress or conflict?
- What can organizations do to make flexitime and telecommuting more attractive to workers?

Family and community care

In an effort to attract and retain a high quality, diverse workforce, ever more organizations are striving to create *family friendly workplaces*. We can point to four interrelated components that can contribute to this aim. These are:

1. programmes and policies that promote employees' quality of life;
2. workplace cultures and climates that reflect 'family' or employee-centred assumptions and beliefs;
3. workplace relationships (for instance with supervisors and co-workers) that are respectful of employees' work *and* private responsibilities;
4. work processes, systems, structures or practices that are designed to serve the dual agenda, namely mutually beneficial outcomes for both the organization and for employees.

Source: Pitt-Catsouphes (2002).

Although a number of different programmes and policies will contribute to a family friendly workplace, perhaps the most significant of these is *family leave*.

It is rather difficult to give an exact definition of what we mean by *family leave*, as such policies can vary widely from country to country, or indeed from organization to organization. Over the last decades women in most industrialized countries have increasingly entered the paid workforce out of economic necessity and/or to pursue careers outside the home. As a result, governments have developed policies to help parents care for their young children while not suffering negative consequences in terms of their employment. Most broadly, *family leave* is defined as any period of paid or unpaid leave granted in order to care for the birth or adoption of a child. In some countries and organizations family leave also includes time away from the workplace to care for an ailing relative, whether a child, spouse or parent.

There is good evidence that family leave policies enable women to retain their jobs and careers when choosing to have a family (OECD, 2007). Such policies also help to increase the talent and gender diversity of the workforce. It is important to understand that family leave policies, unlike many other organizational policies, necessarily represent a synthesis of work, family and cultural forces. They tie together the competing and often conflicting roles of husband/wife, worker, parent, cultural participant and so forth, that individuals must constantly adopt and discard. In addition, family leave taps into two fundamental and emotionally charged areas of our lives, namely our occupations and our families, through which we define ourselves and find fulfilment. These two areas are also linked to the wider ideological discourse of cultural, religious, spiritual and moral norms. Put simply, family leave is not just another organizational policy that dictates how employees spend their time; it is a policy which can shape the very definition and nature of employment.

The benefits of family leave policies are accepted by many countries, especially in northern Europe, where they are hugely popular. However, there remain lingering doubts as to the cost effectiveness and the long-term repercussions. With that in mind, much research has been undertaken into family leave in the hope of devising a perfect programme in which the needs of the individual, the organization and society at large are all given sufficient consideration.

Although there is disagreement on how best to implement family leave policies, the resulting practices generally lead to an increase in the number of women returning to work after the birth or adoption of a child. Furthermore, family leave programmes normally have a positive effect on the mental well-being of workers and their children (Bower, 1988; Tulman and Fawcett, 1991). They can also lead to increased employee commitment and overall job satisfaction (Brown, Ferrara and Schley, 2002).

Thus, family leave programmes are viewed positively by both employers and employees, while researchers agree that they help to encourage workplace diversity.

However, even in countries that have established national family leave policies, the actual implementation of these still requires careful negotiation between employer and employee (Meisenbach, Remke, Buzzanell and Liu, 2008; Miller, Jablin, Casey, Horn and Ethington, 1996). Kirby (2000), for example, uncovered a lack of negotiation between worker and supervisor regarding leave. Across organizations, the implementation of organizational policy on family leave greatly depends on the role and message consistency of the supervisor, so that practices can be inconsistent even in organizations with a clear policy (Sahadi, 2007). Furthermore, a worker's ability to make full use of leave policies can be hampered by power dynamics that make negotiation uncomfortable, difficult or even impossible (Liu and Buzzanell, 2004; Meisenbach et al., 2008). Some workers may limit their claims for leave due to the fear that this will be perceived negatively by superiors. And prevailing cultural norms may oppose the uptake of family leave, particularly in the case of men (Fox, Pascall and Warren, 2009). Clearly, merely drawing up a policy will not assure that workers embrace the notion of family leave. Organizations must also create cultures that support the implementations of these practices (Kirby and Krone, 2002).

Nearly 85 per cent of Swedish fathers take paternity leave, making Sweden one of the most 'father-friendly' countries in the world. A new parental leave policy reserves at least two months of paid leave for the 'minority' parent (generally the father). If the leave is not claimed then the income is forfeit. This change is credited for the sharp increase in the number of men taking paternity leave. Interestingly, a cultural shift can be detected, whereby Swedish men who do not take parental leave are questioned about this decision and even criticized. Masculinity is being redefined to include a more involved parenting style. Definitions of what makes a good husband, partner and father are evolving, perhaps encouraged by the change in workplace policy (Bennhold, 2010).

Thus we see that cultural norms in Sweden are changing. Not all countries, however, have such a generous paternity leave policy in place, nor do they have a culture that supports men who take paternity leave. While changes in *national* policy and culture are difficult to achieve, what can workers and managers do to create an *organizational* culture that encourages the adoption of family leave practices?

ORGANIZATIONAL PRACTICES IN THE CHANGING WORKPLACE

Although organizations have made great progress in developing programmes to help workers manage their work-life interface, this is an ongoing process in which it is necessary to reconsider the nature of the contemporary workforce. In the face of increasing diversity, policies that benefit the majority of employees may simultaneously act in ways that discriminate against minority groups. If the goal is to continue to increase workplace diversity and utilize that diversity, then alternatives to the standard polices must be found. One obvious approach is to take better account of the diversity of the contemporary family, as it is constituted in industrial or post-industrial economies.

The idea of family in most western societies no longer corresponds with the traditional nuclear family model consisting of a married heterosexual couple with young, dependent children (Erickson, Martinengo and Hill, 2010; Lucas and Buzzanell, 2006; Stout, 2010). Single parenting has become widespread in many European countries, although households with two parents still dominate (Margherita et al., 2009). There has also been an increase in patchwork or blended families, in which each partner brings children from previous relationships. Thus it is now common to find families in which one or other adult is responsible for children who are not his or her own. Divorced couples may seek full-time or part-time custody of their children, and their childcare needs will vary accordingly (van der Klis and Karsten, 2009; Warren, Fox and Pascall, 2009). Another conception of family which falls outside the so-called norm, and yet requires the same kind of support as 'traditional' families, is the same-sex marriage or civil partnership. Regardless of the specific family structure, most parents in paid employment will need assistance in caring for their families, even after the period of maternity or paternity leave is over.

Leaving the issue of childcare, we note that all workers, regardless of their familial situation, claim the right to a private life outside the workplace (Alberts, Tracy and Trethewey, 2011). As members of extended families and friendship networks, many of us are occasionally obliged to provide care and support to others. Apart from the traditional responsibilities of caring for a partner or spouse, ever more individuals must look after ageing parents while engaged in paid employment. And because the average age of first-time parents is increasing (Pierret, 2006; OECD, 2011), many find themselves looking after young children and ageing parents simultaneously. Today in Europe the average age of first-time mothers is 30 years (Eurostat, 2011). These individuals, squeezed between their obligations towards the previous and the next generation, constitute the so-called 'sandwich generation'. It comes as little surprise that such dual responsibilities can have a negative impact on the work-life interface, and be the cause of severe stress. Indeed, such pressure may, over the long term, lead to stress-related illnesses or even an increased likelihood of workplace accidents, endangering both the caregiver and their co-workers, while also increasing health-related costs. This type of stress inevitably lowers workplace productivity (Teasdale, 2006; Seaward, 1999) and brings the extra financial burdens of absenteeism and staff replacement, interruptions in the workflow and crisis management. Whatever kind of family constellation people choose to create, they should receive appropriate support from their employer in order to be able to reconcile their private and work lives.

While discussions on the work-life interface often focus on time management and the needs of carers, we know that other important concerns must be addressed in connection with rising workforce diversity. For example, one vital but little considered issue is how our work affects our local communities (Voydanoff, 2005).

While it is impossible to explore all the various issues that relate to the work-life interface, in this next section we highlight two very different groups of workers who are often left out of the discussion: lesbian, gay, bisexual and transgendered (LGBT) individuals and the disabled.

THE BODY AT WORK AND THE WORK-LIFE INTERFACE

LGBT Employees

It sometimes happens that heterosexual students question why LGBT dimensions should be included in diversity work, as they tend to perceive sexuality and sexual orientation as a private matter unrelated to the workplace. At the same time they are unaware that heterosexuals often unconsciously display their sexuality at work without adverse consequences.

> *Heteronormativity* refers to the institutions, understanding and practices that privilege and make heterosexuality (the view that a person can be only a heterosexual man or heterosexual woman) the norm.

Example

After returning from their summer holidays, employees at the Danish company Hope A/S gather during the Monday morning coffee break to talk about their experiences. Lena, for example, tells her colleagues that she, her husband and their two children enjoyed some relaxing weeks in their family summer house. Sam excitedly talks about the trip she and her boyfriend made by car to visit some of France's vineyards. Having told her story, Sam turns to Chantal to inquire how she spent her holiday. Chantal only briefly mentions that she went sailing with a friend.

Lena and Sam, by explicitly referring to a husband and boyfriend, identify both their heterosexuality and the fact that they are in a relationship. They also practice heteronormativity by assuming the heterosexual partnerships to be the 'expected' kind. Chantal, in contrast, makes only vague reference to a 'friend'. In fact, her friend is her wife, with whom she is raising a child. Based on her perceptions of the workplace climate and its implicit heterosexism, Chantal feels it likely that she would face overt or subtle discrimination (Chapter 8) were she to come out to her colleagues as a lesbian. Therefore she chooses to conceal her sexuality from her colleagues, and to avoid lengthy discussions about her private life. Instead she describes her wife as an anonymous friend.

In the 'The Rainbow Manager' (Elisson, 2011), Helen Westin, a Swedish businesswoman, describes her experience of a job interview conducted by a recruitment consultant. During the interview the consultant mentioned what she and her husband had done the previous weekend. Ms Westin responded by talking about what she and her girlfriend had done. When she had finished speaking, the recruitment consultant blurted out: 'Is it important for you to throw your sexuality in the faces of everybody you meet?'

It is clear that the consultant held the view that heterosexuality is the norm, and might therefore have been unaware that she had also 'thrown her sexuality' at Ms Westin.

In this example, as in many workplace encounters, heterosexuality is taken to be the norm. When LGBT individuals attempt to openly discuss their personal relationships, some heterosexual co-workers consider this to be unnecessarily provocative or even 'political'. They may even accuse the LGBT individual of 'flaunting' their sexuality or imposing their 'personal issues' into the workplace (Riley, 2008).

Organizations must recognize that sexuality is performed in the workplace; it is a prime example of the ways in which our work and private lives intersect (Trethewey, 1999). As Gedro (2007, p. 154) points out: 'Heterosexuality's performance happens in behavioural contexts of modern work with the placement of a spouse's picture on a desk . . . or during conversations at the coffee pot of what one did over the weekend or on vacation.'

It is to be applauded that a transformation in societal norms in many American-European cultures over the past decades has resulted in a ban on many types of discrimination at the workplace. However, sexual orientation or the taken-for-granted heterosexuality remains the most ignored dimension of workforce diversity in business research and practice. Not all forms and types of sexuality are equally accepted. Many LGBT individuals hide their sexual identities in their workplace because they see the constant dominance of heteronormativity as a source of prejudice, stereotypical ways of thinking and indeed discrimination (Huffman, Watrous-Rodriguez and King, 2008). This fear of discrimination at work, and the concealing of sexual orientation or gender identity, contribute to a feeling of disconnection, which can lead to a high degree of work-related stress. Huffman, Watrous-Rodriguez and King (2008) have discussed the concept of *minority stress*, defined as a unique form of psychological pressure resulting from a lack of concord between the values, culture and experiences of the dominant group and those of a minority group. Heterosexual colleagues may be unaware of the stress that LGBT persons often experience at work, whether closeted or out, or that some LGBT workers may expend valuable energy hiding their private lives, with adverse effects on their efficiency, productivity, psychological and indeed physical well-being (Griffith and Hebl, 2002). Some studies suggest that organizations that adopt anti-discrimination policies and promote acceptance of all sexualities and genders enjoy higher levels of worker productivity (Colgan, Creegan, McKearney and Wright, 2007; van den Bergh, 1999). This performance gain is not just the contribution of LGBT employees, but the entire workforce.

Gender identity is the way in which a person chooses to self-identify as male or female or something in between or beyond this categorization.

Sexual identity describes how a person identifies his or her sexuality in terms of sexual orientation. *Sexual orientation* refers to a pattern of emotional, romantic and/or sexual attraction to males, females, both of these or neither.

If they decide to disclose their sexuality, LGBT employees should hope to receive support and acceptance from the organization and their heterosexual co-workers (Griffith and Hebl, 2002). Unfortunately, this is often not the case. Congdon (2009), for example, recalls a situation in which Jane, an efficient and productive employee, came out to colleagues at work. This disclosure resulted in a wave of gossip about her sexuality amongst Jane's colleagues. However, when senior management learned about the gossip, rather than reprimanding Jane's colleagues and attempting to improve the interpersonal dynamics among the employees, they confronted Jane about her sexuality. In view of this hostile diversity climate, she chose to leave the organization.

Diversity climate is a shared understanding among organization members of an organization's diversity related structures and actions. It comprises the perception of fairness regarding inclusion and exclusion of people from diverse backgrounds.

This is certainly not an isolated example. Therefore, it is vital that organizations strive to become more inclusive and to reduce workplace discrimination in order to foster a workforce that is tolerant of difference in whichever form (Congdon, 2009; Griffith and Hebl, 2002; Huffman et al., 2008).

There are, of course, more positive examples of workplace treatment of LGBT individuals. Sine, a HR manager at IBM Denmark, was approached by one of her female employees, Lise, who told her that she intended to take some time off as parental leave beginning next month. Sine was at first confused, as Lise did not appear to be pregnant. However, she quickly suspected that it was not Lise giving birth, but her same sex partner. Lise had never spoken about her sexuality at work, and did not want her colleagues to know the reason for her future departure. Sine, being a parent herself, convinced Lise not to conceal the fact that she was having a child, as this would only lead to further complications and stress at work. After some discussion, Sine and Lise wrote a short e-mail together announcing that Lise and her female partner would soon be parents. According to Sine, not only did the rest of the staff receive the news very well, but also Lise herself seemed to be more open at work and willing to take the initiative.

The box below discusses some other positive organizational outcomes when a tolerant and LGBT-friendly climate is created.

Example

The Stonewall UK business case

Although some organizations continue to avoid association with LGBT identities or causes, there is a clear business case that supports a focus on sexual orientation in the workplace:

Brand and reputation

- Demonstrate your commitment to diversity to your staff, community and clients.
- Network with employers in your sector, mark yourself out as a leader in your area and benefit from cross-sector networking.

- Benefit from brand loyalty and access to the untapped LGBT market worth an estimated £70 billion a year by showing your support for the LGBT community.
- The public sector procurement market is worth 15% of Gross Domestic Product (GDP), or £220 billion. The Equality Act requires private sector companies to demonstrate their diversity credentials in winning public sector contracts.

Recruitment and retention

- People perform better when they can be themselves. Concealing one's sexual orientation at work reduces productivity – employees need to be able to communicate and build supportive, cooperative relationships with colleagues, clients and service users. Progressive employers recognize that their workforce should reflect the diversity of the population in order to serve the needs of customers and service users. By 2011 only

14.4% of Britain's workforce will be white, male, non-disabled, under 35 and heterosexual. Position your organization as an employer of choice for diverse talent.
- Prejudice has human costs for staff – bullying at work contributes to £12 billion lost to employers each year through stress-related absenteeism.

Risk mitigation

- Avoid bottom-line costs for employers in legal fees, recruiting, inducting and training new staff, and regaining the trust of key stakeholders. So far, £120,000 is the largest sum awarded by an employment tribunal for sexual orientation discrimination. There is no limit to the amount that can be awarded.
- Equality Act – all publicly funded bodies must show how they proactively consider the needs of LGBT staff and service users.

Source: Stonewall UK, 2011.

Organizations can increase their diversity by developing anti-discriminatory policies and structures. 'Companies described as LGBT-supportive organizations have rejected heterosexist policies and instituted "gay-supportive" policies that show support for and acceptance of sexual orientation diversity' (Huffman et al., 2008, p. 240). Every year the US organization Human Rights Campaign (http://www.hrc.org) publishes the Corporate Equality Index. AT&T and Bank of America are two companies that have received top marks as the best employers for LGBT individuals (The Human Rights Campaign, 2012). Yet policies alone may prove insufficient (Chapter 8). In some cases it has been found useful to seek out the support of heterosexual workers, so-called 'straight allies', within the organization 'who believe that lesbian, gay and bisexual people should experience full equality in the workplace. Good straight allies recognize that gay people can perform better if they can be themselves and straight allies use their role within an organization to create a culture where this can happen' (Miles, 2011). Straight allies, who can be found at all levels of the organization, support the view that it is the responsibility of every employee to strive to create an inclusive workplace culture. Their actions can range from a manager deciding to make equality an essential part of business leadership, to individual colleagues challenging homophobic practices (Miles, 2011). Of course, the quality and nature of the support will depend on the position of the straight ally within the organization (Kirby, 2000; Kirby and Krone, 2002). A study by Huffman et al., (2008) found that support from a supervisor has the greatest impact on job satisfaction, while collegial support boosts overall life satisfaction. However, LGBT employees still need

Table 9.1 Management actions to promote a supportive environment

- provide mentoring opportunities;
- plan social networking events;
- self-evaluate own actions towards employees
- interact with employees from diverse groups;
- initiate intercultural training and workshops for employees and managers;
- let job applicants know in the interview process that the organization fosters diversity and inclusion;
- ask minority employees to point out current practices that are not supportive;
- welcome same sex partners to social events;
- do not assume any 'majority/minority' status of any employee;
- assess the climate for minority employees;
- ask the human resources department to include specific minorities (such as LGBT) in the content of current diversity training;
- schedule meetings with leadership/members of the internal LGBT support group, if already established;
- get in touch with and follow the activities of LGBT organizations that monitor workplace discrimination or harassment;
- allow employees time off for whoever the employee deems to be 'family';
- use all-inclusive language (for example 'partner' versus 'spouse') and respond negatively to homophonic statements.

Source: Adapted from Huffman, Watrous-Rodriguez and King (2008).

organizational support to ensure full acceptance and understanding. Table 9.1 lists a number of actions which managers can take to create a LGBT-supportive environment.

Another way to address discrimination and to help LGBT workers manage their work-life interface is to consider the heteronormative nature of the language used at work. A policy that encourages the use of non-discriminatory vocabulary sets the tone for all organizational members. For example, organizations can change the wording of their work-life policies to ensure that these apply equally to all sexes and genders, and to all family constellations. This subtle revision of official language can trigger more fundamental changes within the organizational culture by increasing tolerance and creating positive attitudes to diversity. A more inclusive climate will encourage co-workers to respect LGBT employees as well as raising sensitivity to their concerns. In fact, all staff members will develop greater awareness of their own sexual orientation and gender identity, and what the repercussions can be at the workplace.

A proactive approach should include an assessment of the organizational climate for LGBT managers and employees, diversity training to educate all employees to be more inclusive, equalized organizational structures and practices for LGBT and heterosexuals. Managers should become role models for all employees by striving to create an inclusive organizational culture. In addition to issues of employee interaction, other concrete measures contained in policies and regulations are important factors in influencing the working climate for gays and lesbians. A recent study (Köllen, 2011) of 487 homosexual employees in the German banking sector found that the equalization of benefits for married spouses and registered life-partnerships in companies was by far the most influential factor affecting the organizational climate for gay and lesbian employees. Other practices such as publishing articles on homosexuality in staff magazines or on the Internet significantly help to remove barriers to discussion, and thereby contribute to a more inclusive organization. 'Focusing on LGBT issues is an essential component of a diversity strategy that fosters a supportive workplace for all – it ultimately builds a stronger organization in which employees have the necessary tools and support to realize their full potential' (Riley, 2008, p. 22).

Review Questions

- What can heterosexual co-workers do to make workplaces more LGBT inclusive?
- What actions can leaders take to reduce discriminatory practices towards LGBT individuals?
- What can an organization gain from becoming more LGBT inclusive?

Employees with disabilities

Discussions on diversity generally focus on race, ethnicity, gender, and even religion or beliefs. However, in recent years the issue of disability has become more prominent. This is due to a wider recognition of many forms of disability, attitudinal changes, and a range of technological innovations that have allowed more disabled adults to commute to work, to move with greater ease around the workplace and to perform work-related tasks. This increase in the numbers of disabled workers has, at the same time, highlighted the problems of discrimination which they face. Of course, discriminatory work practices against disabled individuals are illegal in most of Europe and North America. Companies are required to accommodate individuals with disabilities so that they are able to participate in all workplace activities. The EU directive 2000/78/EU of 27 November 2000 (Europa, 2000) established a general framework for equal treatment in employment and occupation, including the disabled. It should perhaps be noted here that disability is a rather broad term. The United Nations Convention on the Rights of Persons with Disabilities states that: 'Persons with disabilities include those who have long-term physical, mental, intellectual or sensory impairments which in interaction with various barriers may hinder their full and effective participation in society on an equal basis with others (article 1)' (UN, 2006).

This definition encompasses a broad range of individuals with diverse needs and abilities. In addition to the previously mentioned EU directive, individual member countries within the European Union have established their own definitions of disability (Chapter 2). Therefore, it is rather difficult to formulate one universallyapplicable definition to indicate precisely the nature of disability. Disabled individuals do, however, have one characteristic in common: all possess a recognized physical or mental impairment (Wertlieb, 1985). Some of these may be visible, for example in the case of wheelchair users, while others can be difficult to detect, such as visual or hearing impairments, certain forms of cognitive disability or chronic illnesses. Whatever the form of impairment, all disabled persons will at some time suffer the stigmatization of being regarded as 'different' (Goffman, 1986). An additional problem for disabled persons is that their impairments are frequently taken by others in society and at work as a basis from which to conceive other negative traits. It is often assumed, for example, that a disabled worker will have a higher degree of dependency than a 'normal' individual and is therefore not suited to most forms of paid employment (Colella and Varma, 2001; Wertlieb, 1985). Such beliefs are reflected in discriminatory practices that place unfair burdens on disabled individuals, and can have negative consequences at job interviews or in terms of promotion. It is not surprising that persons with disabilities experience higher levels of under- and unemployment when compared to the general population (Bruyere and Erickson, 2000).

Workers with disabilities have the same right to a healthy work-life balance as the non-disabled. However, if their impairment necessitates special accommodation or assistance from an organization, then their work-life interface also becomes an organizational responsibility. In other words, their health requirements – which most workers consider a private matter – demand organizational response and adaptation.

Sensitive work-life policies can help disabled workers improve their performance and better manage their personal interests. Unfortunately, even after the introduction of strict legislation to end discrimination in the workplace, some employers persist in discriminatory practices in the belief that it would be prohibitively expensive for them to accommodate disabled workers. However, research indicates that this is not the case. The physical aids and technical adaptions which may be required by disabled workers are not that much more expensive than typical induction and training costs incurred for all new employees (Schartz, Hendricks and Blanck, 2006). In addition, many governments provide grants for workplace accommodation. One American study has found that accommodation is, in fact, a relatively inexpensive process, and highly effective at reducing workplace limitations for *all* employees (Schartz, Hendricks and Blanck, 2006).

Despite these arguments, disabled employees' requests for accommodation are still frequently denied. The prejudice of immediate superiors often limits the assistance offered to the disabled worker, even if the organization has adequate resources to draw on. The prevalence of such workplace prejudice seems to depend on a range of factors, including the type of disability and perceptions of employee performance (Florey and Harrison, 2000).

Because disabled workers often meet with resistance, they may choose to conceal their impairment where possible. However, as in the case of LGBT workers who 'pass' as heterosexuals, disabled workers who reject the assistance they need to function optimally in the workplace face additional workplace stress and burnout because of the increased energy spent hiding their impediment (Gewurtz and Kirsh, 2009).

Dedicated policies and workplace accommodation are, unfortunately, usually insufficient to attain a healthy work-life balance. Studies have found that other factors such as acceptance, understanding and tolerance from co-workers are required for disabled persons to enjoy a positive work experience (Gewurtz and Kirsh, 2009). A supportive organizational culture can help to ease the disabled worker's integration into the daily working routine.

WEBLINK

The EU has developed a strategy which aims to make disabled persons active participants in the workforce and society at large: http://www.europa.eu/legislation_summaries/employment_and_social_policy/disability_and_old_age/em0047_en.htm.

Interestingly, as organizations have come to address issues of health and disability as part of their work-life strategies, able-bodied workers are increasingly seeking accommodation and assistance for occupational hazards such as stress-related illness or repetitive strain injuries. Many of the accommodations that were once offered only to disabled adults, such as mobile workstations and telecommuting, are now granted to other employees who request them (European Agency for Safety and Health at Work, 2000).

THE WORK-LIFE INTERFACE IN THE CONTEMPORARY ORGANIZATION: AN ORGANIZATIONAL CULTURE OF CARE

The workplace is in a continual state of flux. The forces of globalization, shifting economic structures and increasing diversity have already made work-life interface policies from just 15 years ago out of date. It is no longer sufficient for organizations to merely devise work-life interface policies; they must ensure that these policies are meticulously implemented to create workplace practices that address workers' needs in their total work environment. This task is certainly considerable, but not impossible. Even small, yet significant, changes can positively impact an individual's experience of the workplace.

As we know, supportive work-life cultures are often maintained by family-friendly work policies (for example childcare benefits) as well as programmes to support healthy time and resource management (such as flexitime). However, merely establishing a work-life policy as part of the standard workplace code of practice will not necessarily ensure that workers engage in positive work-life practices (Mescher, Benschop and Doorewaard, 2010). Organizations must also create a culture that encourages and supports employees to implement policies and alter standard practices, namely *a culture of care* (Buzzanell and D'Enbeau, 2009; Friedman, Christensen and Degroot, 2000; Kirby, 2000; Kirby and Krone, 2002; Medved and Kirby, 2005; Townsley and Broadfoot, 2008). Although it is perhaps less difficult than one might imagine to create a supportive organizational culture, the process cannot be rushed. Long-term cultural change that promotes stronger work-life practices, similar to those commonly found throughout Scandinavia, is one of the best ways to ensure fully developed and empowering work-life policies (Ellingsæter, 2009), which, in turn, also benefit the employer.

A first step in initiating cultural change is to address minor everyday practices. For example, ensuring that group meetings are scheduled for times when childcare is available (that is during nursery or kindergarten opening hours) can be a great help to many workers, and not just those with young children. This policy helps to ensure that all workers are present at meetings, thus preventing childless workers from being assigned burdensome tasks ahead of these 'missing' colleagues. It also allows all workers to plan for leisure and community activities. One of the most important strategies towards developing a more positive organizational culture is to encourage supervisors and managers to practice the policies that are already in place. Organizations should also consider introducing training programmes to instruct managers on how they can contribute to a positive work-life culture. This may seem trivial, but the following example demonstrates how important it is for those at the top to lead by example:

A member of the diplomatic service of a European country is serving in a country suffering violent conflict, which prevents her family from living with her. As a staff member serving abroad, she is entitled to a week-long holiday every six weeks. Although she is often highly reluctant to take this holiday due to the burden of work, she believes that it is necessary to take this leave in order to indicate to her staff that they are free to do likewise. The diplomat knows that mere verbal or written expressions of encouragement would be inadequate for her staff, and that it is necessary for her to set an example. As a manager, she recognizes the importance of *practising* rather than just preaching work-life interface policies.

Managers and employees should be given the power to tailor work-life policies to specific needs as they see fit. For example, maternity or paternity leave is designed to accommodate the parents of a new born, but few policies allow parents to take leave for some weeks or months to care for an older child who is recovering from an illness. Empowering workers and managers to collectively create work-life practices is a form of decentralized decision-making that can more precisely address individual needs. This may lead to the development of more efficient ways of performing tasks, to the re-designing of jobs or patterns of work. Such practices will help to reduce workplace stress and burnout, as well as family discord (Kossek, Lewis and Hammer, 2010; Kvande, 2009). Policy enacted through dialogue (Buzzanell, Dohrman and D'Enbeau, 2011; Medved, 2004; Tracy and Rivera, 2010; Wood, 1994) ensures that workplace policies retain a degree of flexibility (even those that appear written in stone) and provides space for the tailoring of work-life practices so that the needs and expectations of both the organization and the individual worker are met. A culture of care is thereby created, helping the organization to attract quality workers and create a more diverse workforce.

Chapter Review Questions

- What is meant by the work-life interface?
- Which groups were first included in the concept of a healthy work-life balance? Why?
- In which ways will an organization benefit from employees who have achieved a work-life balance?
- What can organizations do to help employees achieve a better work-life balance?
- Why should LGBT individuals be included in the work-life concept?
- How can more accessible and inclusive workplaces be created for disabled people?
- What is meant by an organizational *culture of care*?

Case Study

Not so irreplaceable

'Okay, thanks so much for finishing the report. I'll take a look at it later tonight, but I know our client will be pleased. Talk to you tomorrow. Bye!'

Mia felt a bit guilty taking the phone call during her daughter's hockey game. However, as she surveyed the scattered groups of parents watching the game, she thought, 'At least I made the effort to turn up!' But upon reflection, she really couldn't blame anyone for their absence. After all, it was 4.00 pm in the afternoon and most parents were still at work. Those at the game were either housewives or househusbands (a diminishing group in this economy!) or shift workers. The truth is that she would also have missed her daughter's game if she had stayed at her old law firm of Smith, Romano and Hansen. Although day-care centres closed between 5.00 and 6.00 pm, most associates worked past 7.00 pm. Associates at the law firm had a reputation of staying late and going into the office on the weekend. An eighty-hour working week was not uncommon. There was always something that needed attention. Even after returning to work from maternity leave, Mia had done her best to keep up with the other associates, which meant she often arrived home too late to put her children, Mette and William, to bed. Thank goodness that Irina, their Ukrainian au pair, had been so helpful. But it was only a few months after William was born that Mia had realized she could not work the hours the law firm expected and continue to enjoy a good relationship with her family. After looking at her budget, she had determined that part-time work would not support her family, but flexitime and job sharing would.

Later, when William and Mette were already sleeping, Mia opened her laptop and read the report that her colleague, Mikkel, had written. She had promised to read it over and provide comments before their big meeting tomorrow. With a high-speed Internet, laptop, smartphone and useful web services like Dropbox, Mia found working at home quite easy. She made a few edits, saved the document and sent Mikkel a quick e-mail to let him know that she was finished. She really liked working with Mikkel.

Of course, she missed her old associates; but her new colleagues were really friendly. Also, they shared similar family and life values, making it much easier to work with them. Her colleagues were from various parts of the country, and there were even a few foreign workers. The organizational strategy of the new law firm, Yoke, Biddle and Bruni, was to ensure the satisfaction of clients, while also addressing the needs of employees for a healthy work-life balance. Their organizational strategy was to create and maintain a culture of care for their employees and clients.

The key premise of this organizational strategy is the idea that 'No One is Irreplaceable'. While that may seem demeaning or demotivating, the intention is to create shared areas of responsibility, so that individual workers can take time for urgent personal matters without seriously disrupting the workflow. To illustrate, each client is assigned at least two lawyers to his or her case. Although the lawyers work together, sharing all insights and information, only one of the lawyers is required to be present in the law firm at any given time. So, while Mia was watching Mette's hockey game, Mikkel was at the office to answer any queries from their client.

This arrangement differs from traditional team-based organizational strategies, in which each team member is assigned a specific task or contributes a unique skill. Team members at Yoke, Biddle and Bruni are able to perform any kind of legal work for the client. Every team member is replaceable, which means they can put in as many (or as few) hours as they are able without sacrificing the level of service offered to the client.

As one would expect, this type of strategy requires an unusual functional arrangement in the assignment of responsibilities. Mikkel and Mia's manager, Louise, serves as the general manager for the law firm. She meets all new clients and determines what type and level of service they will require. Then she puts together teams of lawyers, based on the amount of work each team member is able to contribute, and assigns these to the client. The teams have two to six members.

One of Louise's ongoing challenges is to retain enough clients for the firm to maintain a profit, while not overstretching employees. It is a tough balance, but the law firm steadily attracts clients because of their good service, the lawyers' professionalism and compassion, and the firm's high degree of efficiency. They are able to meet their clients' needs quickly and fully while charging a competitive rate.

Most workers, like Mikkel and Mia, work approximately 35 hours a week, alternating between mornings and afternoons as their personal schedules dictate. The lawyers at the firm can work as few as ten hours a week, giving them a great deal of freedom. Mia often works with Mikkel because they are both experts in labour law and have compatible schedules, but she also works with Rochelle and Jennifer when handling family law cases. Mia is particularly close to Rochelle because they are from the same small town, and have children who attend the same school. Rochelle has advanced multiple sclerosis and uses a wheelchair to get around. The job sharing scheme and flexitime allow Rochelle to schedule her work meetings around her doctor appointments. She is even able to schedule breaks in her day for the performance of physical therapy. The team members draw up a client work schedule to ensure that all tasks are completed properly and in a timely fashion. This schedule is maintained online so all employees have immediate access to it and are able to make amendments when necessary.

It took Mia some time to get used to the new organizational structure, as this is very different from the traditional model she was used to at her previous law firm. However, now that she has become accustomed to the new strategy, she much prefers it. The amount of redundant work is greatly reduced, and colleagues do not compete with one another to the same extent for clients and billable hours. Mia certainly has to communicate and collaborate more with her colleagues; but there is a less competitive atmosphere than at other firms, and colleagues are more willing to share ideas. The end result is that everyone enjoys a lighter workload. Of course, she sometimes misses the larger pay check she received at Smith, Romano and Hansen. But the extra time she is able to spend with her partner and children is irreplaceable, even if Mia herself is replaceable at work.

Test Your Understanding

- From Mia's perspective, what are the benefits of flexitime and job sharing? In what ways do these organizational strategies help her to achieve work-life balance?
- What does the firm of Yoke, Biddle and Bruni gain from its culture of care?
- How do you think clients respond to the organizational strategy of job sharing and flexitime?

- As a manager, what specific challenges does Louise face because of the job sharing and flexitime policies?
- How do the organizational practices of flexitime and job sharing contribute to a culture of care? Do they help to create and/or maintain greater diversity for the law firm?
- Which conditions allow for the introduction of flexitime and job sharing? What individual factors and circumstances influence whether flexitime or job sharing are viable options?

REFERENCES

A. K. Abendroth and L. den Dulk (2011) 'Support for the Work-Life Balance in Europe: The Impact of State, Workplace and Family Support on Work-Life balance Satisfaction', *Work, Employment & Society*, 25, 234–56.

J. K. Alberts, S. J.Tracy and A. Trethewey (2011) 'An Integrative Theory of the Division of Domestic Labor: Threshold Level, Social Organizing and Sensemaking', *Journal of Family Communication*, 11, 21–38.

K. Bennhold (2010) 'In Sweden, the men can have it all', *International Herald Tribune*, 1 and 4.

B. Bower (1988) 'From Here to Maternity', *Science News*, 134, 220–22.

E. Brandon (2010) 'Why the Retirement Age Is Increasing' *US News and World Report*, http://www.money.usnews.com/money/retirement/articles/2010/11/15/why-the-retirement-age-is-increasing, date accessed 5 January 2012.

T. J. Brown, K. Ferrara and N. Schley (2002) 'The Relationship of Pregnancy Status to Job Satisfaction: An Exploratory Analysis', *Journal of Business and Psychology*, 17, 63–72.

S. M. Bruyere and W. A. Erickson (2000) 'HR's Role in Managing Disability in the Workplace', *Employment Relations Today*, 27, 47–66.

P. M. Buzzanell and S. D'Enbeau (2009) 'Stories of Caregiving: Intersections of Popular Culture, Academic Research, and Women's Everyday Experiences', *Qualitative Inquiry*, 15, 1199–224.

P. M. Buzzanell, R. L. Dohrman and S. D'Enbeau (2011) 'Problematizing Political Economy Differences and their Respective Work-Life Policy Constructions' in D. K. Mumby (ed.) *Reframing Difference in Organizational Communication Studies: Research, Pedagogy, Practice* (Los Angeles: Sage): 245–66.

A. Colella and A. Varma (2001) 'The Impact of Subordinate Disability on Leader-member Exchange Relationships', *Academy of Management Journal*, 44, 304–15.

F. Colgan, C. Creegan, A. McKearn and T. Wright (2007) 'Equality and Diversity Policies and Practices at Work: Lesbian, Gay and Bisexual Workers', *Equal Opportunities International*, 26 (6), 590–609.

Commission of the European Communities (2008) *Report from the Commission to the European Parliament, the Council, the European Economic and Social Committee and the Committee of the Regions – Implementation of the Barcelona Objectives Concerning Childcare Facilities for Pre-school-Age Children, COM(2008) 638 final* (Brussels: Commission of the European Communities).

M. B. Congdon (2009). 'Sexual Minority Issues in Human Resource Development', *Advances in Developing Human Resources*, 11, 3–6.

A. H. Eagly and L. L. Carli (2007) 'Women and the Labyrinth of Leadership', *Harvard Business Review*, 85 (9), 62–71.

*J. Edlund (2007) 'The Work Family Time Squeeze: Conflicting Demands of Paid and Unpaid Work among Working Couples in 29 Countries', *International Journal of Comparative Sociology*, 48, 451–80.

B. Ehrenreich and A. R. Hochschild (2002) *Global Woman: Nannies, Maids, and Sex Workers in the New Economy* (New York City: Henry Holt and Company).

P. Elisson (2011) *Regnbågschefen* (Stockholm: Liber).

A. L. Ellingsæter (2009) 'Leave Policy in the Nordic Welfare States: A "Recipe" for High Employment/High Fertility?', *Community, Work & Family*, 12, 1–19.

*J. J. Erickson, G. Martinengo and E. J. Hill (2010) 'Putting Work and Family Experiences in Context: Differences by Family Life Stage', *Human Relations*, 63, 955–79.

Eurofound (2004) Foundation Forum: Debate 3 – living to work – working to live, http://www.eurofound.europa.eu/events/2004/forum2004/debate3.htm, date accessed 20 January 2012.

Europa (2000) 'EUR-Lex – Recherche simple', *EUR-Lex,* http://www.eur-lex.europa. eu/LexUriServ/LexUriServ.do?uri=CELEX:32000L0078:SV:NOT, date accessed 11 August 2011.

European Agency for Safety and Health at Work (2000) *Repetitive Strain Injuries in EU Member States: Summary of an Agency Report* (Belgium: European Agency for Safety and Health at Work), http://www.osha.europa.eu/en/publications/factsheets/6, date accessed 12 January 2012.

European Centre for the Development of Vocational Training (2010) Jobs in Europe to become more knowledge- and skills-intensive, http://www.cedefop.europa.eu/EN/Files/9021_en.pdf, date accessed 9 January 2012.

Eurostat (2011) Population and Conditions. Theme: Mean Age of Women at Childbirth, http://www.epp.eurostat.ec.europa.eu/portal/page/portal/product_details/dataset?p_product_code=TPS00017, date accessed 16 January 2012.

A. Felstead, N. Jewson, A. Phizacklea and S. Walters (2002) 'Opportunities to Work at Home in the Context of Work-Life Balance', *Human Resource Management Journal*, 12, 54–76.

A. T. Florey and D. A. Harrison (2000). 'Responses to Informal Accommodation Requests from Employees with Disabilities: Multistudy Evidence on Willingness to Comply', *Academy of Management Journal*, 43, 224–33.

E. Fox, G. Pascall and T. Warren (2009) 'Work-family Policies, Participation, and Practices: Fathers and Childcare in Europe'. *Community, Work & Family*, 12, 313–26.

*S. D. Friedman, P. Christensen, and J. Degroot (2000) 'Work and Life: The End of the Zero-sum Gain', *Harvard Business Review on work and life balance* (Boston: Harvard University Press), pp. 1–30.

D. Geary (1972) 'Socialism, Revolution and the European Labour Movement, 1848–1918', *The Historical Journal*, 15 (4), 794–803.

J. Gedro (2007) 'Conducting Research on LGBT Issues: Leading the Field All Over Again!', *Human Resource Development Quarterly*, 153–8.

R. Gewurtz and B. Kirsh (2009). 'Disruption, Disbelief and Resistance: A Meta-synthesis of Disability in the Workplace', *Work*, 34, 33–44.

E. Goffman (1986) *Stigma: Notes on the Management of Spoiled Identity* Reissue (New York, NY: Simon & Schuster).

J. Greenhaus and N. J. Beutell (1985) 'Sources of Conflict Between Work and Family Roles', *The Academy of Management Review*, 10, 76–88.

*J. Greenhaus, K. M. Collins, and J. D. Shaw (2003) 'The Relation between Work-family Balance and Quality of Life', *Journal of Vocational Behavior*, 63, 510–31.

J. Greenhaus and R. Singh (2003) 'Work-family Linkages' in S. Sweet and J. Casey (eds) *Work and Family Encyclopaedia*, http://www.wfnetwork.bc.edu/encyclopedia_entry.php?id=263andarea=All, date accessed 10 July 2011.

A. Gregory and S. Milner (2009) 'Editorial: Work-life Balance: A Matter of Choice?', *Gender, Work and Organization*, 16, 1–13.

K. H. Griffith and M. R. Hebl (2002) 'The Disclosure Dilemma for Gay Men and Lesbians: "Coming Out" at Work', *Journal of Applied Psychology*, 87, 1191–99.

J. G. Grzywacz and D. S. Carlson (2007) 'Conceptualizing Work Family Balance: Implications for Practice and Research', *Advances in Developing Human Resources*, 9, 455–71.

J. R. Hayman (2009) 'Flexible Work Arrangements: Exploring the Linkages Between Perceived Usability of Flexible Work Schedules and Work/life Balance', *Community, Work & Family*, 12, 327–38.

S. Hewlett and C. Luce (2005) 'Off-ramps and On-ramps: Keeping Talented Women on the Road to Success', *Harvard Business Review*, 83, 43–54.

A. R. Hochschild (1997) *The Second Shift: Working Parents and the Revolution at Home* (New York: Viking).

*A. H. Huffman, K. M. Watrous-Rodriguez and E. B. King (2008) 'Supporting a Diverse Workforce: What Type of Support is most Meaningful for Lesbian and Gay Employees?', *Human Resource Management*, 47, 237–53.

M. Hyland (2003) 'Flextime' in S. Sweet and J. Casey (eds) *Work and Family Encyclopaedia*, http://www.wfnetwork.bc.edu/encyclopedia_entry.php?id=13andarea=All, date accessed 10 July 2011.

C. Hymowitz (2012) 'Behind every great woman', *Business Week*, http://www.businessweek.com/magazine/behind-every-great-woman-01042012.html?chan=magazine+channel_top+stories, date accessed 7 January 2012.

ILO (2012) Origins and History, http://www.ilo.org/global/about-the-ilo/history/lang--en/index.htm, date accessed: 15 January 2012.

S. Jayson (2007) 'Married women unite! Husbands do less housework', *USA Today*, http://www.usatoday.com/news/health/2007-08-28-housework_N.htm, date accessed 5 January 2012.

*C. Kelliher and D. Anderson (2009) 'Doing More with Less? Flexible Working Practices and the Intensification of Work', *Human Relations*, 63, 83–106.

E. Kirby (2000) 'Should I Do as You Say or Do as You Do? Mixed Messages about Work and Family', *Electronic Journal of Communication/La Revue de Electronique de Communication*, 10, http://www.cios.org/www/ejcmain.htm, date accessed 20 January 2012.

E. Kirby and L. M. Harter (2001) 'Discourses of Diversity and the Quality of Work Life: The Character and Costs of the Managerial Metaphor', *Management Communication Quarterly*, 15, 121–7.

*E. Kirby and K. J. Krone (2002) ' "The Policy Exists But You Can't Really Use It": Communication and the Structuration of Work-family Policies', *Journal of Applied Communication Research*, 30, 50–77.

Knowledge@Wharton (2011) A Recession for Perks? What Companies Offer and What Employees Want, http://www.knowledge.wharton.upenn.edu/articlepdf/2800.pdf?CFID=178743831&CFTOKEN=36717171&jsessionid=a830588d9537a34210d839555035683f3f29, date accessed 5 January 2012.

J. Kodz, S. Davis, D. Lain, M. Strebler, J. Rick. P. Bates, J. Cummings and N. Meager (2003) *Working Long Hours: A Review of the Evidence: Volume 1 - Main Report*, Department of

Trade and Industry (UK), http://www.employment-studies.co.uk/pubs/summary.php?id=errs16, date accessed 12 January 2012.

T. Köllen (2011) 'The Contribution of Diversity Management to Create a Supportive Working Climate for Gays and Lesbians' in C. Leicht-Scholten (ed.) *Going Diverse: Innovative Answers to Future Challenges: Gender and Diversity Perspectives in Science, Technology and Business* (Birmingham: Budrich UniPress), pp. 161–70.

*E. E. Kossek, S. Lewis, and L. B. Hammer (2010) 'Work Life Initiatives and Organizational Change: Overcoming Mixed Messages to Move From the Margin to the Mainstream', *Human Relations*, 63, 3–19.

E. Kvande (2009) 'Work-life Balance for Fathers in Globalized Knowledge Work. Some Insights from the Norwegian Context', *Gender, Work & Organization*, 16, 58–72.

M. Liu and P. M. Buzzanell (2004) 'Negotiating Maternity Leave Expectations: Perceived Tensions Between Ethics of Justice and Care', *Journal of Business Communication*, 41, 323–49.

K. Lucas and P. M. Buzzanell (2006) 'Employees "without" Families: Discourses of Family as an External Constraint to Work-life Balance' in L. H. Turner and R. West (eds) *The Family Communication Sourcebook* (Thousand Oaks, CA: Sage) pp. 335–52.

S. M. MacDermid, K. Roy and A. M. Zvonkovic (2005) 'Don't Stop at the Borders: Theorizing Beyond Dichotomies of Work and Family' in V. L. Bengston, A. C. Acock, K. R. Allen, P. Dilworth-Anderson and D. M. Klein (eds) *Sourcebook of Family Theory and Research* (Thousand Oaks, CA: Sage), pp. 493–516.

D. MacLeod and N. Clarke (2009) *Engaging for Success: Enhancing Performance through Employee Engagement*, Department for Business, Innovation and Skills, http://www.bis.gov.uk/files/file52215.pdf, date accessed 7 January 2012.

A. Margherita, S. O'Dorchai, and J. Bosch (2009) 'Eurostat – Reconcilitation between Work, Private and Family Life in the EU', *Eurostat F2 Labour Market Statistics*.

*H. S. McMillan, M. L. Morris, and E. K. Atchley (2010) 'Constructs of the Work/Life Interface: A Synthesis of the Literature and Introduction of the Concept of Work/Life Harmony', *Human Resource Development Review*, 10, 6–25.

C. E. Medved (2004). 'The Everyday Accomplishment of Work and Family: Exploring Practical Actions in Daily Routines', *Communication Studies*, 55, 128–45.

C. E. Medved and E. Kirby (2005) 'Family CEOs: A Feminist Analysis of Corporate Mothering Discourses', *Management Communication Quarterly*, 18, 435–78.

R. J. Meisenbach (2010) 'The Female Breadwinner: Phenomenological Experience and the Gendered Identity in Work/family Spaces', *Sex Roles*, 62, 2–19.

R. J. Meisenbach, R. V. Remke, P. Buzzanell and M. Liu (2008) ' "They allowed": Pentadic Mapping of Women's Maternity Leave Discourse as Organizational Rhetoric', *Communication Monographs*, 75, 1–24.

S. Mescher, Y. Benschop, and H. Doorewaard (2010) 'Representations of Work-Life Balance Support', *Human Relations*, 63, 31–9.

N. Miles (2011) *Straight Allies: How to Help Create Gay-friendly Workplaces*, Stonewall Workplace Guides.

V. D. Miller, F. M. Jablin, M. K. Casey, M. L.-V. Horn and C. Ethington (1996) 'The Maternity Leave as a Role Negotiation Process', *Journal of Managerial Issues*, 8, 286–309.

J. Misra, S. Moller, and M. J. Budig (2007) 'Work Family Policies and Poverty for Partnered and Single Women in Europe and North America', *Gender & Society*, 21, 804–27.

K. Moe and D. Shandy (2010) *'Glass Ceilings & 100-hour couples: What the Opt-out Phenomenon Can Teach Us about Work and Family* (Athens, GA: University of Georgia Press).

T. Mohn (2011) 'Plights of the Expat Spouse', *New York Times*, http://www.nytimes.com/2011/06/21/business/21expats.html?_r=1andref=americansabroad, date accessed 20 June 2011.

B. Morris, L. Munoz and P. Neering (2002) 'Trophy husbands arm candy? Are you kidding? While their fast-track wives go to work, stay-at-home husbands mind the kids. They deserve a trophy for trading places', *Fortune Magazine*, http://www.money.cnn.com/magazines/fortune/fortune_archive/2002/10/14/330033/index.htm, date accessed 7 January 2012.

S. E. Needleman (2011) 'Employee Perks Return Amid Fears of Poaching', *In Charge,* http://www.blogs.wsj.com/in-charge/2011/06/28/employee-perks-return-amid-fears-of-poaching, date accessed 5 January 2012.

OECD (2007) *Babies and Bosses – Reconciling Work and Family Life: A Synthesis of Findings for OECD Countries* (Paris: OECD Publishing).

OECD (2011) *OECD Family Database* (Paris: OECD Publishing).

A. Ollier-Malaterre (2009) 'Organizational Work-life Initiatives: Context Matters', *Community, Work & Family*, 12, 159–78.

D. Orr (2004) 'The Same Old Story of Women in the Workplace; There is Female Frustration at the Failure of Attempts to Make the Workplace a More Humane Place', *The Independent*, 17.

P. Peters, L. den Dulk, and T. van der Lippe (2009) 'The Effects of Time-spatial Flexibility and New Working Conditions on Employees' Work-life Balance: The Dutch Case', *Community, Work & Family*, 12, 279–97.

C. R. Pierret (2006) 'The "Sandwich Generation": Women Caring for Parents and Children', *Monthly Labor Review*, 129, 3–9.

M. Pitt-Catsouphes (2002) 'Family-friendly Workplaces' in E. E. Kossek and M. Pitt-Catsouphes (eds) *Work and Family Encyclopaedia,* http://www.wfnetwork.bc.edu/encyclopedia_entry.php?id=871andarea=All, date accessed 10 July 2011.

*M. Pitt-Catsouphes, E. E. Kossek, and S. Sweet (2006) *The Work and Family Handbook: Multi-disciplinary Perspectives and Approaches* (Mahwah, NJ: Lawrence Erlbaum Associates).

J. Polach (2003) 'HRD's Role in Work-life Integration Issues: Moving the Workforce to Change in Mindset', *Human Resource Development International*, 6, 57–68.

D. M. Riley (2008) 'LGBT-friendly Workplaces in Engineering', *Leadership and Management in Engineering*, 8, 19–23.

D. Rosenberg McKay (2012) Job Sharing: An Interview, http://www.careerplanning.about.com/od/jobsharing/a/job_sharing.htm, date accessed 13 January 2012.

A. Roulstone, L. Gradwell, J. Price and L. Child (2003) 'Thriving and Surviving at Work: Disabled People's Employment Strategies', http://www.jrf.org.uk/publications/how-disabled-people-manage-workplace, date accessed 5 January 2012.

H. Russell, P. J. O'Connell, and F. McGinnity (2009) 'The Impact of Flexible Working Arrangements on Work-life Conflict and Work Pressure in Ireland', *Gender, Work & Organization*, 16, 73–97.

J. Sahad (2007) 'Flex-time, time off: Who's getting these perks?', 28 June 2007 and accessed 11 April 2012 at http://articles.cnn.com/2007-06-28/us/money.worklife.balance_1_excellence-in-workplace-flexibility-families-and-work-institute comp time?_c=PM:US.

H. A. Schartz, D. J. Hendricks, and P. Blanck (2006) 'Workplace Accommodations: Evidence Based Outcomes', *Work*, 27, 345–54.

L. Schiebinger and S. Gilmartin (2010) 'Housework Is an Academic Issue: How to keep talented women scientists in the lab, where they belong.' *AAUP*, http://www.aaup.org/AAUP/pubsres/academe/2010/JF/feat/schie.htm, date accessed 5 January 2012.

M. R. Seaward (1999) 'The Sandwich Generation Copes with Elder Care', *Benefits Quarterly*, 15, 41–8.

J. Shen, A. Chanda, B. D'Netto and M. Monga (2009) 'Managing Diversity through Human Resource Management: An International Perspective and Conceptual Framework', *International Journal of Human Resource Management*, 20, 235–51.

K. W. Smola and C. Sutton (2002) 'Generational Differences: Revisiting Generational Work Values for the New Millennium', *Journal of Organizational Behaviour*, 23, 363–82.

P. Stone (2007) *'Opting out? Why Women Really Quit Careers and Head Home* (Los Angeles: University of California Press).

Stonewall UK (2011) Business Case, http://www.stonewall.org.uk/at_work/diversity_champions_programme/4889.asp, date accessed 10 October 2011.

H. Stout (2010) 'When Roles Reverse: The Rise of the Stay-at-home Husband, *Marie Claire*.

J. Sturges and D. Guest (2004) 'Working to Live or Living to Work? Work/life Balance Early in the Career', *Human Resource Management Journal*, 14, 5–20.

S. Tavernise (2012) 'Day Care Centers Adapt to Round-the-clock Demand', *New York Times*, http://www.nytimes.com/2012/01/16/us/day-care-centers-adapt-to-round-the-clock-demands.html?_r=2&pagewanted=1, date accessed 15 January 2012.

E. L. Teasdale (2006) 'Workplace Stress', *Psychiatry*, 5(7), 251–4.

The Human Rights Campaign (2011) 'Corporate Equality Index 2012', *The Human Rights Campaign Foundation,* http://www.hrc.org, date accessed 5 January 2012.

N. C. Townsley and K. J. Broadfoot (2008) 'Care, Career, and Academe: Heeding the Calls of a New Professoriate', *Women's Studies in Communication*, 31, 133–42.

S. J. Tracy and K. D. Rivera (2010) 'Endorsing Equity and Applauding Stay-at-Home Moms: How Male Voices on Work-Life Reveal Aversive Sexism and Flickers of Transformation', *Management Communication Quarterly*, 24, 3–43.

A. Trethewey (1999) 'Discipline Bodies: Women's Embodied Identities at Work', *Organization Studies*, 20, 423–50.

L. Tulman and J. Fawcett (1991) 'Factors Influencing Recovery from Childbirth' in L. Tulman and J. Hyde (eds) *Parental Leave and Childcare: Setting a Research and Policy Agenda* (Philadelphia: Temple University Press), pp. 294–303.

UN (2006) FN:s konvention om rättigheter för personer med funktionsnedsättning, http://www.handisam.se/Tpl/NormalPage____75717.aspx, date accessed 15 August 2011.

N. van den Bergh (1999) 'Workplace Problems and Needs for Lesbian and Gay Male Employees', *Employee Assistance Quarterly*, 15, 21–60.

M. van der Klis and L. Karsten (2009) 'The Commuter Family as a Geographical Adaptive Strategy for the Work-Family Balance', *Community, Work & Family*, 12, 339–54.

P. Voydanoff (2005) 'The Effects of Community Demands, Resources, and Strategies on the Nature and Consequences of the Work-Family Interface: An Agenda for Future Research', *Family relations*, 54, 583–95.

T. Warren, E. Fox and G. Pascall (2009) 'Innovative Social Policies: Implications for Work-life Balance among Low-waged Women in England', *Gender, Work & Organization*, 16, 126–50.

E. C. Wertlieb (1985) 'Minority Group Status of the Disabled', *Human Relations*, 38, 1047–63.

W. H. Whyte, (1956) *The Organization Man* (New York: Simon & Schuster).

J. T. Wood (1994) *Who Cares? Women, Care and Culture* (Carbondale: Southern Illinois University Press).

Working Well (2009) Working Well: A Global Survey of Health Promotion and Workplace Wellness Strategies Executive Summary, http://www.worldatwork.org/waw/adimLink?id= 36309, date accessed 5 January 2012.

C. W. Yost (2011) Escape the 10 Tyrannies of Work/life 'Balance', http://www.fastcompany. com/1716044/escape-the-10-tyrannies-of-worllife-ldquobalancerdquo, date accessed 9 June 2011.

SUMMING UP DIVERSITY IN ORGANIZATIONS

Mary Ann Danowitz,
Edeltraud Hanappi-Egger and
Heike Mensi-Klarbach

Diversity in Organizations: Concepts and Practices was conceived with two objectives in mind. The first was to prepare current and future employees, in particular managers, for the implementation and improvement of diversity management so that diversity can serve to increase organizational performance. The second was to help all employees engage with diversity in their daily work. The individual chapters have addressed various key issues, presenting proposals and research findings on how to develop inclusive organizations. One fundamental idea we have tried to convey is the powerful 'doing' perspective of diversity, which sees markers of difference as social constructions. Rather than conceptualizing and treating diversity in a rigid fashion, this perspective encourages us to strive to change stereotypical thinking, as well as discriminatory structures and practices. For example, categorization by gender or age is all too frequently linked to a pre-determined and static cluster of features and traits. In contrast, the doing perspective makes clear that differences associated with gender or any other category are constantly being 'done' or enacted in everyday interaction, and anchored by specific organizational structures and practices. As the concept of 'doing' difference is dynamic, it offers the possibility of reversing or 'undoing' exclusive structures and practices. Furthermore, we have highlighted the fact that the creation of an inclusive organization is a complex and intensive process, rather than a one-off action. It requires the setting of concrete goals within a specific organizational context that are then continuously reviewed and evaluated. In the following we summarize, chapter for chapter, these and other key themes of the book.

PART ONE

Part One set the stage by reviewing relevant theoretical strands while providing a conceptual framework for diversity and diversity management. Diversity in organizations was placed within the wider field of organizational studies, at the nexus of organizational theory and behaviour. The historical dimensions behind current concepts and theories in the study of diversity were summarized. This was followed by an overview of the legal, political and cultural context of the European Union and its impact on organizations, in particular commercial enterprises. The framing was completed with a discussion of rationales that can sustain change in organizations towards greater inclusivity, namely the business and moral cases. This showed how diversity in organizations can be discussed in regard to greater equality or improved performance as separate issues, but that it is more fruitful to regard these moral and business rationales as mutually dependent.

Chapter 1 introduced some 'Theoretical perspectives on diversity in orga-nizations' and their historical roots in order to deepen our understanding of gender and diversity in organizations. It was shown that the first management publications to deal with gender focused on the issue of 'women' at work and their apparent 'needs'. This essentialist approach can still be found in difference-oriented diversity concepts, which posit rigid social categories in terms of age, religion, sexual orientation, ethnicity, disability and gender. The 'doing' approach was briefly introduced as an alternative to these essentialist concepts. Finally, the role of gender and diversity was examined in relation to organization studies.

Chapter 2 explored the 'European diversity context' by outlining guiding principles and directives on equality and anti-discrimination. Due to the divergent political and cultural contexts, different approaches to diversity management are adopted in Europe and the United States. It was shown how supranational EU directives interact with national laws and policies to positively influence equal opportunity and diversity management, supporting organizations in their efforts to achieve inclusion. Finally, the authors noted the large range of policies and laws of EU member states, which, together with the reigning social values and attitudes, will facilitate or inhibit efforts towards inclusivity.

Chapter 3 looked at 'The business and moral cases of diversity', showing how these are not mutually exclusive arguments, but in fact serve to strengthen one another. In addition, it was pointed out that 'what gets measured gets done', emphasizing the crucial importance of quantifying the economic impact of diversity management in order to embed diversity issues both strategically and sustainably within organizations. Several concepts to evaluate diversity management were then presented and critically investigated.

PART TWO

The second section of the book focused on the necessity of raising the gen-eral awareness of diversity issues as well as underlining the significance of the socio-cultural context. The chapters showed how cultural differences are always relevant when dealing with diversity, and that these are more complex and require more attention in multinational companies. Furthermore, the practices of 'doing gender and doing diversity' were analysed to explain how differences and inequalities are maintained and reproduced through daily interactions.

Chapter 4 addressed 'Gender and diversity across cultures'. A case study entitled 'A dilemma from Thailand' was presented in order to illustrate how doing business across borders requires a degree of sensitivity to the cultural context of gender and diversity relations. A three-level approach of body, culture and language was introduced to enable a structured analysis of the potential impact of cultural differences.

Chapter 5 explored 'The doing perspective on gender and diversity' by arguing the importance of viewing gender and other diversity markers not as fixed traits or qualities of individuals, but rather as differences, categories, hierarchies and inequalities which are created and recreated through our everyday social interaction. The 'doing' perspective was used to make sense of organizational practices, texts and visual images as well as to identify and challenge stereotypical modes of thinking that are often taken-for-granted and therefore go undetected. This perspective enables us to scrutinize masculine forms of management, notions of competence, and the double bind that women and minorities (such as non-whites) face as managers. Crucially, the 'doing' perspective constitutes a useful tool to help transform organizational practices and societal arrangements, thereby fostering equality, diversity and inclusion.

PART THREE

In the third section the spotlight turned to concrete steps that can be undertaken to make organizations more inclusive. The underlying idea was that these steps must constitute a strategic process of change initiated from above. It was noted that the nature and content of this process depend to a large extent on the macro- and micro-organizational context and the commitment of organizational leaders. The discussion then shifted to the significance of organizational analysis in helping to initiate and steer the process. Finally, the book closed by emphasizing the need for new norms and practices to improve the work-life interface for individuals.

Chapter 6, entitled 'Diversity as strategy', gave an overview and comparison of various diversity models which have been developed by researchers in the field. It was shown that an organization's treatment of diversity management is dictated by the choice of diversity strategy, which in turn depends on the macro-environment (that is the international, national and societal level), the micro-environment (that is the regional and local business context) as well as the organizational context (internal diversity climate). A multi-layered contextualized model was presented to illustrate these factors and their impact on diversity.

Chapter 7 discussed the necessity of conducting an 'organizational analysis' to ensure the holistic implementation of diversity management. The authors stressed the importance of developing analytical tools to define the initial treatment of diversity in an organization and subsequently to evaluate the impact of diversity initiatives. Such evaluation helps to identify potential improvements to an organization's strategy and implementation of initiatives. Several different approaches to analysis were presented.

Chapter 8, entitled 'Organizational implementation: Diversity practices and tools', addressed the implementation of practices of diversity management. It was argued that in order to transform organizational structures and practices, clear accountability for diversity work is required, along with sufficient resources (knowledge, money and human resources), support from top management, intelligent diversity policies, measurable goals, transparency, clearly defined processes and long-term commitment. The authors showed how discriminatory practices can be hidden within organizational structures. The main such practices are traditional functions of human resources such as workforce planning, recruiting, performance appraisal, promotion and professional development. Resistance to diversity should be anticipated and handled with care, as it can generate considerable costs in terms of lower organizational profits and productivity. For individuals, the repercussions are thwarted careers as well as stress-related mental and physical illness.

Chapter 9, 'Work, life and a culture of care', described how current demographic trends and other societal changes are affecting attitudes towards and within the workplace, particularly in relation to the work-life interface. It showed the areas and ways in which organizations should constantly strive to meet the expectations and demands of diverse employees who wish to improve their work-life balance. At the same time the increasing prevalence of 'burn out' has led to a re-examination of the contemporary workplace and the degree of organizational support required by individual workers.

CONCLUSION

If the intention is to achieve long-term sustainable change, diversity work cannot be viewed as merely a task for the human resources department. Instead, the commitment and support of organizational leaders must be secured to encourage the implementation of diversity measures at all organizational levels. An inclusive workforce can only be achieved through a combination of relevant laws and policies, public tolerance and egalitarianism, and a majority of organizations committing themselves to diversity management. Thus a fundamental prerequisite for the positive handling of diversity is a government that guarantees the rule of law, upholds human and equal rights, and provides equitable access to social services for all citizens. The historical dismantling of discriminatory practices in Europe and the strong influence of the EU in supporting diversity management provide clear evidence of the truth of this proposition. Multinational companies operating in countries where a less supportive legal and social framework is in place must ensure, therefore, that they maintain a strong commitment to diversity; the organizational leadership must remain advocates of inclusion, while showing a degree of understanding of local sensibilities. For example, a company doing business in a foreign country which still regards homosexuality as a crime may nonetheless be quietly supportive of its gay, lesbian, bisexual and transgendered employees. This kind of diversity management reminds us as individuals, and as members of organizations, that the fostering of diversity not only has a direct impact on performance, but also a moral relevance. Hence, organizational commitment to diversity management and workforce inclusion is not merely a question of good business. It clearly is good business ethics as well.

APPENDIX

CONVENTION FOR THE PROTECTION OF HUMAN RIGHTS AND FUNDAMENTAL FREEDOMS

This page contains the text of the Convention through Section I Article 14, prohibition of discrimination, as amended from the date of its entry into force on 1 June 2010.

The governments signatory hereto, being members of the Council of Europe,

Considering the Universal Declaration of Human Rights proclaimed by the General Assembly of the United Nations on 10th December 1948;

Considering that this Declaration aims at securing the universal and effective recognition and observance of the Rights therein declared;

Considering that the aim of the Council of Europe is the achievement of greater unity between its members and that one of the methods by which that aim is to be pursued is the maintenance and further realisation of human rights and fundamental freedoms;

Reaffirming their profound belief in those fundamental freedoms which are the foundation of justice and peace in the world and are best maintained on the one hand by an effective political democracy and on the other by a common understanding and observance of the human rights upon which they depend;

Being resolved, as the governments of European countries which are like-minded and have a common heritage of political traditions, ideals, freedom and the rule of law, to take the first steps for the collective enforcement of certain of the rights stated in the Universal Declaration,

Have agreed as follows:

Article 1 – Obligation to respect human rights

The High Contracting Parties shall secure to everyone within their jurisdiction the rights and freedoms defined in Section I of this Convention.

Section I – Rights and freedoms

Article 2 – Right to life

1. Everyone's right to life shall be protected by law. No one shall be deprived of his life intentionally save in the execution of a sentence of a court following his conviction of a crime for which this penalty is provided by law.

2. Deprivation of life shall not be regarded as inflicted in contravention of this article when it results from the use of force which is no more than absolutely necessary:

   a. in defence of any person from unlawful violence;

   b. in order to effect a lawful arrest or to prevent the escape of a person lawfully detained;

   c. in action lawfully taken for the purpose of quelling a riot or insurrection.

Article 3 – Prohibition of torture

No one shall be subjected to torture or to inhuman or degrading treatment or punishment.

Article 4 – Prohibition of slavery and forced labour

1. No one shall be held in slavery or servitude.
2. No one shall be required to perform forced or compulsory labour.
3. For the purpose of this article the term 'forced or compulsory labour' shall not include:

   a. any work required to be done in the ordinary course of detention imposed according to the provisions of Article 5 of this Convention or during conditional release from such detention;

   b. any service of a military character or, in case of conscientious objectors in countries where they are recognised, service exacted instead of compulsory military service;

   c. any service exacted in case of an emergency or calamity threatening the life or well-being of the community;

   d. any work or service which forms part of normal civic obligations.

Article 5 – Right to liberty and security

1. Everyone has the right to liberty and security of person. No one shall be deprived of his liberty save in the following cases and in accordance with a procedure prescribed by law:

   a. the lawful detention of a person after conviction by a competent court;

   b. the lawful arrest or detention of a person for non-compliance with the lawful order of a court or in order to secure the fulfilment of any obligation prescribed by law;

   c. the lawful arrest or detention of a person effected for the purpose of bringing him before the competent legal authority on reasonable suspicion of having committed an offence or when it is reasonably considered necessary to prevent his committing an offence or fleeing after having done so;

   d. the detention of a minor by lawful order for the purpose of educational supervision or his lawful detention for the purpose of bringing him before the competent legal authority;

   e. the lawful detention of persons for the prevention of the spreading of infectious diseases, of persons of unsound mind, alcoholics or drug addicts or vagrants;

   f. the lawful arrest or detention of a person to prevent his effecting an unauthorised entry into the country or of a person against whom action is being taken with a view to deportation or extradition.

2. Everyone who is arrested shall be informed promptly, in a language which he understands, of the reasons for his arrest and of any charge against him.

3. Everyone arrested or detained in accordance with the provisions of paragraph 1.c of this article shall be brought promptly before a judge or other officer authorised by law to exercise

judicial power and shall be entitled to trial within a reasonable time or to release pending trial. Release may be conditioned by guarantees to appear for trial.

4. Everyone who is deprived of his liberty by arrest or detention shall be entitled to take proceedings by which the lawfulness of his detention shall be decided speedily by a court and his release ordered if the detention is not lawful.

5. Everyone who has been the victim of arrest or detention in contravention of the provisions of this article shall have an enforceable right to compensation.

Article 6 – Right to a fair trial

1. In the determination of his civil rights and obligations or of any criminal charge against him, everyone is entitled to a fair and public hearing within a reasonable time by an independent and impartial tribunal established by law. Judgment shall be pronounced publicly but the press and public may be excluded from all or part of the trial in the interests of morals, public order or national security in a democratic society, where the interests of juveniles or the protection of the private life of the parties so require, or to the extent strictly necessary in the opinion of the court in special circumstances where publicity would prejudice the interests of justice.

2. Everyone charged with a criminal offence shall be presumed innocent until proved guilty according to law.

3. Everyone charged with a criminal offence has the following minimum rights:

   a. to be informed promptly, in a language which he understands and in detail, of the nature and cause of the accusation against him;
   b. to have adequate time and facilities for the preparation of his defence;
   c. to defend himself in person or through legal assistance of his own choosing or, if he has not sufficient means to pay for legal assistance, to be given it free when the interests of justice so require;
   d. to examine or have examined witnesses against him and to obtain the attendance and examination of witnesses on his behalf under the same conditions as witnesses against him;
   e. to have the free assistance of an interpreter if he cannot understand or speak the language used in court.

Article 7 – No punishment without law

1. No one shall be held guilty of any criminal offence on account of any act or omission which did not constitute a criminal offence under national or international law at the time when it was committed. Nor shall a heavier penalty be imposed than the one that was applicable at the time the criminal offence was committed.

2. This article shall not prejudice the trial and punishment of any person for any act or omission which, at the time when it was committed, was criminal according to the general principles of law recognised by civilised nations.

Article 8 – Right to respect for private and family life

1. Everyone has the right to respect for his private and family life, his home and his correspondence.

2. There shall be no interference by a public authority with the exercise of this right except such as is in accordance with the law and is necessary in a democratic society in the interests of national security, public safety or the economic well-being of the country, for the prevention

of disorder or crime, for the protection of health or morals, or for the protection of the rights and freedoms of others.

Article 9 – Freedom of thought, conscience and religion

1. Everyone has the right to freedom of thought, conscience and religion; this right includes freedom to change his religion or belief and freedom, either alone or in community with others and in public or private, to manifest his religion or belief, in worship, teaching, practice and observance.
2. Freedom to manifest one's religion or beliefs shall be subject only to such limitations as are prescribed by law and are necessary in a democratic society in the interests of public safety, for the protection of public order, health or morals, or for the protection of the rights and freedoms of others.

Article 10 – Freedom of expression

1. Everyone has the right to freedom of expression. This right shall include freedom to hold opinions and to receive and impart information and ideas without interference by public authority and regardless of frontiers. This article shall not prevent States from requiring the licensing of broadcasting, television or cinema enterprises.
2. The exercise of these freedoms, since it carries with it duties and responsibilities, may be subject to such formalities, conditions, restrictions or penalties as are prescribed by law and are necessary in a democratic society, in the interests of national security, territorial integrity or public safety, for the prevention of disorder or crime, for the protection of health or morals, for the protection of the reputation or rights of others, for preventing the disclosure of information received in confidence, or for maintaining the authority and impartiality of the judiciary.

Article 11 – Freedom of assembly and association

1. Everyone has the right to freedom of peaceful assembly and to freedom of association with others, including the right to form and to join trade unions for the protection of his interests.
2. No restrictions shall be placed on the exercise of these rights other than such as are prescribed by law and are necessary in a democratic society in the interests of national security or public safety, for the prevention of disorder or crime, for the protection of health or morals or for the protection of the rights and freedoms of others. This article shall not prevent the imposition of lawful restrictions on the exercise of these rights by members of the armed forces, of the police or of the administration of the State.

Article 12 – Right to marry

Men and women of marriageable age have the right to marry and to found a family, according to the national laws governing the exercise of this right.

Article 13 – Right to an effective remedy

Everyone whose rights and freedoms as set forth in this Convention are violated shall have an effective remedy before a national authority notwithstanding that the violation has been committed by persons acting in an official capacity.

Article 14 – Prohibition of discrimination

The enjoyment of the rights and freedoms set forth in this Convention shall be secured without discrimination on any ground such as sex, race, colour, language, religion, political or other opinion, national or social origin, association with a national minority, property, birth or other status

Source: Council of Europe (n.d.) The European Convention of Human Rights, http://www.conventions.coe.int/treaty/en/Treaties/Html/005.htm, accessed 19 January 2012.

GLOSSARY

The *business case for diversity* focuses on the intrinsic value-added offered by diversity, for instance a positive relation between the number of female board members and board effectiveness.

The *business case for diversity management* concentrates on the economic benefits stemming from diversity programmes and practices, such as a positive relation between training in diversity and productivity.

Business ratios are concentrated economic information, preferably quantitative in nature, while indicators are employed when subjects can only be depicted incompletely (Gladen, 2003; see Chapter 3 references).

Culture consists of explicit and implicit patterns of behaviour (knowledge, language, values and customs) and the complex interaction of symbols, values and behaviours of distinct human groups.

Deconstruction is a specific method of discourse analysis which is designed to reveal subtexts, power relations and unspoken ideologies in written text.

Direct discrimination is the unfair treatment of and individual or group solely on the grounds of a personal characteristic such as age, disability, ethnic origin or race, religion or beliefs or sexual orientation.

Directives require states to achieve a certain outcome by a certain date, but leave it to the national authorities to choose how they go about implementing the provisions

Disability refers to a physical, mental or psychological impairment that can hamper work performance or hinders the participation of a person in following their chosen professional life.

A *diversity charter* is a short document voluntarily signed by a company or a public institution outlining measures it will undertake to promote diversity and equal opportunities in the workplace, regardless of race or ethnic origin, sexual orientation, gender, age, disability and religion.

Diversity climate is a shared understanding among organization members of an organization's diversity-related structures and actions. It comprises the perception of fairness regarding inclusion and exclusion of people from diverse backgrounds.

Diversity dimension (or *diversity marker*) refers to one of these specific social categories.

Diversity and gender mainstreaming seeks to promote equality at all levels and in all areas by taking equality issues into account during policy formation, implementation and evaluation.

Diversity management can be defined as a management concept which, acknowledging the value of difference, strategically and systemically strives to promote equity among its workforce in order to create added value.

A *diversity manager* or *chief diversity officer* is responsible for guiding efforts to define, assess, nurture and cultivate diversity as an organizational resource. Following the organization's diversity policy, the diversity manager works to promote a culture of diversity and inclusion through the support and coaching of managers and employees, while monitoring cultural diversity within the organization. Diversity officers support line managers in achieving the designated diversity goals.

A *diversity strategy*, based on its defining vision, specifies not only goals and objectives to foster inclusion, but also the most appropriate courses of action and the allocation of resources necessary to achieve those goals.

'Doing' gender is a routine accomplishment. As human beings in society, we automatically assign a gender categorization to all those we meet, while in turn we ourselves are similarly categorized. Thus we all lead lives under constant gender assessment. According to the 'doing' perspective, gender does not simply reflect biological differences between women and men, but is created through practices of social interaction, for example at the workplace. Both women and men contribute to the establishment and perpetuation of gender differences.

The *'doing' perspective* brings into sharp relief the range of common daily practices that contribute to the (re)construction of differences and inequalities in certain socio-cultural conditions. This perspective avoids the rigid and artificial categorization of individuals as women/men, black/white, young/old and the assignment of a dubious list of characteristics.

Equal opportunities refers to an equal distribution of opportunities of education, training, employment, career development and the exercise of power, so that individuals are not disadvantaged on the basis of their sex, race, language, religion, economic or family situation, or any other factor.

Essentialism refers to the idea that people have an immutable 'essence' that is the root cause of their behaviour. In particular, it is assumed that biological traits are responsible for social behaviour (for example gender-specific skills).

EU regulations have binding legal force throughout all member states. States usually do not have to take actions themselves to implement regulations, which override any conflicting domestic law or decision.

Flexitime (also called flextime or flexible working hours) is a type of flexible work arrangement that allows employees to vary their work schedules, within certain ranges and dimensions, according to their needs (Hyland, 2003).

Gender identity is the way in which a person chooses to self-identify as male or female or something in between or beyond this categorization.

A *gender order* comprises the ways in which a particular society organizes the roles and responsibilities of men and women. Gender orders frame and condition practices in organizations. Although based on cultural conventions, they are reflected in legislation, for example, concerning maternity and parental leave and the availability of child care. Religion can also contribute to a gender order. Societal gender orders are not monolithic; rather they display inconsistencies and even conflicting elements. Furthermore, they are not static, but are susceptible to change when challenged.

Harassment is a particular form of discrimination that encompasses verbal or written comments, gestures or other forms of behaviour regarded as intimidating, humiliating or offensive by the recipient.

Heteronormativity refers to the institutions, understanding and practices that privilege and make heterosexuality (the view that a person can be only a heterosexual man or heterosexual woman) the norm.

Homosociality can be defined as the seeking and preference for the company of people who are perceived as similar in some significant way, for example, in terms of gender. In management, homosociality means that managers tend to feel more comfortable when working with people whom they think resemble themselves. Obviously this can have a considerable impact on recruitment and promotion decisions in organizations.

Homosocial reproduction refers to the phenomenon that individuals involved in the recruitment or promotion process select candidates who most closely resemble themselves.

Inclusion means enabling and valuing the participation of all employees so that they contribute fully to the organization.

Indirect discrimination is a more complex phenomenon in which a rule or practice which appears neutral has a negative impact upon a person or a group of persons who display a specific characteristic. The author of the rule or practice may be unaware of these repercussions.

Individual resistance to diversity is displayed by individual workers within an organization. This resistance may include instances of overt prejudice, discrimination and harassment, as well as more subtle forms of exclusion, avoidance, distancing or even silence in the face of acts of discrimination and harassment by others.

Intangible assets can be defined as assets other than material and financial assets, which bring value to an organization (Stoi, 2004, citing Lev, 2001).

Job sharing is an employment scheme in which two or more workers share a position. They do not work at the same time, but rather each works a half day, a half week or every second week, for example.

Knowledge-intensive firms or *organizations* are those in which the prime commodity is knowledge, in whatever form. Examples are law firms, universities and banking institutions. Of course, even if an organization's primary objective is in manufacturing or some other practical activity, it may still need to maintain a strong knowledge base. For example, large engineering or construction companies will generally have accounting, communication and management departments, which essentially operate as in a knowledge-intensive firm.

Mainstreaming seeks to promote equality at all levels and in all areas by taking equality issues into account during policy formation, implementation and evaluation.

The *moral case* argues that discriminatory structures and practices be eliminated in order to achieve equality of opportunity. The business case formulates concrete economic goals to be realised by implementing diversity practices.

Occupational segregation is the tendency of particular social groups (for example men, women and immigrants) to be overly represented in certain kinds of jobs at different hierarchical levels in the organization. For example, immigrant women are often employed in low level, low paid jobs such as in the fields of caring and cleaning, while majority men are overly represented in technically-oriented fields, such as construction or engineering jobs.

Organizational climate refers to employees' perceptions, attitudes and expectations of the work environment including the atmosphere, practices, procedures and rewards.

Organizational culture refers to values, artefacts (office design, logos and websites), norms (guiding principles and shared implicit and explicit expectations and roles, behaviour and practices) that influence social interaction.

Organizational resistance to diversity manifests itself in organizational policies and practices. For instance, holding training sessions after normal working hours or on weekends, when workers with child care responsibilities may not be able to attend, is a relatively overt form of organizational resistance to diversity. Another, more subtle, example of organizational resistance is refusing to acknowledge diversity as an issue of relevance to the organization, and thus generating a culture of silence around the topics of diversity and discrimination.

Organization studies are systematic investigations of structures, practices and ways of 'acting' in organizations. These include:

Organization theories, which deal with the structural framework of organizations and industries (the macro-level), and

Organizational behaviour, which concerns the actions and interactions of individuals and groups (the micro-level).

Overt resistance to diversity consists of behaviours or attitudes that are performed or displayed openly, and that are plainly apparent to observers. For instance, using racist language to belittle a co-worker can be considered overt resistance to diversity.

Positive action refers to proportionate measures intended to foster full and effective equality for members of groups that are socially or economically disadvantaged, or otherwise face the consequences of past or present discrimination.

Qualitative intentions can be defined as strategic positions, which are used to quantify targets.

Only *quantified targets* can be measured and evaluated, while qualitative intentions are usually formulated rather vaguely and thus evade economic evaluation.

Rationalism is a school of thought which emphasizes the importance of intellect and empirical fact in opposition to feelings, intuition, coercive power or religious conviction.

Scientific management (also called *Taylorism*) refers to an understanding of management as a scientifically informed process of organizing work as efficiently as possible. 'Scientific' in this context refers to a neutral and objective form of management which does not take account of any hidden assumptions, such as those regarding gender and diversity.

Sexual identity describes how a person identifies his or her sexuality in terms of sexual orientation. *Sexual orientation* refers to a pattern of emotional, romantic and/or sexual attraction to males, females, both of these or neither.

Social categories refer to a system of classifying individuals in terms of social categories such sex, religion, age and so on.

Soft law encompasses other EU measures such as guidelines, declarations and opinions that are not legally binding, but which are a more flexible means to achieve policy objectives by influencing practice.

Stereotypes are popular beliefs about social groups or types of individuals: for example men and women, particular ethnic groups, or people of a particular age. They are standardized and simplified conceptions based on prior, often deeply held, assumptions. Gender stereotypes abound in relation to management. For example, men are stereotypically assumed to be competitive and active, while women are regarded as empathetic and caring.

Subtle resistance to diversity is much less obvious than overt resistance; it is frequently concealed and can therefore be difficult for observers to accurately perceive or describe. For example, choosing to remain silent after witnessing acts of overt discrimination or harassment can be considered subtle resistance to diversity, as can forming exclusive friendship groups with members of one's own social category, while avoiding members of other social categories.

Tolerance is a fair, objective and permissive attitude towards opinions and practices that differ from one's own.

Transgender is an umbrella term used to designate any group of people whose lifestyle appears to conflict with the gender norms of society.

Early definitions of *work-family stress* or *conflict* included any form of discord in the workplace perceived to stem from the conflicting demands of a worker's private and professional lives. Contemporary definitions tend to take a wider view of such discord to look at the effects *beyond* the workplace, namely in the home and in the community, particularly the impact on familial and other relationships.

Work-life balance practices let employees determine how and when they work. They help workers create schedules that give them greater autonomy within the workplace.

Workplace wellness refers to programmes designed to improve the health and well-being of employees (and their families), in order to enhance organizational performance and reduce costs. *Wellness programmes* typically address specific behaviors and health risk factors, such as poor nutrition, physical inactivity, stress, obesity and smoking. These factors commonly lead to serious and expensive health problems and have a negative impact on workforce productivity' (Working Well, 2012).

INDEX

Notes: bold = extended discussion or term highlighted in text; *page number in italics* = glossary definition; f = figure, n = footnote, t = table.